W9-CCI-150

Looking to Grow

Traditionally, garages, attics, and basements were not considered part of a house itself; they were all created to serve purposes other than to be lived in. It is possible, in fact, to have a house with none of

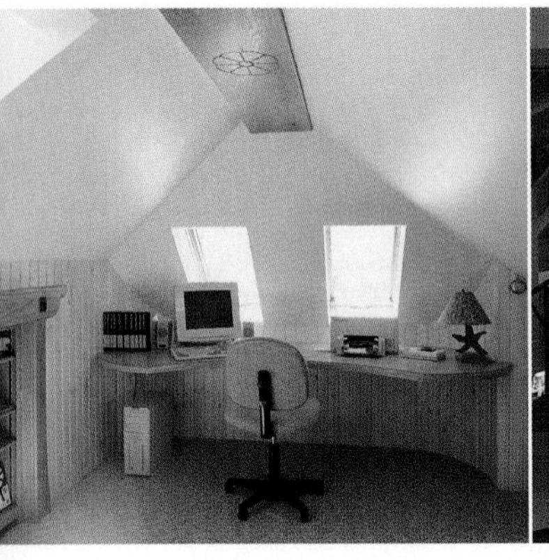

ABOVE: An attic can be converted into a simple yet fully functional home office (left) or a roomy, relaxing retreat from the hustle and bustle of daily family life (right).

BELOW: The basement library makes stunning use of concrete and stone.

these spaces. Yet, as families grow and property lines shrink, these areas present very attractive and affordable opportunities for expanding a home's living space.

Garages

Whether out of necessity or simply from recognizing that cars are durable enough not to require a roof over their heads, the garage has long been a popular choice for conversion. Garages, however, are a relatively new addition to housing construction. As automobiles became more common after 1910, detached garages began to appear to house them. By the middle of the 20th century, the attached garage had become the norm in new house construction. And by the end of the century, it was not uncommon to see houses with enormous garages suitable for several vehicles—or potentially substantial additions of living space.

Attics

Attics also are good choices for conversion, provided they have sufficient space without needing to alter the roof line. Generally, the steeper the roof, the more likely it is that the attic can be converted. But no matter what the height, the roof must be framed with rafters; if it sits on top of a web of modern trusses, conversion is almost certainly out of the question.

The standard attic is really no more than a necessary by-product of roof design. In nonarid climates, where roofs are sloped to allow rainwater to run off quickly, attics provide the structure for such a roof. In dry climates, flat roofs—and, thus, no attics—are commonly found. Even when houses with sloped roofs are built in these climates, the slope is often too moderate to produce an attic in which a person can stand up, much less one that can be turned into livable space.

Basements

Houses generally sit on top of basements, crawl spaces, or slabs; the foundation choice is often determined by climate and soil conditions as well as budget and personal preferences. In houses with basements, this space is often underutilized and begging for a makeover.

Sunset

converting garages, attics & basements

BY JEFF BENEKE AND THE EDITORS OF SUNSET BOOKS

SUNSET BOOKS • MENLO PARK, CALIFORNIA

Sunset Books
Vice President, General Manager: Richard A. Smeby
Vice President, Editorial Director: Bob Doyle
Production Director: Lory Day
Director of Operations: Rosann Sutherland
Art Director: Vasken Guiragossian

Staff for this book
Sunset Books, Senior Editor: Marianne Lipanovich
Consulting Editor: Bridget Biscotti Bradley
Copy Editor: Carol Whiteley
Indexer and Proofreader: Barbara J. Braasch
Photo Researcher: Kathleen Olson
Production Coordinators: Patricia S. Williams, Eligio Hernandez
Consultant: Larry Haun

Art Director: Robin Weiss
Principal Illustrator: Rik Olson
Additional Illustrations: Troy Doolittle, Top Dog Illustrations
Principal Photographer: Mark Rutherford
Additional Photography: Carolyn L. Bates, 6 top left, top right, 10; Van Chaplin, 118 (courtesy Southern Living Magazine); Jay Curtis, 101; Delta Faucet Co., 82; Empire Comfort Systems, 47; Philip Harvey, 6 bottom, 16, 52 left, 95, 138, 144, 150, 151, 182; The Iron Shop, 174; Philip Wegner Kantor, 148, 149; Kurt Lavenson, 102, 103; Colin McCrae, 120; Stephen Marley, 123; Stephen O'Hara, 163; Robin Stancliff, 5; Brian Vanden Brink: 8, 9, 14, 19, 121, 133, 147, 152; Tom Wyatt, 164.

Cover: Design by Vasken Guiragossian. Photography by Brian Vanden Brink. Rockport Post & Beam, Builders.

10 9 8 7 6 5 4 3 2 1
First Printing March 2001

Library of Congress Catalog Card Number: 00-109156.
ISBN 0-376-01099-1.

Printed in the United States.
For additional copies of Converting Garages, Attics & Basements or any other Sunset book, call 1-800-526-5111 or visit us at www.sunsetbooks.com

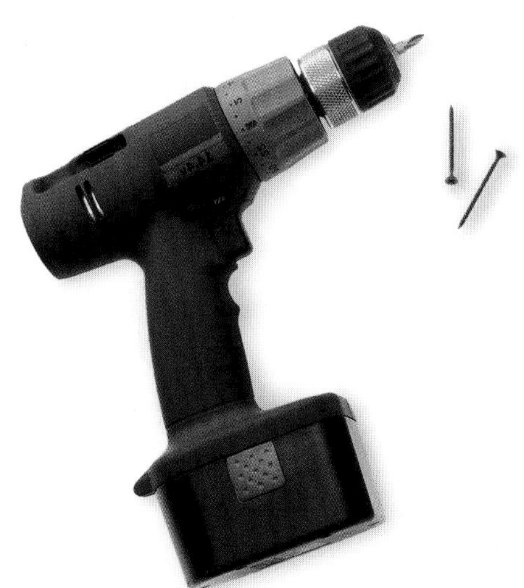

Contents

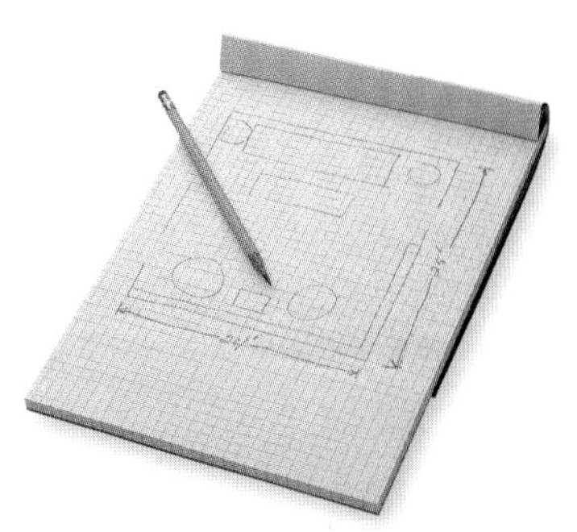

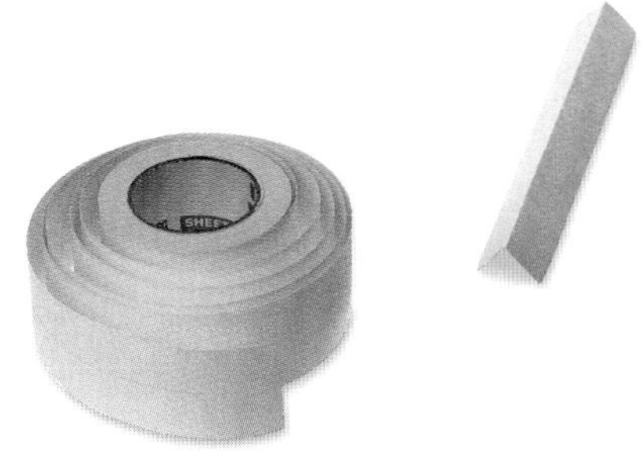

Planning and Preparation

Some home improvement projects, such as a leaking pipe or a broken window, demand immediate attention. Converting a garage, attic, or basement into a well-designed living space, however, is a major undertaking, and should not be rushed or started without careful planning. Such a conversion may involve significant expense, and almost certainly will affect the long-term value as well as the comfort of your home.

This chapter offers advice on how best to plan your project. Even if the conversion you envision is a relatively simple one, there are a host of decisions required to keep the project on track and to keep you on the good side of the local building inspector and zoning office. Here you'll find tips on evaluating the advantages and disadvantages of turning your garage, attic, or basement into living space, plus preliminary ideas on what it means to design such a space, legally and aesthetically. If you need professional help, you'll find advice on choosing the best person for the job.

Conversion Pros and Cons

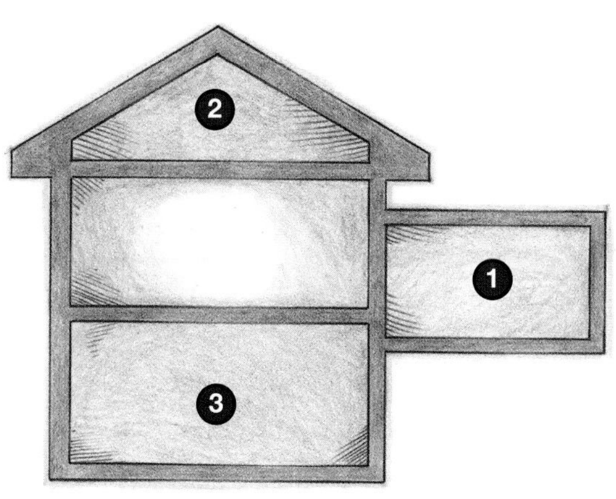

1. GARAGE

Pros:
- **Floors and walls may require only moderate amount of work**
- **Easy exterior access**

Cons:
- **Where to park the car**
- **May be difficult to heat**
- **Can be a challenge to make the exterior look more like part of the house**
- **Driveway leading right up to the house can be awkward**

Best uses:
- **Family room, play or exercise room, bedroom, media room, shop or hobby space**

2. ATTIC

Pros:
- **Often a quiet, peaceful living space or retreat**
- **Usually not being used for any other purpose**

Cons:
- **Old ceiling joists may have to be reinforced to serve as new floor joists**
- **Headroom may be insufficient**
- **Access may be difficult**
- **May be difficult to heat and cool**

Best uses:
- **Bedroom, home office, study**

3. BASEMENT

Pros:
- **Existing walls and floor may be sufficient**
- **Often has easy access**
- **May be large enough to create several rooms**

Cons:
- **May be moist and dark**
- **Ceiling may be too low**
- **Heating and cooling systems could restrict usable space and be noisy and ugly**

Best uses:
- **Small "in-law" apartment, bedroom, play or exercise room, media room, shop or hobby space**

Basements are most common in cold climates, since they provide ample space to house bulky heating systems. The walls of the basement actually constitute the foundation for the house. In older houses, basement walls may be made of stone and the floors may be made of dirt, while in newer houses both surfaces are often formed with poured concrete.

A Good Investment?

Even a modest conversion is going to cost you some money and time, so it makes sense to consider if the investment will be worth it. There are two ways of looking at this matter. First, how valuable is the conversion to you in terms of livability? Do you really need the extra space? How much will it improve life under your roof? What are your other options?

The second consideration is financial. How much money will you need to invest in the project? What percentage of that investment are you likely to recoup if and when you sell the house? Finally, could the conversion actually reduce the value of your house to future buyers (say, for example, for someone who really wants a garage)? A real estate agent or an appraiser may be able to offer good advice based on the conditions in your local market.

If you have a cramped two-bedroom, one-bathroom house and a growing family or the need for an in-law unit, converting a basement into another bedroom with a full bathroom could markedly increase the immediate value of the house to you while adding substantially to the house's eventual resale value.

Conversely, the cost of making the same change in a house that already has three or four bedrooms and a couple of bathrooms might not be recoverable at resale time, yet the conversion might meet your immediate needs for extra space. Faced with the choice of converting space in your existing house or moving, a conversion might be very worthwhile, regardless of whether or not you recover all or most of the investment when you sell the house.

Planning a Room

Planning involves making numerous careful and thoughtful decisions. The big decisions (what kind of room? how big?) are often the easiest. It is the small things—the details—that can cause the biggest headaches.

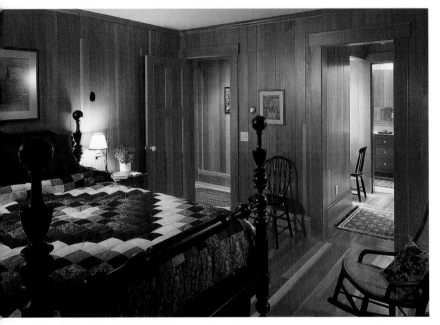

This basement has been transformed into a new suite, with full-size bedroom, bathroom, and closet.

Try to plan every detail of your new space—electrical wiring, phone lines, light fixtures, storage, plumbing needs, doors and windows, furniture—before any dust starts flying. And don't rely on your memory to store your thoughts and plans; instead, keep a written record, including notes, sketches, measurements, and photos clipped from magazines.

ROOM SIZES AND LAYOUTS

When you convert a basement, attic, or garage, you create a new entity, what the building codes refer to as a "habitable room" or "living space." Taking that step means that you must respect a set of requirements about the size of the space, as well as other criteria designed to ensure that the new room is safe and functional.

Building codes and industry guidelines often specify necessary minimum requirements. One widely recognized code requirement is that all habitable rooms (rooms used for sleeping, living, cooking, or dining) have an area not less than 70 square feet and not less than 7 feet wide or long. At least half of any habitable room must have a minimum ceiling height of 7 feet 6 inches (kitchens, bathrooms, and hallways are often considered exceptions, with 7-foot ceilings allowed). Hallways typically must be at least

Minimal Room Dimensions

Building codes vary, but most codes require habitable rooms to have at least 70 square feet of floor space and a ceiling height of at least 7½ feet. Bedrooms, kitchens, and bathrooms often have more specific requirements.

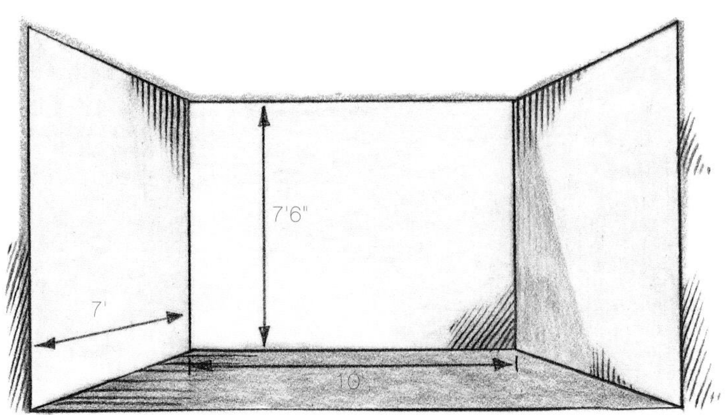

Swinging Doors

Hinged doors are classified as right-handed or left-handed, depending on which side the hinges are placed. Doors placed near the middle of a wall consume almost twice as much floor space as doors set near a corner, as shown. When preparing a floor plan, remember to account for the space needed for the door to swing open and closed. Also consider if you want doors to open into or out of the room.

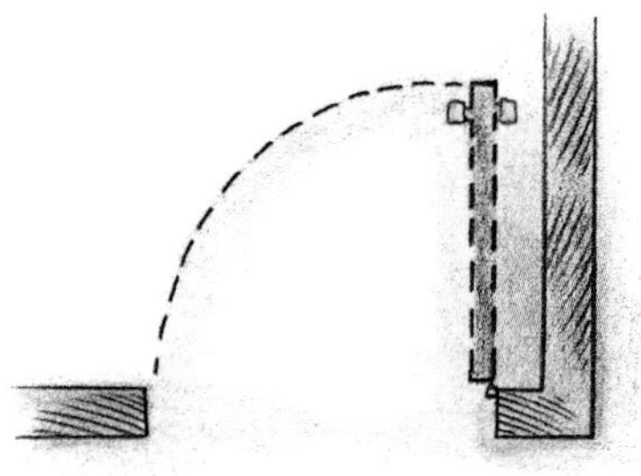

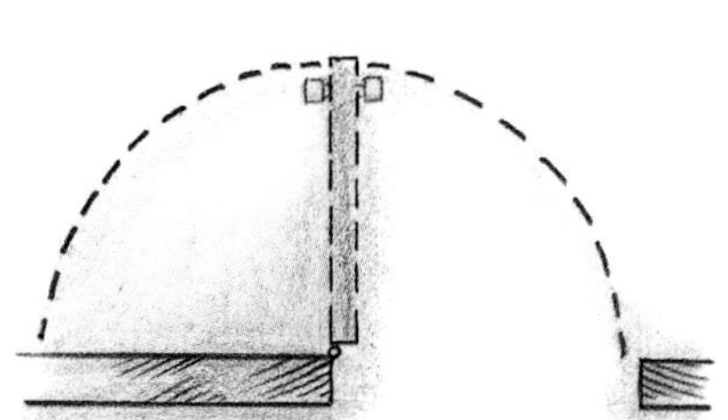

36 inches wide. Building codes vary from region to region, so check the requirements in your area before proceeding.

Also, if you are remodeling a room for a disabled or elderly person, or if you're simply looking down the road, be aware of the growing trend toward "universal" or barrier-free design. Special heights, clearances, and room dimensions may be necessary.

When considering room sizes, it is wise to remember one rule of thumb: An empty room always looks larger than a room filled with furnishings. When you start making sketches of the room or rooms you envision, make them to scale. And be sure to think about the different furnishings and equipment the room will need to house, depending on its purpose (see below). Some standard clearances for fixtures and furnishings are shown on pages 10, 11, and 12. For information on making your own scaled drawings, see pages 16-17.

Play or Exercise Room Decide what you want to put in the room before getting too far along in the planning process. A stationary bicycle takes up little space, while a Ping-Pong or pool table requires much more (including plenty of space around the table to allow for use). For a kid's play room, plan for lots of shelves and drawers—set low at kid height—so that toys, games, and books can be reached easily.

Continued on page 10

SAFETY TIP

It is always best to provide at least two escape routes from every part of the house in case of fire. Your building code may be less demanding, but bear in mind that codes are generally minimal, not necessarily optimal, standards. Your code, for example, may require only one egress (i.e., escape) window from a bedroom in a converted attic, but also providing a stairway to the outside would give you superior protection (albeit at a much higher cost). If stairs are not feasible, keep an escape ladder available in an attic room.

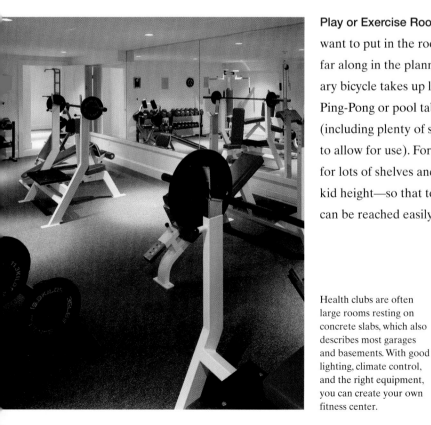

Health clubs are often large rooms resting on concrete slabs, which also describes most garages and basements. With good lighting, climate control, and the right equipment, you can create your own fitness center.

This bathroom takes advantage of its attic location with skylights set in the roof over the tub. Additional lighting is provided by recessed downlights over the sink.

Home Office or Study Equipment and space requirements vary widely, depending on final use. Make a list of all furniture and equipment you are likely to need, such as a desk, computer and printer, and work table. In addition, remember to plan for storage (files, work in progress, and books and reference materials), meeting space, and additional seating. Also, plan for any special wiring needs.

Living Room Try to route traffic around, rather than through, this room. Use furniture, shelving units, or partitions such as screens or plants to create pathways and define areas. Changing the ceiling height within a room also creates a sense of separate spaces.

Try to create quiet conversation areas (seats facing each other, close together) or somewhat secluded reading areas (one or two chairs set away from the TV or conversation area). For a TV/media center, locate seating to surround the screen.

Bathroom Minimal bathroom size is generally dictated by local building codes and bath industry guidelines that specify certain clearances between, beside, and in front of bathroom fixtures. Some standard fixture sizes and recommended clearances are shown below and at right. Check the size of any fixtures you're considering and local code before proceeding.

Bathrooms require ventilation, either with an exhaust fan or, in warm climates, with operable windows or skylights. Plumbing walls must be deep enough to accommodate drain, waste, and vent lines. Also consider storage needs for towels, supplies, and, perhaps, bedding and dirty laundry. Several sample compact layouts are shown at right.

Continued on page 12

Standard Bathroom Clearances

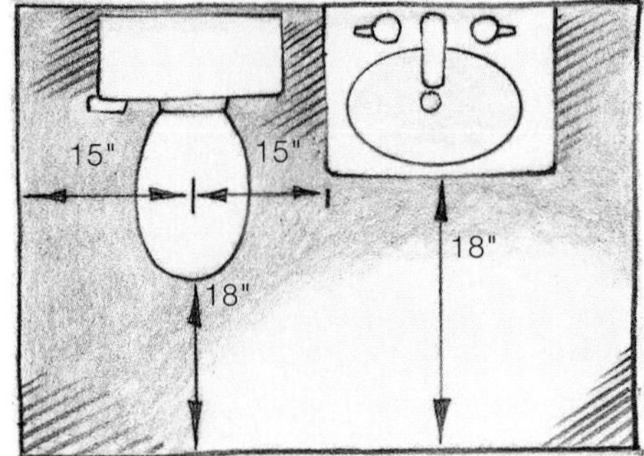

Standard Sizes of Bathroom Fixtures

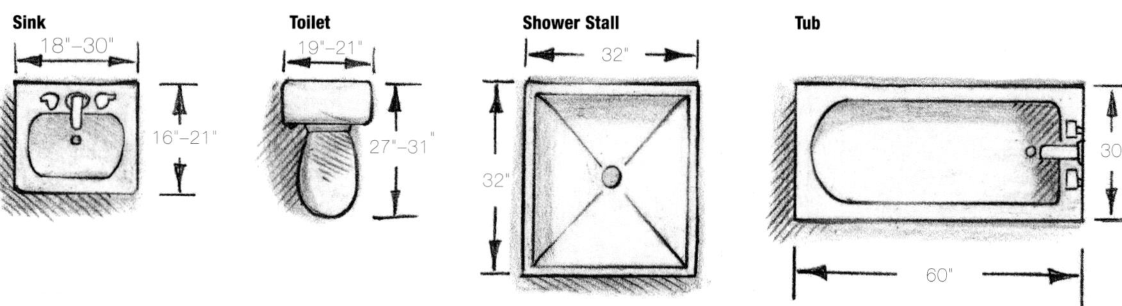

Bathroom Layouts

Half Bathrooms

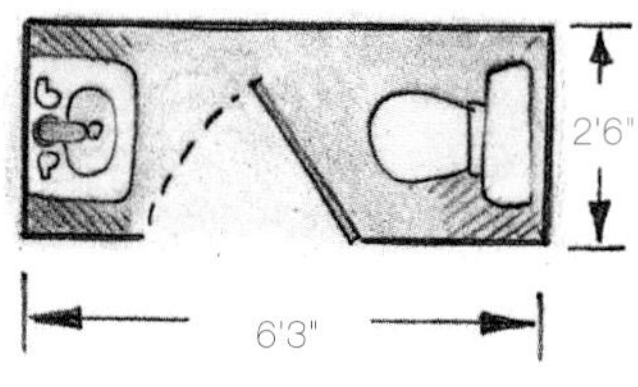

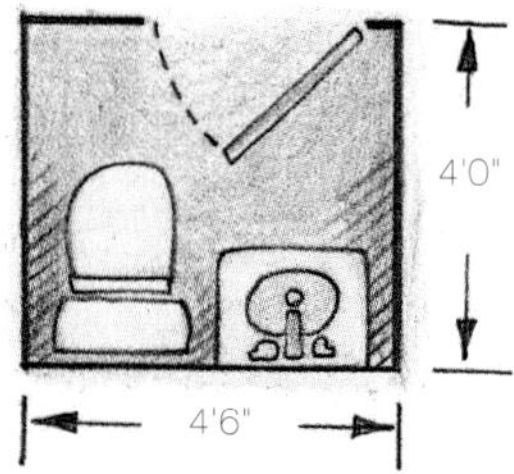

Full Bathrooms

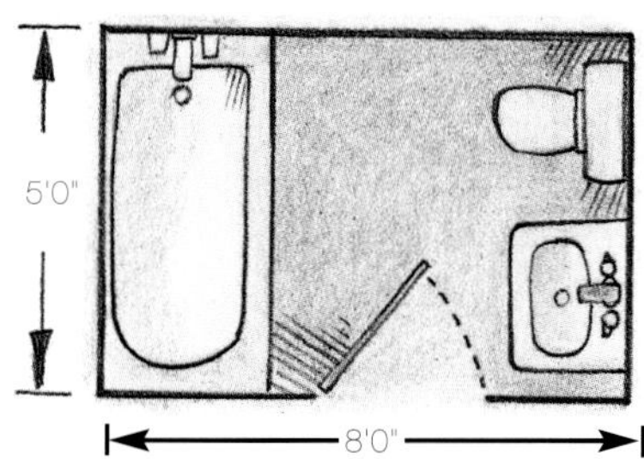

Space Savers

While showrooms and magazine ads are filled with products that fit standard needs, manufacturers also offer a wide variety of products whose sole purpose is to solve space or configuration problems. For fixtures and appliances to suite tight spaces or meet your special requirements, such as the one shown on page 95, talk directly with the manufacturers or browse their Web sites for information.

Pocket doors (at right) can be great space savers. They do not create dead space because they don't swing into the room but rather slide into the wall.

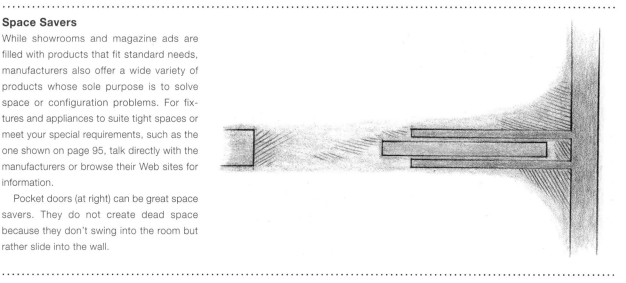

Bedroom Provide room for the bed or beds, preferably with access from both sides—especially if more than one person will be sleeping there. Some standard clearances for bedroom furnishings and bed sizes are shown below and at right. Plan for storage for clothes (clean and dirty), a bedside stand or two, and perhaps a desk or dressing table.

If there's room, consider adding a comfortable chair and reading lamp. Also consider space for displaying and storing other items, such as a television or stereo equipment, a favorite collection, or often-used sporting equipment.

Typical Bed Sizes

DAY BED	30" x 75"
SINGLE	39" x 75"
DOUBLE	54" x 75"–80"
QUEEN	60" x 80"
KING	76" x 80"

Comfortable Master Bedroom

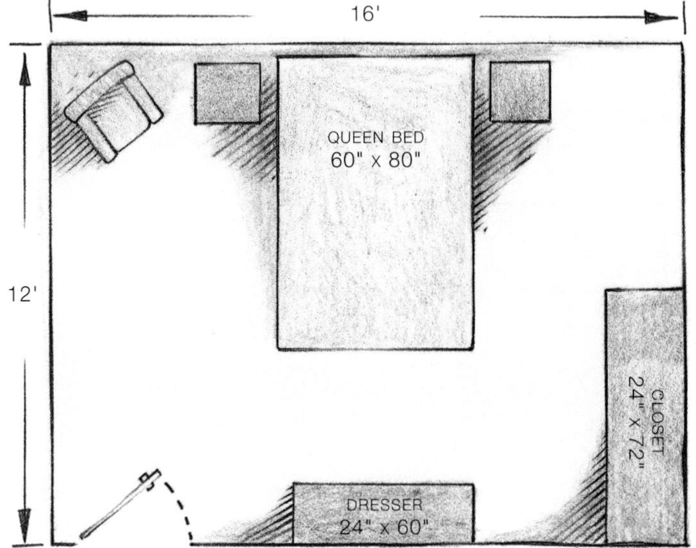

Basic Small Bedroom

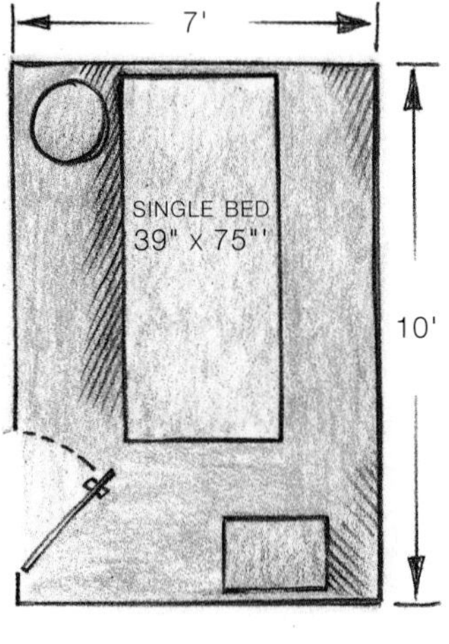

Laundry Plan for adequate space in front of the machines for loading and unloading and behind the machines for plumbing and exhaust systems. Include shelves for storage of detergent, bleach, and other items. Consider creating surfaces for folding and ironing. Some standard clearances for laundry rooms are shown at right.

Laundry Room Clearances

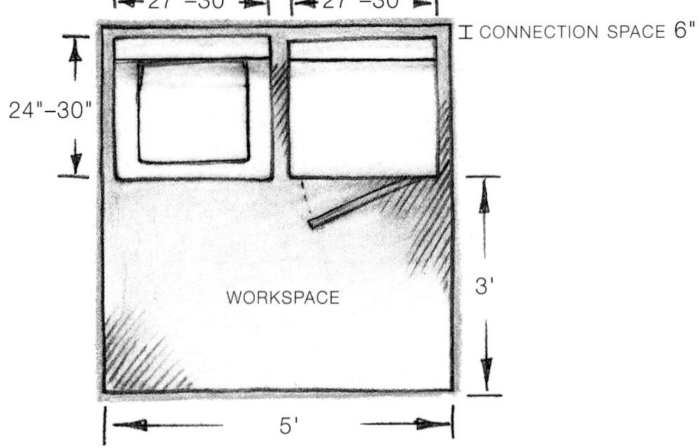

Keeping It Legal

Most communities have zoning ordinances and building codes to protect standards of health, safety, and land use. Any remodeling done to your house must comply with these standards. Your building plans may have to be approved by local officials before you can begin work, and the work in progress may have to be inspected periodically.

If you hire a contractor, such as an electrician or a plumber, to do some of the work, you may be able to avoid dealing with the building inspector or planning commission yourself.

Zoning Ordinances

Designed to regulate land use, zoning ordinances establish barriers between commercial, industrial, agricultural, and residential areas. If you are planning to convert any part of your house into a space to be used for business purposes, even if it is just a small home office, you may run into zoning obstacles. Urban areas—and especially condominium associations—tend to be the most restrictive.

If you run a simple desk-and-computer-based business, chances are good that you will not violate local provisions. However, if your workspace is quite large, you have frequent visitors or several employees, you sell goods from your home, or you want to hang a sign, you may face a host of restrictions.

Furthermore, if your neighborhood is zoned for single-family residential use only, you could run into legal trouble if you try to rent out a converted basement, for example, without first obtaining permission from the planning board or zoning office. Check the applicable "home occupation accessory use" provisions at City Hall.

Building Codes

Building codes are concerned principally with construction practices: structural design and strength, and durability of building materials. Codes outline minimal standards you must meet when you build. Codes vary from region to region, just as interpretations of some provisions may vary from inspector to inspector. It is highly recommended that, before you begin any work, you discuss your plans with the person who will be conducting any required inspections at your home.

In most cases, the projects discussed in this book involve creating "living space" out of a part of the house that was not previously lived in. As discussed on pages 10–11, that could entail a host of changes you will be required to make whether or not you need or want them. And you may be required to obtain separate permits for carpentry, electrical, plumbing, and mechanical tasks (especially heating and cooling). Your local building department will be able to tell you which permits you need for the work you are doing.

To obtain a building permit you may be required to supply a drawing of the intended changes and pay a fee. Be sure to inquire about the inspection schedule, and clarify if there are any restrictions that may apply to the work you are allowed to do yourself. Bear in mind that building permits typically are good for no more than one year, so it is wise to obtain the permit just before you plan to begin work and to schedule the work to conclude before the permit expires.

Common Code Requirements

Building codes commonly provide specifications for the types of materials that can be used for certain jobs or portions of jobs. Most building codes cover the following.

FRAMING
- Type and size of lumber
- Spacing and spans of studs and joists
- Type and spacing of nails and screws

ROOM
- Minimal square footage
- Minimal ceiling height

STAIRS
- Tread depth
- Riser height
- Handrail size and location
- Minimal headroom

WINDOWS AND DOORS
- Size and number required
- Minimal energy standards

ELECTRICAL
- Type of cable
- Number and location of receptacles
- Required ground-fault circuit interrupters (GFCIs)

PLUMBING
- Regulations on use of plastic pipe
- Types of solder allowed
- Size of pipes required for various purposes
- Venting requirements
- Types of traps and connections

FIRE
- Egress requirements
- Number and location of smoke alarms
- Types of materials allowable

Shedding Light

Garages, attics, and basements are not usually well-lit rooms. That makes it especially important to prepare a careful and thorough lighting plan for the space to be remodeled. Good lighting design seeks the best mix of natural and artificial lighting.

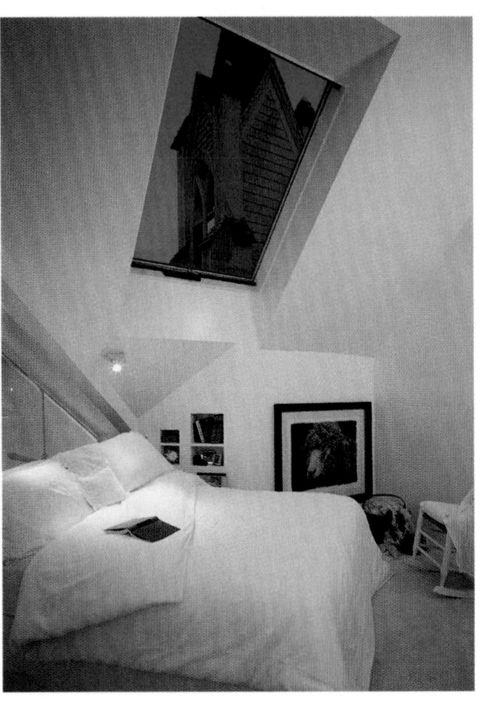

If carefully planned, skylights can provide natural light, as well as ventilation, heating, cooling, and a good view. When poorly chosen or improperly installed, however, they can cause excessive heating in the summer and drafts and condensation in the winter.

Natural Lighting

Sunlight is free light, so it makes sense to use as much of it as you can in your converted space. Natural light is more evenly distributed than artificial light, and thus casts fewer shadows. It is also less tiring to the eyes.

Designing with natural light involves selecting and locating windows and skylights to allow sunlight into a room. A south-facing window (north-facing in the southern hemisphere) will let in the most light; a window oriented north provides soft, diffuse light. Windows on two adjacent walls provide a rich multidirectional source of natural light.

A window located near light-colored walls will allow light rays to bounce off the walls, creating more light in the room. Remember, however, that sunlight is not controlled with a switch, it must be managed when necessary with shades, blinds, overhangs, and tinted glass.

Types of Artificial Lighting

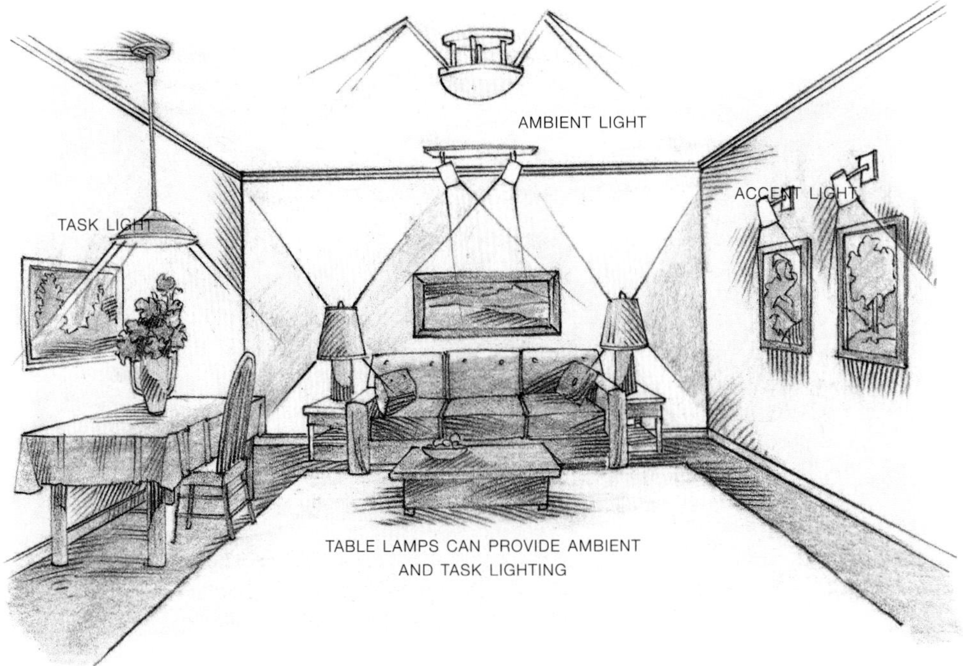

Lighting Tips, Room by Room

LIVING ROOM

- Place task lighting to facilitate reading, game playing, or other activities.
- For listening to music or watching TV, low-level ambient lighting is best (consider installing a dimmer switch).

HOME OFFICE OR STUDY

- Combine ambient light with task lighting at your desk or work surface. Place the task light to the side to cut glare and shadows.
- For computer work, low-level ambient lighting may be sufficient.

BEDROOM

- Instead of a ceiling light, think of installing a valance on the wall to provide indirect ambient lighting.
- For reading in bed, consider wall-mounted fixtures controlled with switches located next to the bed.

DINING ROOM

- Place ambient lighting over the table.
- For tables set against a wall, use wall sconces that bounce light off the wall.
- Use dimmer switches to control the mood of the room.

BATHROOM

- Provide enough ambient lighting to illuminate the entire room, including tub and shower.
- For vanity lighting, place lights on both sides of the mirror to reduce shadows on the face.

Artificial Lighting

Artificial lighting is necessary in any room for illumination at night, when light levels are low, or to meet a specific need. Lighting designers divide artificial light into three categories: ambient lighting, task lighting, and accent lighting for highlighting.

Ambient, or general, lighting illuminates an entire room or space. It permits people to see the entire area and to move around safely. Ambient lighting is frequently provided by a ceiling fixture, although lamps can also be used. It is usually best to keep ambient lighting to a low or moderate level of illumination.

Task lighting provides light for specific, more visually demanding tasks, such as reading, drawing, or sewing. Normally used in conjunction with ambient lighting, it better illuminates small objects and objects with low contrast. Task lighting can be supplied by recessed or ceiling-mounted track lights as well as by table and desk lamps.

Accent lighting, or highlighting, is used for decorative purposes. It generally focuses on artwork or interesting architectural details and usually requires either ceiling- or wall-mounted fixtures.

Choosing Light Bulbs

Light bulbs and tubes are grouped into general categories according to the way they produce light. The two most common types of bulbs are incandescents and fluorescents.

Incandescents create light when electricity passes through a wire filament inside the glass casing. Though inefficient, incandescents are excellent at rendering color, which is important in many workspaces, and they can be easily dimmed. Halogen incandescents are often used in specialized task lamps, low-voltage track fixtures, and recessed downlights.

Fluorescents are coated cylindrical glass tubes that are filled with gases and a small amount of mercury. Fluorescents can be much more energy efficient than incandescents, especially if they are left on for long periods of time (they lose efficiency when switched on and off regularly).

Fluorescents require ballasts to start up and to regulate the current. Electronic ballasts are more efficient, lighter, quieter, and flicker less than magnetic ballasts. Newer fluorescents are much better at rendering color than their predecessors.

Making Plans

Measuring all of the perimeters and elements of your planned renovation will increase your awareness of the existing space. Scale drawings also serve as a good foundation for design and may satisfy your local building department's permit requirements. If you decide to consult a professional about your project, you may save money by providing those measurements and drawings.

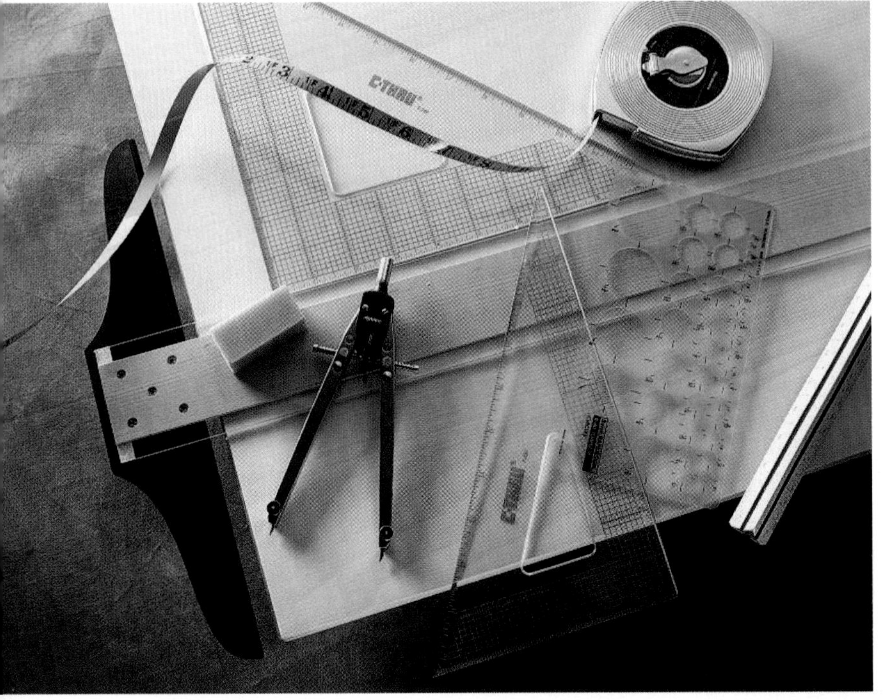

Basic drafting tools, such as a drafting board and T-square, an art gum eraser, a compass, a triangle, a circle square, a tape measure, and an architect's scale, are all helpful when making scale drawings.

Use drawings to bring your ideas to life, to check fit, to experiment, and to revise and revise and revise. The time you spend drawing plans will be some of the best-spent time in the entire project. Good plans, drawn to scale on paper, will save much labor down the road and will ensure the most efficient use of materials.

There are several computer software programs that can help you create floor plans and elevations easily and quickly. Computer-aided design (CAD) software shows you how a room looks in three dimensions and allows you to move walls and windows and drag furniture and fixtures in and out at will. You can also purchase design and layout kits that contain graph paper and appliance and cabinet templates that are scaled to size.

MEASURING A ROOM

Take and record all measurements accurately, since even a fraction of an inch counts in fitting together all of the elements of a layout. First, draw a rough sketch of the perimeter (including doors, windows, recesses, and projections) and any relevant adjacent areas. Make your sketch large enough to record all the dimensions directly on it.

Then take your measurements—they should be exact to ⅛ inch. Use a 25- or 30-foot tape measure with a sturdy, 1-inch-wide tape. Keep the tape taut as you measure. Double-check all dimensions.

Measuring for floor plans

A floor plan gives you a bird's-eye view of the layout of your space. To make this two-dimensional drawing you will need to measure along all of the walls, including any openings. You will also need to measure any desired fixtures as well as furniture and appliances. Also take measurements to establish the locations of light fixtures, switches, outlets, and other features of the room.

Measuring for elevations

Elevations, or straight-on views of each wall, show the visual pattern created by all the elements against that wall. To create such drawings you will need to know the height and width of all elements, including openings, fixtures, furniture, and appliances.

Drawing floor plans to scale

For neat, readable floor plans, take careful measurements and be accurate converting them to scale. You will probably want to use a scale of ½ or ¼ inch to 1 foot.

You can use graph paper (four squares per inch), a pencil, and the kitchen table to make your drawings, but using a few inexpensive drafting tools is really easier and much more versatile. An art gum eraser, a straightedge, several pencils, and a pad of tracing paper are all you need. Optional are a drafting board, a T-square, one or more triangles, a compass, a circle template, and an architect's scale.

Attach the paper to the drawing board or other smooth surface with masking tape. Use a ruler or T-square to draw horizontal lines, a triangle to draw vertical lines, and a template or compass for drawing the doors' direction of swing.

Complete the floor plan by including all of the elements you've sketched out, using the architectural symbols shown at right. A very basic floor plan is shown at right as well.

Drawing Your Plans

Floor Plan

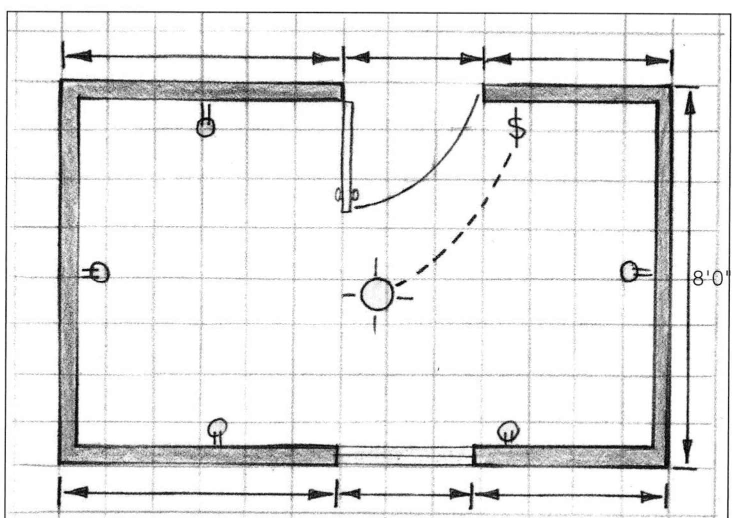

Architectural Symbols

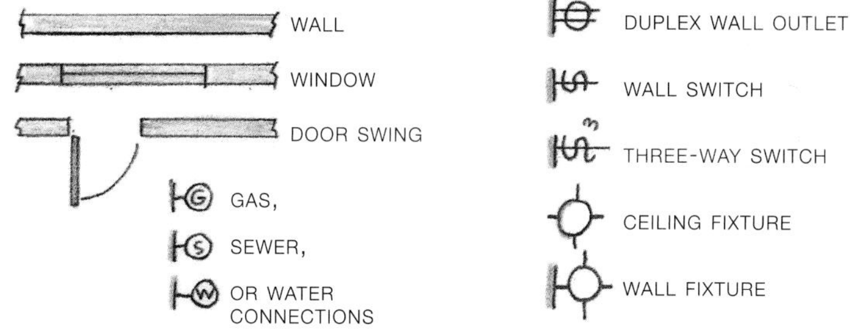

SEQUENCE OF WORK

Aside from good scaled drawings of your project, one of the most important elements of planning is establishing a logical sequence of the work to be done. The specific tasks vary from project to project, but you can use the following list to help you prepare one tailored to your own needs. As you near the end of one task, start arranging delivery of materials for the next one.

- Structural changes: walls, floors, doors, windows, skylights
- Rough utility changes: wiring, plumbing, heating/air conditioning
- Insulation
- Wall and ceiling coverings
- Painting
- Light fixtures
- Cabinets, shelves
- Countertops, backsplashes
- Floor materials
- Fixtures, appliances
- Furniture
- Decorative elements

Finding Good Help

This is a book for do-it-yourselfers, but that doesn't mean that you necessarily need to plan on doing everything yourself. Learning how to judge your own limits and when to seek professional help are among the most valuable skills in any do-it-yourselfer's toolbox. Also, you may be required to hire a licensed professional for some jobs.

Building professionals often have received lengthy training and education. They may be licensed (licensing policies vary by state and by trade), and they can call upon years of hands-on experience. Picking and choosing the right pros for the right tasks can save you time, may even save you money, and certainly will save you a lot of aggravation.

Most of the projects discussed in this book do not involve structural changes in the house, which would require cutting into the major skeleton that holds up your house. If your project does require removing—even temporarily—a supporting (or "load-bearing") wall, for example, you should seek the advice of a structural engineer, architect, or building contractor before proceeding. And if you are unsure of whether or not the changes you wish to make involve structural alterations, seek professional help.

Also seek professional help for any of the specialized tasks you don't want to tackle yourself, such as plumbing, wiring, and HVAC (heating, ventilation, and air conditioning). Simple wiring and plumbing jobs are not necessarily difficult to do, but these kinds of jobs have very little margin for error and can be dangerous if you don't know what you are doing.

CHOOSING A PROFESSIONAL

Below is a summary of some of the types of professionals you may want to consult. Following that are tips on how to find the best professionals for your job.

Architects and designers An architect or designer can design the project, draw plans and prepare specifications that are acceptable to building department officials, and even select and supervise a contractor, if you desire.

Some builders are very good designers—you may even find one who promotes himself or herself as a "designer-builder"—but not all. The two skills overlap, but they are not all that similar. Both are equally important: Great construction and expensive materials cannot mask poor design any more than great design can cover for shoddy construction techniques.

The simpler your project, the less likely you are to need design assistance; but don't take the design for granted. Finding the right materials, blending styles, matching colors, deciding on the proper scale, planning for the room's ultimate comfort and resale value, and meeting building code requirements are all factors that can be addressed by good design.

General contractors Licensed general contractors do more than swing hammers. They coordinate all aspects of a construction project, right down to drawing plans and obtaining permits. They have a broad understanding of the entire building process, schedule each phase of work, and hire and supervise the crew.

Subcontractors These professionals specialize in one area of construction. Electricians and plumbers are obvious examples, but you can find "subs" with expertise in flooring, framing, tiling, bath and kitchen remodels, drywalling, cabinetmaking, and a host of other skills.

Interior designers Even if you feel completely confident that you can build walls, run new wiring, and finish drywall, you may be amazed at the advice a trained interior designer can give you. Making an old basement look and feel like a comfortable living space can be tricky. The knowledge that someone specially trained to work with the materials, textures, colors, and furnishings brings to a project can give shape and character to a room.

DEALING WITH PROFESSIONALS

The process of finding good help is not particularly difficult, but it can be frustrating and time consuming. Often, the best construction professionals keep busy through "word-of-mouth" referrals and regular clients. Such professionals are often the best people to hire, but you may have to wait a long time before your job fits into their schedule.

Ask around Collect as many referrals as possible from friends, co-workers, neighbors, and the folks at the local lumberyard.

Interview prospects Call all of the potential contractors who interest you. Any who do not return your phone call should probably be scratched from your list immediately, since inaccessibility is one of the greatest aggravations in a construction project. Ask how long they have been in the business, what kinds of work they do, how busy they are. Try to get a sense of how comfortable you could be with each person. Which ones listen to you and show a keen interest in your vision? Which act as though they know better than you do what you want? Finally, ask for the names of former clients.

A design professional can help you make the most of a converted space and create a style that blends with your personal tastes and the rest of the house.

Check references Find out if the contractor stayed on schedule and within budget. Ask the homeowners if they would hire him or her again. Check with the local Better Business Bureau to see if any complaints against the contractor are on file. See if your state has a contractor's licensing board that offers information to consumers. Make sure the contractor is insured for damage, liability, and worker's compensation.

Compare bids Ask for bids or estimates from three or four contractors who interest you the most. Each bid should include a list of materials, labor costs, a schedule, and other fees. Make sure that bids include details on handling change orders and penalties the contractor will pay if the work falls behind schedule. Be suspicious of bids that are significantly lower than the others.

Sign a contract You may not need a signed contract for subcontractors who will work on a small project, but any large job should be based on a contract that spells out all aspects in detail. Read and understand the contract thoroughly before you sign it, and be prepared to negotiate over terms or clauses that you do not like.

Techniques: Roughing In

The "roughing in" phase of a construction project includes all the behind-the-scenes work that is later covered up by wall, ceiling, and floor surfaces. For many, it is an especially enjoyable part of the job because the work is relatively straightforward, the results come quickly, and minor blemishes can be ignored, since they will be hidden. But doing the job properly is important if the rest of the project is to fall into place easily.

This chapter provides a basic introduction to the techniques you are likely to need in your garage, attic, or basement conversion. These include frame carpentry, designing an effective plumbing system, tips on snaking electrical cable through walls and floors, and information on how to install receptacles and switches safely. Extending your existing heating and air conditioning systems is a job usually best left to a professional, but you will find some suggestions here that may help you in your early planning. You will also learn how to repair cracks and holes in masonry quickly and effectively.

Framing a Wall

Frame carpentry is the process of constructing the skeleton that holds a house and its parts together. The principal components of that structure are wall studs, floor joists, and roof rafters. In remodeling work, most of the framing involves walls, which will be the focus of this section. If you are planning to convert an attic, you will also want to study the section that focuses on strengthening joists and rafters (see pages 126–127).

Below you will find descriptions of the materials and techniques needed to frame a wall. Then on pages 26–27 there are step-by-step instructions for constructing a wall and setting it in place.

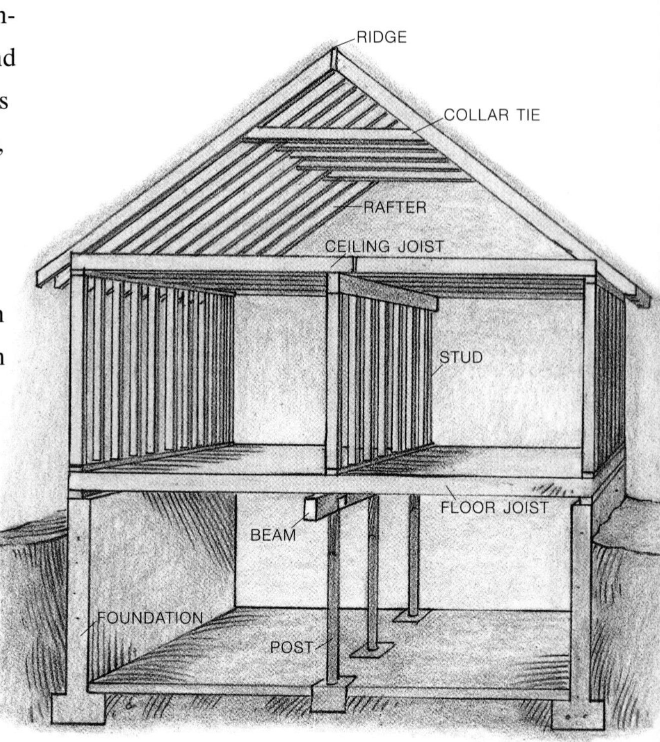

Lumber

Lumber used for structural framing is known as dimension lumber. But the dimensions by which you choose and buy the various sizes of wood don't refer to the actual sizes; the dimensions refer to the nominal sizes. Thus, when you buy a 2 x 4 ("two by four"), the piece of wood actually measures 1½ inches by 3½ inches. The table at right compares nominal and actual sizes for standard pieces of lumber.

Standard Lumber Dimensions

NOMINAL SIZE	ACTUAL SIZE
1"	¾"
2"	1½"
4"	3½"
6"	5½"
8"	7¼"

Nails

In frame carpentry, nails are the most common type of fastener. They are also very often misused. A framed structure is only as good as the nails that hold it together, so it is critical that you use the right-sized nail, the right number of nails at each joint, and the proper nailing technique.

Common Nails

PENNY SIZE	LENGTH	NAILS PER POUND
6d	2"	181
8d	2½"	106
10d	3"	69
12d	3¼"	63
16d	3½"	49

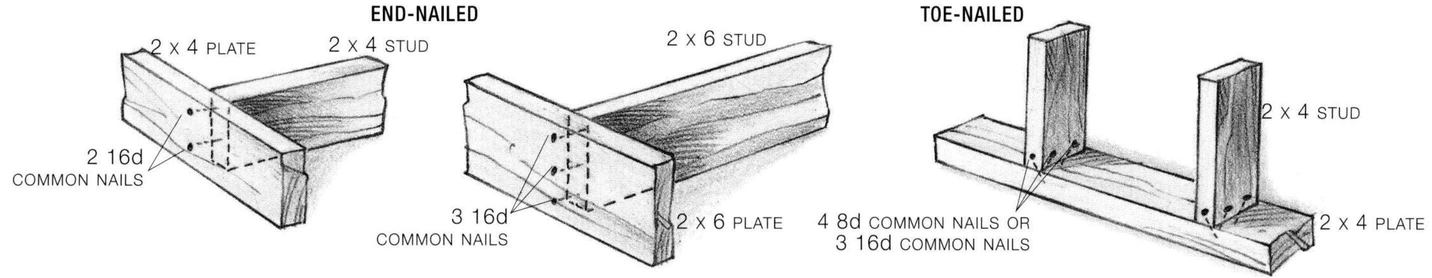

Two types of nails are used for framing: common and box. Box nails have a more slender shank than common nails, making them less likely to split wood but more likely to bend when they are hammered.

Nail length is referred to by the letter "d," or by the word "penny"; for example, a 3-inch-long nail is called a "ten penny," or a "10d." The chart below left provides relevant information on the most frequently used common nails.

Nailing Techniques

When framing walls, joints are generally formed where a stud meets a top and a bottom, or sole, plate. There are two methods for forming these joints with nails: end-nailing, in which nails are driven straight through the plate and into the stud; and toe-nailing, in which nails are driven through the stud at an angle into the plate. When done properly, a toe-nailed joint is stronger, but for framing nonstructural walls, either technique is fine.

End-nailing is done when you can form the frame flat on the floor, while toe-nailing is the method for attaching studs to plates that are already in place. Smaller nails are often used for toe-nailing to prevent the lumber from splitting, but using smaller nails means that you must use more of them in each joint. The illustrations above offer some typical examples, but your building inspector can supply specific nailing recommendations.

Working with a Circular Saw

In frame carpentry, no power tool sees more use than a circular saw. The most common style has a 7¼-inch blade, although if you are shopping for a new saw you might want to consider buying a trim saw with a 5½-inch or 6-inch blade instead. This lighter tool can cut through 2-by lumber and is especially easy for beginners to use. Stay away from low-cost power tools, though; a mid-priced professional product will perform much better.

Circular saws, like all power tools, require the utmost respect. When using one, wear ear, eye, and respiratory protection, and always place the wood to be cut across a pair of sawhorses or on a small table. Position the wood so that the part to be cut off will fall to the ground, as shown below. Do not make the cut between the sawhorses, as the wood

may pinch the blade. Measure and mark the wood, then make your cut on the waste side of the line.

Make sure the saw blade is turning at full speed before it makes contact with the wood. Guide, but don't force, the blade through the cut. Follow the line by eye, or use a speed square to guide the saw, as shown on the previous page.

Making Your Framing Plumb, Level, and Square

Building frames that are plumb, level, and square will make your conversion job much easier. Abutting walls will align perfectly, windows and doors will fit just right, and drywall edges will line up with nailing surfaces.

A surface is called plumb when it is perfectly vertical, and it is level when it is perfectly horizontal. Both planes can be checked with a carpenter's level; a 2- or 4-foot level is sufficient for most work. A surface is level when the bubble in the middle vial is exactly centered between the lines. The surface is plumb when the two end bubbles are centered.

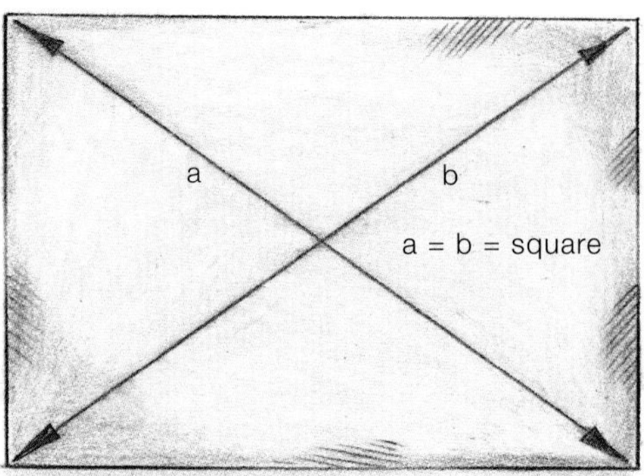

When a wall is plumb and level, it will also be square. To determine if a wall or floor, is square, measure the diagonals. If they are identical, the surface is square.

Continued on page 26

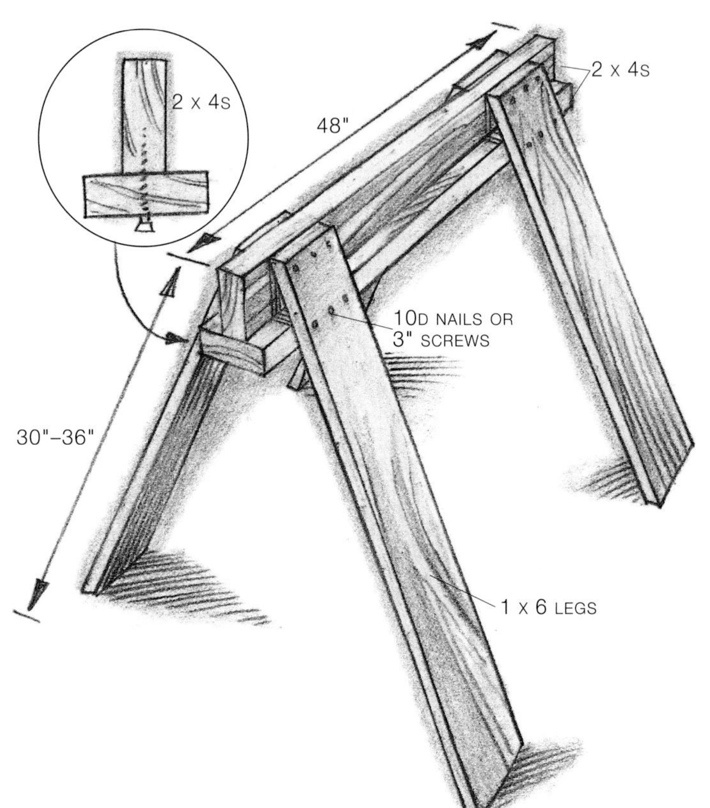

Making Sawhorses

While carpentry has seen quite a number of changes over the years, one constant element has been the sawhorse. A pair of sawhorses provide a safe, sturdy surface on which to measure, mark, and cut lumber. Sawhorses can also become part of an instant workbench when you lay a sheet of plywood over them.

The sawhorse shown here can be built quickly using only three materials: 2 x 4s, 1 x 6s, and either 10d nails or 3-inch screws. Make two of them, then disassemble or store them until you're ready to put them to work. Cut an eight-foot 2 x 4 in half, then fasten the two pieces in an inverted T, as shown. Cut four 1 x 6 legs to the length you prefer: 30 to 36 inches is usual. Attach each leg with nails or screws.

Anatomy of a Stud Wall

Headers

Headers are lengths of wood that span the tops of window and door openings. A built-up header (near right) is usually made with two 2 x 4s, 2 x 6s, or 2 x 8s set on edge, with a ½-inch plywood spacer in between them; the spacer builds out the thickness of the header so that it is flush with both walls. Technically, built-up headers are required only in load-bearing walls. Most of the walls needed in the types of remodeling projects covered in this book are partition walls, and, since they do not have to support a heavy load, can be built with two 2 x 4s installed on flat (center right).

Top plates

When two walls meet at a corner, they are tied together with an overlapping double top. A double top plate is not necessary, however, on relatively short partition walls, especially if you are building only a single wall to be joined to two existing walls.

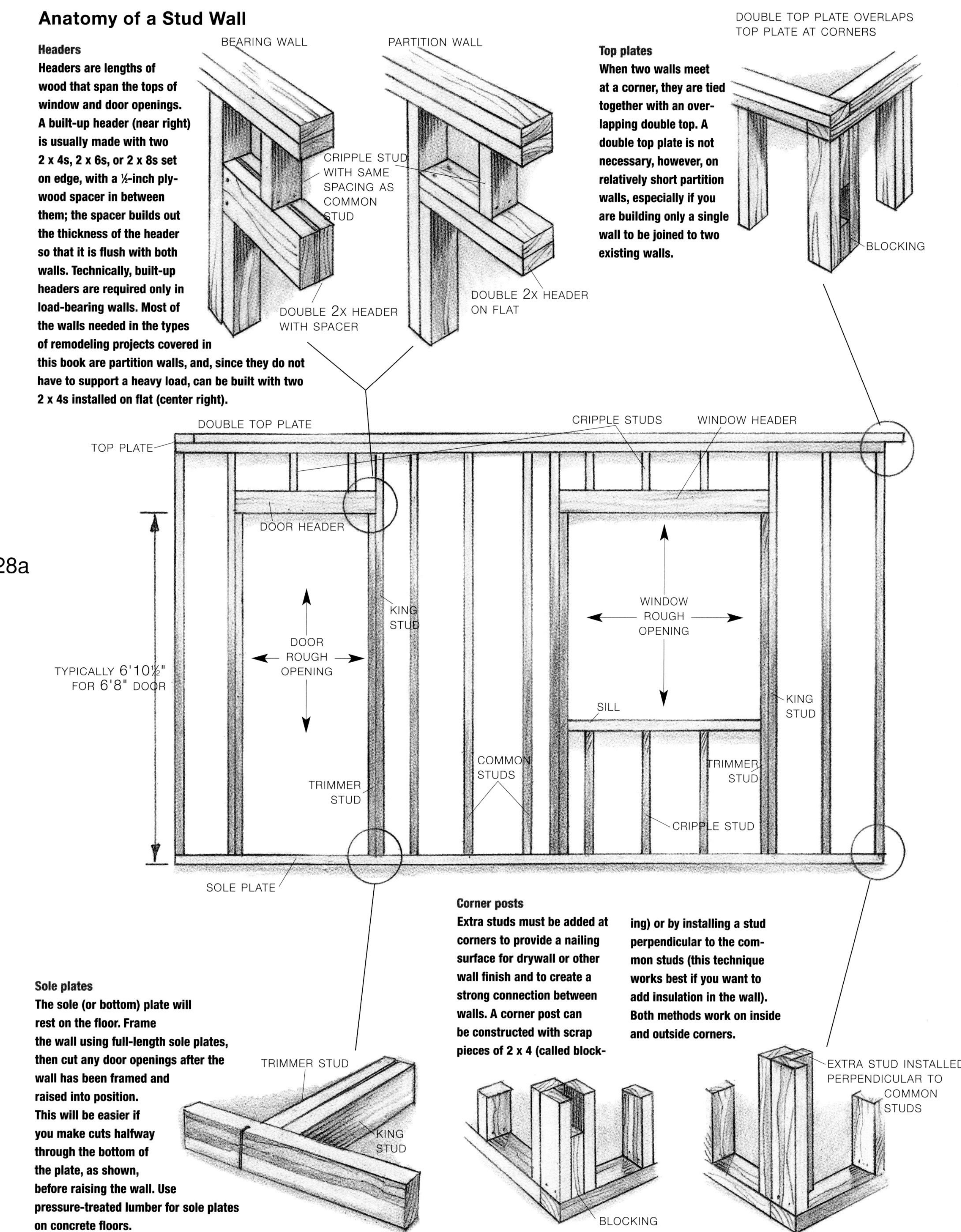

Corner posts

Extra studs must be added at corners to provide a nailing surface for drywall or other wall finish and to create a strong connection between walls. A corner post can be constructed with scrap pieces of 2 x 4 (called blocking) or by installing a stud perpendicular to the common studs (this technique works best if you want to add insulation in the wall). Both methods work on inside and outside corners.

Sole plates

The sole (or bottom) plate will rest on the floor. Frame the wall using full-length sole plates, then cut any door openings after the wall has been framed and raised into position. This will be easier if you make cuts halfway through the bottom of the plate, as shown, before raising the wall. Use pressure-treated lumber for sole plates on concrete floors.

Building Walls

Framing a wall is done in three stages: assembling the wall components while they lie on the floor; raising the wall section into position, checking it for plumb, and bracing it securely; and fastening the wall section to the floor framing and to the other wall sections or the existing walls. The first two stages of this process are shown in the photos on the facing page. As seen on page 25, all wall framing requires a sole plate, evenly spaced wall studs, and a top plate; horizontal fire blocks between studs may also be required. Walls with doorways or window openings need extra studs, as well as headers and sills to span the opening.

The standard ceiling height for interior spaces is 8 feet. Because ceiling materials encroach on this height, you will have trouble installing 4 x 8 gypsum wallboard (drywall) or sheet paneling unless you frame the walls slightly higher—8 feet ¾ inch is standard. When you subtract the thickness of the sole plate and the doubled top plates, this leaves 7 feet 8¼ inches (92¼ inches) for the wall studs. Lumberyards frequently stock studs precut to this length.

It is best to frame a wall on the ground, then lift it up into place. This is usually possible in most garage, attic, and basement remodeling projects. If you do decide to frame on the ground, build the walls a little short (about ½ inch or less). That way, they will be easier to move into place when you raise them; place wood shims or strips of ½-inch plywood between the top plate and the ceiling before nailing the wall in place. If you are framing more than one wall, frame and raise each one before moving on to the next.

Attaching Wood to Masonry

If you are raising a new wall in a basement or garage, you will probably have to fasten the sole plate to a concrete floor. Sometimes you also have to fasten a stud to a concrete or cement-block wall. There are a variety of masonry anchors available for these jobs, but most are time consuming and troublesome to use. Some building inspectors may allow you to attach partition walls with a bead of silicone adhesive. But the surest way to make the connection is with a powder-actuated fastener (see below), more commonly known among pros as a "stud gun." These tools use a gunpowder cartridge to shoot a special pin or nail through wood and into concrete.

Hammer-activated stud guns are inexpensive, but unless you think you will have more use for the tool again in the future you might be better off spending about the same amount of money to rent a heavy-duty model at a tool rental shop. Or you may be able to hire a construction pro who owns a stud gun to do the job for you. These tools are not toys, and even though the newer models are much quieter and recoil less than older ones, you should pay careful attention to the instructions.

Framing on the Ground

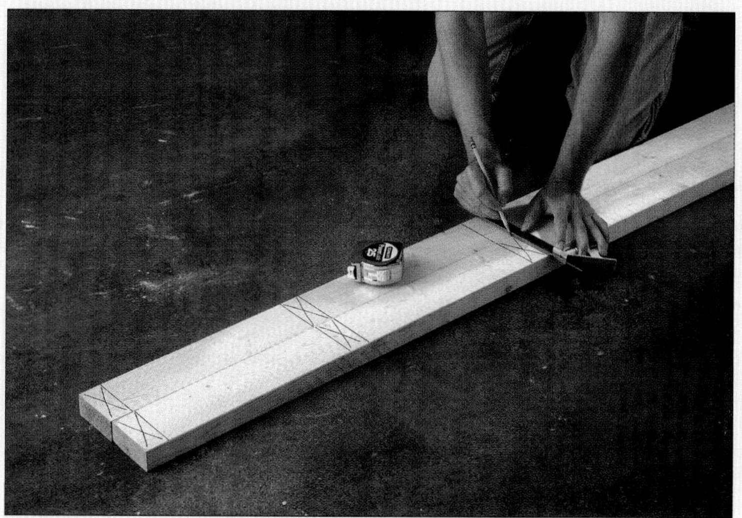

1 LAY OUT THE PLATES
Cut the sole and top plates to length. If you need more than one piece of wood for each, locate the joints at stud centers; offset any joints between top and sole plates at least 4 feet. Lay the plates side by side with the ends aligned. Use a tape measure to mark the stud placement 16 inches on center (O.C.) on one plate. Then use a square to extend the marks to the other plate. Mark the plates for the corner posts you are using (see page 25), and indicate where window and door rough openings will be located. Note that you need a full ("king") stud and a shorter ("trimmer") stud on each side of a rough opening. Feel free to move the rough openings so that the king stud coincides with a common stud—this will save you a 2 x 4.

2 ASSEMBLE THE PIECES
Measure and cut the wall studs to length. Separate the plates on the ground, stud markings inward. Align the studs with the markings and drive nails through the plates and into the ends of the studs. Use two 16d nails at each joint. Build and position any window sills and headers you need (see page 25), then cut and install "cripple" studs to fit below the window openings. If the wall includes a door opening, cut the bottom of the sole plate as shown on page 25. Cut and install the double top plate.

3 RAISE THE WALL
Mark the intended location of the sole plate on the floor (use a pencil or snap a chalk line). Slide the wall into position, then carefully raise it upright (you may need a helper or two). Check the wall for plumb (see page 24), add shims if necessary, then nail the wall in place with 16d nails or a powder-actuated fastener (see "Attaching Wood to Masonry," opposite). The top plate should be nailed to ceiling joists if they run at a right angle. If they run parallel with the wall, either locate the wall directly under a joist to which the plate can be nailed or add nailing blocks between the joists.

Plumbing Basics

If your room conversion plans call for a new bathroom, kitchen, or laundry room, you will need to do a bit of rough plumbing before you can install the new fixtures. This section contains a brief introduction to household plumbing systems and instructions for joining both copper and plastic pipe. Additional plumbing techniques are also described in the sections on converting attics (pages 120–145) and basements (pages 146–189).

Rough plumbing is often a challenge, even for those who have experience with jobs such as replacing bathtubs, unclogging drains, and repairing leaky pipes. Take some time to understand how the major plumbing

Drain, Waste, and Vent System

Drain-waste pipes carry wastewater and solid wastes away from the house. Vent pipes carry away sewer gas and maintain atmospheric pressure in drainpipes and fixture traps; traps are filled with water at all times to keep gases from coming up the drain. Though they serve separate functions, the drain-waste and vent pipes are tied together, and the entire system is usually referred to as DWV.

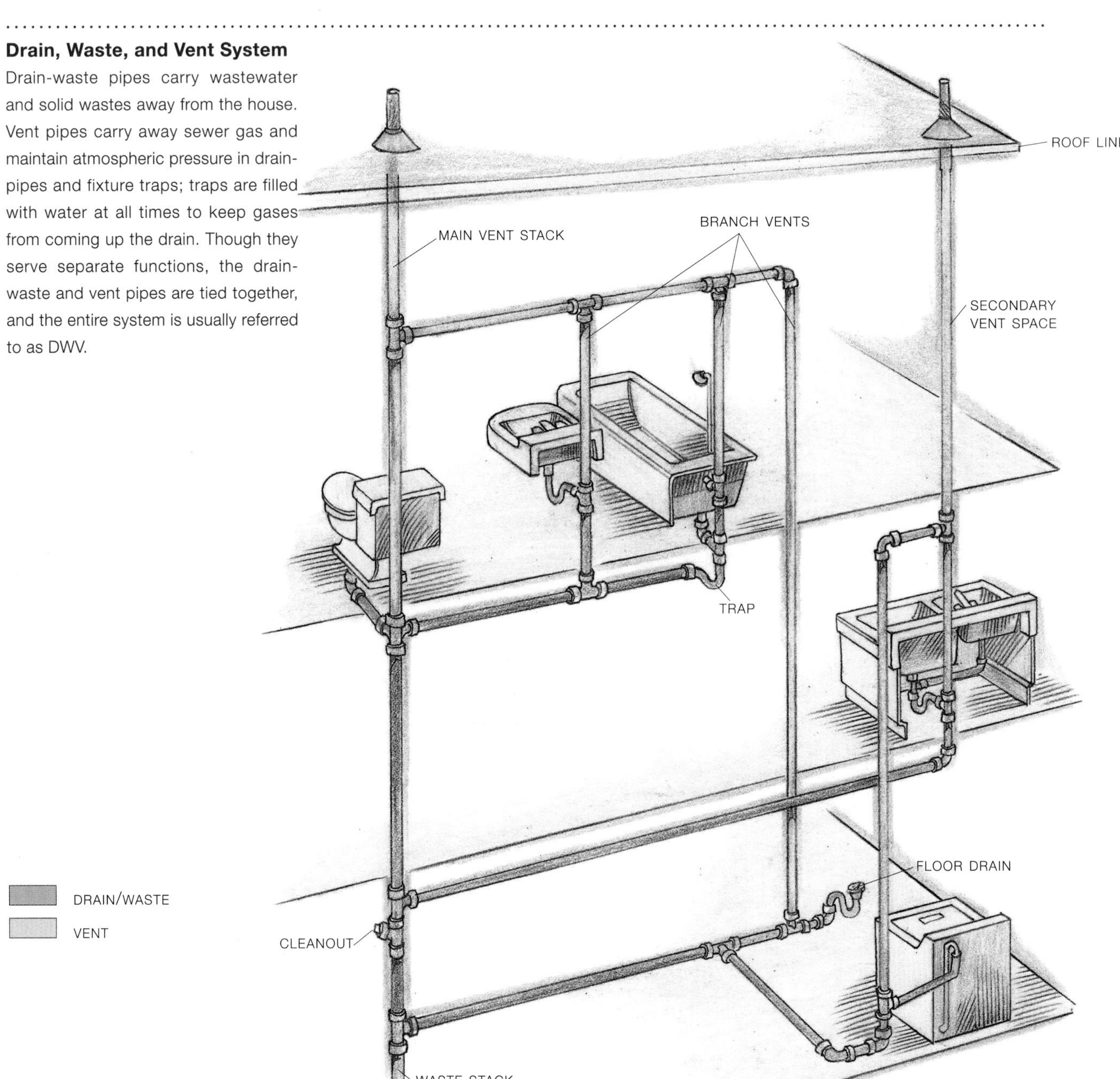

systems in your house work before you start trying to tap into them. If you feel at all uncertain about your skills, consider hiring a plumber to tackle the rough work, then plan on doing the finish work yourself. For a more detailed introduction to plumbing systems and techniques, see Sunset's *Complete Plumbing.*

Tying into a Cast-iron Pipe

If you need to tie a new drain-waste pipe into a cast-iron waste stack, you will need to cut through a thick piece of cast iron. This is best accomplished with either a snap cutter or a reciprocating saw equipped with a suitable metal-cutting blade. Before cutting, attach a riser clamp to the framing above

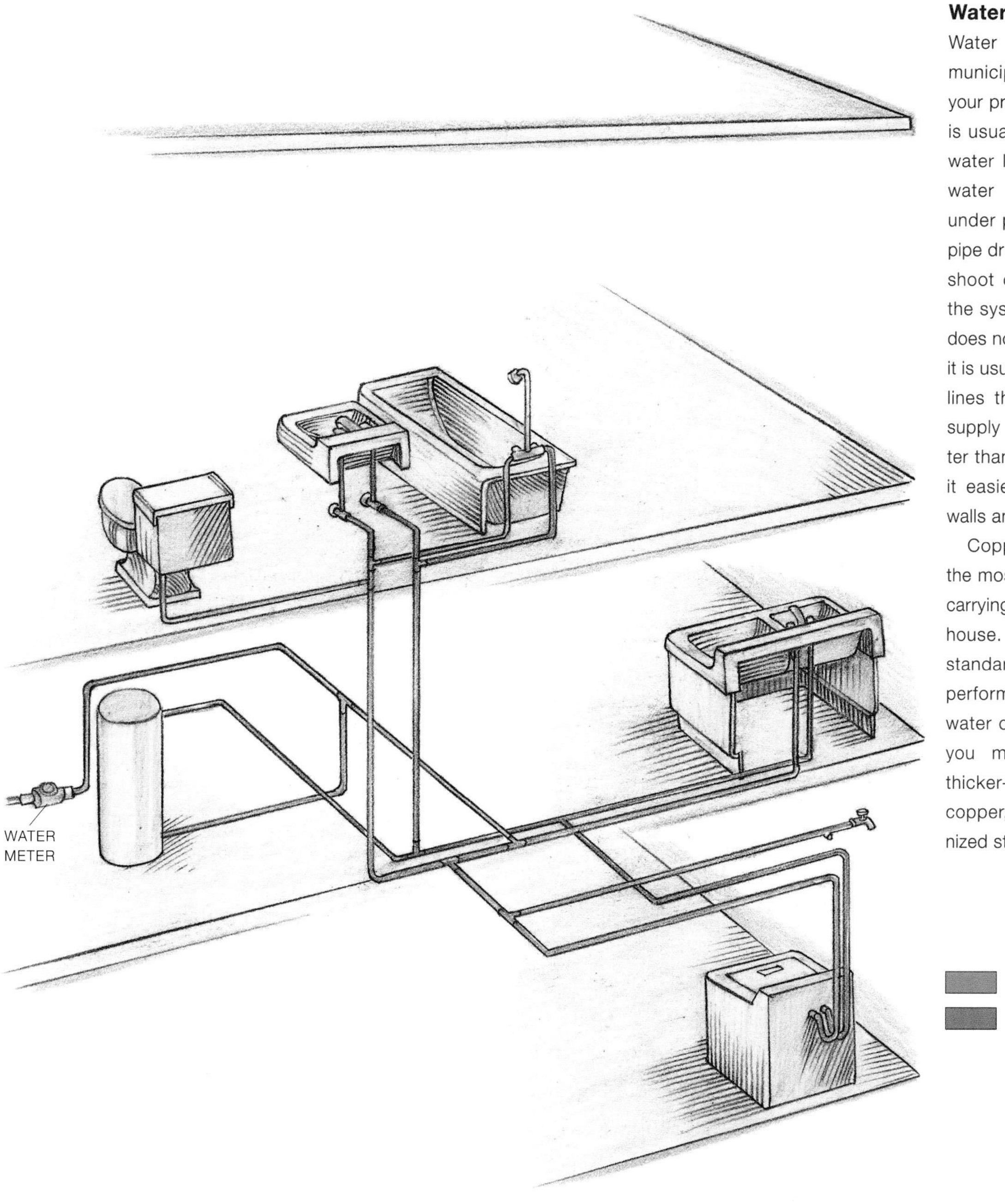

WATER METER

COLD

HOT

Water Supply System

Water enters the house from a municipal water line or a well on your property. A main shutoff valve is usually located near where the water line enters the house. The water supply system operates under pressure—leaks in a drainpipe drip, but those in a supply line shoot out continuously. Because the system is under pressure and does not rely on gravity to function, it is usually easier to extend supply lines than it is DWV lines. Also, supply pipes are smaller in diameter than DWV pipes, which makes it easier to snake them through walls and floors.

Copper tubing is far and away the most common type of pipe for carrying fresh water throughout the house. In some regions, however, standard type M copper does not perform well because of unique water conditions. In those cases, you may be required to use thicker-walled type L or type K copper, or else plastic or galvanized steel.

the waste stack to keep it from dropping when you remove a section.

Measure the length of the new tee, then mark the waste stack, adding about ¼ inch to make sure the tee fits. Wear eye protection and gloves.

Wrap the cutter's chain around the pipe, with the cutting wheels on the first mark, and connect it to the handle, as shown above. Hand-tighten the chain, then carefully crank it until the pipe cracks. Repeat the process on the other mark, then knock out the section.

If you are using a reciprocating saw, be sure to set the blade to a non-orbiting (i.e., metal-cutting) position. Use a lubricant to prevent the blade from heating up and wearing out prematurely.

Slip the new tee and no-hub couplings into place. Tighten the couplings, preferably with a special torque wrench that prevents overtightening.

WORKING WITH COPPER

Cut copper tubing with a tubing cutter or with a hacksaw. Copper tubing is soft, so you'll want to be careful not to damage it as you work. Do not use wrenches and vises, which could crush the metal.

Soldering is the best way to join copper tubing (see facing page). Soldered joints are made with copper fittings that have smooth interiors and, in most cases, internal shoulders, or stops. To solder, or "sweat," a joint, you will need a small propane torch; some emery cloth, 00 steel wool, or very fine sandpaper; a can of soldering flux; and some lead-free plumber's solder. CAUTION: Use only solder that's labeled lead-free when making joints in any potable water supply or in a DWV system.

WORKING WITH PLASTIC

Rigid plastic pipes and fittings are normally joined with solvent cement. Flexible PE tubing is joined with barbed insert fittings. Barbed inserts are forgiving, but solvent cement sets within seconds; if you don't get the alignment right the first time, you'll need to cut the fitting off and start over.

Before you cut any pipe, make exact measurements. Rigid pipes will not give much if they're too long or too short. Minor measuring and cutting errors are rarely a problem when you're using flexible tubing because it usually has enough play.

The quickest, cleanest way to cut plastic pipe and tubing up to about

Watch the Slope

Since the drain-waste system works on gravity, all drain-waste pipes are installed at a slope. Although building codes allow for some variation, the ideal slope is a drop of ¼ inch for every foot of horizontal run. Pipes that are sloped too much can be as troublesome as those that slope too little.

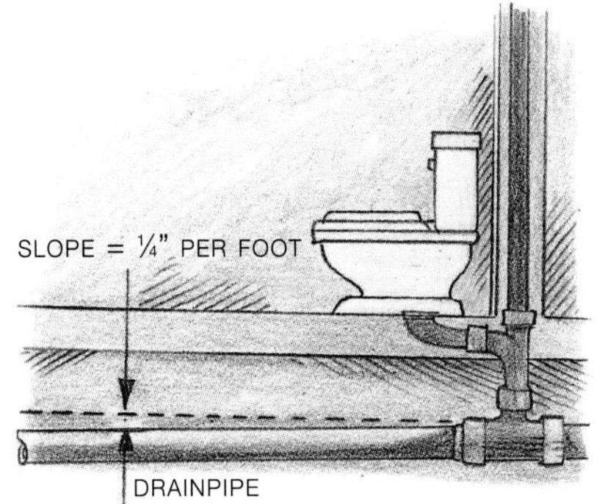

Soldering a Joint

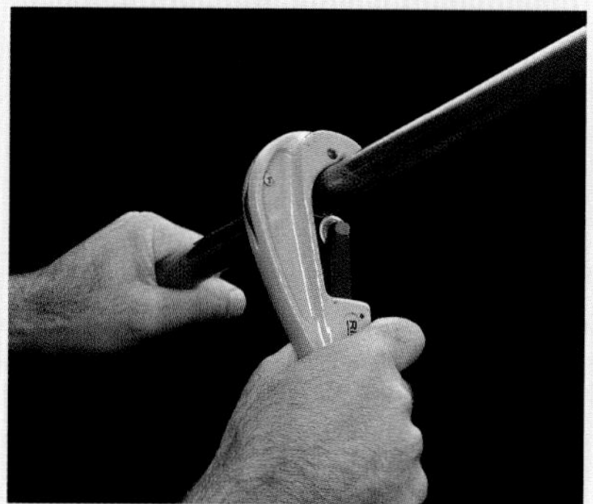

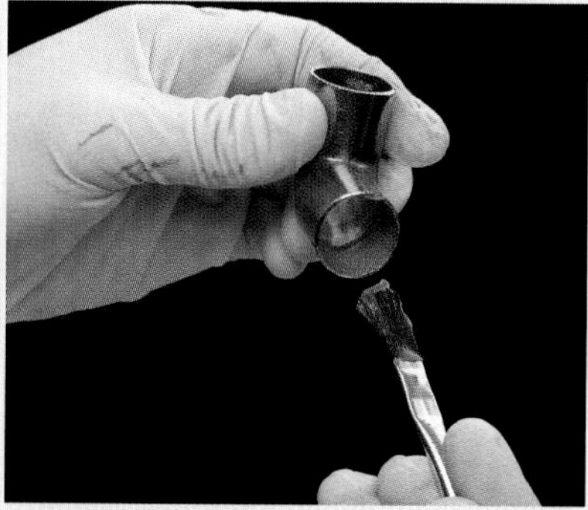

1 CUT THE PIPE
Cut new lengths of copper pipe with a tubing cutter designed for copper. To use the cutter, twist the knob until the cutter wheel makes contact with the surface. Rotate the cutter around the tube, tightening after each revolution, until the pipe snaps in two. You can also cut copper with a fine-tooth hacksaw or a mini-hacksaw, but it's more difficult to make a straight, clean cut.

2 CLEAN THE FITTING
After you've cut the tube, clean off inside burrs with a round file or with a retractable reamer often found on tubing cutters. Use emery cloth, 00 steel wool, or sandpaper to smooth and polish the last inch of the outside end of the pipe until it's shiny. Also clean the inside of the fitting from the end down to the shoulder. You can use the emery cloth or steel wool, but a pipe brush makes cleaning easier.

3 APPLY FLUX
With a small, stiff brush, apply flux that's made for sweat-soldering purposes around the inside of the fitting and around the outside of the pipe end. Place the fitting on the end of the pipe and turn the pipe or the fitting back and forth once or twice to spread the flux evenly. Then position the fitting correctly. Wear gloves when applying flux, as the chemicals can irritate your skin.

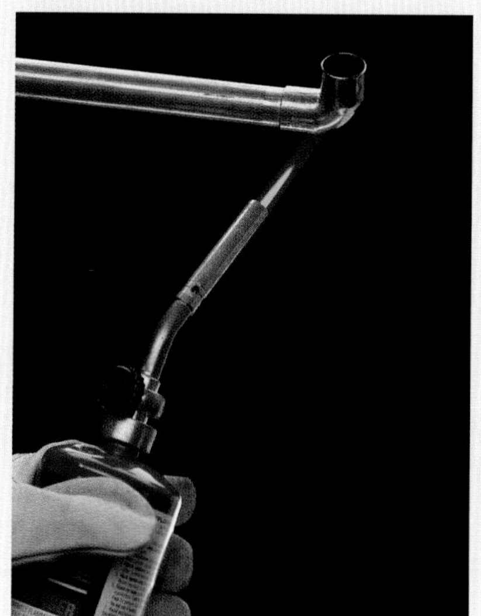

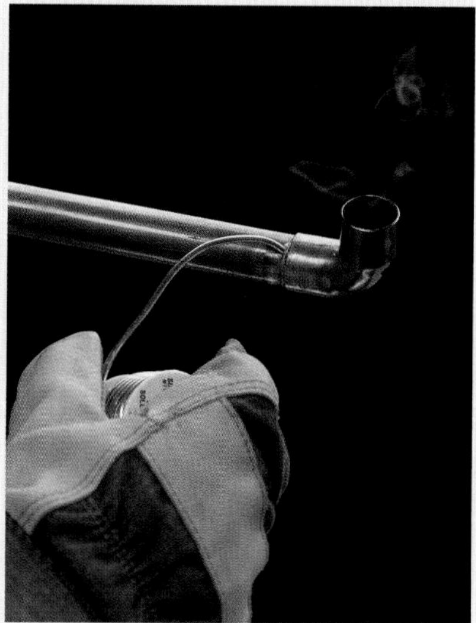

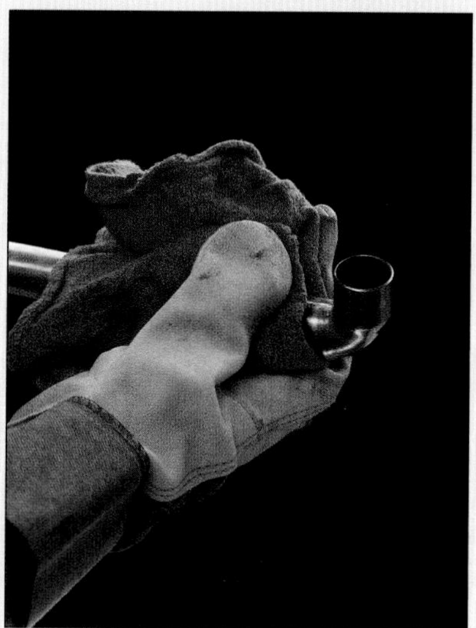

4 HEAT THE FITTING
Turn the propane torch's control valve on, then light the nozzle end with a striker tool. Adjust the flame so it's steady and strong. Position the torch nozzle about 4 inches from the fitting and move the flame back and forth to distribute the heat evenly. Get the fitting hot but not too hot—the flux will burn away if it's overheated. The joint is hot enough when solder melts upon contact. Test by touching the solder wire to the joint occasionally. The instant the solder melts, the joint is ready.

5 APPLY SOLDER
Turn off the torch and touch the solder wire to the edge of the fitting; capillary action will pull molten solder in between the fitting and the pipe. Keep applying until a line of molten solder shows all the way around the fitting.

6 WIPE OFF THE EXCESS
Once the solder cools (in just a few seconds), gently wipe off surplus flux with a damp rag. Keep your hands away from the joint—the pipe can get quite hot as far as 1 to 2 feet on either side of the joint. Also be careful not to bump or move the newly soldered joint for an hour or two, until the solder hardens.

1 inch in diameter is with PVC scissors. You can also cut rigid pipe with a PVC saw and a miter box or with a power miter saw. If you use a saw on an installed pipe, brace the pipe with your free hand to prevent excess motion that could affect the straightness of the cut.

After cutting, use a knife or a reaming tool to remove any burrs inside and outside the pipe end. Inspect the end for cracks, gouges, and deep abrasions. Cut a replacement piece if necessary. Then test-fit the pipe in the fitting. It should enter the fitting but stop partway. When the assembly is inverted, the fitting shouldn't fall off. A successful solvent weld cannot be made if the fit is too tight or too loose.

Joining PVC Pipe and Fittings

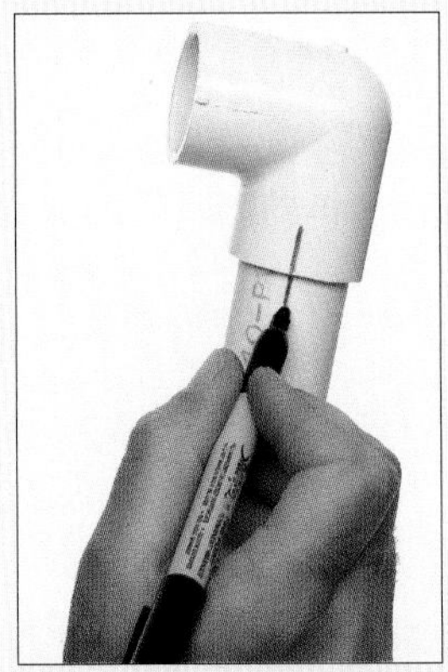

1 MARK THE ALIGNMENT Put the fitting onto the pipe end temporarily and mark the pieces for proper alignment before cementing. Once the cement (which acts as a lubricant) is applied, the pipe will slip further into the fitting, so make your marks long enough to take this into account.

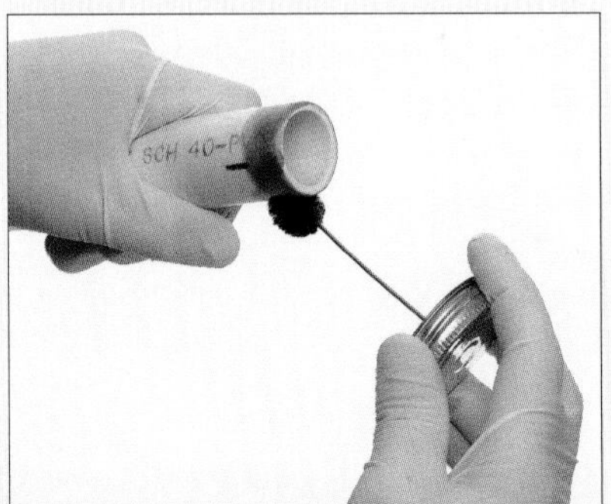

2 APPLY PRIMER Before gluing PVC, spread a layer of PVC primer (often called purple primer) around the end of the pipe and inside the fitting down to the shoulder. The primer should dry in a minute or so.

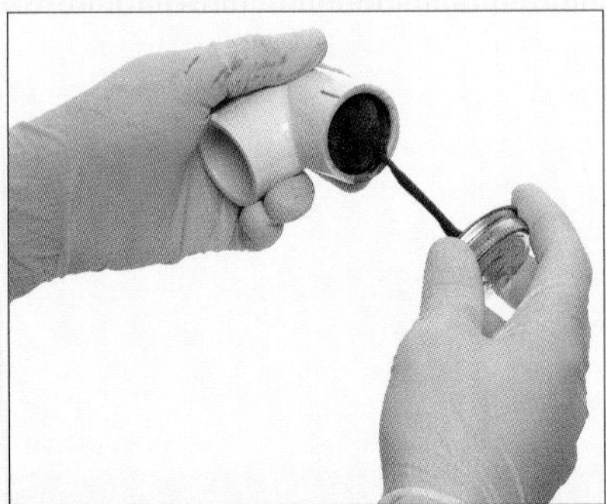

3 APPLY SOLVENT CEMENT Once the primer is dry, apply the PVC solvent cement. Work in a well-ventilated area, avoid breathing fumes, and keep the flammable cement away from sources of flame. Following the manufacturer's instructions, apply cement liberally to the pipe, then more lightly to the fitting socket. If the temperature is below 40°F, use a special low-temperature solvent cement.

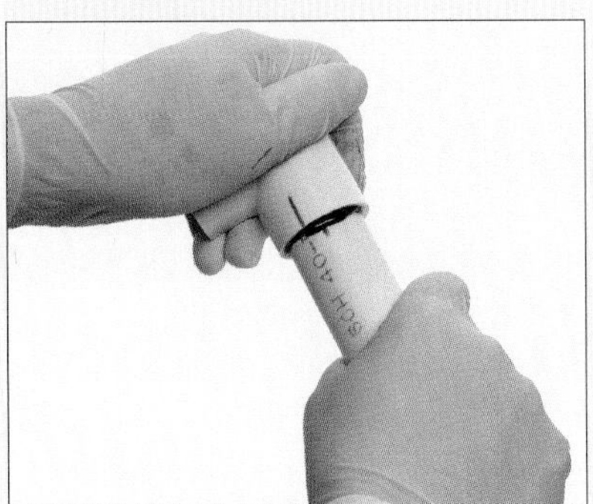

4 SECURE THE FITTING Slip the fitting onto the pipe so your marks are offset ¼ inch or so, then immediately twist the fitting into correct alignment. Hold for a few seconds while the cement sets. Inspect the joint between pipe and fitting. There should be a narrow band of solvent all around.

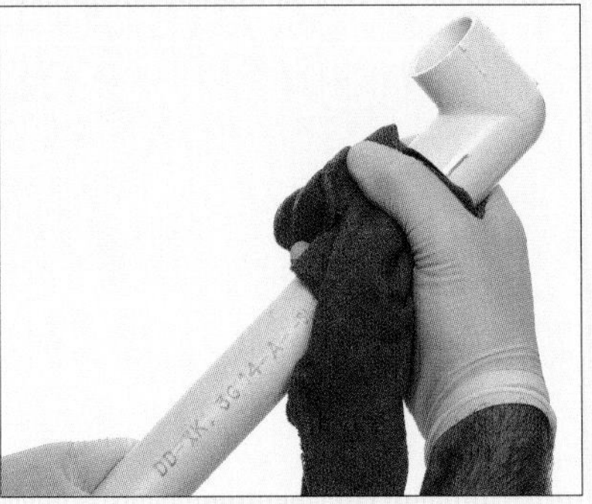

5 CLEAN UP THE EXCESS Wipe off excess cement with a damp rag. Solvent-welded joints can be handled gently within a minute, but wait at least 2 hours before pressurizing with water (and even longer under cold, damp conditions). Then you can turn on the water and inspect for leaks.

Adding Wiring

The first question you should ask yourself when considering any alterations or additions to your present electrical system is "what do I have to work with"? Once you know what type of electrical service you have, you can start planning additions or changes as required.

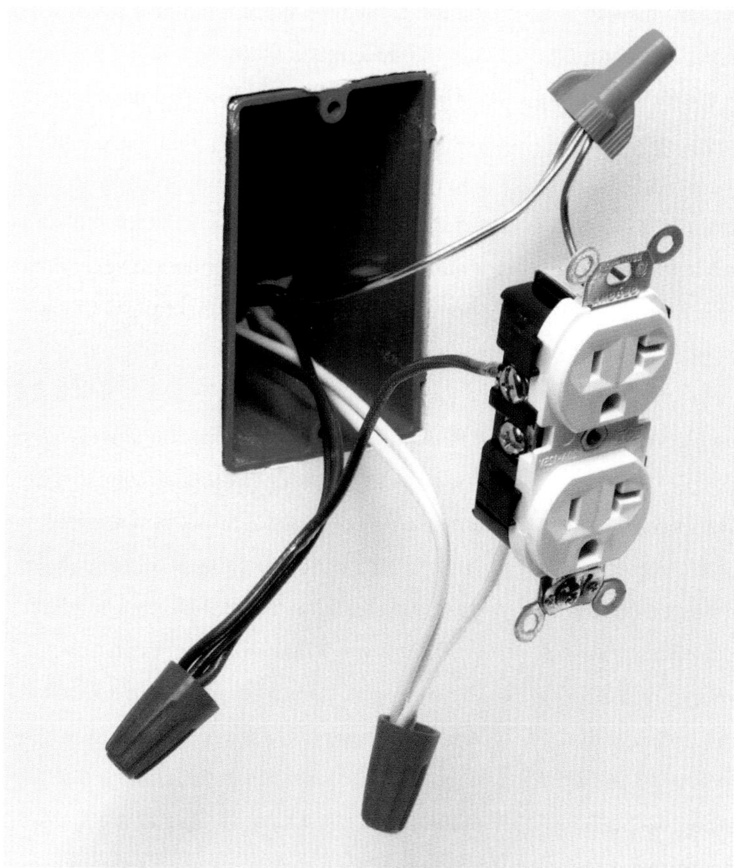

You can usually find out your service rating by looking at the service entrance panel, which contains the main disconnect. If you cannot find the service rating there, call the utility company or your local building inspection department rather than trying to figure out the service rating yourself.

Once you have established the service rating, make a simple map of all the lamps, light fixtures, switches, and appliances on each of the circuits.

The next step is to determine your present usage, or electrical load. Several formulas are available to calculate electrical usage; check with the National Electrical Code, the utility company, or your building inspection department. For more information, see Sunset's *Complete Home Wiring*.

WORKING WITH YOUR EXISTING SERVICE

There are three approaches you can take to accommodate the electrical needs of your converted space: extend the existing circuits, add new circuits, or install a subpanel. Check with your local building department to see if you will need a permit for the planned work and whether or not it must be done by a licensed electrician.

Even if you determine that it is permissible to do the work yourself, it may be a better idea to obtain a permit and get a follow-up inspection. This gives you a solid guarantee that the work is done properly and also gives you access to expert advice from a pro—your electrical inspector. Needless to say, you never want to embark upon such a wiring project without a clear understanding of how to do the job safely and correctly.

Extending a Circuit This is usually the easiest approach, and if you only need a light fixture and a couple of outlets, it may be all you need to do. There are two general categories of circuits. Dedicated circuits serve a single appliance, such as a range, garbage disposer, dryer, or furnace. These circuits should not be altered. General purpose circuits can serve several outlets and fixtures. Presuming you are careful not to overload (see below), you can tap into one of these circuits at any switch, receptacle, or light fixture, as long as it has both a hot wire and a neutral wire that are directly connected with the power source at the service panel. You cannot tap into a switch box that is wired with two hot wires and no neutral wire or to a switch-controlled light fixture at the end of a circuit.

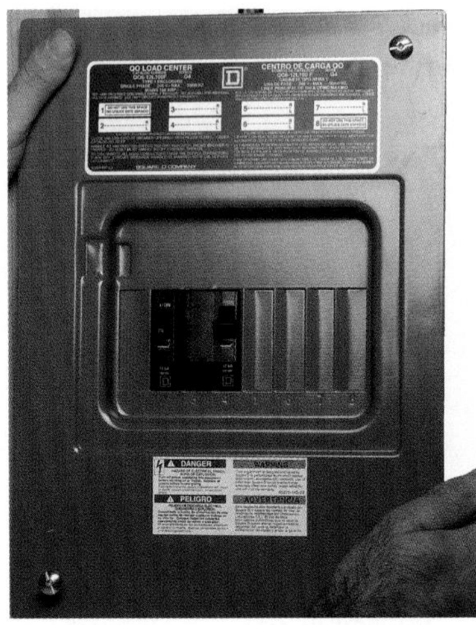

Adding a Circuit If your existing circuits can't handle a new load, or if you are adding major electrical appliances, you will have to add one or more new circuits. Again, before launching into such a job, make sure that the new load you are planning will not exceed the service rating for your existing electrical service.

Adding a Subpanel If you plan to run several new circuits into your converted space, a subpanel may come in handy. You will need to have two branch circuits removed from the main service panel to make room for a two-pole breaker for subfeeds; the subfeeds can then be routed to the new subpanel. Once the subpanel has been installed, you can route new circuits from it rather than from the main service panel.

ADDING NEW SERVICE

If your current wiring system cannot accommodate your proposed additions, you have one additional option: upgrading the service entrance equipment.

For all practical purposes, the minimum size service you'll need is a 100-amp, three-wire service that can deliver 24,000 watts. Higher service ratings are also available, depending on your electrical load. For example, the next larger standard ratings are 125, 150, and 200 amps.

Don't cut any corners when estimating your new service rating. In fact, you should leave an extra margin of service for the future. It is much easier and cheaper to install the larger service entrance equipment the first time than it is to increase your service a short time later.

The type of service equipment you'll need will depend on both its location and on how you plan to run your circuits. If your service entrance is centrally located, for example, you will probably want to run all branch circuits directly from it. On the other hand, if your service entrance panel is in an out-of-the-way spot, it may be preferable to have a smaller service entrance panel and use subpanels, fed by a set of subfeeds from the main panel, elsewhere in your home.

Don't Overload

When tapping into an existing circuit, you do not want to overload it. Overloaded circuits lead to circuit breakers tripping repeatedly or fuses burning out. Before adding any wiring, it's a good idea to prepare a wiring map of your house. Turn off the breaker or unscrew the fuse on each circuit, one at a time, then go around the house seeing which fixtures and outlets are dead. Draw a color-coded map of where each circuit runs.

Next, calculate the wattage on each circuit. Light bulbs and electronic devices usually have a watt rating stamped on them. For devices that use motors, check the amp (ampere) rating on the motor plate and multiply the amps by 120 volts to find the wattage. Check only those devices that are regularly plugged in. The maximum allowable load on a 15-amp circuit is 1,800 watts (or 2,400 watts on a 20-amp circuit), but the ideal load is about 20 percent less. The fuse or breaker controlling the circuit will be marked with the circuit's amperage. If a circuit is already near its maximum load, don't try to extend it. Either look for another circuit to tap into or add a new circuit.

First and Most Important: Be Sure the Circuit Is Dead

Before working with any wiring, make it an iron-clad rule to check first that power to the area you're working on is turned off at the service panel or subpanel.

Before you touch bare wire ends, use a neon tester, as shown at left, to confirm that the circuit is dead. Touch one tester probe to a hot wire or terminal and the other to a neutral wire or terminal, the grounding conductor, or the grounded metal box. The tester will light up if the circuit is live.

Be careful! If by some chance you did not turn off the right circuit or if there is a short in the system, the wires you are testing may still be hot. Make sure to hold the tester probes by their insulation—not by their metal ends—or else you may get a shock or cause a short circuit.

If a lamp or an appliance does not work, that doesn't necessarily mean that the circuit is dead; the appliance itself could be faulty. To check, insert the probes of the neon tester into the slots of a receptacle, as shown below. If the tester lights up, the circuit is still hot.

PREPARING CABLE AND WIRES

Wire is cut to length at the rough-wiring stage; splitting and stripping are done when wiring switches and receptacles. To cut wires or cable to length, use lineman's pliers or diagonal cutters. To open up flat cable, such as two-wire NM (with or without a ground), use a cable ripper or knife to score the sheath lengthwise (see page 36). If you're working with round, three-wire cable, which is needed to wire three-way switches, use a pocket knife or utility knife so you can follow the curve of the twisted wires without cutting into their insulation.

Do not cut cable while it rests on your knee or thigh. Cut it on a flat board or wall surface. Also, never cut toward your body—always work away from it.

Once you have exposed the wires and cut off the outer sheath and any paper or other separation materials, you're ready to strip the insulation off the ends of the wires with wire strippers or a multipurpose tool. Be careful not to nick the wire when you are stripping off its insulation. A nicked wire will break easily when bent to form a loop for a connection to a screw terminal. If you do nick a wire, snip off the damaged end and begin again.

Continued on page 36

Multi-purpose tool

Wire strippers

Diagonal cutters

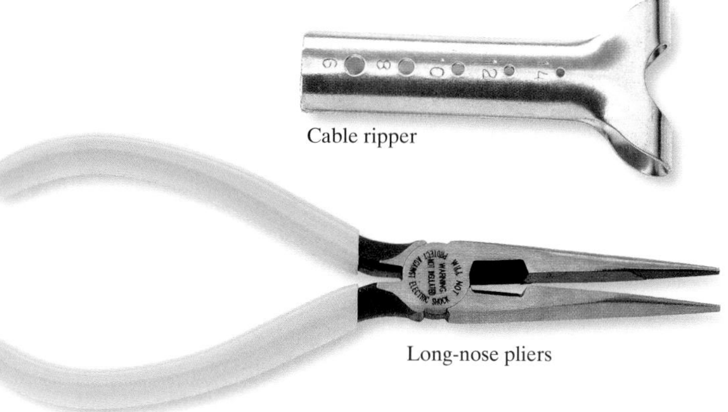

Cable ripper

Long-nose pliers

Ripping Cable

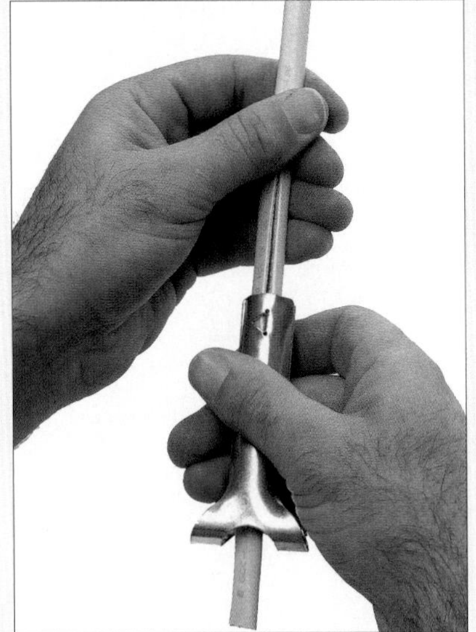

1 SLICE THROUGH THE SHEATH
To cut flat cable, first slide a cable ripper up the cable. Press the handles of the cable ripper together and pull toward the end of the cable. This action will score the outer sheath.

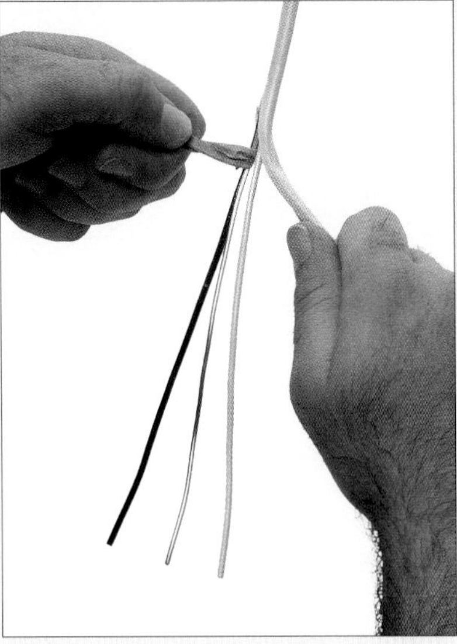

2 EXPOSE THE WIRES
Bend the cable back to crack the score, then peel open the outer sheath of insulation. Pull the outer sheath and all separation materials away from the cable end, exposing the wires.

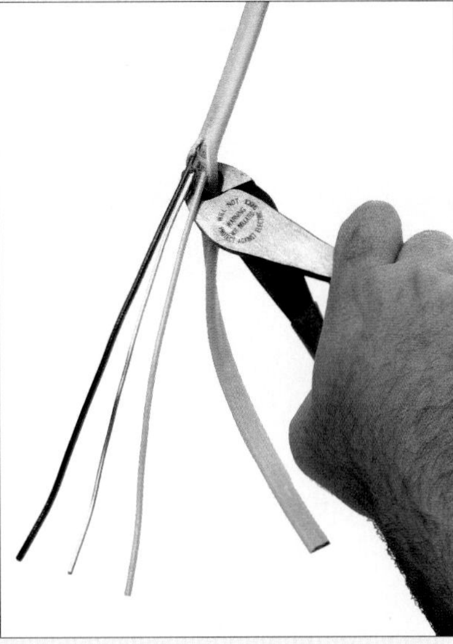

3 CUT OFF THE SHEATH AND SEPARATION MATERIALS
Using a pair of diagonal-cutting pliers or utility scissors, cut off the opened sheath and paper or other separation materials, leaving just the insulated wires.

Stripping Wire

1 GRIP THE WIRE
Using wire strippers, insert the wire into the matching slot. Holding the wire firmly in one hand, with your thumb extended toward the end of the wire, position the strippers on the wire with your other hand and press the handles together.

2 SLIDE OFF THE INSULATION
Rock the strippers back and forth until the insulation is severed and can be pulled off the wire in one quick motion. Once you get the hang of it, wire stripping is easy.

ROUTING CABLE

In new construction, all rough wiring is completed before wall, ceiling, and floor coverings are put in place. The procedures for doing so are shown in the pages that follow. If you must run cable and mount switches and receptacles on a masonry wall, see pages 168–169.

Nonmetallic sheathed cable (type NM) is used for most new work. To make your work easier, plan to run cable along the surface of structural members (studs, joists, rafters, etc.) whenever possible. Where you must route it at an angle to the members, you will have to drill holes through which to run the cable.

When drilling holes for cable, use the smallest drill bit practical—typically ¾ inch. To avoid weakening the joists or studs excessively, drill through the center of the boards. If a hole is less than 1¼ inches from the edge of the board, you must tack a metal plate over the edge, as shown on page 38.

Make a rough sketch of the route for your cable, including critical measurements such as the height of boxes from the floor and the distance between boxes. Total all the lengths. Then, for box-to-box runs, add at least 4 feet (2 feet for each box) for mistakes, box connections, and unforeseen obstacles. When cable goes to a box from either a service entrance panel or a subpanel, add at least 6 feet (4 for the panel, 2 for the box).

Continued on page 39

A cordless right-angle drill bores a string of ¾-inch holes through a run of new wall studs. Whenever possible, drill through the centers of framing members, well away from the edges.

A run of 12-2 NM cable makes its way through parallel holes toward a new receptacle box.

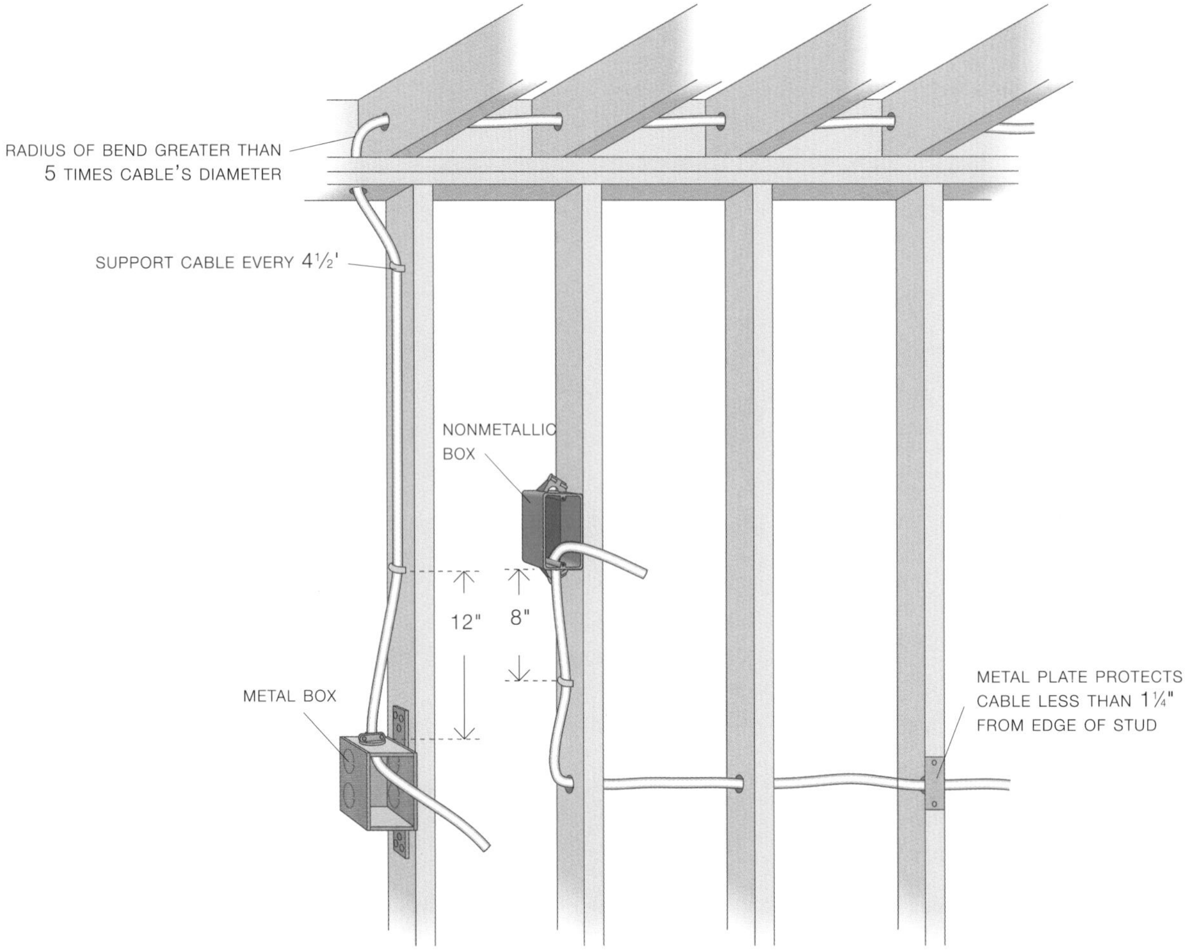

RADIUS OF BEND GREATER THAN 5 TIMES CABLE'S DIAMETER

SUPPORT CABLE EVERY 4½'

NONMETALLIC BOX

12"

8"

METAL BOX

METAL PLATE PROTECTS CABLE LESS THAN 1¼" FROM EDGE OF STUD

What's the Best Way to Secure Cable?

In new exposed wiring, cable must be stapled or supported with straps every 4½ feet and within 12 inches of each metal box and 8 inches of each nonmetallic box. When using cable staples (left), be careful not to staple through or smash the cable. Staple the face of the cable, not the side. Use metal plates (right) to protect cable that is installed less than 1¼ inches from the front edge of a stud or other structural member.

Cable staples or supports are not required when cable is fished behind walls, floors, or ceilings. However, in such concealed work, the cable must be clamped to boxes using built-in cable clamps, metal cable connectors, or plastic cable connectors (if the box is nonmetallic). There is one exception: NM cable does not need to be clamped to a nonmetallic box if it's stapled within 8 inches of the box.

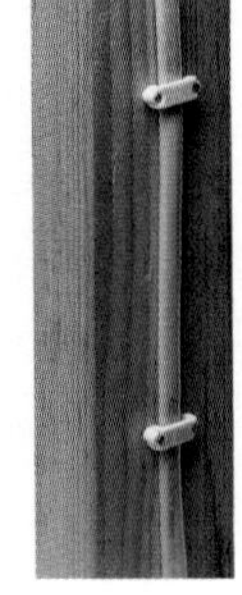

MOUNTING BOXES

Boxes that house wiring come in a variety of types and sizes. You first need to decide which kinds of boxes you need and where you want them. Put your plans on paper, noting where boxes will be needed.

When shopping for boxes, make sure they have the right mounting holes for the devices you plan to install. Also be sure the boxes have suitably placed knockout holes for routing cable in and out. Boxes may have built-in clamps for securing cable, or you may have to purchase separate cable connectors. Most importantly, buy boxes that are big enough for the job at hand. A box's cubic-inch (or "box fill") rating varies depending on its depth and whether it is plastic or metal. To be safe, choose the deepest boxes that will fit your wall or ceiling. A slightly oversized box makes it easier to make the necessary connections; an undersized box constitutes a code violation.

Keep receptacles a uniform 12 to 18 inches above the floor. Switch boxes are typically installed 48½ inches from the top plate. This allows the ceiling to be covered with ½-inch drywall and the top sheet of drywall to be installed horizontally without having to make a cut for the box. (If the ceiling height is greater than 8 feet, however, measure up 48 inches from the floor instead.) Be sure to avoid placing a switch box on the hinge side of a door opening. Remember that every box must be accessible.

Boxes are installed using an external nail or flange (collar), an internal screw, or a hanger bar. Several standard installations are shown below and on the following page. If you want to hang a box between two studs or joists but don't have a hanger bar, you can nail a 2 x 4 between the members and attach the box there.

Boxes should be installed flush with the finished wall or ceiling. If the covering is not yet in place, tack or hold a scrap of your finish material to the stud or joist next to your box and use it to align the box's front edge.

Continued on page 40

Ceiling box with flange

Nail the flange to the side of an exposed ceiling joist, aligning its front so that it will be flush with the finished ceiling material. Some boxes have "spiked" flanges, which allow you to anchor the boxes first with a tap of the hammer before driving the nails home.

Screw-on handy box

The back or side of this box can be attached directly to framing—or, in this case, a scrap block mounted between wall studs.

Nail-on wall boxes

These nonmetallic boxes are simple to install: just butt them against a wall stud and nail them home. Some versions are side-mounted with integral nails; others are front-mounted (the thin mounting flange is covered by the wall material). Note that in the photo at left, a scrap of drywall helps align the side-mounting box with the finished wall material. The flange on the front-mounting model shown at right adjusts to align the box.

Pancake box

Simply screw this ceiling box to a joist or an exposed beam. Position the box so that it will hide the hole drilled for the cable. But do not make wire or cable splices in this type of box—it's big enough to accommodate only two conductors and a grounding wire.

Adjustable hanger bar

This ceiling box spans two joists. The two-piece bar can be narrowed or expanded to fit various joist spacings. The box also slides along the bar, allowing you to fine-tune the fixture's placement.

JOINING WIRES TO TERMINALS

Many switches and receptacles come with two sets of connection points where wires can join them: screw terminals and back-wired terminals. Screw terminals are tried-and-true connection points. To make these hookups, you need to strip insulation off the wire ends (see page 36), then use long-nose pliers to bend the wire ends into hooks (see below). The only other tool you need is a standard screwdriver. However, screw terminals can accommodate only one wire; if you need to join several wires at a single screw terminal, use a pigtail splice.

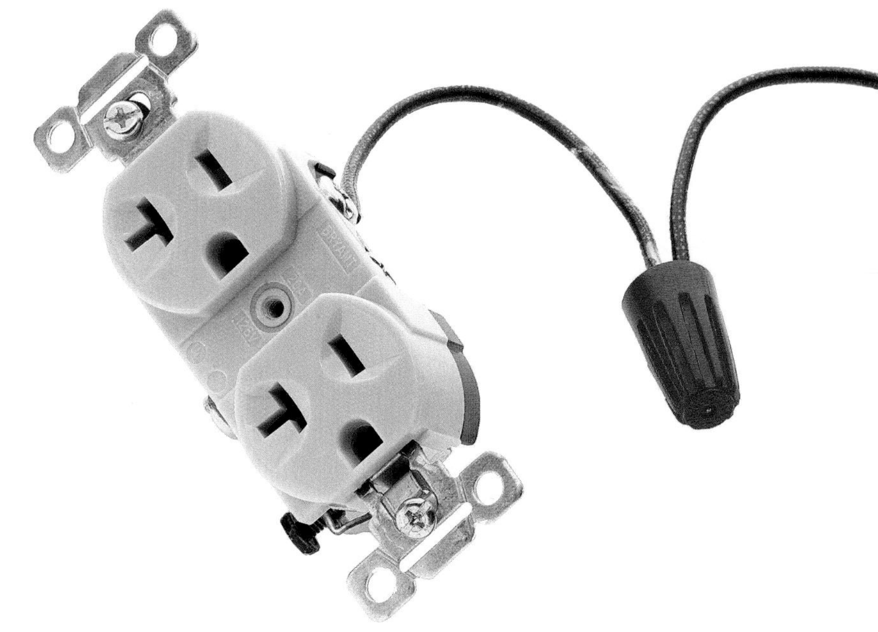

Joining Wires to Screw Terminals

1 FORM A HOOK
To make wire-to-screw terminal connections, first strip about ½ inch to ¾ inch of insulation off the wire end. Then, using long-nose pliers, form a two-third to three-quarter loop in the bare wire: starting near the insulation, make progressive right-angle bends, moving the pliers toward the wire end until a loop is formed.

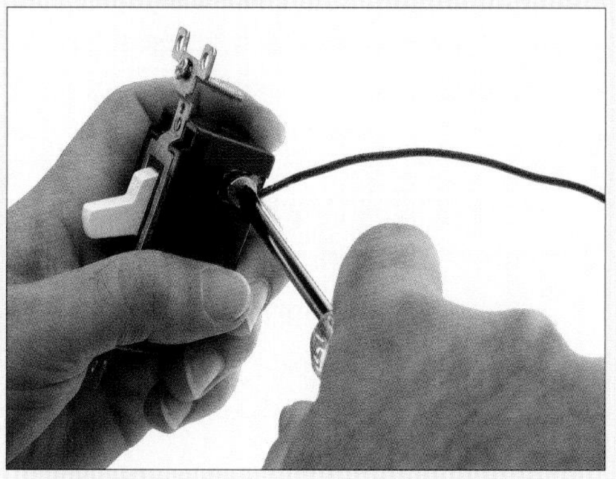

2 SECURE A TERMINAL CONNECTION
Hook the wire clockwise around the screw terminal. As you tighten the screw, the loop on the wire will close. If you hook the wire backward (counterclockwise), tightening the screw will tend to open the loop.

WIRING SWITCHES

Most switches in a home are of the single-pole type: an on-off toggle controls a light or receptacle from a single location. However, a whole range of specialty switches, including dimmers, pilot switches, and timers, expand on the tried-and-true switching function. A pair of three-way switches will let you control a light fixture or receptacle from two locations. Two three-way switches working with a four-way switch will let you operate a device from three locations.

CAUTION

Before wiring any switch, be sure to disconnect the circuit by removing the fuse or by switching off the circuit breaker. For a 240-volt circuit, you may have to remove two fuses or trip a two-handled breaker.

Installing Single-Pole Switches

Single-pole switches have two terminals of the same color (usually silver or brass) for wire connections, and an obvious right side up. All switches are wired into hot wires only; with a single-pole switch, it makes no difference which hot wire goes to which terminal. Most new designs are wired the same way as standard single-pole switches. Switches marked AL-CU may be used with either copper or aluminum wire. Unmarked receptacles and those marked with a slash through the AL symbol can be used with copper wire only.

Traditional 120-volt switches had no grounding wires because their plastic toggles were considered shock-proof. However, for extra safety, many switches now have grounding terminals. Installation of such switches is similar to that of grounded receptacles: join the incoming circuit grounding wires to a jumper connected to the green switch terminal, securing the wires with a wire nut or compression sleeve. If the housing box is metal, you will also need to include a short grounding jumper to the box's grounding screw or grounding clip.

Begin by removing the outer sheath of insulation and all separation materials from the cables inside the box (see page 36); strip the insulation from the wire ends. Then connect the wires as follows:

- Join the neutral (white) wires, if any, and cap with a wire nut.
- Join the grounding wires with a wire nut or compression sleeve. For a metal box, include a grounding jumper from the box.
- Connect the hot wires to the switch's screw terminals. It makes no difference which wire goes to which terminal. Secure the grounding jumper to the green grounding terminal.
- Fold the wires behind the switch and carefully push the switch into the box. Screw the switch to the box; align the switch vertically by adjusting the screws in the mounting slots. If the switch isn't far enough out to be flush with the drywall or other surface material you will be using on the wall, you can later shim it out using the break-off portions of the switch's plaster ears or special washers sold for that purpose.

Making Sound Connections

Always strip your wires so that, once attached, no more than 1/32 of an inch of bare wire extends beyond the screw head—or, for that matter, beyond any connector. At the same time, don't let the insulation extend into the clamped area. If necessary, unscrew the connection and start again.

Wiring Diagrams: Single-Pole Switches

Because of cable-routing logistics, your circuit wires may run from the service entrance panel or a subpanel to a switch in one of two ways: through the switch box to the fixture that the switch controls, or to the fixture box first, with a switch loop to the switch box. Three typical setups are shown here. The single-pole switches shown include grounding terminals. If your switch doesn't include them, just omit the grounding jumper between the cable grounding wires and the switch.

POWER ENTERS SWITCH BOX

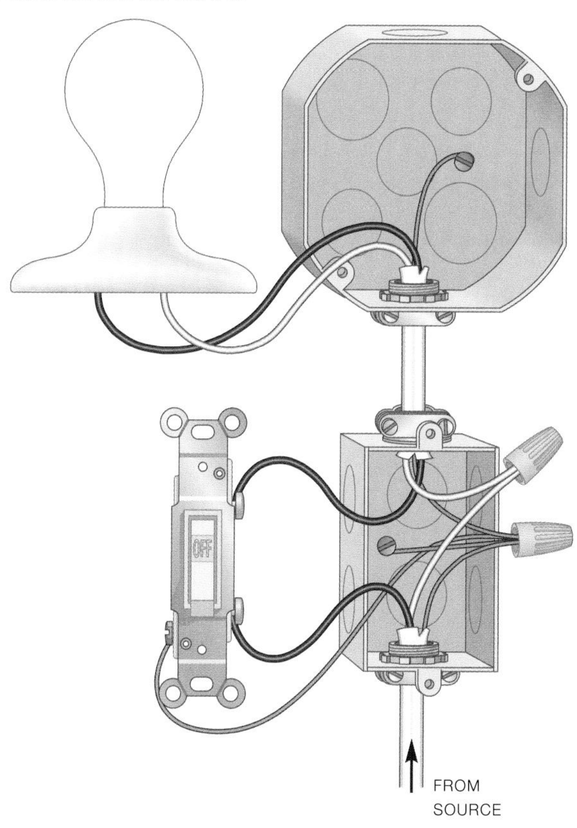

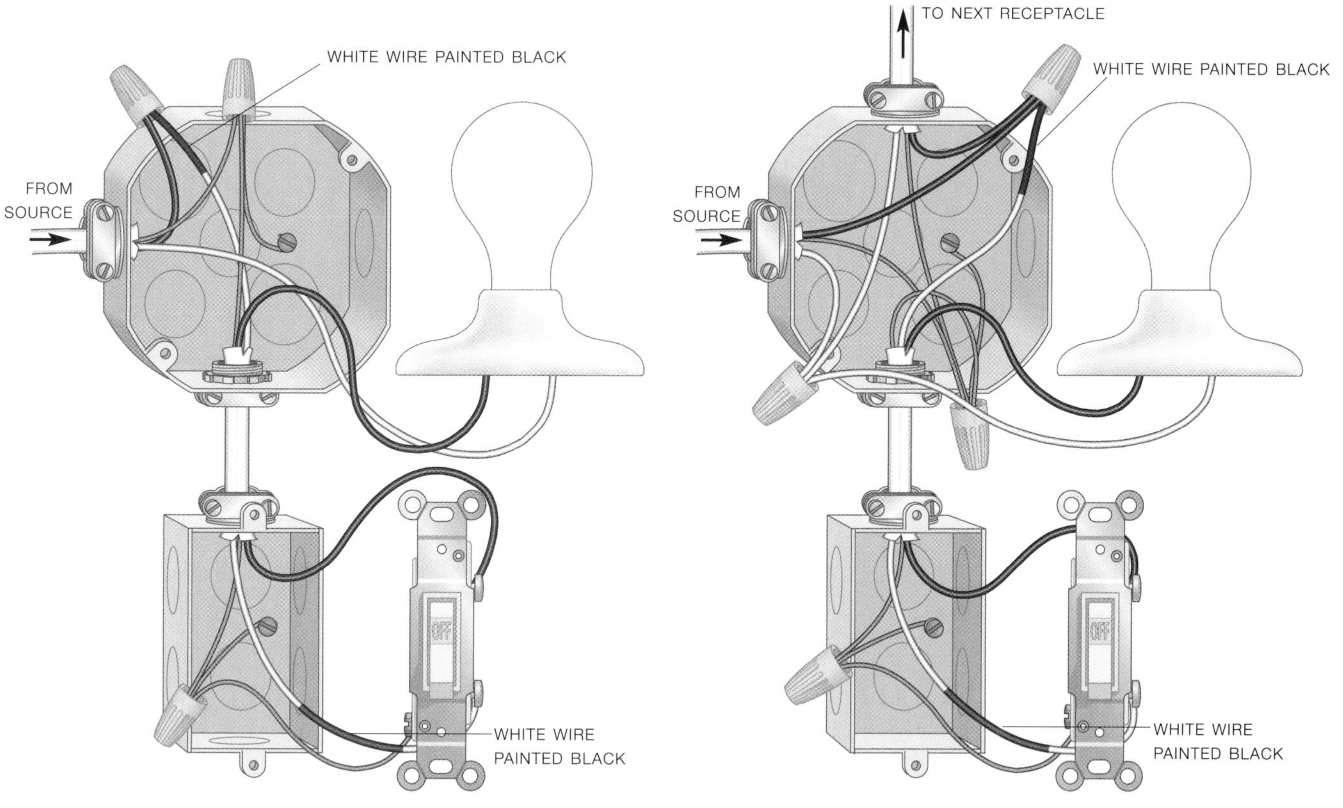

Split-Circuit Receptacles

Occasionally it may be appropriate to have the outlets of a duplex receptacle operate independently. For example, you might want one outlet to be controlled by a switch and the other to be always hot. Or you may wish to wire a receptacle's two outlets into different circuits. To make the outlets operate independently, use pliers to remove the break-off fin that connects them.

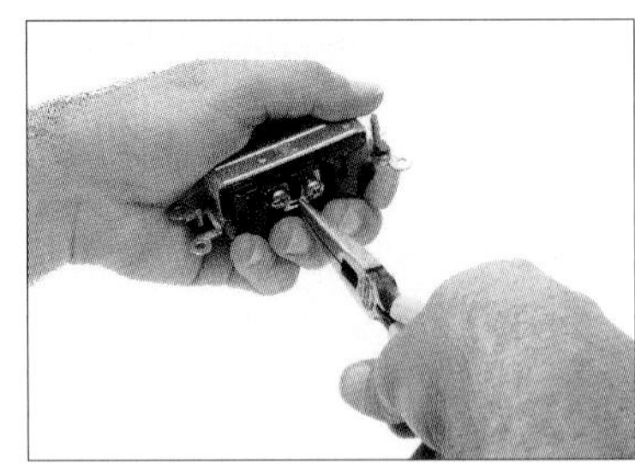

CAUTION:

Before wiring any receptacle, be sure to disconnect the circuit by removing the fuse or by switching off the circuit breaker. For a 240-volt circuit, you may have to remove two fuses or trip a two-handled breaker.

WIRING RECEPTACLES

Receptacles are designed for either 120-volt, 120/240-volt, or straight 240-volt use. Receptacles are also rated for a specific amperage.

The drawings on page 45 show typical wiring configurations for receptacles in the middle or at the end of a circuit. Use them as a reference when you are planning a wiring route or installing a receptacle.

How to wire a receptacle

First, remove the outer sheath of insulation and all separation materials from the cables inside the housing box (see page 36); then strip insulation from the individual wire ends. Next, connect the wires as follows:

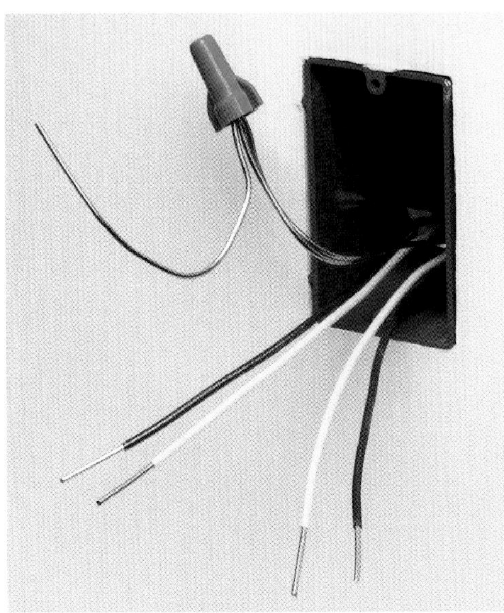

- Use a wire nut to join the circuit's grounding wires with a grounding jumper from the receptacle (above). For a metal box, include a jumper from the box.
- Join pairs of hot (black) and neutral (white) wires entering and leaving the box. Add a jumper from each splice.
- Attach the hot jumper to one brass screw terminal and the neutral jumper to the silver terminal (as shown below). Secure the grounding jumper to the green grounding screw. Tighten unused screw terminals.

- Now, carefully fold back the wires and screw the receptacle to the box. Adjust the screws in the mounting slots until the receptacle is straight. If the receptacle isn't positioned to be flush with the drywall or other surface material you are planning to add, you can later shim it out using the break-off portions of the receptacle's plaster ears or washers sold for that purpose.

Receptacle Wiring Diagrams

The usual arrangement is for receptacles to be wired in such a way that all outlets are always hot. In other cases, the power may need to be routed first through a fixture box and/or a switch box. A wall switch may also control a receptacle.

The drawings on this page assume that your housing boxes are metal; if they're not, you still have to ground each receptacle, but there's no need to also ground the boxes. Always attach the grounding wire to the green grounding screw on the receptacle. Remember, you must be able to pull out and disconnect a receptacle without interrupting the grounding continuity of the circuit.

If you want to add a receptacle to a circuit that doesn't have a grounding wire, you can use either a grounding type and run a separate grounding wire to an approved ground; install a GFCI; or, in some areas, use an old-style, nongrounding receptacle.

RECEPTACLE AT THE END OF THE CIRCUIT, ALWAYS HOT

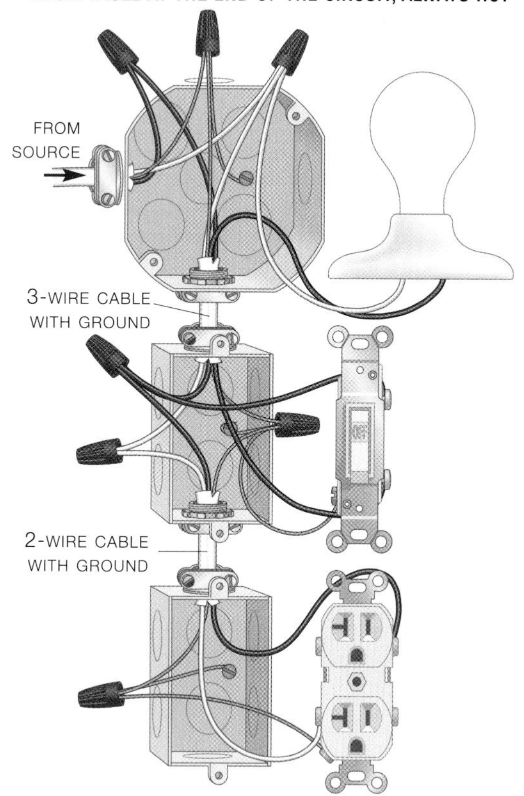

RECEPTACLES AT THE END OF THE CIRCUIT

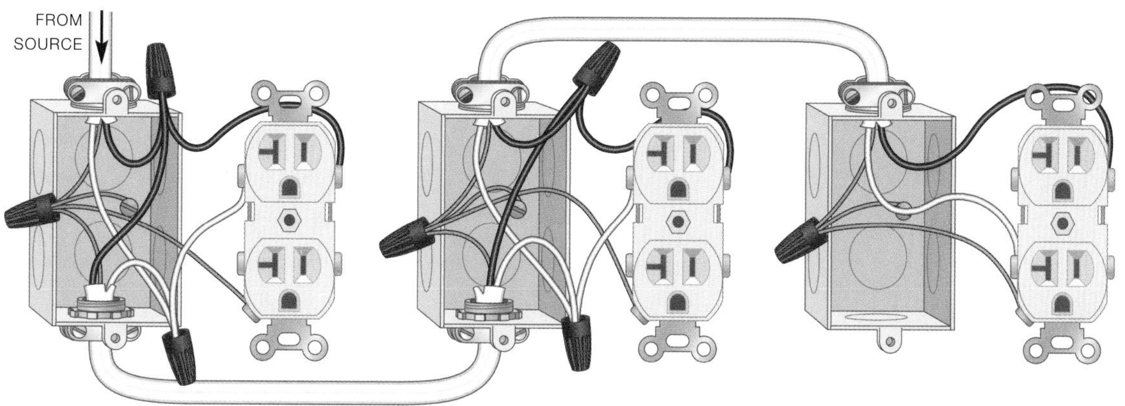

SWITCH-CONTROLLED RECEPTACLE

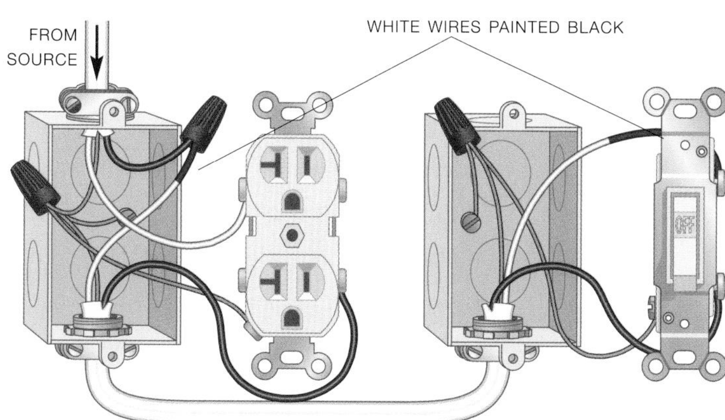

Heating and Air Conditioning

One of the biggest challenges in creating new living space is ensuring that the rooms will have adequate heating, cooling, and ventilation. There are two basic ways of addressing the matter: by adding on to an existing system or by creating an independent system. If you intend for your remodeled space to become a regularly used part of the house, it's best whenever possible to heat it by tapping into the existing system. In most cases, this is a job that should be left to an experienced contractor.

The most common residential heating systems are forced air and hydronic, or circulating hot water. Forced-air systems utilize a furnace to heat air, which is then distributed through a system of supply and return ducts (top left). The same network of ducts can be used to distribute cooled air as well. Forced-air systems are generally easier to extend than hydronic, especially with the insulated flexible ducts that are now available.

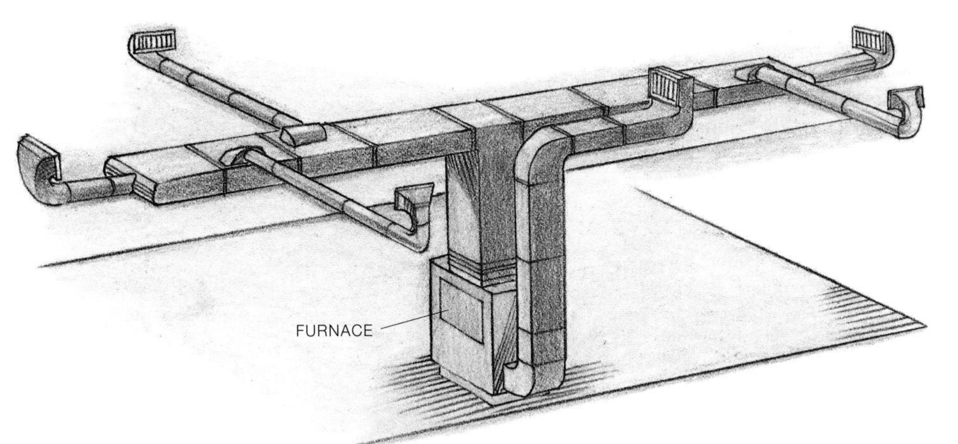

In a traditional hydronic system, a boiler heats water, which is then delivered by pipes throughout the house to radiators or baseboard units (bottom left). In newer radiant hydronic systems, the heated water passes through pipes or tubing buried in floors, ceilings, or walls. Extending hydronic systems has become easier with the appearance of reliable, flexible plastic tubing that can be snaked through walls and ceilings. When floor space is at a premium, consider installing wall-mounted panel radiators rather than baseboard units.

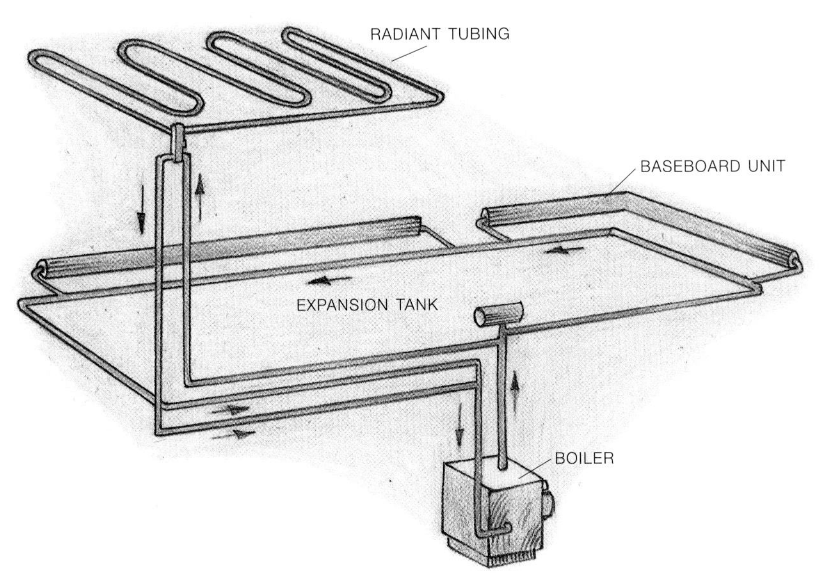

Even if the main part of your house does not have hydronic heat, you may still want to consider adding a new system to heat just the converted space. Adding hydronic heat may be affordable if a water heater is used rather than a more expensive boiler to heat the water. Talk with an experienced hydronics contractor for further guidance.

The first step in extending your heating system is to have a contractor perform a heat-loss calculation for the house, including the space to be converted. With this information you will be able to determine if your current system will be able to handle the extra load. If the conclusion is that your current system is already stretched to its limits, don't despair. It's possible that by adding insulation, resizing ducts, or increasing blower speed you may be able to create sufficient excess capability. As you look into your existing system, you may also want to consider replacing your old furnace or boiler with a newer, more efficient model.

Choosing an Independent System

There are many choices in independent heating systems. Each has its own lists of pros and cons.

Electric heaters Electric baseboard and wall heaters are inexpensive to install, but can be very expensive to operate. In a cold climate, electric baseboards are a poor choice for a room that will be used often, unless there are no other options. On the other hand, in a moderate to warm climate, this kind of heat may make the most sense for a room that will not be used often. Cost aside, electric heat has several things going for it: it is quiet, clean (since there is no combustion in the house), and unobtrusive. It does not require a large furnace or boiler.

Space heaters Space heaters are portable devices that can be fueled by gas, electricity, or kerosene. They typically don't cost much, and, since they are portable and deliver heat only where you want it, they can be an economical choice for some uses. For kerosene and gas units though, you will want to consider the merits and potential dangers of ventless installation. Be aware, too, that building codes in some areas restrict the use of certain types of space heaters.

Woodstoves and fireplaces A woodstove might be a good choice for heating a converted garage, attic, or basement, provided you have room for a safe installation and a proper chimney. Prefabricated fireplaces are another option worth considering. They can be fueled by gas or wood, and direct-vent models can be vented through the wall, eliminating the need for a chimney. Vent-free gas fireplaces are growing in popularity, but there is some concern with the effect these units have on indoor air quality. Before considering a vent-free product, consult consumer and public health publications.

CAUTION: DON'T CHOKE YOUR HEATER

Any heater or appliance that runs on fossil fuel requires combustion air to function safely. If your basement or garage contains gas- or oil-fired devices and you are planning to seal them up as part of a remodeling job, you run the risk of reducing combustion air enough to cause back-drafting (i.e., exhaust fumes being sucked back into the space). This potentially dangerous situation can be addressed by installing a powered exhaust system, upgrading to high-efficiency sealed combustion equipment, or providing an alternative source of fresh air. Consult with a mechanical contractor.

Masonry Repairs

The best time to repair cracks in concrete or mortar joints is as soon as you discover them. If you plan to cover the floors or walls of your basement or garage, take the time to repair all cracks and other damage before the problems get buried. If cracks that were previously repaired have opened up again, you may have an underlying structural problem that should be evaluated by a construction professional.

Cracks in concrete that are under ¼-inch wide can be repaired with a premixed product. For cracks in garage and basement floors, use a concrete crack sealer. For basement walls, use a concrete patching caulk, which is applied with a caulk gun.

Repairing larger cracks or small holes in floors or walls requires more preparation to ensure that the repair will hold. Use patching mortar for these fixes, and follow the instructions at right, below.

If the walls of your basement or garage are built of concrete blocks, check to be sure that none of the blocks are loose and that the mortar in the joints is not cracked. Repair any loose joints or cracks with joint filler, as shown at right.

Repairing Mortar Joints

To repair loose or cracked mortar joints between concrete blocks, remove mortar with a cold chisel to a depth of about 1 inch. Brush out debris. Dampen the joint with water (a spray bottle works well), then pack the joint with mortar using a joint filler. Finish the joints with a curved jointer or other finishing tool to match the adjacent joints.

Repairing Small Cracks

1 PREPARE THE CRACK
Use a stiff brush to clean all dirt and loose material from the crack. Vacuum any debris that the brush cannot reach.

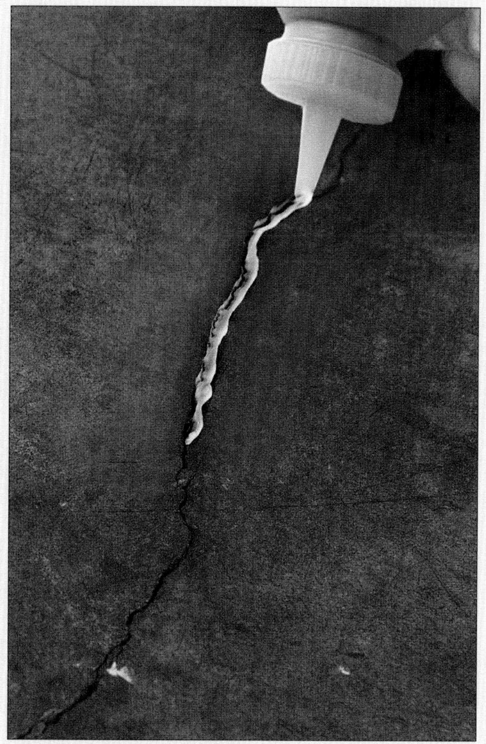

2 SEAL THE CRACK
Cut off the tip of the sealer or caulk, then apply in ¼-inch layers. If necessary, push the sealer or caulk deep into the crack with a putty knife. Allow each layer to set, as directed by the manufacturer, before applying the next one.

Repairing Large Cracks and Small Holes

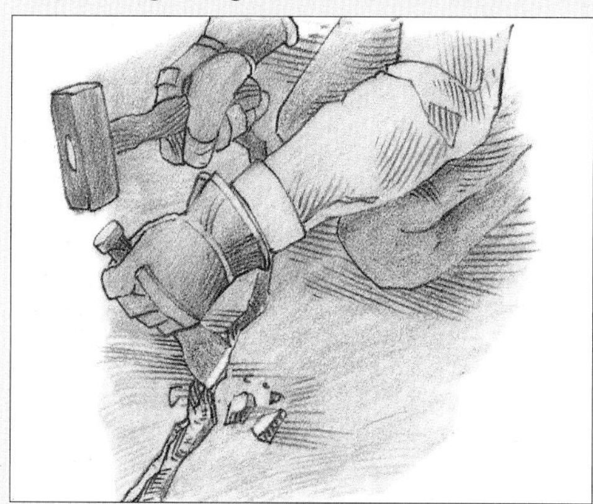

1 PREPARE THE CRACK OR HOLE
With a small sledgehammer and a cold chisel, enlarge the crack slightly. Undercut the crack by holding the chisel at an angle; by making the bottom of the crack wider than the top, the patching mortar will stay in place better. Follow the same approach for a small hole, undercutting the edges. Clean all debris out of the crack or hole with a brush or shop vacuum.

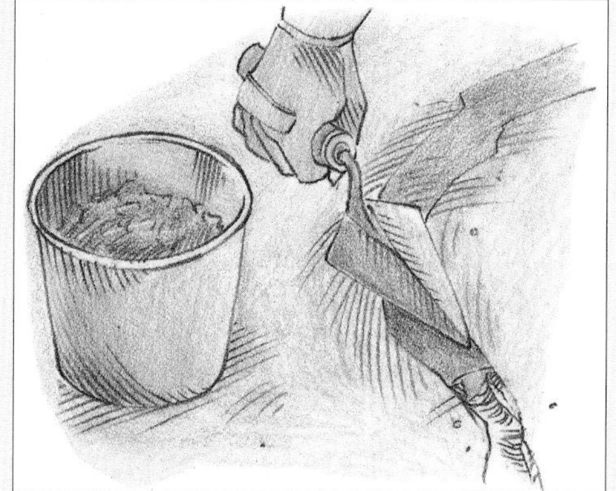

2 APPLY THE PATCH
For a crack, use a pointing trowel to force patching mortar deep into the crack. For a hole, use a margin trowel or pointing trowel to fill the hole. Smooth the patch flush with the surrounding concrete.

Techniques: Closing In

With the framing, wiring, rough plumbing, and other "behind-the-walls" work completed, the next step is to cover it all up. This chapter is devoted to the process of choosing and installing the surface materials for your ceiling, walls, and floor. After finishing the work detailed in this chapter your remodeled space will have much of its final appearance.

A variety of products is available for each of these surfaces, and they can be finished in a multitude of textures, colors, and effects. The following pages focus on the most common surfacing materials, which are generally also the most convenient to use.

Ceiling and wall installations are within the capabilities of nearly anyone with the patience to work carefully. Floors can be a bit more challenging. Creating a professional-looking floor may be trickier than you think; don't be afraid to subcontract the job. Use this section of the book to help you choose materials and understand what to look for when you talk to a contractor.

Insulation and Soundproofing

Proper insulation can improve the comfort level of a house in nearly any climate. Not only does it allow you to heat and cool your house at less expense, but insulation can also double as a very effective soundproofing material, muffling noises from outside the house or from adjacent rooms.

As a first step toward insulating your home, reduce air leaks by sealing gaps with caulk (above) and spray foam (below).

In a remodeling project, insulation must be approached with an eye toward the condition of the rest of the house. If you create a new, superinsulated living space in what is otherwise a largely uninsulated house, you may find that the imbalance creates too much temperature variation from room to room. On the other hand, maximizing the insulation in the new space may allow you to reduce the heating and cooling load that will need be delivered to the room, thereby reducing both immediate and long-term costs.

STOP THE LEAKS

As effective as insulation can be, it will only work properly if you also plug and seal any gaps leaking air into or out of your house. Although newer, energy-efficient houses are constructed to be tightly sealed against leakage, older houses can leak enormously. Common sites for air leakage include:

- Between sill plates and the foundation
- Plumbing penetrations
- Around electrical outlets
- Behind built-in cabinets and baseboards
- Around windows and doors
- Around chimneys and flues

As you seal the gaps in your remodeled space, consider taking the time to extend your efforts to the rest of the house. Caulk and spray foam, used as directed, are the best materials for filling most gaps.

Choosing Weatherstripping

Weatherstripping is used to seal leaks around doors and windows. There are many different products available. Some of the best are listed below and shown opposite.

Rubber tape or closed-cell foam tape is sold in self-adhesive rolls. These are cut to fit along doorjambs and on the tops and bottoms of double-hung window sashes.

Felt is used to seal inside edges around doors and windows. It is sold in rolls, either plain or with metal reinforcement, and is attached with tacks or staples.

V-strips are available in self-adhesive plastic or bronze, and must be tacked or stapled in place. Use them on the inside tracks of sliding windows and around door jambs.

Tubular gaskets are made of rubber or vinyl, and are attached by their flange with tacks or staples. They are especially useful around doors and windows with irregular gaps.

Door sweeps seal gaps along the bottoms of doors.

Moisture Control

Warm air inside your home can contain a lot of water vapor. As this air makes contact with the cool edges around the exterior of the house, the moisture can collect in wall and ceiling cavities, causing mold and mildew to form, paint to peel, and wood to rot. Vapor retardants, such as plastic (polyethylene) sheets, the backing on "faced" fiberglass batts, vinyl wallpaper, and vapor-blocking paint, block warm, moist air from escaping. In most parts of North America, vapor retardants should be placed on the warm, interior side of walls, floors, or ceilings. In hot, humid climates, however, any vapor retardant should be installed outside the insulation.

Choosing Insulation

There are several types of insulation available, and all work well if installed correctly. Choose the product that best suits your needs and installation abilities.

Fiberglass is sold in batts that fit between wall studs or ceiling joists. Larger fiberglass blankets can be set on top of joists in an attic, while loose fiberglass can be blown into cavities. You can now buy fiberglass that is wrapped or made with "low-itch" fibers, thus eliminating a major irritant for many people. Fiberglass is readily available, inexpensive, and easy to install. See the next two pages for instructions on installing batts.

Cellulose is a loose-fill insulation that is growing in popularity. Made primarily from recycled newspapers and treated with a fire retardant, cellulose is usually blown into wall and ceiling cavities with a special blowing machine. Blowers can be rented at many tool rental stores, and home centers will sometimes loan you a free one if you buy your cellulose there. Though trickier to install than fiberglass batts, cellulose is a good choice for filling existing walls. Just cut a hole large enough for the hose, then patch the hole when you're finished blowing in the cellulose. Be sure to get thorough instructions from the dealer.

Rigid panels of foam or polystyrene are particularly useful on basement walls and on concrete floors in basements and garages. Rigid panels offer high insulation value without a lot of thickness.

INSTALLING FIBERGLASS BATTS

In terms of price, availability, and ease of installation, it's hard to beat fiberglass insulation. Here are some tips to make using this material easier.

- Buy the right size. For 2 x 4 walls, you will want 3½-inch-thick batts. However, you should be able to find thicknesses to fit just about any depth you have. Don't buy overly-thick batts and try to squeeze them in; doing so will actually reduce the insulation value. Choose 15-inch widths for framing that is set 16 inches on center, or 23-inch widths for framing that is spaced 24 inches on center.
- Decide on the right length. For standard 8-foot walls, you can buy batts that are precut to 93 inches. You can also buy longer rolls and cut them to the length you need. For bays containing wiring and other obstructions, you may want to use precut 4-foot batts. Split and install the bottom batt first, as described in the illustration below, then stack another batt on top.
- To protect yourself, wear gloves, eye protection, long sleeves, and a dust mask. Fiberglass can be itchy and irritating to your skin, eyes, and lungs.
- Before setting a batt into place, fluff it a bit to its full thickness; fiberglass does not insulate properly if it is compressed. After fluffing, cut and install it so that it just fills the entire cavity, without being forced.

Fiberglass Techniques

1 CUTTING FIBERGLASS Place the fiberglass over a piece of plywood. Measure the batt to the length or width you need, then lay a 2 x 4 or other straightedge at the point to serve as a guide. Slice through the fiberglass with a utility knife.

2 WORK AROUND OBSTRUCTIONS Don't try to jam the full thickness of a fiberglass batt behind wires or pipes. Instead, peel the batt in half, slide half of it behind the obstruction, then place the other half on top. Around electrical boxes, split the batt enough to slide half behind the box. Cut out the front section with scissors or a utility knife for a snug fit around the box.

3 ATTACHING FACED BATTS Faced batts have flaps around the edges, which are stapled to studs or joists to hold them in place. The face serves as a vapor retardant and should be located on the "warm" side of the wall. The flaps are typically stapled to the outside edges of the framing, but some installers prefer to staple the flaps to the inside of the bay.

Quiet

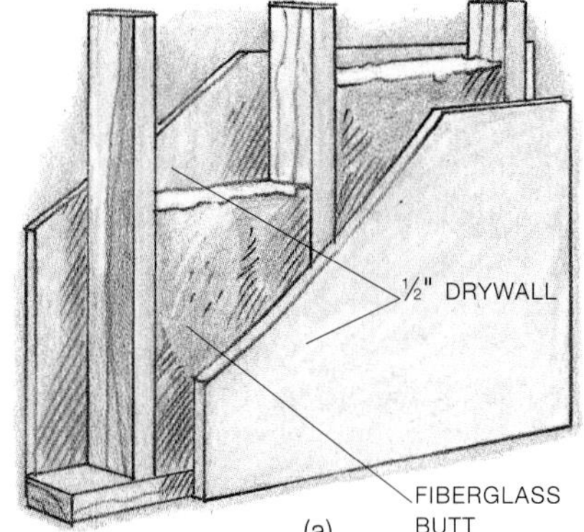

Quieter

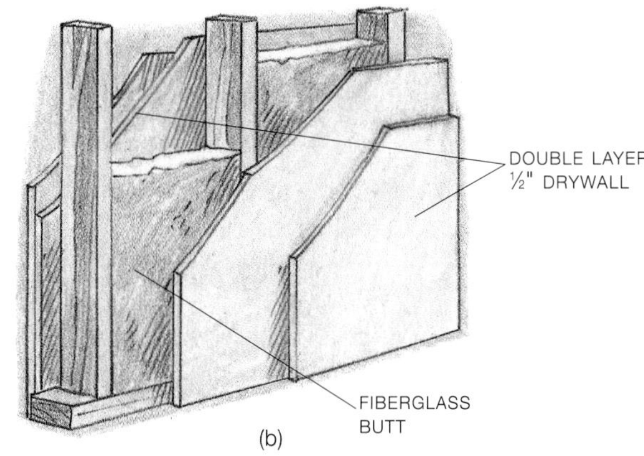

Quietest

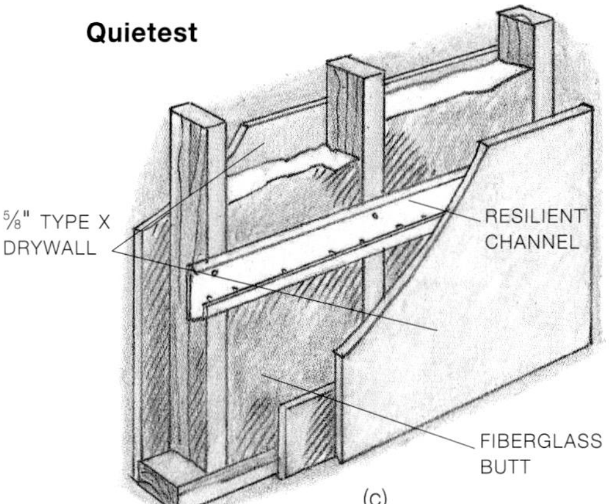

Three Alternatives for Soundproofing a Wall

(a) Install fiberglass batts between the studs or joists. Regular insulation works well, but you can also look for special noise-control batts that have been introduced by insulation manufacturers. If you don't want to disturb existing walls, insulation can be blown in through small holes drilled in the walls, which can be patched when you are done.

(b) Attach extra surface material, such as acoustical tiles or panels or added layers of drywall. Standard drywall is ½ inch thick; using ⅝-inch sheets will be an improvement. Type X (fire-resistant) drywall is also good since it is denser than normal drywall.

(c) Add resilient channels, which reduce vibration by separating the drywall or other surface material from the joists or studs. Resilient channels are available through drywall suppliers.

- To fill small cavities around windows or elsewhere, tear small strips of fiberglass and push them into place with a putty knife. Fill the space without compressing the insulation.

ADDING SOUNDPROOFING

When you seal and insulate a house, you not only reduce air leakage, but you also make it quieter. That's because noises pass through gaps and empty walls just as easily as hot and cold air. In addition to insulating, however, there are other steps you can take to reduce sound transmission.

To reduce the noise level within a room, finish it with sound-absorbing materials, such as carpeting, heavy furniture, wall hangings, and thick curtains.

To keep noises in one room from being disruptive in another, first seal any gaps. You can use caulk, spray foam, and weatherstripping materials to block sounds from passing through openings. Typical problem areas are around loose-fitting doors, heating vents, and back-to-back electrical outlets. An even more effective solution is to add mass to the walls, ceilings, or floors. As shown in the illustrations above, you can add weight and density by simply layering additional materials within the structure of the wall.

Ceilings

While the ceiling is usually not a prominent feature of a room, it serves the practical purposes of dampening noise and hiding pipes, wires, and ducts. Choosing the right ceiling material, moreover, can brighten a room with light and color. The most common ceiling choices are drywall, suspended ceiling systems, and ceiling tiles.

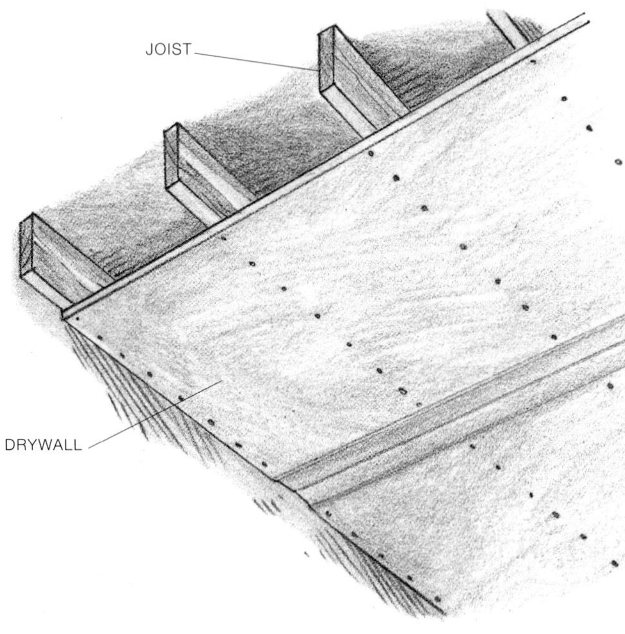

Drywall Also called gypsum wallboard, drywall is inexpensive and—for a highly experienced crew—quick to install. The drywall is attached directly to joists with screws, as shown at left, below. Because of the size and weight of the panels, however, drywall ceiling installations are trickier than installations on walls.

Tiles Ceiling tiles are available in a variety of decorative and acoustic styles. Typically 1 foot square, tiles are usually stapled to 1 x 3 furring strips that are attached to joists (see the facing page). You can also attach tiles to special tracks available from ceiling tile manufacturers.

Suspended Ceilings Easy to install and more forgiving than drywall, suspended ceilings provide an effective, reasonably attractive surface, while providing easy access to wiring, plumbing, and ductwork (see below). The panels absorb sound and, should you want to change the color or texture, you can replace them. If headroom is a problem in your garage, attic, or basement, however, a suspended ceiling may not be the best choice. For detailed information on installation, see pages 58 and 59.

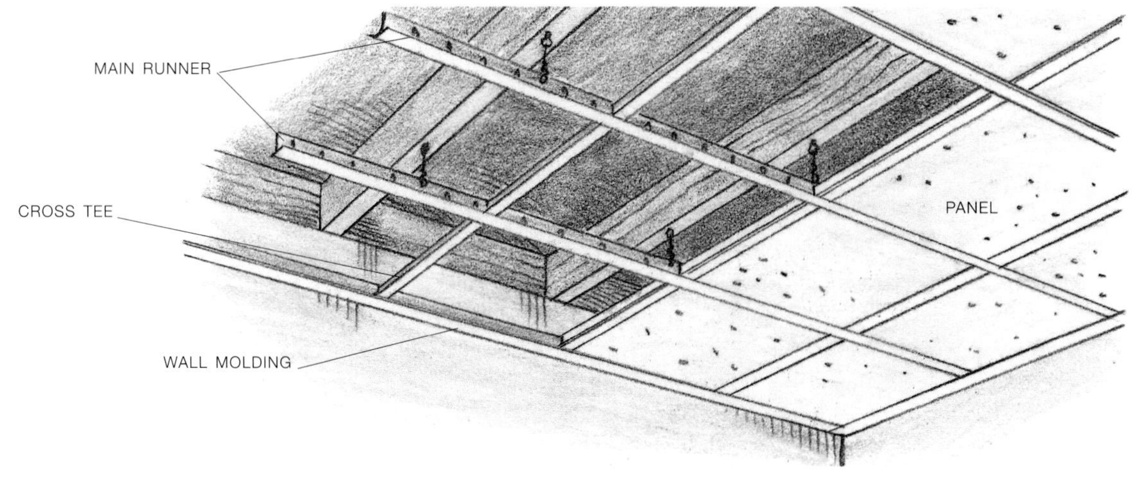

Installing Ceiling Tiles

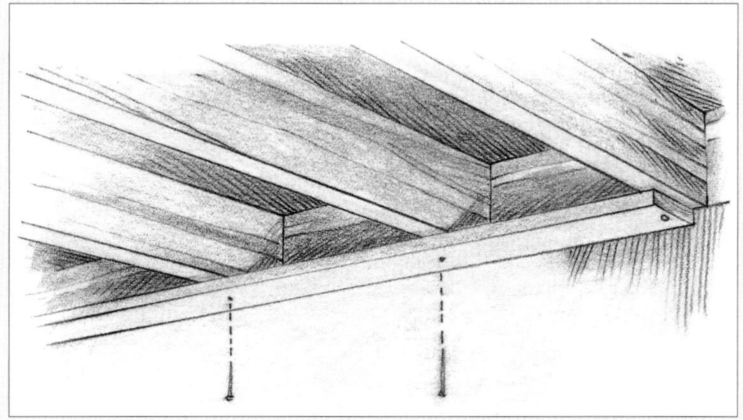

1 ATTACH THE FURRING STRIP
Fasten furring strips to the ceiling joists with 2-inch nails. Place the first strip along the edge of one wall, perpendicular to the joists. Place the second strip so that the edges of the border tiles will be centered on the strip. (Note: As discussed in Step 3, the border tiles will not necessarily be full-width tiles.) Space succeeding strips 12 inches on center.

2 LEVEL THE FURRING STRIPS
Level the strips with one another, checking with a straightedge. At the high spots, place shims between the furring strips and joists before nailing.

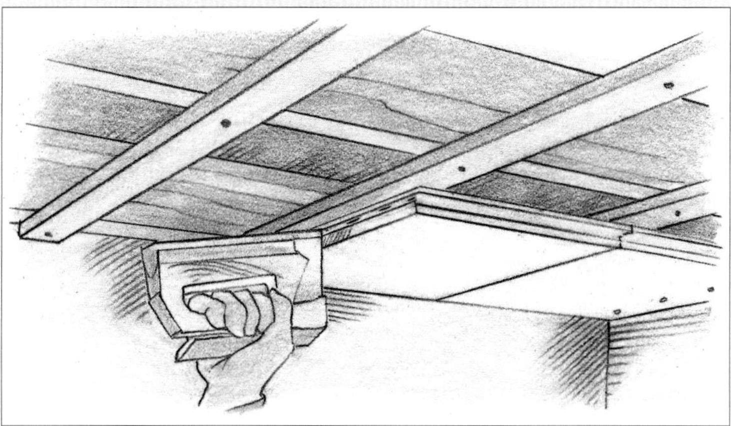

3 LAY OUT THE BORDER TILES
Plan your layout so that the border tiles are the same width on each side of the ceiling, and so that you can avoid using very narrow tiles on the borders (see "Plan the Layout" on the next page). Cut tiles with a utility knife and place the cut edges against the wall. Face nail these tiles in place, positioning the nails where they can be concealed by a molding. Staple the other sides of the tiles to the furring strips through the flanges.

4 INSTALL THE REMAINING TILES
Work outward from the border tiles across the room. Center each tile on the furring strips, as shown, and staple in place.

INSTALLING SUSPENDED CEILINGS

A suspended ceiling is held in place by a metal grid, which is supported from above by wire or hangers. Here are a few considerations when selecting materials for such a ceiling:

- Which grade? Commercial-grade panels cost a bit more, but are considerably more durable than consumer-grade. The latter, however, offers a somewhat wider range of styles.
- Which grid? The standard one-inch grid is easier to work with, and less expensive, than the narrow or concealed grid systems.
- Lighting panels that fit into the grid openings are available from some manufacturers.
- Which panel? Panels are available in 2-foot squares and 2 foot by 4 foot rectangles. The squares are less likely to sag over time and usually look better in a residential setting.

Installing Suspended Ceilings

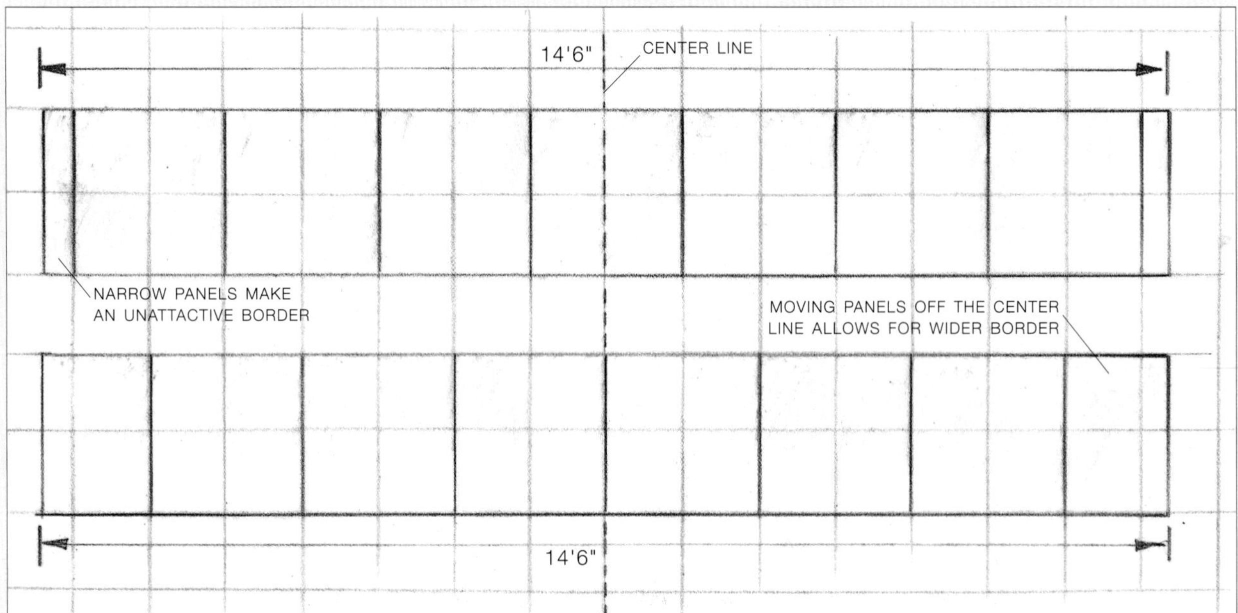

1 PLAN THE LAYOUT

Drawing your layout on paper first is helpful in two ways: it will allow you to know how much material to buy and will make the installation easier. Use graph paper and a pencil to prepare the layout. Your primary concern should be with the borders. Try to keep the opposite borders the same width and make those panels as wide as possible. In the illustration, both examples have opposing border panels that are the same width. However, by reducing the number of full tiles from seven to six, the border panels in the lower example can be 15 inches wide. This will be more visually pleasing than a ceiling with 3-inch borders, as shown in the example at top. On your layout, mark the locations of main runners, cross tees, and hanger wires (see the illustrations that follow for guidelines).

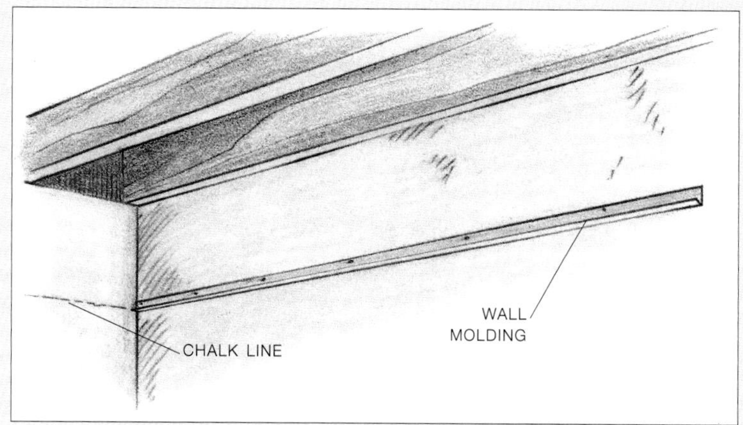

2 ATTACH THE WALL MOLDING

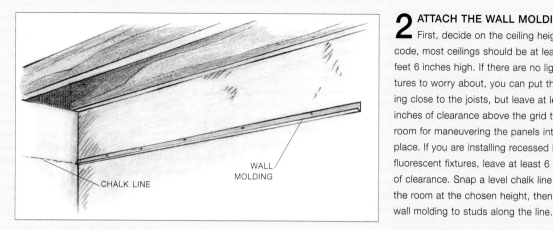

First, decide on the ceiling height. By code, most ceilings should be at least 7 feet 6 inches high. If there are no light fixtures to worry about, you can put the ceiling close to the joists, but leave at least 2½ inches of clearance above the grid to allow room for maneuvering the panels into place. If you are installing recessed lights or fluorescent fixtures, leave at least 6 inches of clearance. Snap a level chalk line around the room at the chosen height, then nail the wall molding to studs along the line.

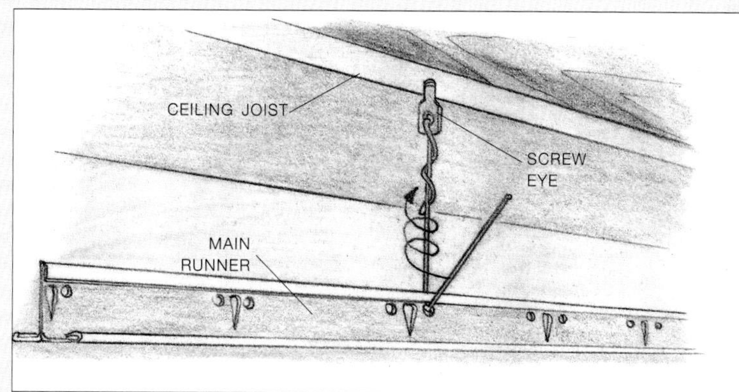

3 INSTALL THE MAIN RUNNERS

Cut the main runners to length with tin snips or a hacksaw and set them on the molding, following the dimensions on your layout. Attach the eye screws or other hardware supplied by the manufacturer to joists, spaced no more than 4 feet apart. Run wire from the screw eye through the runner. Twist the wires, making sure that you do not pull the runners out of level.

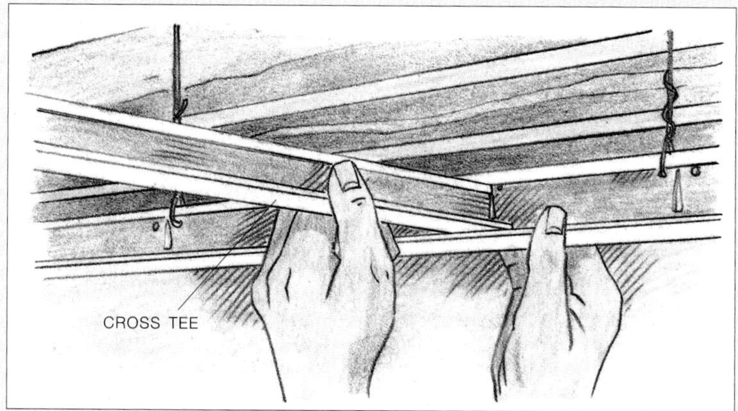

4 ATTACH THE CROSS TEES

Install the cross tees into the main runners and wall molding. Measure the diagonals of each grid to make sure it is square.

5 INSTALL THE PANELS

Slide the panels up at an angle through the grid openings, then lower them into place. If the panels have a directional pattern or texture, be sure to set the panels accordingly. Cut border panels with a sharp utility knife. To avoid smudging panels, work with clean hands.

Installing Drywall

Drywall, or gypsum wallboard, consists of a core of gypsum coated on both sides with paper. The standard drywall thickness for both ceilings and walls is ½ inch, although ⅜-inch and ⅝-inch sheets are also available. The thicker sheets provide better sound resistance and are less likely to sag. Standard sheets of drywall are 4 feet wide and from 8 feet to 16 feet long.

Moisture-resistant drywall has a light green or blue surface; it is used mainly in bathrooms and around laundry facilities or kitchen sinks. *Fire-resistant drywall* is treated to contain fire. It is often required in attached garages, in rooms containing furnaces or other utilities, and in walls and ceilings separating apartment or condominium units. *Abuse-resistant drywall* stands up better to rough treatment than regular drywall. Consider it for a workshop or high-traffic play room.

If drywall is going over an insulated exterior wall, and your insulation is unfaced, install a vapor retardant of 6-millimeter polyethylene or other suitable material. And be sure that you have all the wiring, plumbing, and ductwork completed, before installing the drywall.

PLAN THE LAYOUT

The most time-consuming part of any drywall installation is not hanging the sheets, but finishing the joints. Before ordering any materials, figure out the exact size and location of each sheet, so as to keep this finishing work to a minimum. Here are a few guidelines.

Avoid butted seams The long edges of drywall sheets are tapered to make room for paper tape and joint compound, which are used to conceal the joints between sheets. For best results, always orient the sheets on a ceiling or wall in the same direction, so that the tapered edges will meet.

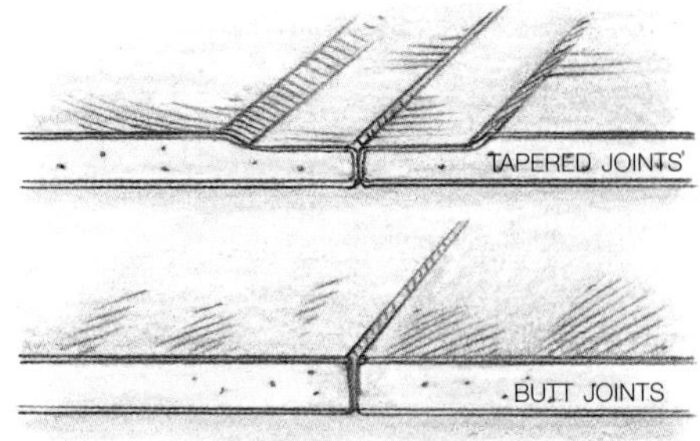

It is more difficult to disguise joints where untapered edges must meet.

Although you may not be able to eliminate butt joints altogether, using long sheets can reduce their number. For example, the very best layout for a 16-foot expanse of wall that is 8 feet high would be two 16-foot sheets of drywall installed horizontally, the one above the other (below).

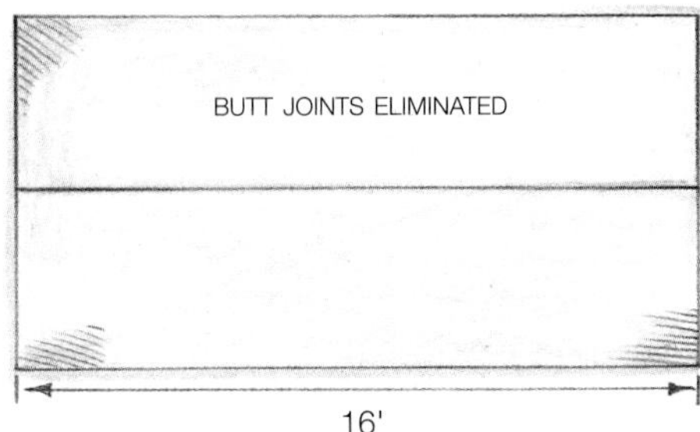

This would leave you with only tapered joints to finish. A less desirable layout for this same wall would involve four 8-foot sheets installed horizontally (below).

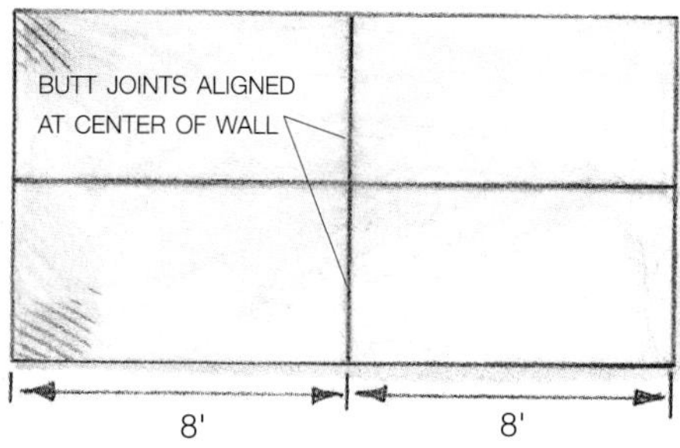

If you cannot avoid butt joints on a wall, try to stagger the joints and to keep them away from the center of the wall (see example below).

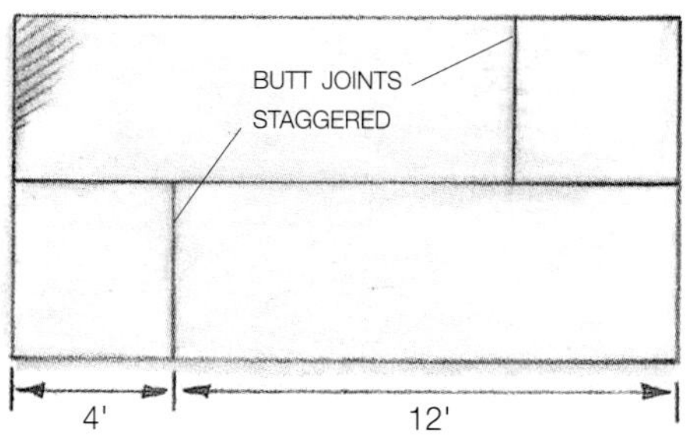

Use the largest sheets possible You can minimize the number of joints to be finished by always using the longest sheets possible. While 8-foot sheets are easier to handle and sometimes cheaper, 14-foot or 16-foot sheets will often span an entire wall, completely eliminating the need for a butt joint. As long as you are able to get the panels into the room and have a couple of helpers, longer sheets will save time.

Both of the layouts below leave you with nothing but tapered seams to finish, but the one on top has eight additional feet of seams to be finished—a lot more work.

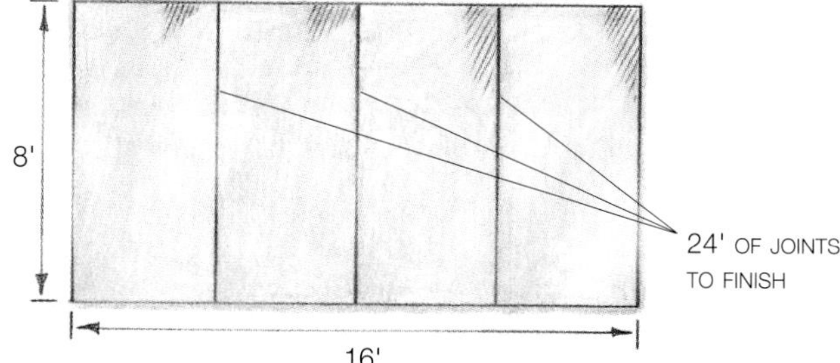

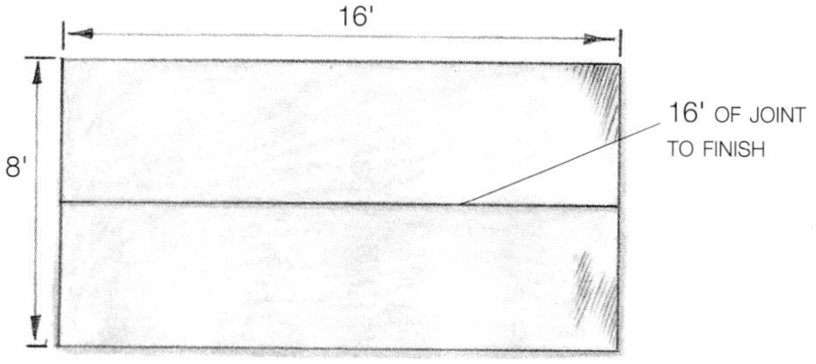

Work perpendicular to framing On walls that are no more than 8 feet high, install the drywall horizontally. This will reduce the length of joints and place the joints at a convenient height for finishing. For walls that are 4 feet wide or less, however, hang the drywall vertically so that you eliminate a joint. If you have walls that are between 8 and 9 feet high, you can still maintain a single horizontal joint by using 54-inch drywall sheets. Drywall on ceilings is usually hung perpendicular to the joists, but it can also go parallel, if this gives you a simpler layout.

Consider Your Access

Even the smallest sheets of drywall are large enough to cause problems when you transport them through doors or up and down stairs. Garages and basements with exterior entrances pose no delivery problems, but attics and basements without an exterior entrance sometimes do. Plan ahead. It is always best to use the longest sheets possible, to reduce the number of joints requiring taping. But limited access may require that you order shorter sheets instead. For attics with large enough openings, consider having the drywall delivered by a boom truck before the windows are installed.

CUTTING DRYWALL

Most drywall sheets will require some cutting, either to adjust the length or width or to make an opening for an electrical box, window, or door. To make clean and accurate cuts, it is worth spending a few dollars to buy tools made especially for cutting drywall. In addition to a 25-foot or 30-foot tape measure, you will need a 4-foot aluminum T-square, a utility knife, a keyhole saw, a drywall saw, and a surface-forming tool.

Take your time when measuring and cutting drywall. If you cut too much off a sheet, you will wind up with a large gap between sheets that requires extra work to finish. If you cut too little, you will break the edges of the sheets when you try to force them into place. Aim for a loose fit, cutting the sheets

Basic Drywall Skills

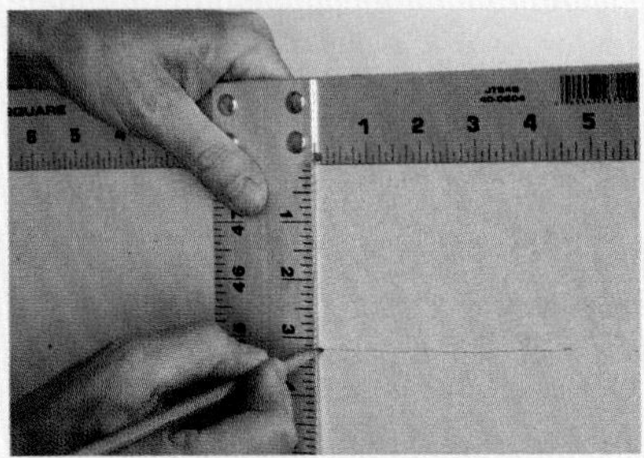

1 MARKING THIN STRIPS To cut thin strips, use the T-square to measure and mark at the same time. Align the top edge of the square with the desired measurement (3 inches in the photo), then mark the cut line along the other edge.

2 CUTTING FULL SHEETS To cut the full width of a sheet, use a tape measure or the T-square to mark the edge of the drywall, then align the T-square with the mark. Hold the T-square against the front of the drywall with your foot as you slide a utility knife along the edge. Always keep a sharp blade in the utility knife, and make a smooth, deep cut.

3 MAKING ANGLED CUTS For an angled cut, measure and mark the appropriate lengths on both sides of the drywall. If you are working alone, make a small notch at one of the marks to hold the string line, then extend the string line to the other mark and snap.

4 SNAP THE DRYWALL With the cut line scored from one end to the other, snap the panel back to form a crease in the backing paper.

5 CUT THE PAPER Working from the back side, split the paper with your utility knife.

6 SMOOTH THE EDGES To remove a small amount from the edge of a sheet of drywall, use a surface-forming tool.

about ¼ inch short. Tapered joints, however, should fit together snugly.

HANGING DRYWALL

It doesn't take much time to cover a ceiling or wall with drywall, especially if you have a helper or two. Before attaching any sheets, however, check the framing for any twists or bows. Finished walls will look much better if they are as flat as possible, and flat walls also make it much easier to install cabinets.

Making cutouts

To make cutouts for electrical boxes and other obstructions, take careful measurements and transfer them to the drywall

sheet—your T-square will come in handy for this step. Before cutting, double-check your measurements. Drill starter holes large enough to allow the keyhole saw to slip through. Cut carefully. To cut small holes for pipes or other objects, use a hole saw in your electric drill.

To save measuring and marking sheets to fit around doors and windows, you can first fasten a full sheet across the opening, then cut it with a drywall saw.

Create a level surface. Inspect the studs or joists to see if they are aligned in a straight plane; you can also hold a long straightedge across the framing. If you find any framing members that stick out more than ¼ inch, replace them or trim them with a saw or a plane (a power planer is a great tool for this job). Sometimes simply removing and renailing the stud or joist will bring it into line. Any low spots should be filled in with shims attached with nails or glue.

If joists are full of irregularities, you can attach 1 x 3 furring strips across them, shimmed to level the surface. Then attach the drywall to the furring strips.

Choose your fastener. Drywall can be attached to wood framing with screws or nails. Screwing is faster, neater, and stronger. The best tool for driving drywall screws is a screwgun, which can be adjusted to drive the screwhead to the perfect depth (see "Drive Carefully," page 64).

You can also drive screws into drywall with a special drywall screw bit, which fits into a drill chuck. The bits are designed to stop turning once the screw has been driven to its proper depth. Screw bits wear out fairly quickly, though, so be sure to have several on hand before you start.

If you use nails, you should use a drywall hammer, which has a convex face that leaves a small dimple around the nail head. A standard, flat-faced hammer is much more likely to break the surface paper. Also, be sure to use ringshank drywall nails.

Note: If you have access to both a screwgun and a drywall hammer, do what many pros do: nail along the edges to quickly get the sheet in place, then finish with screws.

Drywall screws should penetrate the framing at least ⅝ of an inch, so use at least 1⅛-inch screws on ½-inch drywall. Nails need to penetrate at least ¾ of an inch, so you will need at least 1¼-inch nails for ½-inch drywall.

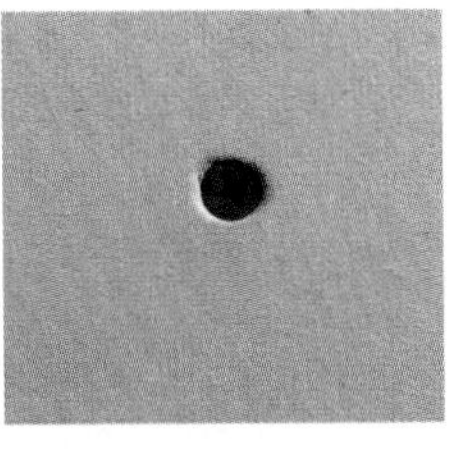
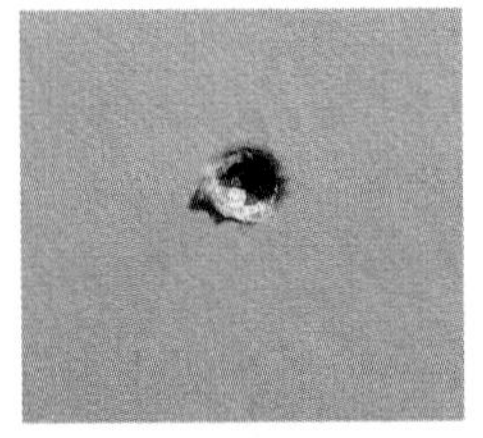
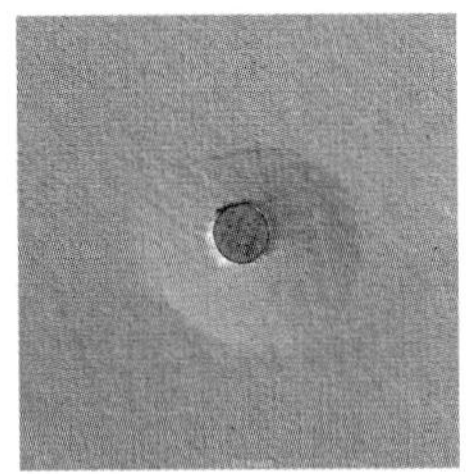
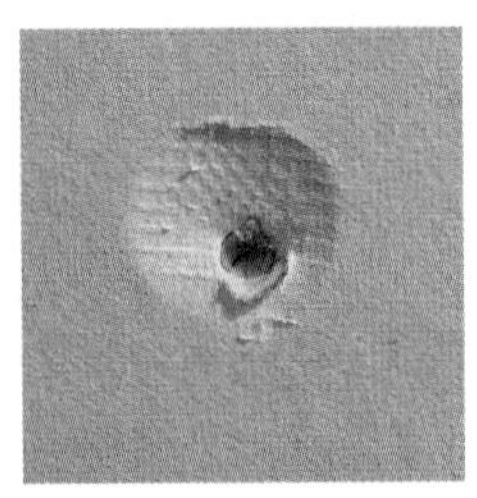

Drive Carefully

Screws and nails must be driven below the surface of the drywall so that they can later be covered with joint compound and sanded to create a smooth surface. But driving the fasteners too deep into the drywall can tear the surface paper and even damage the gypsum core, thereby weakening the connection and creating extra work when it comes time to finish the sheets. A properly driven screw is slightly countersunk, while a well-driven nail will have a very modest dimple around the head, as shown in the photos on the far left. Screw depth can be adjusted on a screwgun, but proper hammering technique can be mastered only with practice.

Attach the drywall. If you are covering both ceiling and walls with drywall, begin with the ceiling. For flat ceilings, a simple T-shaped brace can make the job go quicker. The brace should be about ½ inch longer than the finished ceiling height so that it can be wedged into place. Make a brace by attaching a 4-foot-long 2 x 4 or furring strip to a 2 x 4 leg (below). If you have a helper, lift the drywall into place, then slide the brace under one end while the helper supports the other end. You are now free to fasten with screws or nails. The ends of the drywall should be perfectly centered on studs and joists.

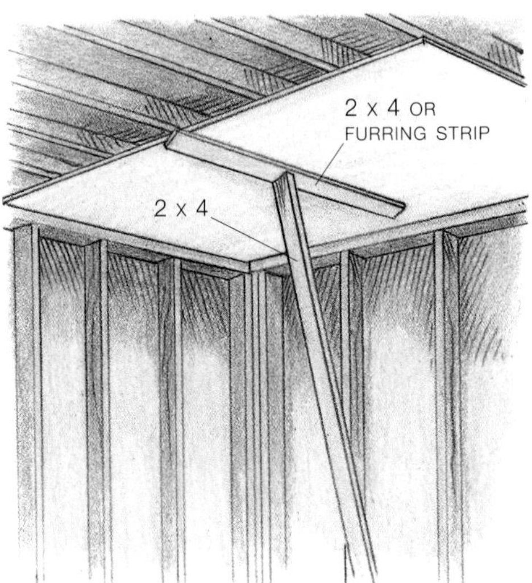

When attaching drywall to ceiling joists spaced 16 inches on center, fasteners should be spaced no more than 12 inches apart. On wall studs, maximum fastener spacing is 16 inches. Place fasteners every 8 inches along the edges, but keep them at least ⅜ of an inch from the edge to avoid damaging the core. If you are using nails, you will need to "double nail" along the face of the panel—that is, drive a second nail 2 inches from the first at each required fastener location.

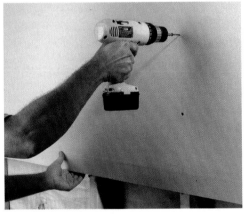

After the ceiling has been covered, attach the top sheets on the wall. First, though, mark the locations of the studs on the ceiling sheets; this will make it easier to drive fasteners into studs when the drywall is in place. Bottom panels should fit tightly against the top panels before fastening. The easiest way to accomplish this is to use a drywall lifter. Commercial models are best, as they have a thin lip that skips easily under the edge (as shown in photo below), but you can also make a simple lifter out of a couple of lumber scraps.

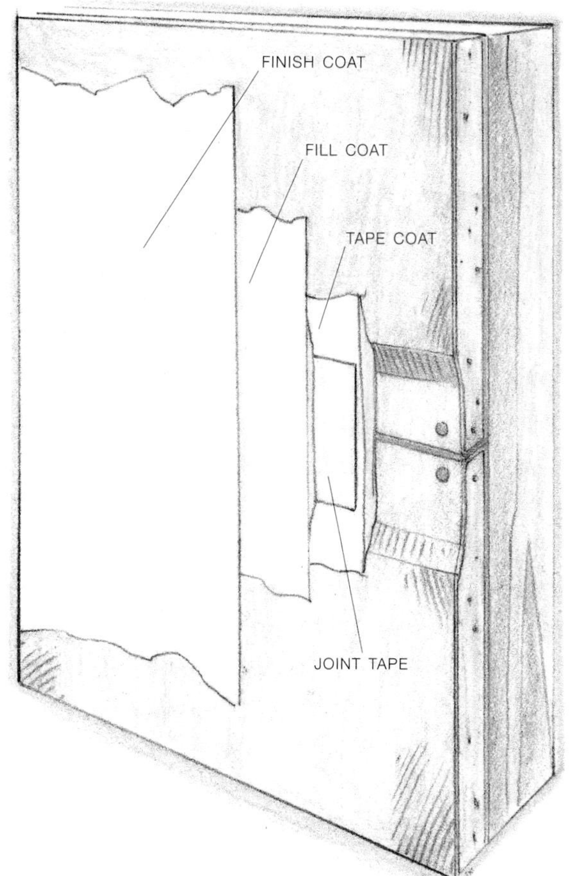

TAPING AND MUDDING

The finishing process for drywall involves applying paper tape and several layers of joint compound ("mud") to seal and smooth the joints. After drying, each layer of compound is sanded. It is not difficult work, but it can be tedious and a bit frustrating for the novice. As you gain experience, however, your speed and technique will improve.

The first job is to make sure that all nail and screw heads are below the drywall surface. Drag a taping knife over the surface and tighten any fasteners you find that are still "proud" of the surface.

Joint compound is available in premixed or powdered forms. Premixed, all-purpose compound is generally the best choice for most finishing work. Premixed joint compound should be stirred just enough to ensure consistency throughout the bucket; overstirring will introduce air bubbles that will show up when the compound dries. Powdered ("setting-type") compounds are useful for filling large gaps between drywall sheets, because they dry faster than premixed, allowing you to tape over the gaps sooner. Mix these compounds with water, preparing only as much as you need or will be able to use within the product's setting time (typically 90 minutes).

When the joint compound has been mixed or stirred, scoop some into a compound tray. Apply a smooth, thin layer of it over the joint with a 6-inch taping knife. Before the compound dries, press joint tape into it, centered on the joint. Holding the tape in place with one hand, gently pull the taping knife over the tape, using just enough pressure to squeeze a little compound out from under the tape.

Immediately apply another thin layer of compound to fill the joint and cover the tape (as shown below). Smooth the surface and feather the edges as best as you can. Repeat these steps for each joint.

Using the 6-inch knife, fill and smooth over all nail or screw heads. Clean all tools and let the compound dry overnight, or longer if necessary. Lightly sand the dried compound to remove any bumps or ridges. Use a 10-inch or 12-inch knife to spread another layer of compound over the joints, feathering the edges. After this second coat has dried, give it another light sanding.

If you take care applying and sanding the first two coats, the third coat should require only a light skimming to create a smooth, seamless surface. Use a wide knife, or a drywall trowel, which is curved slightly to facilitate feathering, to apply the final coat. You might want to thin the compound just a bit with water (add no more than one pint of water per 5-gallon bucket of compound). Sand the compound after it has dried. If you aren't satisfied with the finish, don't be afraid to apply another thin top coat.

Corners On inside corners, apply a smooth layer of compound to each side of the corner. Tear a piece of tape to length, fold it in half vertically, then press it into the corner. Use a corner trowel or a small taping knife to embed the tape (as shown below), and apply successive layers of com-

pound as previously described, gradually soothing the surface.

For outside corners, first cover the corners with a protective metal corner bead cut to length and nailed or screwed through its

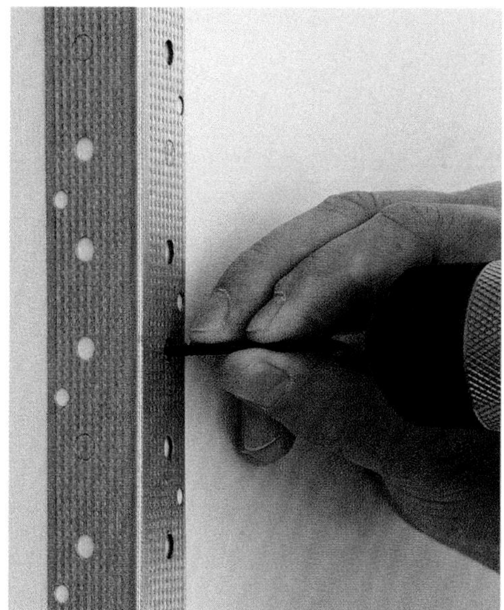

perforations every 8 to 10 inches and 1 inch from the bottom and top. There's no need to tape these joints, although tape may reduce the chance of cracks developing later on. Simply run your taping knife down the metal edge (below) to fill the spaces with compound.

Sanding The final step—sanding—is the messiest and most time-consuming part of the entire process. Use a pole sander for the job (as shown below); it has a 4-foot handle that allows you to reach distant spots and to keep away from the dust you will be creating. Buy a supply of 120-grit sanding screens

or sandpaper to fit the pole sander. Always wear a dust mask when sanding, and cover doorways and vents with plastic to confine the dust. The object of sanding is to blend the taped edges and remove any bumps. But do not sand too much! If you sand through the paper face on the drywall, you will have to apply another coat of compound. Use a shop vacuum cleaner to clean the room when you have finished sanding.

Flooring

Innovations in design and manufacturing have made many flooring materials easier to install by the motivated do-it-yourself homeowner. New flooring materials, effective adhesives, tough sealers, and finishes of improved durability make the possibilities much more attractive to the non-professional, and the results more long-lasting.

It's a good idea to take the time to visit flooring dealers and home improvement centers to see the materials available in your area. Many dealers are happy to let you borrow samples so you can see how they will look in your home. Aesthetics play a very important role in the decision-making process, but you will also want to choose flooring materials based on the amount of traffic that they will have to bear. When choosing a floor for a basement or garage conversion, you will need to be concerned with possible moisture problems and proper insulation. If you are turning an attic into living space, you will probably be interested in minimizing noise transmission by using soft, padded flooring.

Estimating Flooring Needs

Flooring products and installation costs are usually dealt with on a square footage basis (or square yardage, in the case of carpeting). To determine the square footage of a room that is square or rectangular, measure the length along adjacent walls and multiply the two figures. Round the inches in your measurements up to the next foot. For a room with a closet or some other offset space, first divide the room into separate rectangles and determine the square footage of each, then add the two figures together. To the final result (192 square feet in the example below), add 5 to 10 percent to account for waste or errors.

When comparing the prices of flooring products, keep in mind that advertised prices often refer only to the top layer itself, not to any required underlayment, such as carpet pad, foam, or plywood.

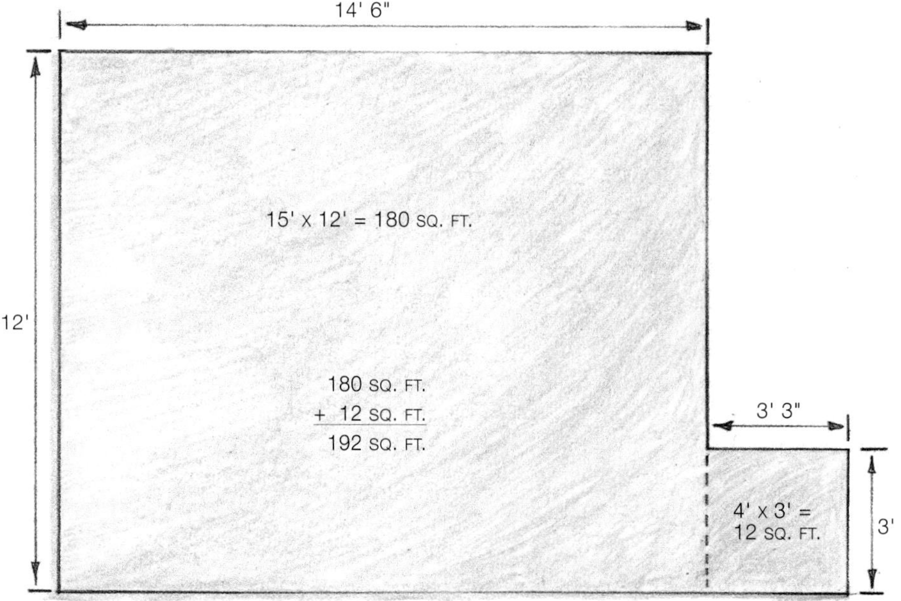

New Floors Shouldn't Cover Old Problems

Don't make any final flooring decisions without considering the type and condition of the subfloor and underlayment your new flooring will cover. With proper preparation, a concrete subfloor can serve as a base for almost any type of flooring. A plywood subfloor over wood framing in an attic may be overly flexible and not suitable for rigid materials, such as ceramic tile, unless it is stiffened. Don't install flooring in an attic until you are certain that the framing is strong enough to support the load. All flooring manufacturers have minimal requirements for the use of their products, so play it safe by checking with them.

Handling Transitions

It is not unusual for carefully considered flooring choices to be scrapped at the last minute because they could not be adequately integrated with adjacent floors. A change in materials is easy enough to cover with a transition strip, but changes in floor height are a different matter. Most building codes require that any difference in height between adjacent floors be no more than ½ inch. This kind of transition can usually be handled by a threshold (top, right) that covers the seam between the floors and minimizes the possibility of tripping.

For larger discrepancies between floors, plan new flooring that can compensate. Use thin flooring material on the high side, and thicker material on the low side (center, right). Or add thickness to the subfloor on the low side with one or more layers of plywood.

If you plan to install new flooring next to existing stairs, be aware that you may create a different type of hazard and possibly a code violation: a step that is too short at the bottom (right) or too high at the top.

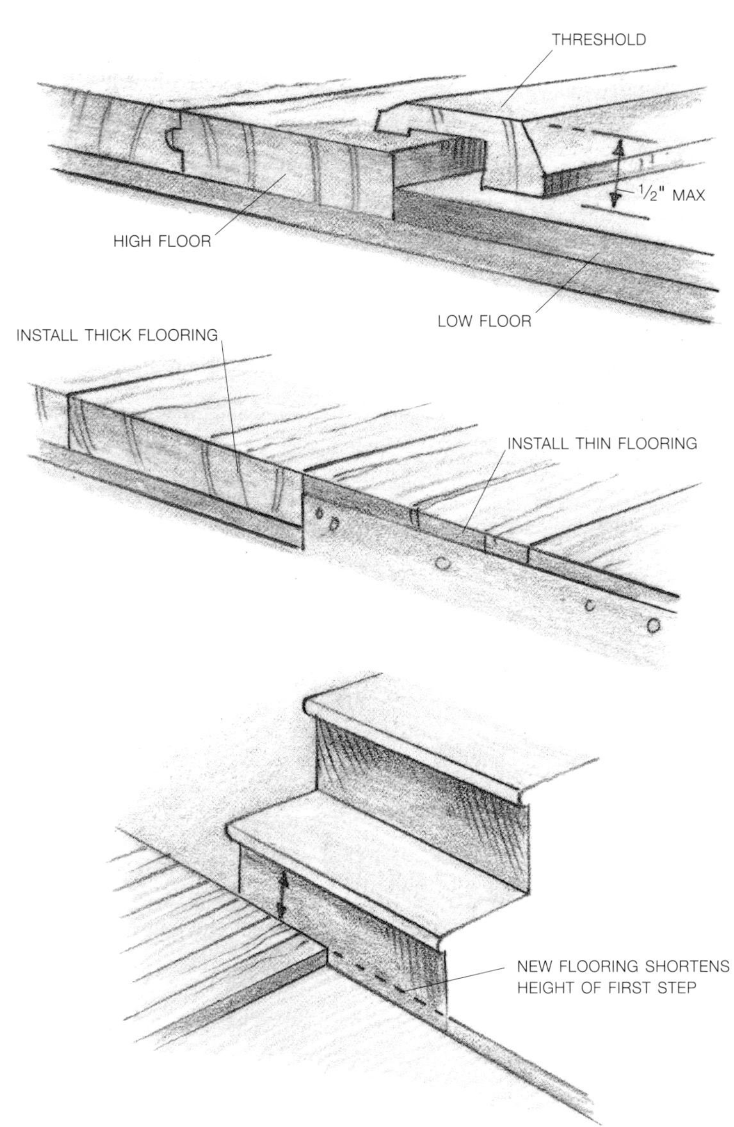

Slab Happy?

If you don't mind concrete and you don't need to insulate the floor, you can finish a concrete basement or garage floor simply by painting it. The most durable products are epoxy-based floor paints, but they're difficult to apply. Latex or oil-based paints are easier to apply, but aren't as durable.

Before being painted, old concrete floors should be cleaned thoroughly, and all cracks and surface damage repaired (see pages 48-49). Concrete with a glossy finish should be "etched" before painting; that is, treated with a liquid deglosser. Consult with your paint dealer about the best masonry primer to use, and choose a paint that is compatible with the primer.

CARPET

Installing carpet is not actually difficult, but it is still a job best left to professionals. Special tools and some experience mean a lot when it comes to stretching carpet, trimming and tucking the carpet to get a neat fit, and creating seams that are as durable and invisible as possible. A trained installer can carpet a room in a couple of hours, usually for a very reasonable fee. Further, if you install the carpet yourself, you may void the manufacturer's warranty.

Cut pile

Loop pile

Even if someone else will be installing your carpeting, however, you'll still need to choose the carpet and pad. You can help keep costs down by shopping around for the best style and type of carpet—prices can range from under $10 per square yard to $50 or more. You will also need to make sure you have a solid subfloor. Carpet should be installed over ¾-inch tongue-and-groove plywood that has been glued and screwed to framing in an attic or to 2 x 4 sleepers on a basement or garage floor (see pages 116–117).

Most residential carpet is installed over a pad, but you can buy carpet that can be glued directly to a concrete slab. This is a job that most do-it-yourselfers can handle, but first make sure that the concrete is dry and that all cracks and holes have been repaired (see pages 48–49). A floor with glued-on carpet won't be insulated, however, so it would not be a good choice for a living space in a cold climate. It also may not be as comfortable as you would like, unless you choose a well-cushioned carpet.

Fibers

Nylon is the most popular carpet fiber. It is tough, mildew resistant, affordable, and can be treated successfully with stain repellent. Polyester is less resilient. Olefin (polypropylene) is a good choice for a basement or garage play room. It stands up well to moisture, fading, staining, and abrasion.

Wool is generally considered the best carpet fiber. It is very resilient and sheds water well, but it is also quite expensive. And if you have pets, you should know that fleas seem to be especially partial to wool carpets.

Styles

The principal difference between carpet styles has to do with whether the yarn has been cut or left in loops. Cut pile (including plush and saxony styles) has a softer feel under foot, making it a popular choice for bedrooms and living rooms. Thicker, deeper pile feels more luxurious, but is a bit harder to clean.

Loop pile is more durable than cut pile and is a good choice in areas that will have a lot of foot traffic, such as family rooms or play areas. Level loop is the more durable; multi-level loop has a mix of short and long loops to create texture or patterns. Berber is a type of loop carpet that made with thicker yarns. Because of its density, Berber can be harder to clean.

Pads

The carpet pad you choose can have a big effect on the comfort factor and durability of your carpet. Thin, low-density foam padding—especially the multicolored "rebonded" variety—is the cheapest and least effective. It compresses easily and wears inconsistently. A better choice is prime urethane, and best of all is rubber.

LAMINATE FLOORING

Similar to plastic laminate countertops, laminate flooring is composed of four layers, as shown in the illustration at right. Durability is provided by a protective, clear top layer of melamine. The appearance of this flooring is created by the design layer, which is made to simulate the look of things like wood or stone or to create a variety of color patterns. The bottom two layers are a high-density fiberboard and a backing.

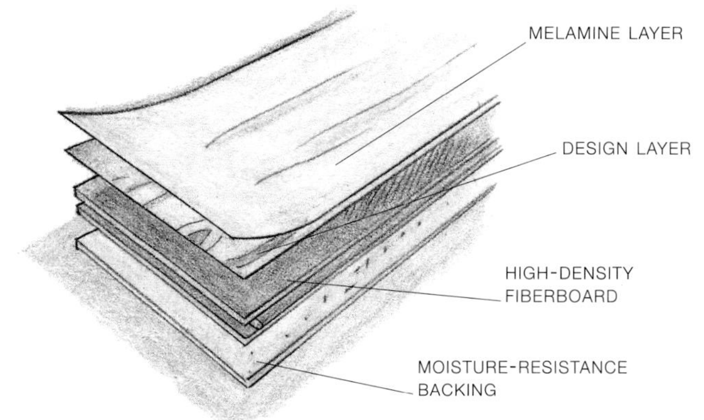

Laminate flooring is tough; it resists dents and stains and is very easy to clean. It is also relatively easy to install. Remember, however, that while much laminate flooring is made to look like wood flooring, there is a critical difference between the two: wood floors can be refinished and repaired easily, laminate floors cannot. Regular laminate should not be used around water or in bathrooms with a shower or tub, but laminate can be installed over a concrete floor if you use a plastic moisture barrier.

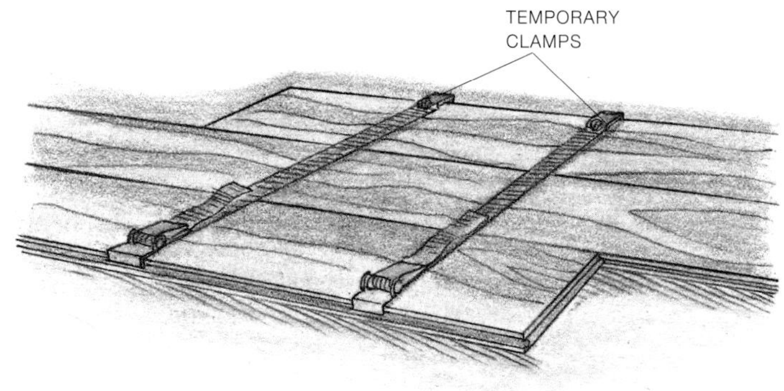

Sold in 4-foot-long planks or square tiles, laminate flooring is not fastened to a subfloor. Instead, individual flooring pieces are glued together along the edges and clamped as shown above, which is why laminate is often called a "floating" floor.

Tips on Installing Laminate Flooring

Installation techniques vary only slightly among manufacturers, and most of the laminate products come with good basic instructions. Here are a few tips that will help you avoid some of the most common problems.

- Leave a ¼-inch expansion gap around the perimeter of the room. This will allow the flooring to expand and contract throughout the year without heaving and buckling. Along walls, cover the expansion gaps with baseboards.
- Get a straight start. Laminate flooring is not flexible, so you must get the first three rows installed as straight as possible to ensure a perfect finish.
- Trim the edges. If the room is not perfectly square, trim the flooring along the wall to create square rows. It is particularly important to ensure that the flooring does not meet appliances or islands at an angle.
- Dry fit before gluing. Always assemble pieces first without glue to check the fit and alignment.
- Plan the transitions. Laminate manufacturers offer a variety of special pieces to cover the transition to other floor surfaces. If your finished floor levels will be at different heights, you will need transition pieces that compensate.
- Use foam. To reduce sound transmission, install laminate flooring over a foam underlayment.

SOLID WOOD

If you want a flooring surface that will last a lifetime, it's hard to beat solid wood. Properly installed, a solid wood floor looks great, wears well, and can be sanded and refinished several times before it has to be replaced. Installing your own wood floor is not a one-day project, however. It takes time and effort, and requires that you rent some big, challenging machines—especially if you plan to sand and finish the floors yourself.

Sanding, staining, and finishing are actually the hardest parts of the job. Unless you feel an urgent need to learn to do these jobs, there are a couple of alternatives you may wish to consider. First, you could install prefinished flooring. Most manufacturers now offer strip flooring with a durable, factory-applied finish. Although it costs more and comes in a narrower range of styles, prefinished flooring will save you the mess and expense of sanding and finishing. Second, if you do choose to buy unfinished flooring, consider hiring a pro to sand and finish it for you.

Solid-wood flooring is available in strips, which are 2¼ inches wide, and planks, which are 3 inches or more in width. Strip flooring is the more popular, for professionals and do-it-yourselfers alike. Red oak and white oak are the most popular types of wood flooring, although you can find a wide range of woods, including maple, cherry, hickory, and yellow pine, if you seek them out. Maple and hickory are among the hardest woods available, but that does not make them the most stable; in fact, both tend to cup or gap as the humidity changes. When putting wood flooring over concrete, you should choose a stable wood, such as red oak.

Strip flooring comes in random-length bundles with a tongue-and-groove pattern cut into the sides and ends. The best grades (usually called "select" or "clear") have few, if any, knots or defects. "Common" (or #2) grade flooring has a few knots and some variation in color and grain. Lesser grades have larger knots and a greater variation in color and grain. Vertical-grain strips are more stable (that is, they will expand and contract less) than flat-grain strips (see illustration below).

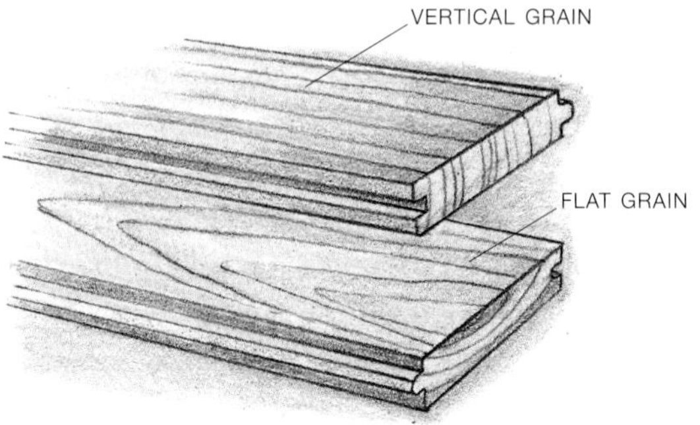

Solid-wood floors should be installed over a plywood subfloor that is and will remain dry. This makes them ideal for attic conversions, worth considering for garages, and, frequently, not a great choice for basements, unless you are prepared to take measures to guarantee a dry floor (see "Wood Flooring over Concrete," on the facing page).

One of the principal rules to remember when installing wood flooring is that wood expands when it absorbs moisture and shrinks when it loses moisture. If the flooring has a high moisture content when it is installed, gaps will appear later when the wood dries out and contracts. And if a wood floor is exposed to high moisture levels after installation, it will begin to cup and buckle.

Both the manufacturers of wood flooring and the suppliers who sell it commonly recommend that you allow the wood to acclimate on site for several weeks before installation. But this process can sometime be counterproductive. During new construction and remodeling, building materials often get damp and stay that way for lengthy periods. Concrete floors, wood framing, and newly finished drywall all contain a good deal of moisture. If you bring kiln-dried wood flooring into such a moist environment and let it acclimate, it may actually absorb water and swell. If you install it in that condition, gaps will begin appearing when you start heating the room. When you acclimate your wood, be sure that it is done in a dry environment. The best idea is to wait until the site has dried out before having the wood delivered.

WOOD FLOORING OVER CONCRETE

Wood flooring can be installed over concrete if the proper precautions are taken. Floors below ground level are potentially more troublesome than others, which is why many flooring professionals recommend other surfaces. But with the right preparation and a reasonably dry basement, solid wood can work.

- Make sure that the concrete is dry. Check for moisture with a 2-foot by 2-foot piece of plastic, as shown on page 154. If you find any moisture, wood would be a poor choice, unless you eliminate the source of the moisture.
- Make sure the concrete is level. The surface should be level to within about ¼ inch every 10 feet. Low spots should be filled with a leveling compound, or use dry mason's sand and level it ("screed" in masonry terms) with a straight board. Take care not to step on the sand until the plywood subfloor or rigid foam insulation is set in place.
- Provide a solid nailing substrate. Although some sources suggest installing wood floors over 2 x 4 sleepers, it is not a good idea. Sleepers do not provide the firm support and nailing acceptance of plywood. A floating subfloor is the best choice, if you are concerned about the wood expanding and shrinking (see "Floating Subfloor on Concrete," page 74). If moisture is not a problem, you can attach the plywood to the slab (see "Plywood Subfloor on Concrete," below).
- Check the manufacturer's warranty. The manufacturer may have strict instructions for installing their product over concrete. Many will void the warranty if 15-pound felt paper is not installed between the concrete and the flooring.

Plywood Subfloor on Concrete

A plywood subfloor provides a good nailing surface for wood flooring.

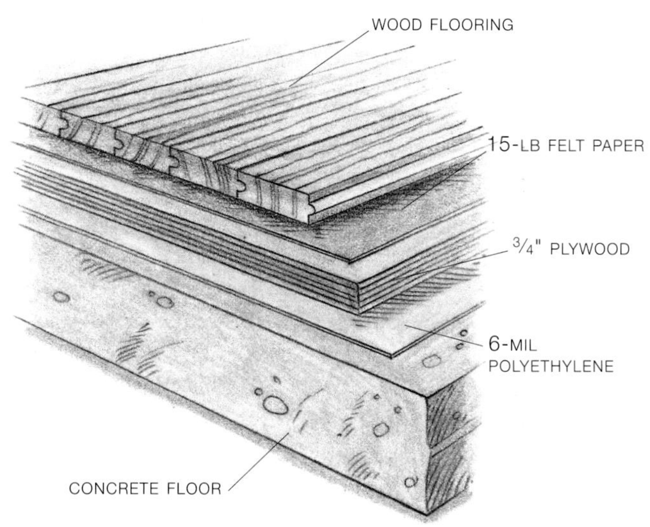

- With the floor clean and level, lay 6-millimeter polyethylene on the floor. Overlap the edges 12 inches, then tape the edges with duct tape.

- Place ¾-inch plywood on the floor, leaving ¼ inch between sheets and ½ inch around the perimeter. Attach the plywood to the concrete with powder-actuated fasteners or other suitable fasteners.
- Add a layer of 15-pound asphalt-saturated felt paper, stapled to the plywood.
- Attach the wood flooring with 1¼-inch flooring nails.

Floating Subfloor on Concrete

Because a floating floor is not nailed in place, it can experience some weather- and moisture-related movement without being damaged. However, because of the double layer of plywood, it raises the floor level substantially, which can present headroom problems in basements.

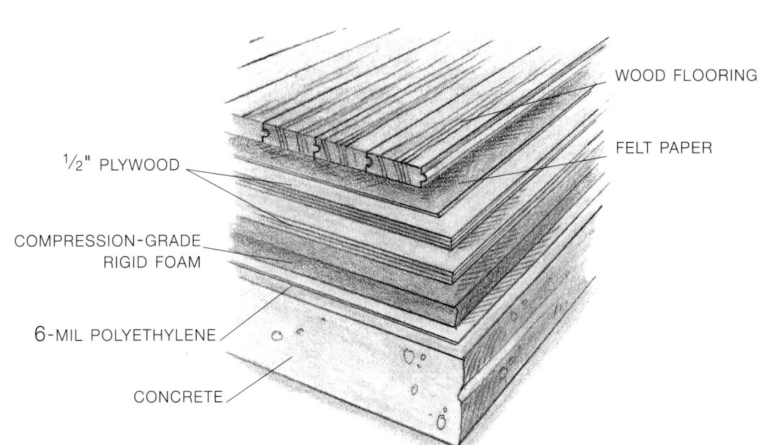

- With the floor clean and level, lay 6-mil polyethylene on the concrete. Overlap the edges 12 inches, then tape the edges with duct tape. Run the poly several inches up the wall.
- Install a layer of compression-grade rigid foam insulation on the floor, leaving a ½-inch gap around the perimeter. Be sure to use only compression-grade rigid foam, which will stand up to foot traffic.
- Place ½-inch plywood on the foam, leaving ¼ inch between sheets and ½ inch around the perimeter. Don't fasten the plywood down; gravity will hold it in place.
- Add a second layer of ½-inch plywood, reversing the orientation of the panels and staggering the joints. Screw the two plywood layers together, but don't let the screw tips penetrate the poly.
- Set 15-pound asphalt-saturated felt paper on the plywood, overlapping the seams several inches. Staple it down.
- Install the wood flooring, as described on the facing page.

INSTALLING WOOD STRIP FLOORING

Wood strip flooring is installed by "blind nailing" through the tongues of the flooring pieces, using a special nailing machine. Rental stores and some flooring suppliers or

Wood Flooring over Joists

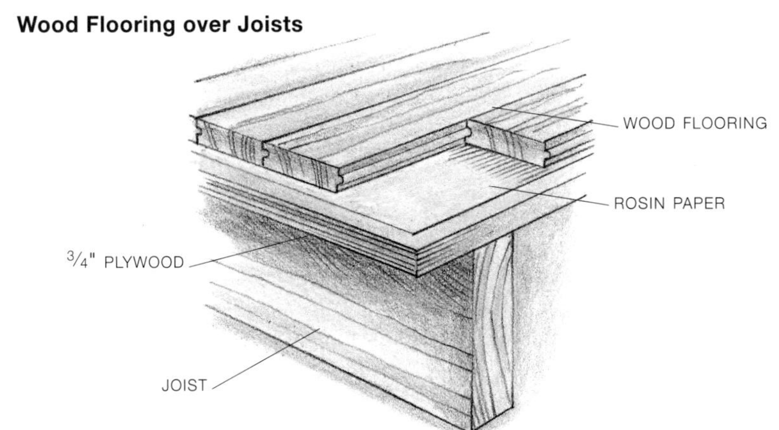

To create a good subfloor for wood flooring in an attic, you have to first make sure that the joists are strong enough to support the load (see pages 126-127). Attach ¾-inch plywood with 2 ¼-inch ring shank nails or with drywall screws driven into the joists. The plywood should be oriented perpendicular to the joists. Staple rosin paper to the plywood, then proceed to install the wood flooring, as described on the next page.

home centers carry manual and power nailers and staplers. A manual nailer is relatively inexpensive to rent, but the process of striking it over and over to drive all the nails you will need can be exhausting. A power nailer will cost more, but will get the job done much more quickly. A power nailer does require a compressor, also available at tool rental centers.

Begin by cleaning the subfloor surface thoroughly. Run a 4-foot level over the plywood subfloor looking for bumps. If you find any, sand them down. Then add a layer of 15-pound felt paper or rosin paper over the subfloor. Felt paper is the better choice over concrete, as it provides additional protection against moisture.

Measure to see if the walls in the room are parallel. If they are not, plan to run the flooring perpendicular to the out-of-parallel walls so the problem will be less noticeable.

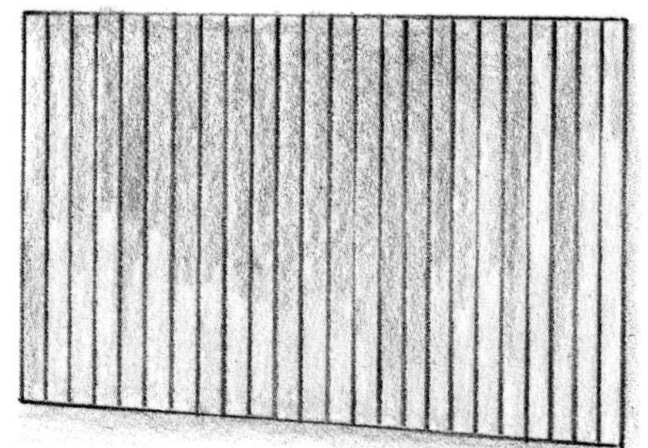

If you do not have this problem, align the first row to run in the direction of the longer dimension of the room.

Lay the first row of wood strips in place with the tongue facing away from the wall; leave a ½-inch gap around the perimeter of the room. This gap allows for the wood to expand and contract without buckling; it will be covered later with baseboard trim. Once you are satisfied with the layout, snap a chalk line to guide you in nailing down the first row.

Before you start nailing boards down, lay out several rows of the flooring strips. Work out a pattern that allows you to avoid repetitive patterns in the ends of the strips, as shown below.

By using random lengths of the flooring strips, you should be able to create a random pattern of the joints between boards (below).

Face nail the first few rows. Blind nailing is the best way to fasten wood flooring, but when you are close to the wall you will need to face nail. Always drill a pilot hole first to prevent the wood from splitting; make the holes slightly smaller than the nail size. Hammer carefully so that you do not hit the wood itself. Use a nail set to drive the nail head about ⅛ inch below the surface; fill these holes later with wood filler, then sand.

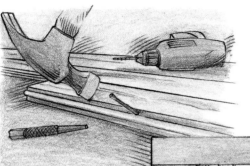

As soon as space permits, start blind nailing the flooring. Even if you can't use a power nailer, at this point, you should be able to blind nail by drilling holes at a 45-degree angle through the tops of the tongues or the inside the

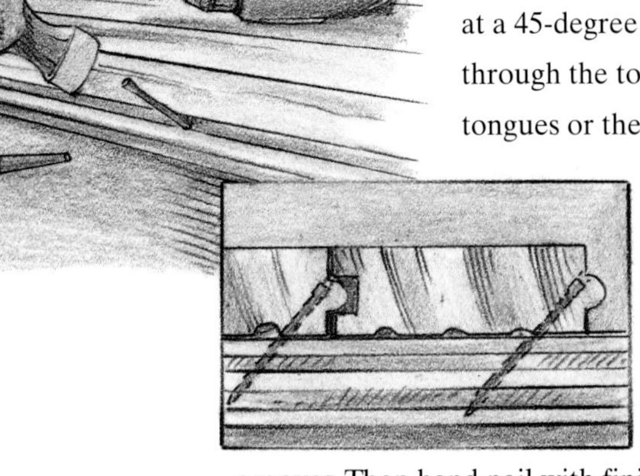

grooves. Then hand nail with finish nails and set the nail head flush with the wood, using a nail set.

Changing Directions

If you are installing wood flooring into a closet or hallway that opens off the room, you may have to align two boards groove to groove. Your flooring supplier can supply you with slip tongues or splines made especially for this purpose. Blind nail the slip tongue through the groove, then proceed to reverse the direction of the boards as shown in the illustration at left, below.

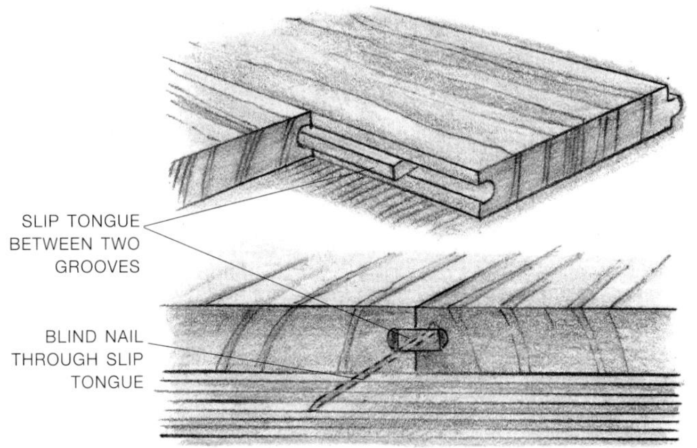

Handling Transitions

If your new wood flooring meets an adjacent flooring surface at a different level, you will need to add a reducer strip. Flooring suppliers carry reducers in several sizes. If

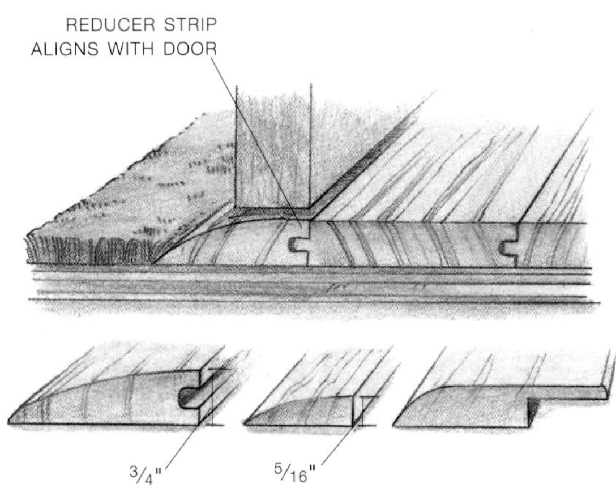

necessary, you can make your own reducer out of a strip of flooring. When using a reducer between two rooms with a door, try to align the edge of the reducer with the door, as shown above.

Using a Power Nailer

To use a power nailer, position the nailer over the edge of the board and strike it with a mallet. If you are using a pneumatic nailer, be sure to get instructions from the rental store. A power nailer pushes the wood against the adjacent row while simultaneously driving a nail through the tongue. Use plenty of nails, spacing them 6 to 8 inches apart.

SANDING

If you install unfinished flooring, you will need to sand and finish it. Professional-grade floor sanders are difficult to master, but rental stores and home centers often carry belt or drum sanders that are easier to use and plug into standard 15- or 20-amp outlets. Be sure to get thorough instructions on how to use the sander before you take it home. You will also need a small edge sander, a buffer, and a supply of sanding belts, discs, and buffing screens.

Floor sanders can remove a lot of wood very quickly. Get detailed instructions before you turn on such a machine.

FINISHING

Polyurethane is the most popular finish for wood floors. Both waterborne and oil-based varieties are durable and tough, and the two types are comparably priced. Waterborne finishes are currently growing rapidly in popularity, among pros and do-it-yourselfers alike. These finishes dry quickly and give off fewer offensive fumes and odors than the oil-based products. Many people continue to prefer oil-based finishes, however, in part because they produce an amber tint to the floor. The waterborne finishes dry clear. With either choice, use an applicator with a long handle to ease the work of applying the finish. A paintbrush can be used in hard-to-reach areas. Read the instructions before you begin. Lightly sand the first coat, after it has had a chance to dry.

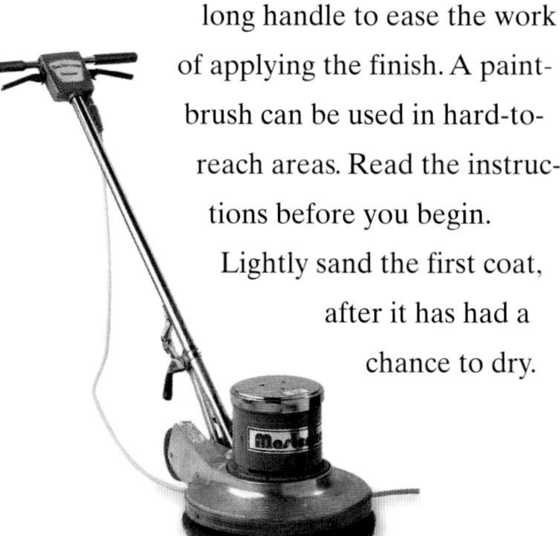

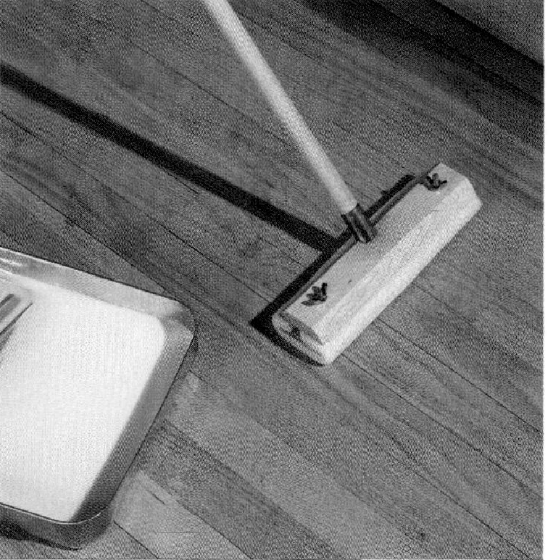

ABOVE: An edge sander can reach parts of the floor that are inaccessible to a regular floor sander.

LEFT: Waterborne polyurethane dries quickly and produces fewer fumes than oil-based finishes.

RESILIENT FLOORING

Resilient flooring is the general name for a variety of thin sheet or tile products that are applied with adhesive. Vinyl is far and away the most popular resilient flooring product today, but cork, linoleum, and rubber are also available.

Long used primarily in kitchens and bathrooms, resilient flooring can also be a great choice for converted spaces. It is relatively inexpensive, easy to install, and available in patterns and colors that suit most decorative needs and tastes. When headroom is limited, as is sometimes the case in garages, attics, and basements, resilient flooring is often the only reasonable choice, since it needs no built-up subflooring.

This section provides instructions for installing vinyl sheets and tiles. Some types of resilient flooring require special adhesives, so be sure also to check the manufacturer's instructions.

Before installing, remove the flooring from its packaging and let it acclimate for several hours, at a minimum. Because this flooring is so thin, any bumps or dips in the underlayment will telegraph through the vinyl, so take extra care to provide a clean, smooth surface. If the vinyl flooring has to meet another, higher flooring surface, increase the vinyl's underlayment as necessary to create equal heights. Choose an appropriate reducer or cover strip to mark the transition between surfaces.

Vinyl Flooring over Concrete

Vinyl sheets and tiles can be installed over the concrete in a basement or garage. However, the concrete must be dry, smooth, clean, and free of cracks or other damage. For information on repairing concrete and controlling moisture, see pages 49 and 153. If you wish to insulate the floor, follow the instructions for installing a floating subfloor on page 74. Instead of adding a second layer of ½-inch plywood, however, use a ¼-inch lauan plywood underlayment, available at lumberyards, to provide a smooth surface for the vinyl.

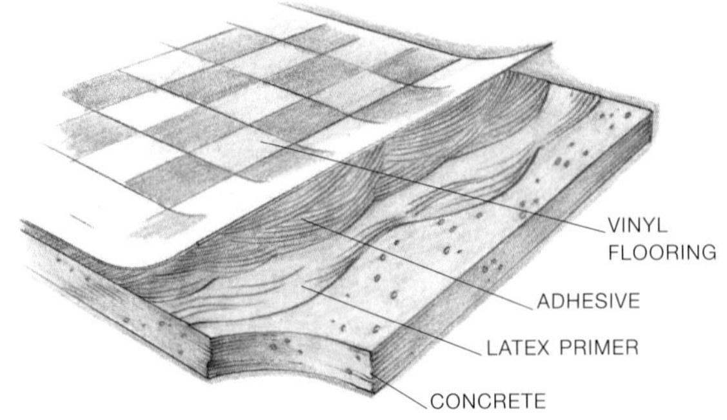

Vinyl Flooring over Wood Framing

If you plan to install vinyl flooring in a converted attic, first make sure the framing is strong enough (see page 126). The joists should be covered with a ¾-inch plywood subfloor and a layer of ¼-inch lauan plywood underlayment. Seal the seams in the underlayment with a floor patch powder mixed with water. Allow the patch to dry, then smooth with 80-grit sandpaper.

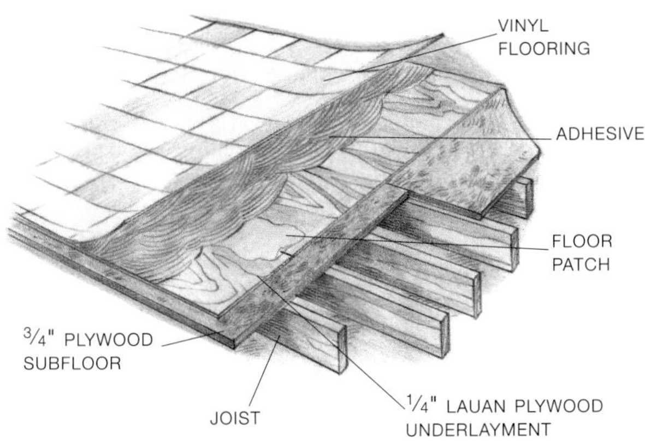

Installing Sheet Vinyl

Vinyl sheets typically come in 6-foot and 12-foot rolls. Six footers are the most common and offer the greatest variety, but 12-foot sheets offer a better opportunity for a seamless installation.

Make a paper template If you are a little uncertain of your skills, the safest way to avoid making cutting errors is to make a paper template of the floor. Use heavy paper, such as craft paper or butcher's paper, or buy one of the template kits offered by some flooring manufacturers. Note that you will need a flat surface large enough to lay the flooring out so that you can set the template on it.

Place sheets of paper around the edges of the room, carefully cutting and fitting around pipes or other obstructions. Tape overlapping sheets of paper together, but don't tape the edges; instead, cut out small holes near the edges and place tape over the holes. When the template is complete, fold it up and transfer it to the vinyl flooring. Trace along the template with a washable felt-tip pen, then remove the template and cut the flooring with a utility knife or flooring cutter. Roll up the flooring and carry it to the installation site.

Cut-to-fit installation without seams If you chose to skip the paper template step, unroll the flooring in a large room. Transfer the floor plan onto the flooring with a washable

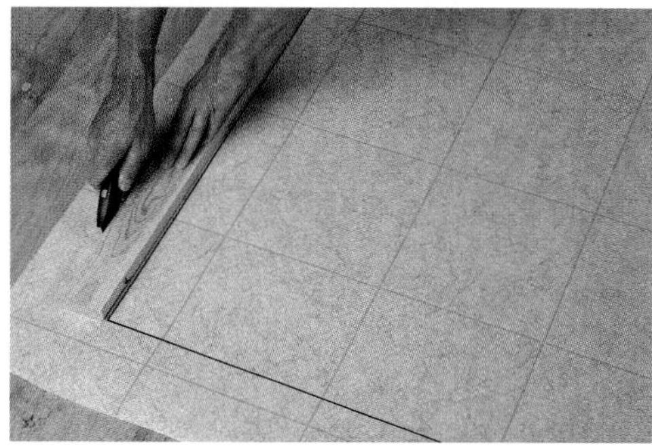

felt-tip pen. Use a carpenter's square or long straightedge to draw straight, accurate lines. With a flooring knife or utility knife cut the flooring roughly 3 inches oversized on all sides. The excess will be trimmed away after you have positioned the flooring. Roll up the flooring and carry it to the installation site.

Cut-to-fit installation with seams Unroll the flooring in a large room. Overlap the edges of the sheets at least 2 inches and tape them together. On flooring with a decorative

pattern, align the sheets so that the patterns are matched. If your flooring has simulated grout or mortar joints, plan to cut along the printed joint. Transfer the floor plan and cut the flooring as described above. Cut the seams using a straightedge as a guide. Cut straight through both pieces of flooring. Remove the flooring scraps and align the seams.

Trim the flooring Make a series of relief cuts at all inside and outside corners to allow the flooring to lie flat on the floor. At inside corners, trim away the excess with diagonal cuts. At outside corners, cut straight down to the point where the wall and floor meet. To trim along the walls, lay a heavy metal straightedge about ⅛ inch from the wall, then cut along the straightedge, as shown above. The gap will be covered later with baseboard trim.

Spread the adhesive The manufacturer will specify the adhesive and type of trowel you should use with your flooring. Roll up

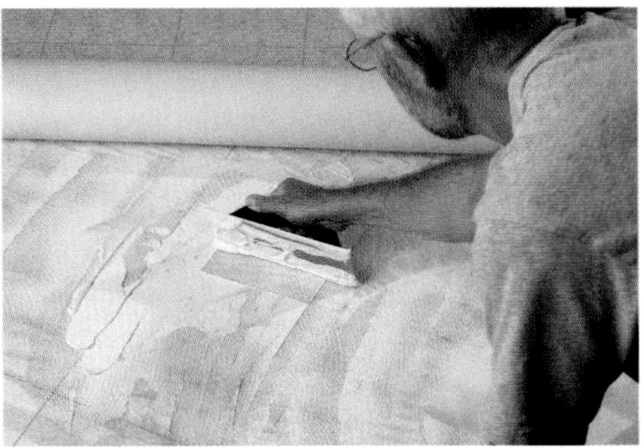

half the flooring and spread adhesive over half the floor. Allow the adhesive to sit for 10 or 15 minutes to become tacky. Carefully roll the flooring back in place. Repeat the process for the other half of the floor. Take special care to align all seams. Working from the middle out, use a roller to smooth down the flooring.

Installing Vinyl Tiles

Vinyl tiles generally come in 12-inch squares. Some tiles are self-adhesive, requiring only that you peel off the backing. If your tile requires the use of adhesive, first mark layout lines as described in step 1 on the facing page, then spread the adhesive and lay the tiles as described in step 2. If you want to experiment with colors and patterns, use graph paper and colored pencils to work out a pleasing design before installing. Once the tiles have been installed, roll them smooth as described for sheet vinyl flooring.

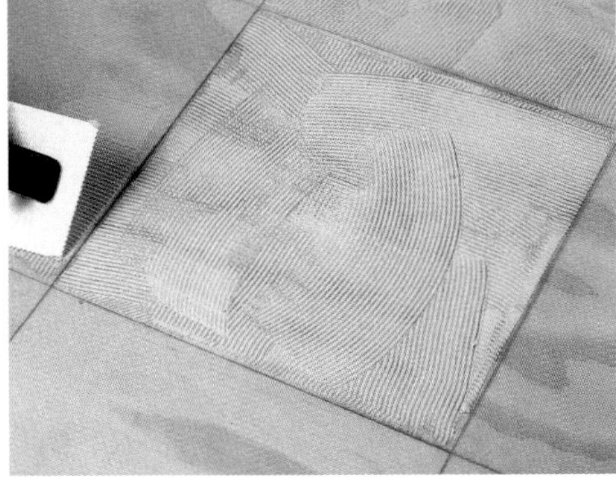

Installing Vinyl Tiles

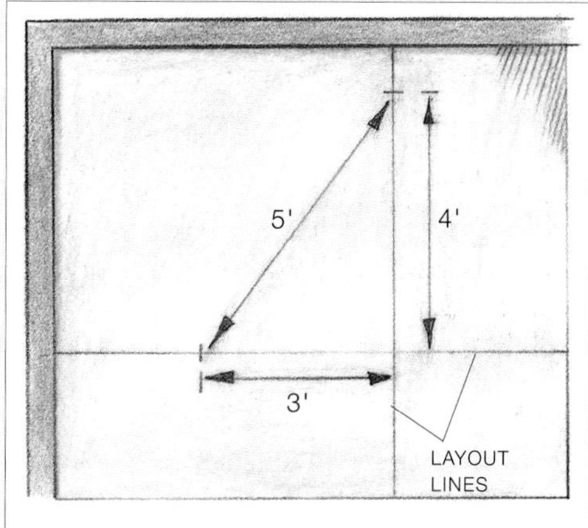

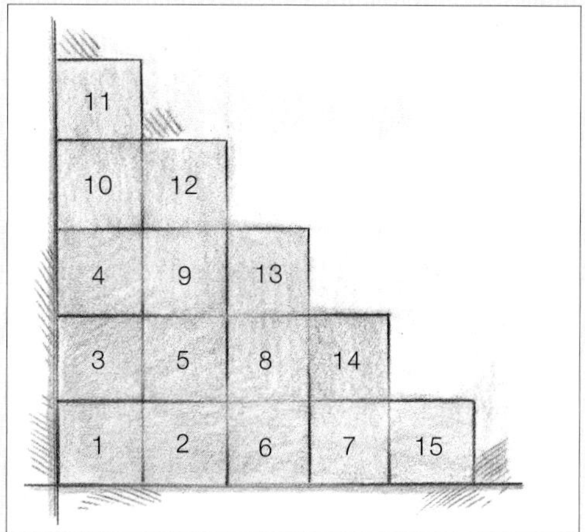

1 MARK LAYOUT LINES Measure and mark layout lines at the centers of opposite walls. After marking the first line, use a framing square as a guide to create a perfectly perpendicular second line. Check for squareness using the 3-4-5 method: Measure from the center 3 feet out on one line and 4 feet out on the other. Make a mark at both spots. Then measure the distance between the marks. If it is 5 feet, the lines are square. If it isn't, adjust the lines.

2 LAY THE TILE If you are using self-adhesive tiles, peel off the backs and press them in place. If you are using adhesive, spread it on with the recommended trowel, taking care not to cover the layout lines. Begin from the center and work out, following the pattern sequence in the illustration.

Trimming Vinyl Tiles

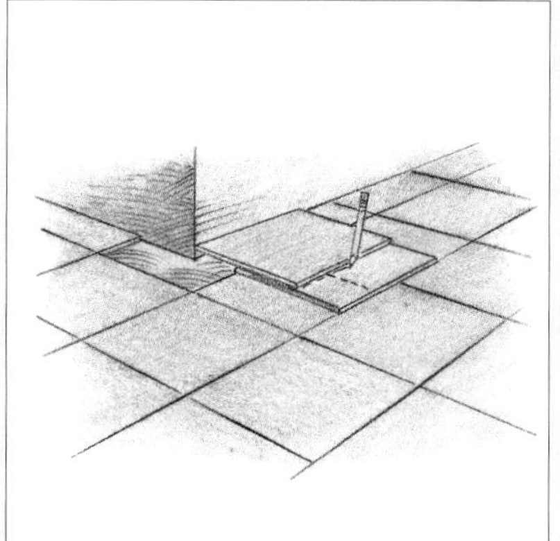

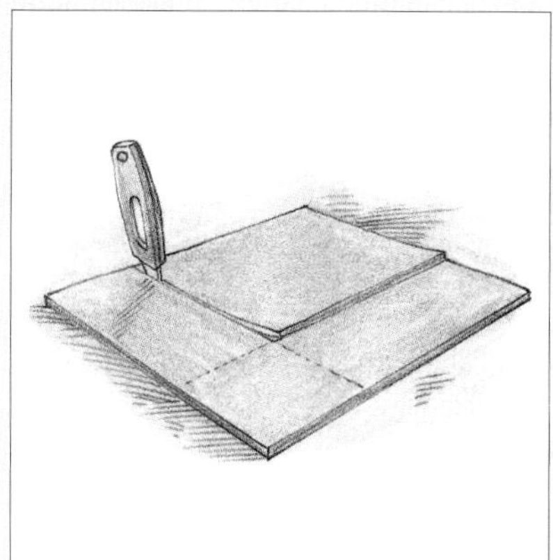

1 To mark cutting lines on a border tile, place a loose tile on top of the last full tile nearest the wall. Set a second tile over the first, keeping its edge back away from the wall ⅛ inch. Mark the first tile for cutting.

2 Use this same marking technique in two stages first, on one side of an outside corner, then on the orther side to mark the L-shaped tiles that will fit in those postions.

3 Cut the tiles with a flooring cutter or utility knife, using a straightedge to guide the blade.

Techniques: Finishing Up

The construction process is a sequence of operations—it begins with noisy tools, heavy lifting, and lots of dirt and debris, and ends with much quieter, detail work. After following the information provided in chapters 1 through 3, your converted space should now be ready for the finishing touches, and this chapter focuses on the principal tasks required to make it ready for occupancy.

Even if you farmed out some of the earlier jobs to subcontractors, you will probably want to handle the work detailed in this chapter yourself. Completing your room will consist of installing doors and windows, trim (or finish) carpentry, installing light fixtures, and adding the sink, vanity, and toilet to a bathroom. Use this section of the book to help you choose materials and decide what projects to tackle. And if you decide to subcontract some of the work, this section will also help you understand what to look for when you start talking to a contractor.

Installing Doors and Windows

When it comes to selecting doors and windows, there are many choices available, in a wide variety of price ranges. Make your selections based on your real needs. In most cases you will want to stick with a style that complements the rest of your house. Consider your climate as well; good-quality exterior doors and windows may cost more initially, but they can save money in the long run by reducing energy bills. Security is also a factor; some doors and windows are easier to break into than others.

Doors and windows have become much easier to put in place. Prehung doors allow you to skip the tedious and troublesome step of installing hinges; windows can be ordered to fit almost any opening and can be installed in an hour or two.

CHOOSING A PREHUNG DOOR

Installing a door in the traditional way means constructing a door frame, positioning it in the rough opening, hinging the door to the frame, and installing a latch or lockset. If you buy a prehung door, much of the work has already been done for you.

The size of the door should have been determined when you framed the walls (see pages 22–27). The rough opening should be plumb and level, 1 inch taller and 2 inches wider than the finished door dimensions. The width of the jambs should equal the width of the wall; if necessary, jambs can be trimmed or extended. Ideally, the door should swing into the room toward the nearest wall, thus consuming the least amount of floor space.

Doors are available in a variety of patterns, from flush (smooth and flat) to paneled to louvered. In terms of styles, you have three primary choices.

- *Hollow-core doors* are lightweight, easy to carry and install, and easy on the budget. They do not provide much sound privacy, however.
- *Solid-core doors* have a wood fiber core that gives them added stability. They are heavier than hollow-core doors and better at sound reduction. Once painted, it is often hard to tell the difference between a solid-core door with molded panels and a solid-wood door with a similar pattern.
- *Solid-wood doors* are more traditional. They are heavy, and thus offer the best noise protection. Extra care is needed in sealing the wood with paint or stain to minimize the expansion and shrinkage that can occur when the humidity changes.

Common Door Styles

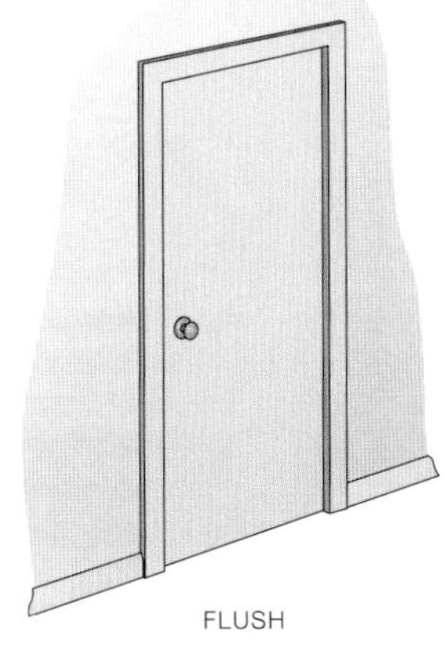
FLUSH

6-PANEL

LOUVERED

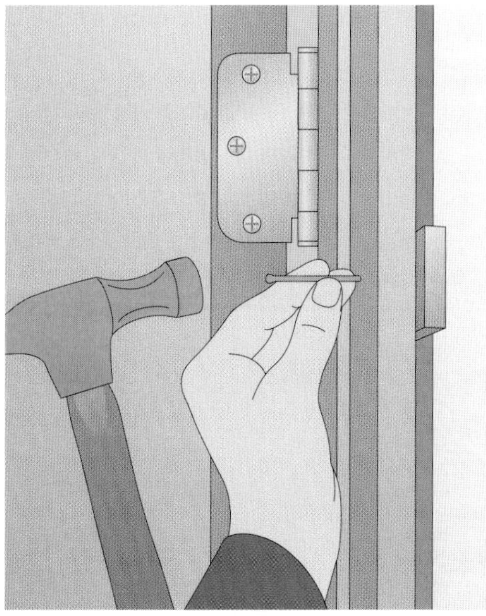

LEFT: **Plumb the side jambs with wood shims between the jamb and the rough opening. Always add shims near each hinge.**

RIGHT: **Drive 8d finish nails through the jamb and shims into the framing. Cut the shims flush with the jambs. The nail heads can be set and covered with wood putty later.**

INSTALLING A PREHUNG DOOR

Begin the installation by removing any packing material or braces from the door assembly. Place the closed door in the rough opening and center it. Check the jamb on the hinge side with a level. Plumb the jamb, if necessary, by tapping wood shims between the jamb and the framing, as shown above left.

Even if the jamb is plumb, you will need to fill the gaps with shims near each hinge. At each shim location, drive an 8d finish nail through the jamb and shims and into the frame, as shown above right.

Note: If your unit has a split jamb, separate the jambs before you start installing the door. One advantage of split-jamb doors is that the casing is already attached. Attach the doorstop side of the jamb first, then slip the other half into the first half and drive 8d finish nails through the center of the stop into both pieces.

Continue the same process around the jamb. On the strike side (opposite the hinge side), nail at the top and the bottom, and above and below the strike itself. Cut the shims flush with the jambs, taking care not to damage the wall or the jambs.

When Plumb Is Not Enough

It is not unusual to install a door perfectly plumb and level, only to discover that an out-of-level floor makes for an unsightly fit. In this case, it is usually best to cut the bottom of the door so it is even with the floor, as shown below.

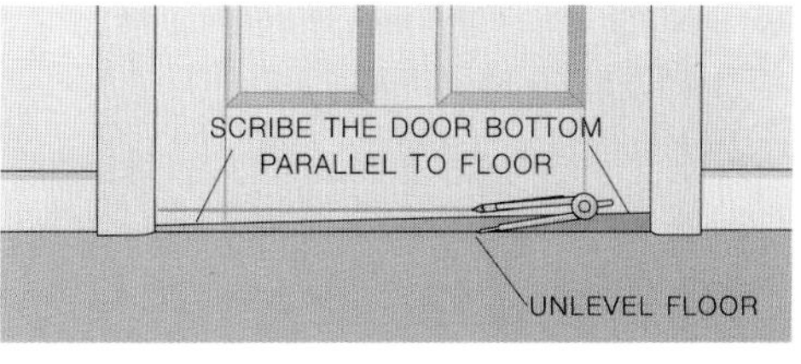

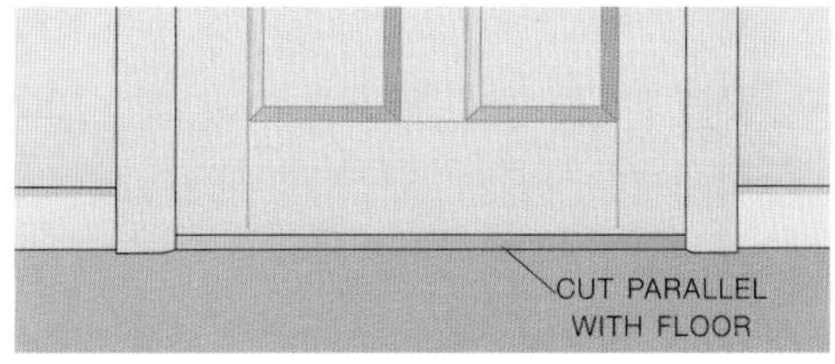

INSTALLING A LOCKSET

A standard cylindrical lockset, the most common style in use today, is easy to install, especially if the lock and latch holes have already been drilled. If you need to drill holes to install a new lockset, be sure that you have the right size hole saw (usually 2⅛ inches for the lock hole) and spade bit (usually 1 inch for the latch hole).

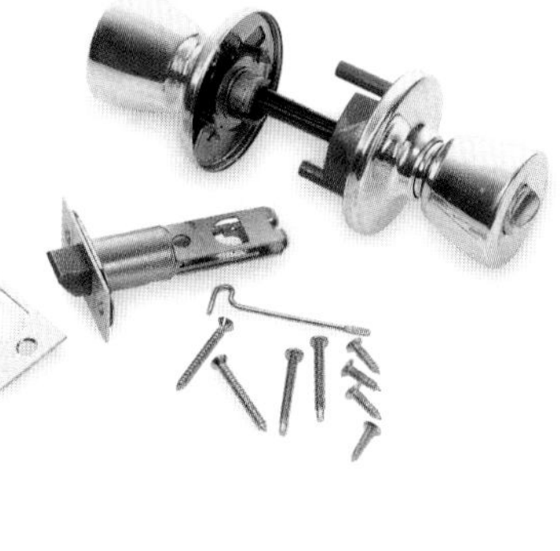

Continued on page 86

You will have the best results using a hole saw with an integral guide bit.

When you're installing a new lockset, make certain the new faceplate and strike plate are flush with the door edge and all door jamb surfaces. If they are not, you will need to adjust the mortises by chiseling out a shallow mortise or by building up a deep one with wood putty.

The steps illustrated below show the preparation and installation process for a standard cylinder lockset. If the lock and latch holes have already been drilled, you can skip steps 1 through 4. Check first to be sure the mortises are the correct depth.

Adding a Lockset

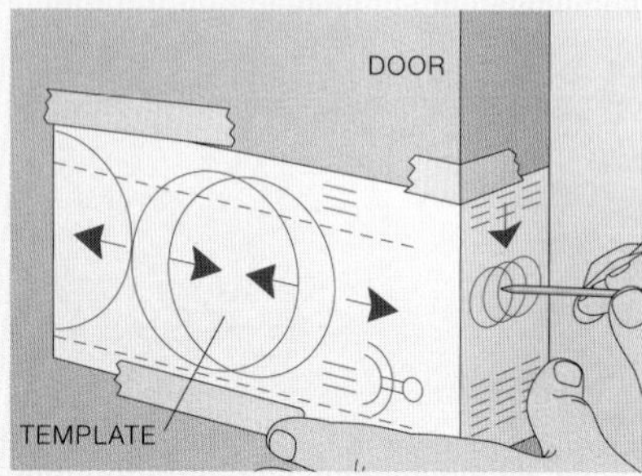

1 LOCATE THE HOLES A template and instructions should be included with your lockset. Place the knob 36 to 37 inches above the floor. Tape the template to the door. Use a nail or awl to mark the centers of the lock and latch holes.

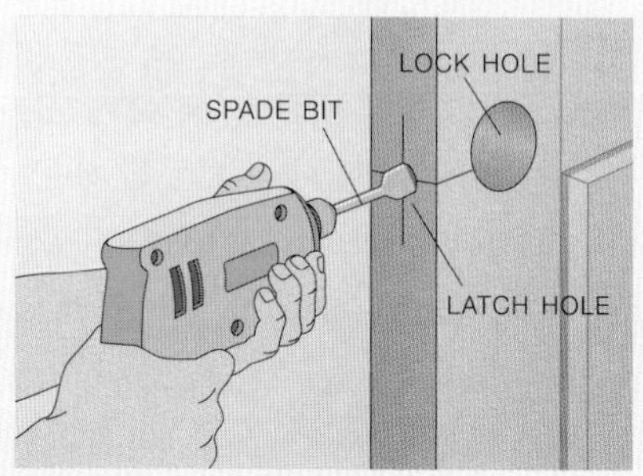

2 DRILL THE HOLES Always bore the lock hole first, using a hole saw. As soon as the guide bit on the hole saw exits the opposite side of the door, stop and continue from that side. This will help prevent tearout when the hole saw exits. Use a spade bit to bore the latch hole, as shown. Take care to drill straight, level holes.

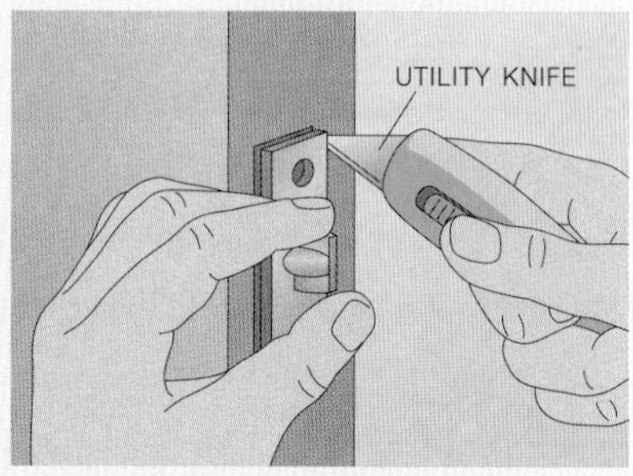

3 MARK THE MORTISE Insert the latch assembly. Holding it square, trace the outline of the latch plate with a sharp pencil. Then use a utility knife or awl to score the outline. Alternatively, trace around the latch plate with a utility knife, as shown.

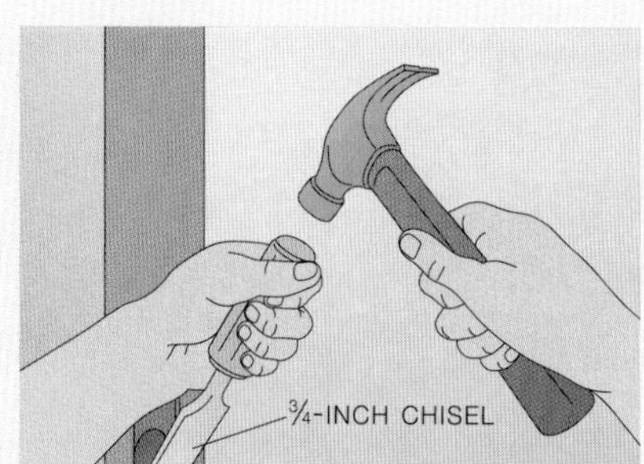

4 CUT THE MORTISE With a ¾-inch chisel and a hammer, score the two long sides; hold the chisel at a 45-degree angle, with the beveled edge toward the wood. Working from the center of the mortise, tap the chisel to the bottom, then to the top. The finished mortise should be about ³⁄₁₆-inch deep. Insert the latch; if necessary, shave off a little more wood.

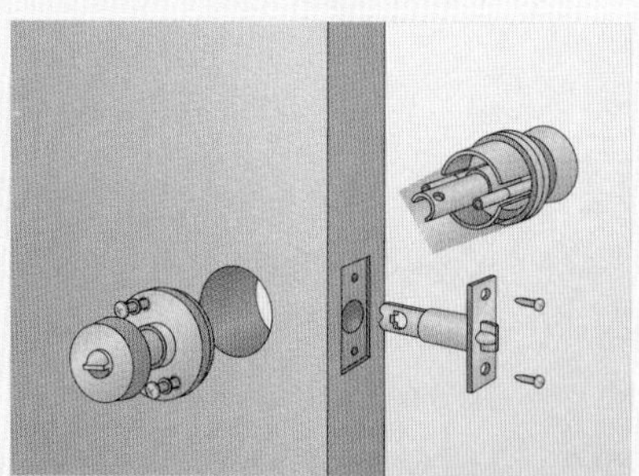

5 INSERT THE LATCH ASSEMBLY AND FACEPLATE Holding the exterior knob and cylinder, slide the cylinder in and engage it with the latch assembly. Attach the mounting plate, handle trim, and knob.

6 INSTALL THE STRIKE PLATE Place the strike plate against the jamb to align with the latch. Score the outline. With a spade bit, bore a hole just deep enough for the latch. Then chisel the mortise. Attach the strike plate to the jamb with screws.

INSTALLING A WINDOW

The most common style of window is double-hung, with an upper outside sash and a lower inside sash that slide up and down. Vinyl-clad windows are a popular choice because they are easy to install and to maintain. Some people prefer traditional wood windows, though, because they tend to be less expensive and they often look better on older homes. Installation will be easier if you work with a partner.

Flanged Window To install a flanged window, as shown below, run a continuous bead of silicone caulk around the rough opening, then center the window in the rough opening. If the house exterior is covered with house wrap, slide the top flange under it. Check the window for level and plumb, inserting shims on the inside as needed to correct the alignment. Using the fasteners specified by the manufacturer (typically, 2-inch galvanized roofing nails), drive nails through the flange at the top corners.

Check the window again for level and plumb, then nail around the flange. If supplied, attach the corner gasket. Cover the flange on all four sides with house wrap tape or 4-inch-wide self-sticking bituminous tape; tape the bottom first, then the sides, then, finally, the top.

Installing a Flanged Window

Installing a Wood Window

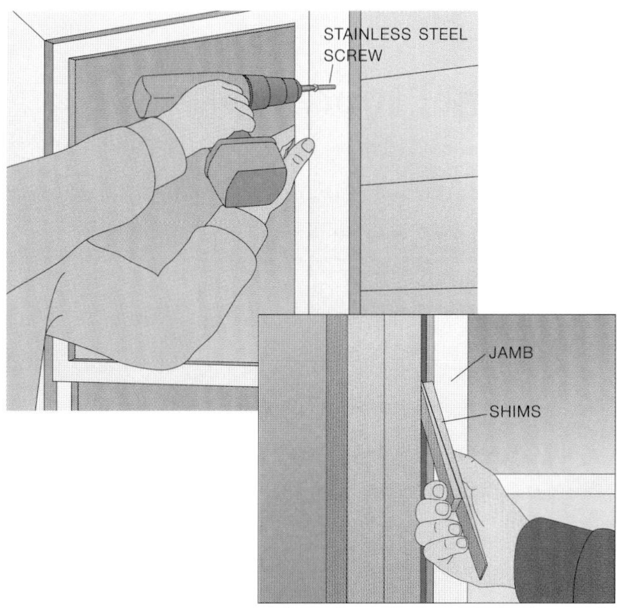

Wood Window For a wood window, shown above, first cover the framing with 8-inch-wide strips of house wrap or felt paper. Staple this protective layer in place, sliding it between the sheathing and the siding. Then cut a piece of drip edge and slide it under the siding on top of the window. Center the window in the rough opening, and level and plumb it as described at left.

When the window is aligned properly, drive 2⅛-inch stainless steel screws, spaced about 12 inches apart, through the top and sides and into the framing. Do not drive screws through the sill. If it is more convenient, you could also use 16d casing nails, driven through predrilled holes. Run a bead of silicone caulk around the entire window unit, and fill the nail holes with paintable (or color-matched) caulk.

Installing Light Fixtures

Most plans for converted garages, attics, and basements call for surface-mounted or recessed light fixtures. Basic installation instructions for both are given below.

For instructions on wiring switches, see pages 42–43. Track lighting is another option worth considering. Track units are sold as systems, with fixtures that fit the manufacturer's track design.

WARNING:
Before tackling any lighting job, disconnect the circuit by removing the fuse or switching off the circuit breaker.

FIXTURES

Small, lightweight ceiling and wall fixtures generally can be screwed directly to the fixture box's mounting ears. Heavier fixtures may need to be fastened to the box with a mounting bar or hickey, or with another method that will hold them securely.

Fixtures with exposed metal parts must be grounded. If you've installed a metal box, the nipple or screws holding the fixture to the box will ground the fixture. A nonmetallic box does not need grounding, but you will have to ground the fixture.

Surface-mounted Fixtures Most surface-mounted incandescent fixtures come with their own mounting hardware, which is adaptable to any standard fixture box. With the cable routed and the box and switch installed, mounting the fixture itself is straightforward, as shown below.

Installing a Surface-mounted Incandescent Fixture

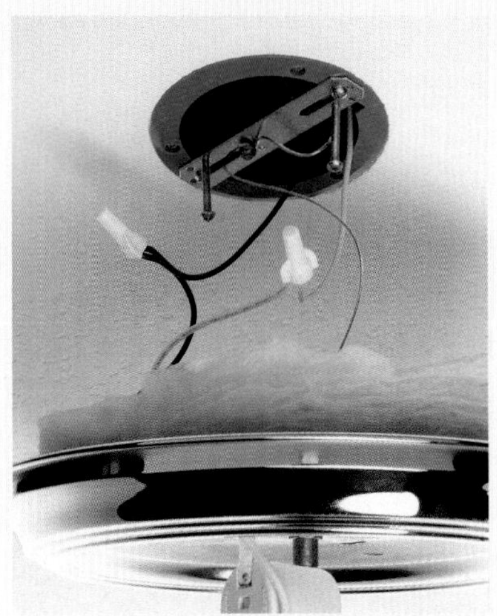

1 MAKE THE CONNECTIONS This fixture attaches to a grounding bar that is first screwed to the nonmetallic housing box. Mounting bolts are then loosely fastened to the bar. Splice the black fixture wire to the circuit hot wire, and the white fixture wire to the incoming neutral wire. This fixture has its own grounding wire; secure it to the grounding screw on the grounding bar.

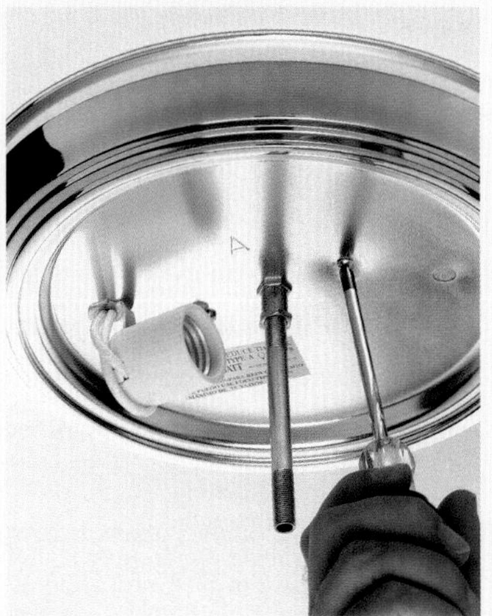

2 SECURE THE CANOPY Carefully fold wires into the housing box, then secure the canopy to the box. This fixture has keyhole slots that slip over the mounting bolts. Push the canopy into place, then tighten the bolts.

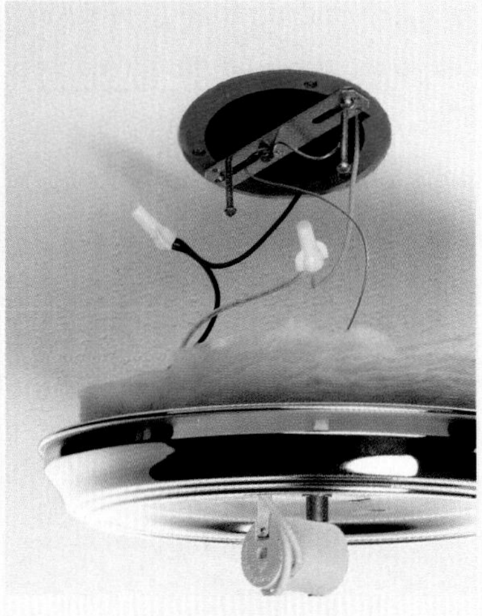

3 ADD THE TRIM Screw in the light bulb or bulbs, then attach the diffusing globe or shade. This globe slips over the long center hickey and is held in place by a threaded end piece.

Note: If the fixture is heavy, have a helper hold it while you work, or hang it from the box with a hook made from a wire coat hanger.

Recessed Downlights New recessed downlights are usually prewired and grounded to their own housing box; however, older-style downlights may require wiring into a junction box attached to a ceiling joist. If you plan to insulate the ceiling, buy an IC-rated fixture for direct contact or plan to remove insulation within 3 inches of the fixture. When you have access from above, choose a new-work downlight. When you don't have access, use an old-work fixture, also called a remodeling fixture.

Adding a Recessed New-Work Downlight

New-work downlights with adjustable hanger bars are easy to install from above. Nail the ends of the adjustable hanger bars to joists on either side, then make wiring connections inside the unit's junction box. Replace the cover plate on the box. Once the ceiling material is in place, clip the fixture trim or baffle into place from below.

Installing a Recessed Old-Work (Remodeling) Downlight

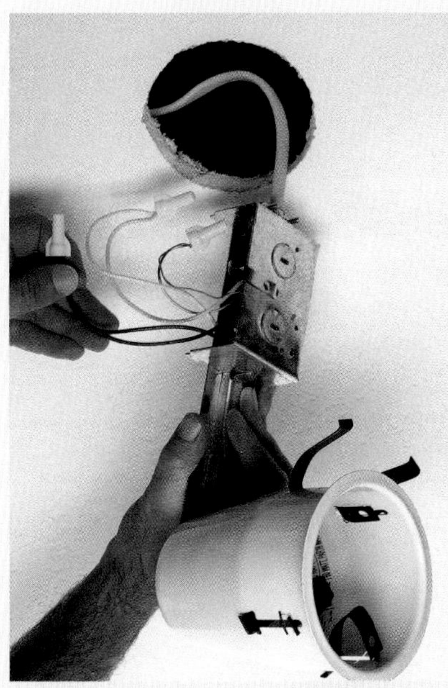

1 MAKE THE CONNECTIONS Cut an access hole in the ceiling, then splice the fixture to the incoming circuit wires. Replace the cover plate on the box.

2 SLIP THE FIXTURE INTO POSITION Thread the fixture, junction box first, into the ceiling. Attachment methods vary; this fixture has spring clips that, when locked into place, grab the ceiling material from above.

3 ADD THE TRIM Trim pieces vary from model to model; the style shown here clips into the fixture. You can choose from trims that aim the light exactly where you want it or those that use diffusers or baffles (as shown) to create softer ambient lighting.

Trim Carpentry

Installing contoured moldings or standard lumber trim along the bottom and top edges of walls and around door and window frames is an exercise in artful deception. Trim covers gaps and hides imperfections, but it also introduces a new architectural feature to the room.

Most of the major elements of modern trim are derived from ancient Greek and Roman architecture. Although the modern trend has been toward minimizing trim work, it is worth considering how attractive, well-placed, and properly installed trim can add to the appeal of a room.

TRIM CHOICES

Most doors and windows are trimmed with a casing (a wood frame that covers the gap between the wall and the jamb—sometimes the casing is already installed on prehung units), and baseboards are almost mandatory protection on most walls. Other types of trim, such as crown molding, chair and picture rails, corner boards, and wainscoting, are additional options. Typical door and window trim styles are shown at right.

It is easiest and best to stain or paint molding before installation, then fill nail holes, lightly sand, and touch up with stain or paint after installation.

Casing Styles

There are several styles of casing that can be purchased at home centers and lumberyards. This prefabricated material typically is thin, with a groove routed in the back to give it

Typical Trim Pieces

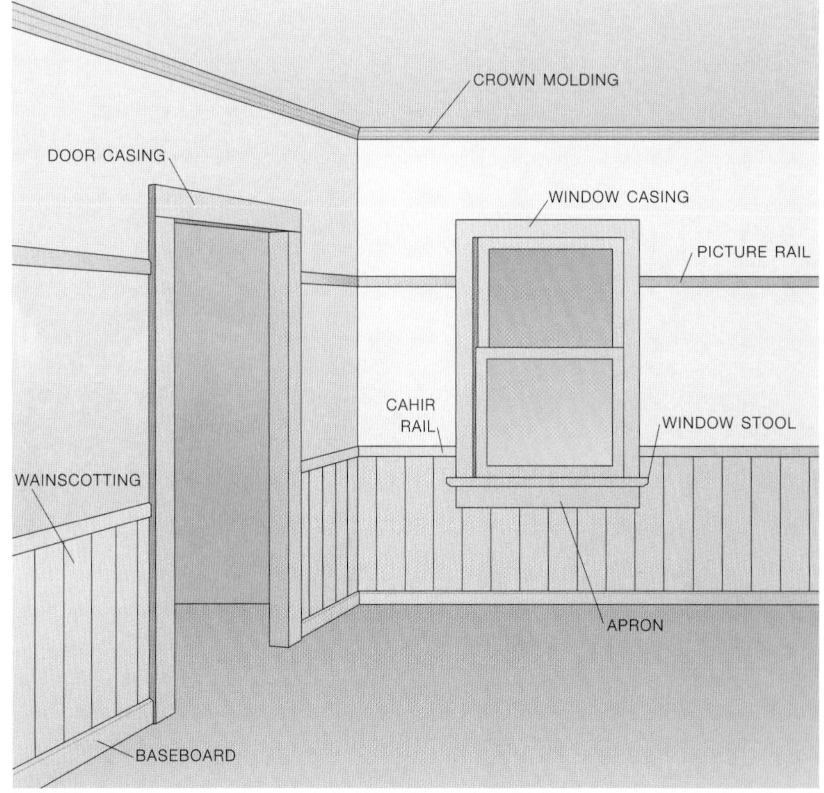

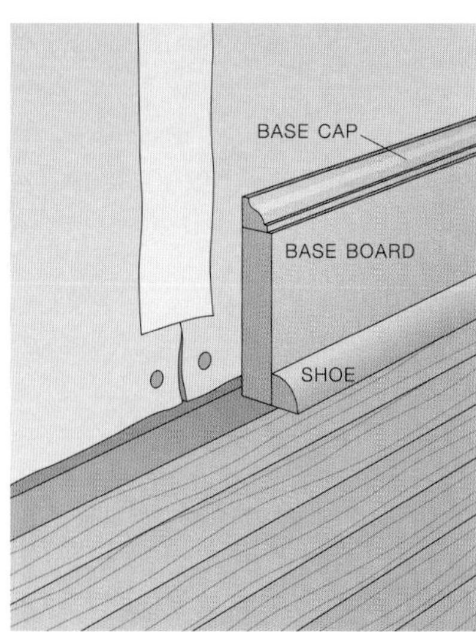

Trim can hide sloppy joints and both planned and unplanned gaps.

Door Casing Trim Styles

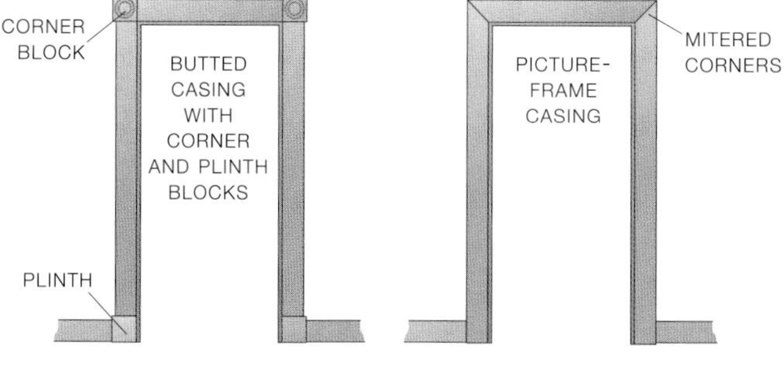

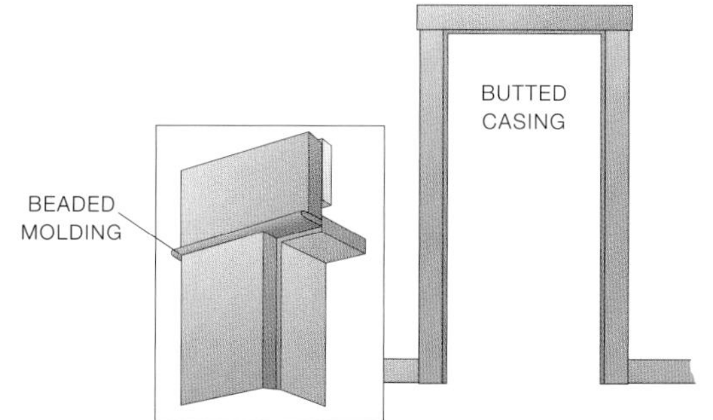

Window Casing Trim Styles

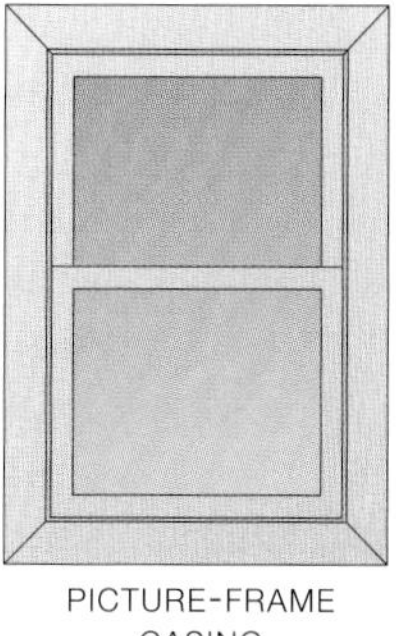

PICTURE-FRAME CASING

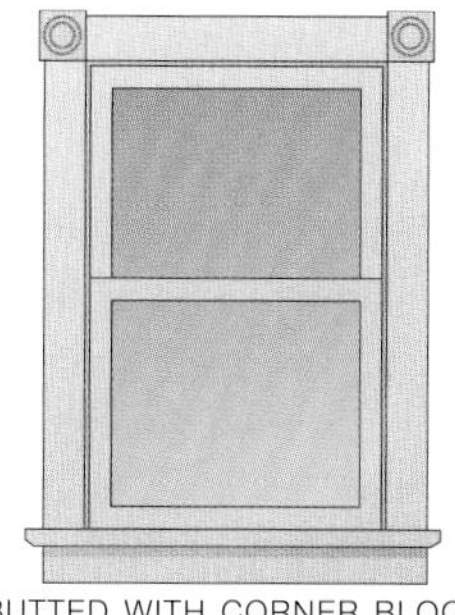

BUTTED WITH CORNER BLOCKS AND STOOL AND APRON

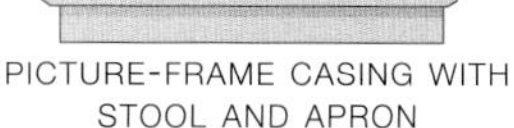

PICTURE-FRAME CASING WITH STOOL AND APRON

BUTTED WITH STOOL AND APRON

some flexibility; this can be a great help when installing the casing over surfaces that are less than perfectly flat. You can also use full-sized boards, such as finished pine or oak. The styles of door and window casings are largely defined by the types of cuts that are made at the corners.

Many trim carpenters now make custom interior trim from medium-density fiberboard (MDF). Sold in 4-foot by 8-foot sheets, MDF cuts easily with a table saw and can be shaped with a router. Because it has a smooth surface, MDF looks great when painted (although it should be coated with an oil-based, not a latex, primer).

Butted Casing This style of casing utilizes square cuts, or butt joints. These casings can be made with pieces of material of the same thickness, with the edges perfectly flush, or thicker material can be used for a head casing, cut a bit longer to form an overhang. Backband can be used around butted casing to cover the end grain. Bead molding can be used beneath the head casing to create a reveal (see page 92).

Picture-frame Casing This kind of casing is formed by using the same casing material on all four edges. The corners are formed with miter joints (see page 94). Although a quick and simple technique, full picture-frame casing does not incorporate a window stool (or sill), which many find an unacceptable compromise. And miter joints have a tendency to develop gaps over time.

Continued on page 92

Trim Profiles

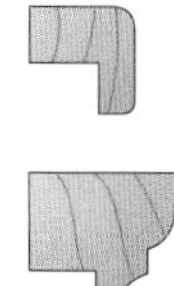

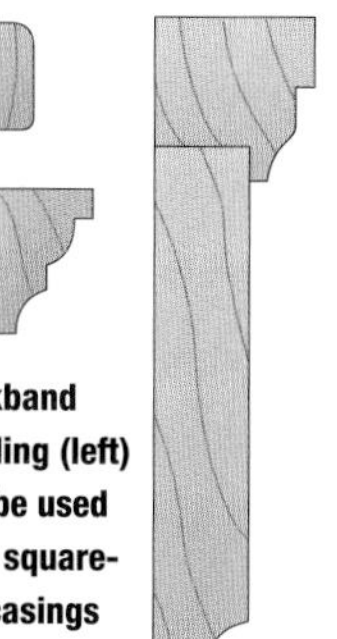

Backband molding (left) can be used with square-cut casings (right).

Casing Profiles

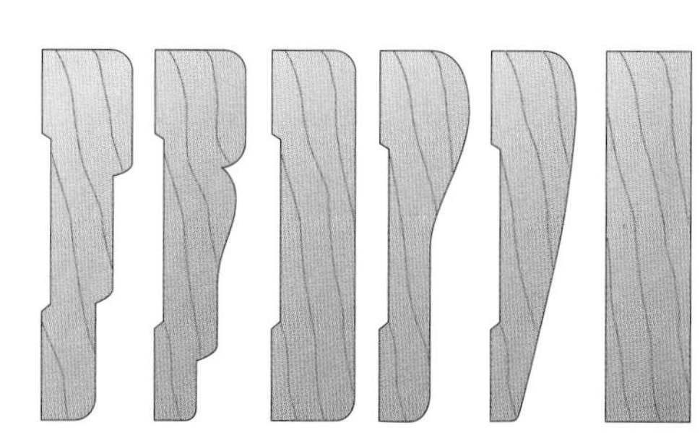

Reveals and Overhangs

Trim carpenters know that it is difficult to create neat, flush edges with trim pieces, and almost impossible to prevent gaps from developing over time due to wood movement. You can minimize the effect of such developments with reveals and overhangs as shown below left.

Reveals are created by stepping the edges of successive layers of wood back from each other. Overhangs can be created by cutting casing pieces longer than necessary and by using thicker pieces. The eye and mind will tend to notice the shadows and shifting planes you create with these devices, rather than the gaps or other irregularities themselves.

The size of the overhang can vary depending on the size of material you are using. The best size for a reveal depends on the size and style of your casing, but, for standard materials and designs, a consistent 3⁄16 inch or 1⁄4 inch is best. Mark the edge of the reveal with pencil, then align the casing with the mark. A combination square is a handy tool for marking reveals; set the square to the desired depth, then slide the square along the jamb with a pencil fixed on the edge, as shown below right.

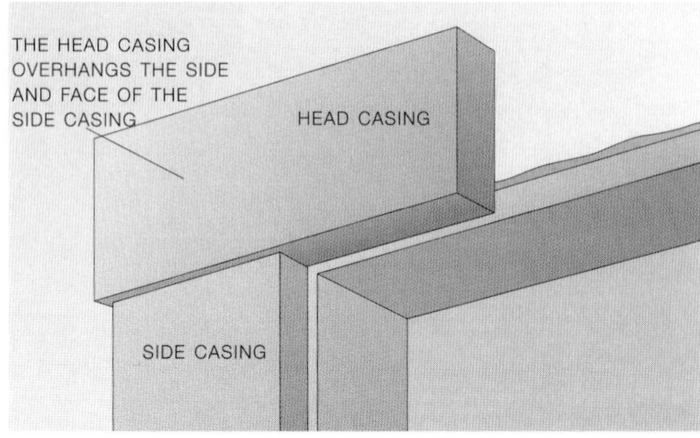

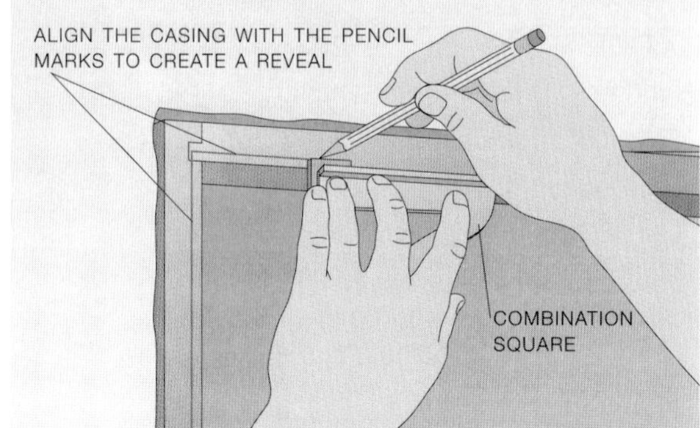

Corner and Plinth Blocks Corner blocks can be used in the upper corners of doors and windows, and plinths are similar devices used at the bottom of door casings. You can buy both types of blocks or make your own. Typically, both blocks are thicker than the casings or adjacent baseboard. This serves two convenient functions: it creates attractive reveals and overhangs while also permitting the use of butt joints (see page 94), which are easier to cut and fit than miters.

Chair and Picture Rails

Chair rails were originally installed to protect plastered walls from being damaged by the backs of chairs, and picture rails were used to facilitate mounting pictures and mirrors. Today, both are more decorative than functional. Chair rails are typically installed about 36 inches above the floor; picture rails are added at least 72 inches above the floor.

Ceiling Molding

Ceiling molding covers the joint between the wall and the ceiling. The simplest technique for installing it is to use flat molding, which is just baseboard molding installed upside down, with nails driven through the molding and into studs. Crown molding is a bit more complicated to install. Nails are driven through the molding and into both studs and ceiling joists. Joints can be coped (see page 94; this is tricky with crown molding) or mitered.

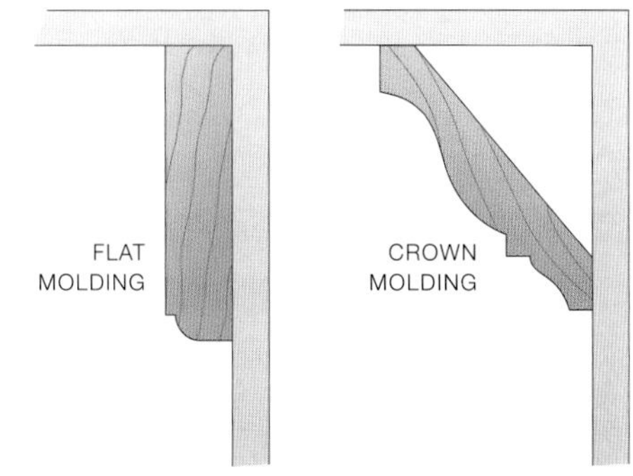

Installing contoured moldings or standard lumber trim along the bottom and top edges of walls and around door and window frames is an exercise in artful deception. Trim covers gaps and hides imperfections, but it also introduces a new architectural feature to the room.

Most of the major elements of modern trim are derived from ancient Greek and Roman architecture. Although the modern trend has been toward minimizing trim work, it is worth considering how attractive, well-placed, and properly installed trim can add to the appeal of a room.

TRIM CHOICES

Most doors and windows are trimmed with a casing (a wood frame that covers the gap between the wall and the jamb—sometimes the casing is already installed on prehung units), and baseboards are almost mandatory protection on most walls. Other types of trim, such as crown molding, chair and picture rails, corner boards, and wainscoting,

Continued on page 94

Installing Casing

Cutting Trim

When cutting trim always try to fit the difficult end first. At right, the inside corner joint was cut first. With the two pieces of trim pushed snugly in place, the wall can be used to mark the miter on the outside corner.

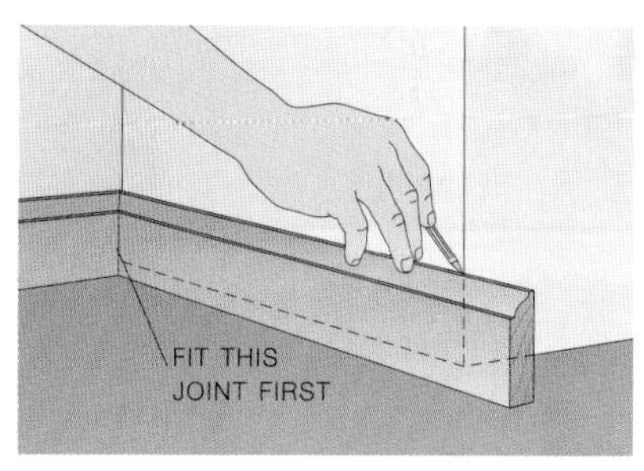

Baseboard Trim

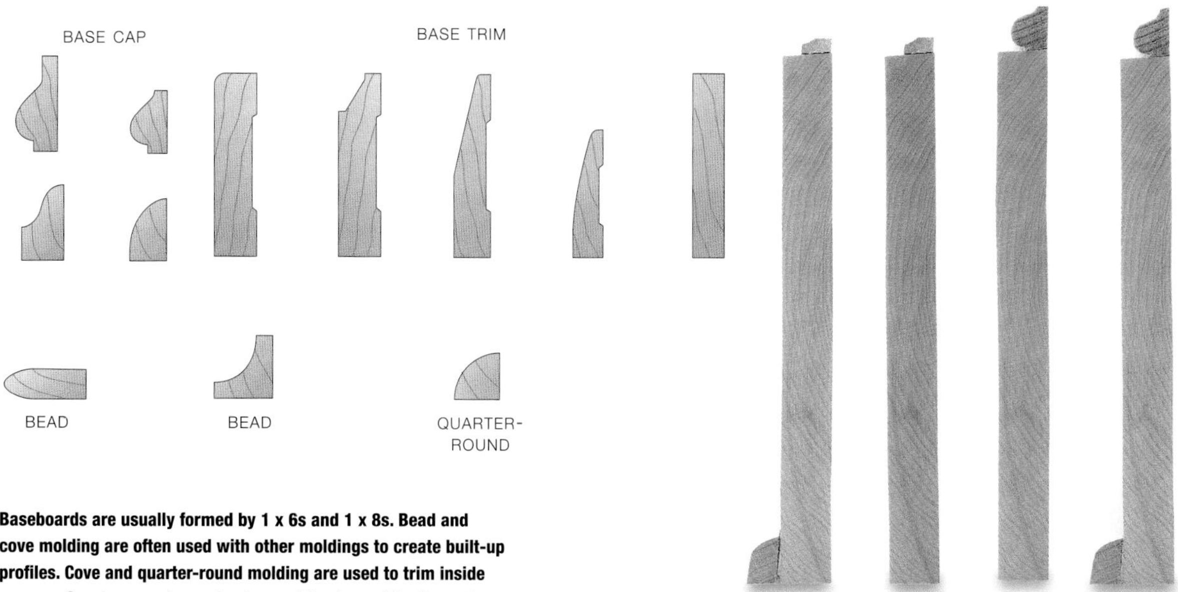

Baseboards are usually formed by 1 x 6s and 1 x 8s. Bead and cove molding are often used with other moldings to create built-up profiles. Cove and quarter-round molding are used to trim inside corners. Quarter-round can also be used in place of the base shoe.

INSTALLING BASEBOARD

Baseboard should always be nailed to wall studs, not to the floor. Use 8d finish nails for ¾-inch baseboard on top of ½-inch drywall; adjust the nail length as necessary to ensure that the nail penetrates the stud.

The trickiest part of baseboard installation is creating neat, durable joints at corners. Here are some of the more common techniques for doing so.

Butt Joints These are the easiest joints to form. You can use just about any kind of saw to make a straight cut through the wood. Butt joints work best on inside corners, especially if you plan to add a base cap, which will cover the top of the joint. On outside corners and flat corners, however, a butt joint will result in exposed end grain, which is tough to stain or paint neatly.

INSIDE CORNER

Miter Joints Miter joints can be used in nearly all corner situations. The corner is formed by cutting the two pieces of trim at a 45-degree angle. If the corner is not perfectly square, however, you will need to adjust the angles accordingly, either with the initial cut or by trimming with a block plane. Miter joints are also prone to open up into unsightly gaps as the humidity level rises and falls, and miters on outside corners can be damaged easily because the wood is cut to a tip. The best tools for cutting miters are miter boxes and power miter saws ("chop saws").

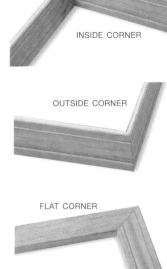

INSIDE CORNER

OUTSIDE CORNER

FLAT CORNER

Coped Joints Coped joints require more work, but they usually produce the nicest-looking corners. The joint is formed by cutting one piece of trim to match the profile of the other piece. Gaps are less likely to form at a coped joint, but if one does appear it will not be as noticeable as it would on a mitered joint. The two methods for coping a joint are shown in the photos below.

Making Coped Joints

1 TRACE THE PROFILE For the first method of coping a joint, place a scrap piece of the trim on the corner of the piece to be cut. Trace the profile in pencil.

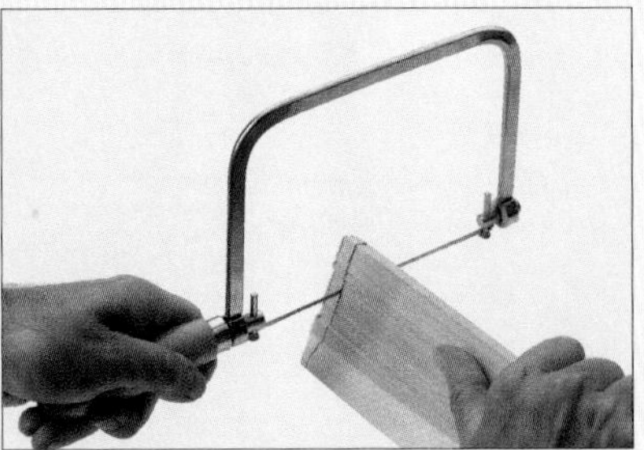

2 CUT ALONG THE PENCIL LINE Carefully cut along the pencil line with a coping saw. Slide one square-cut piece of trim into the corner, then slide the coped piece over it. If necessary, use a file to trim the coped piece until it forms a tight fit.

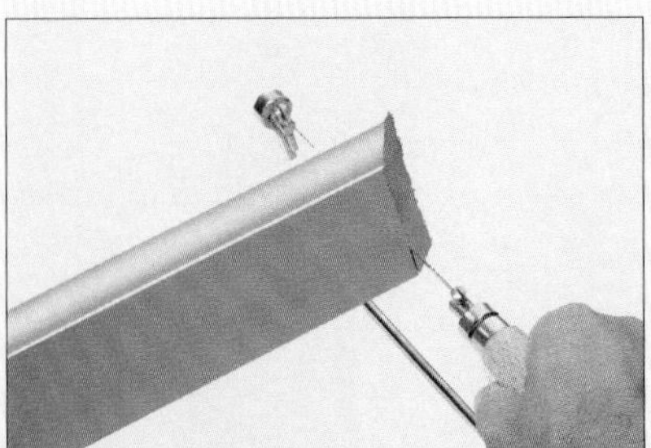

The second method requires that you cut a 45-degree inside corner miter in the trim. Then, with a coping saw, cut along the profile with the saw blade angled, as shown above.

Finishing a Bathroom

You may be surprised at how easy it can be to install the fixtures needed to finish a new bathroom. Local building supply centers, hardware stores, and specialty shops carry a range of vanities, sinks, and faucet and drain hardware to match any decorating style. You may also be able to order special products to fit into unconventional spaces.

Stock vanities range in width from 24 to 48 inches, in 6-inch increments. They also come in a range of heights, usually from 30 to 34 inches tall. If you would like your sink to be higher than standard, you can raise the vanity by building a base under it. Directions for installing a vanity are shown on page 96.

The most common type of top for a vanity is a one-piece molded unit with an integral sink. Another popular choice is a laminate-covered countertop and a set-in sink. Directions for installing a sink-countertop unit are shown on page 97.

There are two types of drop-in sinks you are likely to encounter. The most popular, and easiest to install, is a self-rimming sink, which is shown on page 98. The other option, a rimless sink, is held in place with a metal strip and clips, and should be installed as instructed by the manufacturer.

Along with your vanity and sink, you will need to select a faucet. Good-quality faucets are available in a wide variety of styles and finishes; just be sure when you choose one that the spacing of the tubes in the new faucet matches the holes in the new sink.

Choose a unit that comes with clear installation instructions, and make sure that repair kits or replacement parts are readily available. Since procedures vary with the type of faucet, you should look carefully at the manufacturer's instructions.

Before you begin, have an adjustable wrench on hand. If your new faucet does not come with a rubber gasket, you will also need to have a supply of plumber's putty.

It is usually easiest to install the faucet and drain hardware before putting the sink or sink-countertop unit in place. While you're at it, install the pop-up assembly as well (see page 97). Set the sink-countertop unit upside down on a pair of sawhorses to make it easier to work with it.

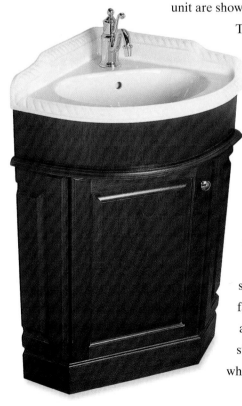

This space-saving corner pedestal sink fits into a tight corner without sacrificing style or looks.

Installing a Vanity

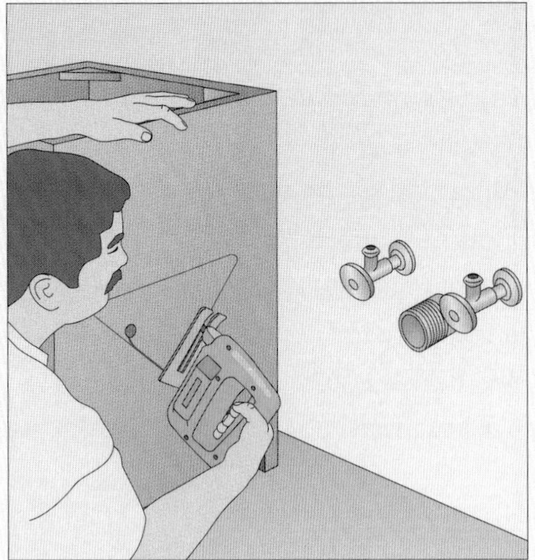

1 CUT OUT THE BACK If the vanity has a solid back, center it over the plumbing lines. Mark the position of the supply and drain hardware and draw a triangle around the marks. Then drill a starter hole and cut the opening with a jigsaw. Alternatively, drill an individual hole for each required opening. On some vanities the back has already been cut out.

2 LEVEL THE VANITY Set the vanity in place against the wall. If there is a wooden baseboard, remove it first. If there is a tile baseboard, scribe the outline of the baseboard on the vanity corners and trim to the line with a coping saw. With the vanity in place, level it from side to side and from front to back using wood shims.

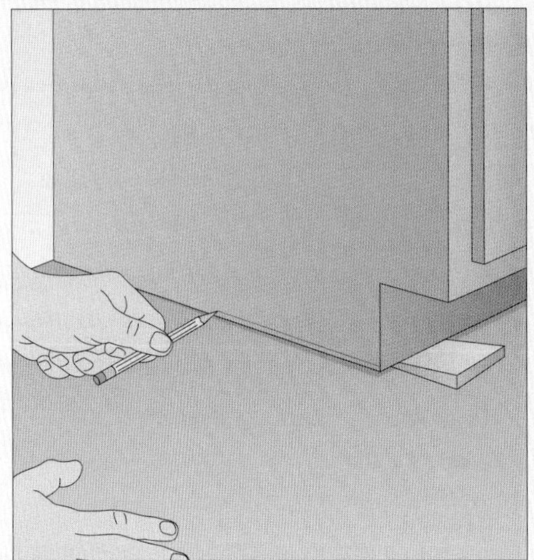

3 SCRIBE THE BOTTOM With the shims in place, scribe the bottom edge of the vanity. To do this, slide a pencil or marker along the floor. Using a saw or belt sander, trim the cabinet to the line. Make corrections as needed so the vanity sits level on the floor. Alternatively, leave the shims in place, trim them with a utility knife, and cover them with molding when the installation is complete. If the back wall is crooked, you may need to scribe and plumb the back of the vanity as well.

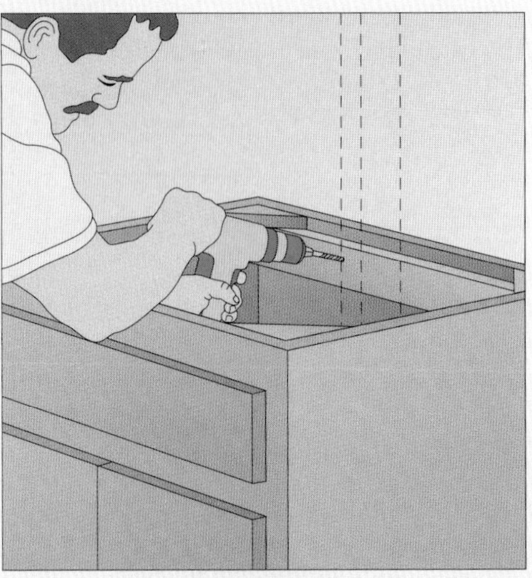

4 ANCHOR THE VANITY Locate the wall studs behind the vanity with an electronic stud finder. (With plaster walls, you may have to drill a small hole, then probe the cavity with a bent hanger to find the studs.) You will probably find the studs centered at 16-inch intervals. Drive 2-inch wood screws through the vanity back brace and into the studs.

Installing a Sink-Countertop

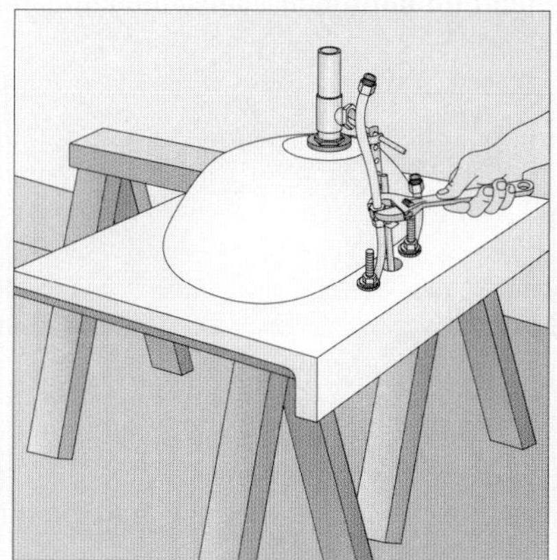

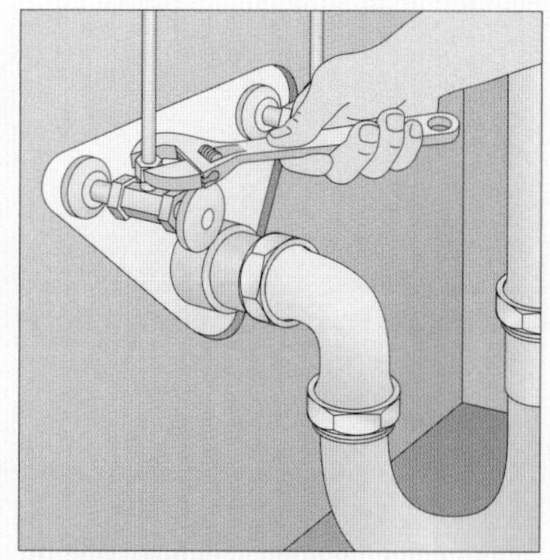

1 INSTALL THE HARDWARE Install the faucet and attach new flexible supply tubes. Pros like to pack the underside of a faucet body with plumber's putty to keep water from penetrating. Set the faucet in the sink holes and attach washers and nuts. When the faucet is aligned with the drain hole, tighten the nuts with a wrench.

2 SET THE SINK-COUNTERTOP Apply a bead of caulk or sealant, as specified by the countertop manufacturer, around the upper edges of the vanity. Center the sink-countertop over the vanity and press it firmly into place. As you press, use a slight twisting motion to ensure a good seal. Some countertops can also be fastened with screws driven up through the corner blocking in the vanity.

3 ATTACH THE SUPPLY TUBES AND TRAP Attach the supply tubes to the shutoff valves. Tighten the nuts by hand, then give a final quarter-turn with an adjustable wrench. Slide the P-trap over the sink tail-piece and attach it to the wall drainpipe. Tighten the slip nuts. Turn on the water supply, then the faucets, to test for leaks.

Installing the Sink Pop-up

The sink pop-up assembly opens and closes the drain on a bathroom sink. The lift rod works through the pivot rod to raise and lower the stopper. Although the mechanism is simple, its several moving parts need adjusting every so often. Pop-ups are usually included with a new faucet.

It is often easier to install and adjust the pop-up on a new sink before setting the sink in place. Position the pivot rod in the middle hole of the clevis and drop in the stopper. Raise the clevis until the stopper seals. Loosen the screw holding the lift rod in place and raise the rod a couple of inches. Tighten the screw and lower the rod. The stopper should open properly, allowing for drainage, and the lift-rod knob should nearly touch the body of the faucet.

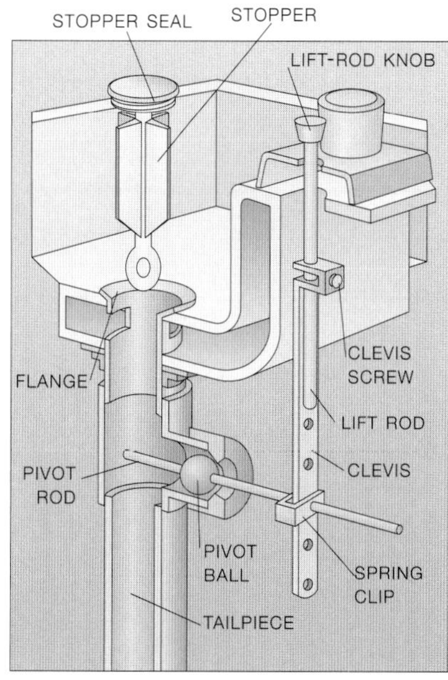

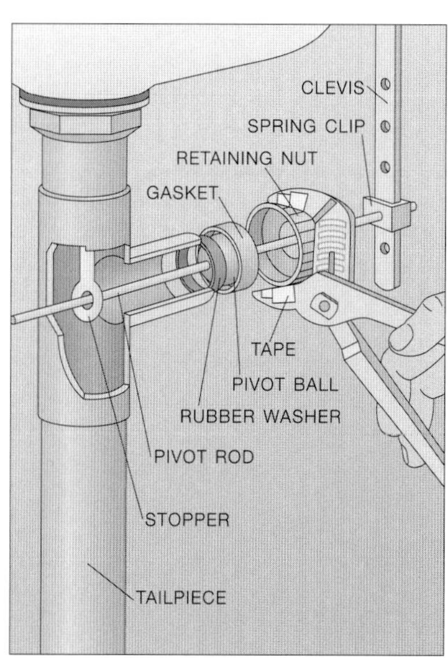

Installing a Self-rimming Sink

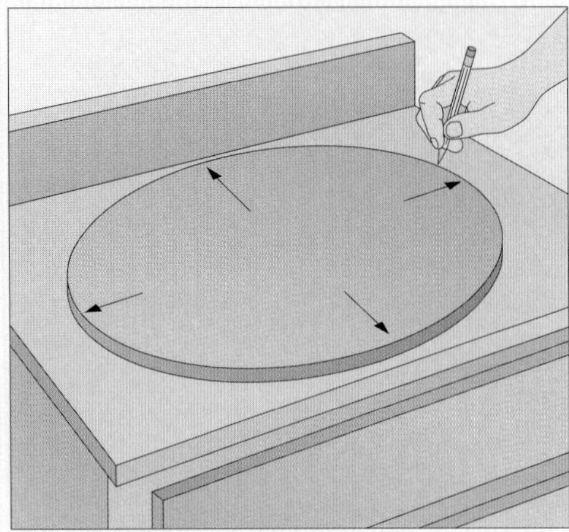

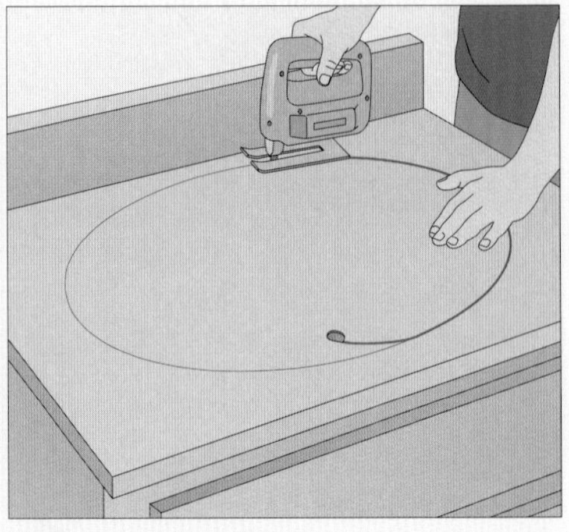

1 LOCATE THE NEW SINK New sinks usually come with a template for marking the cutout on the countertop. Position the template as instructed, maintaining sufficient clearances from the front and back edges. Trace around the template with a pencil.

2 CUT THE HOLE Drill a starter hole inside the cut line, then use a jigsaw to cut the hole for the sink. To protect the countertop from scratches, you may want to wrap the base of the jigsaw with masking tape before you begin cutting the opening.

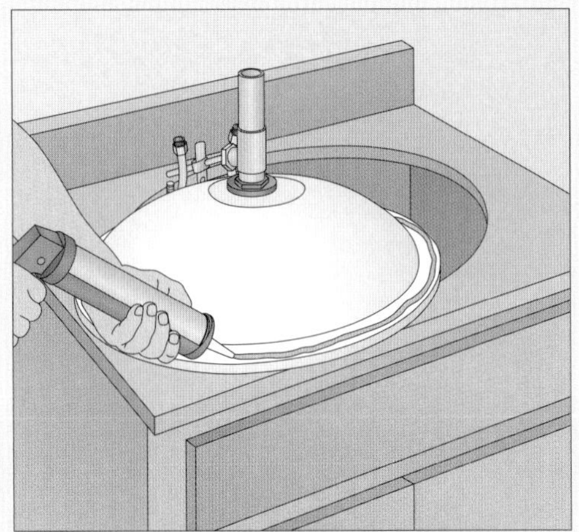

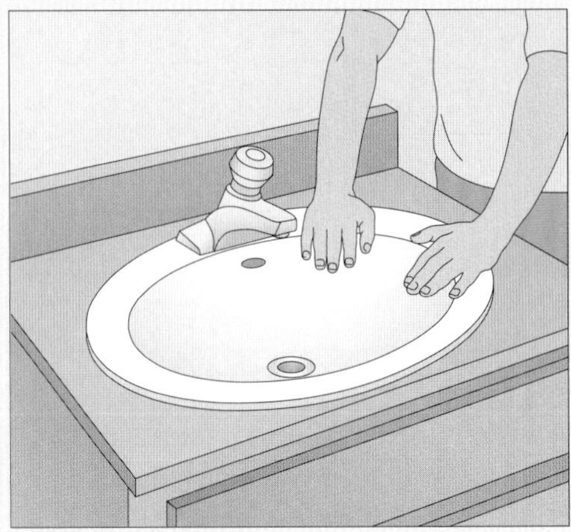

3 PREPARE THE SINK Carefully set the sink into the countertop. Enlarge the cutout, if necessary, to ensure a good fit. Apply a bead of silicone caulk around the bottom lip of the sink.

4 SET THE SINK Center the sink over the cutout, then press it firmly into place with a slight twisting motion. Make sure the sink is centered and square with the front of the countertop. Attach the supply tubes and P-trap. Remove any excess caulk that squeezes out between the sink and the countertop, or fill any gaps between them with additional caulk.

Installing a Toilet

Other than the code requirements for a new toilet, the only crucial dimension to consider when you are installing a toilet is its roughing-in size—the distance from the wall to the center of the drainpipe. Pick a model that is ready to install—one that has a flush mechanism already in the tank. With the toilet, you will get the necessary gaskets, washers, and hardware for fitting the tank to the bowl, but you may need to buy hold-down bolts and a wax gasket.

Putting in a Bowl-mounted Toilet

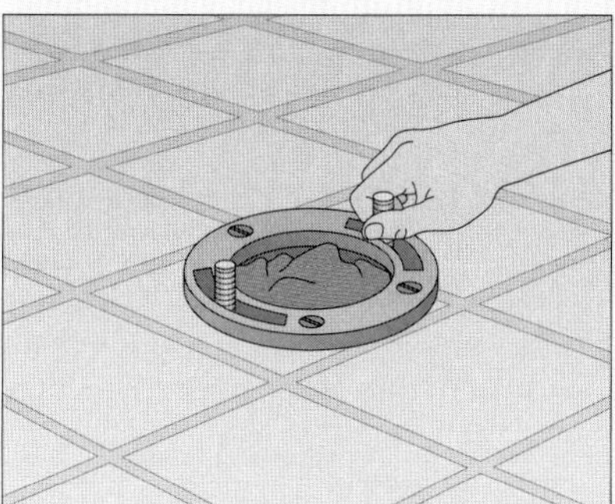

1 PREPARE THE FLOOR FLANGE Cement the plastic floor flange to the drainpipe, then stuff the drainpipe with a rag to block sewage odors. Set the floor bolts in plumber's putty and insert them through the flange. Adjust the bolts so that they line up with the center of the drainpipe.

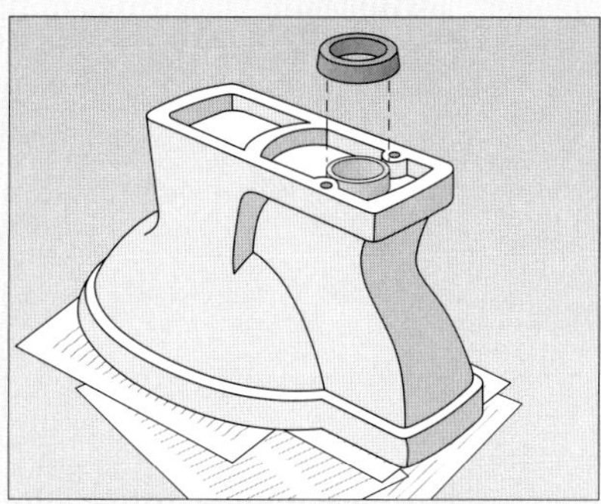

2 INSTALL THE WAX GASKET Set the new bowl upside down on newspapers or a towel. Place the wax gasket over the horn on the bottom of the bowl, with the rounded edge facing the bowl. If you use a wax gasket with a plastic collar, which provides a little extra protection, it is usually easier to set the gasket directly on the flange since the collar may require some twisting to fit properly.

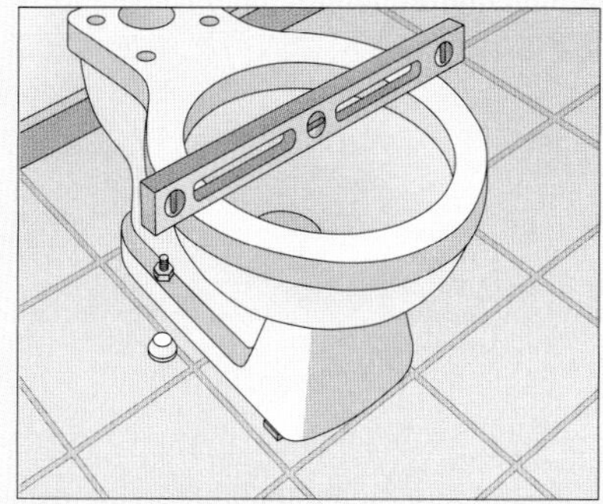

3 SET THE BOWL Remove the rag from the drainpipe. Gently lower the bowl into place atop the flange, using the bolts as guides. Press down firmly while twisting slightly. (Hint: Sitting on the bowl will help seal it.) Check to see that the bowl is level. If it is not, use plastic shims to make it level. Place washers and retainer clips on the floor bolts, then tighten the nuts securely. Do not overtighten! If the floor bolts are too long, trim them with a hacksaw. Press the cap onto the retainer clip.

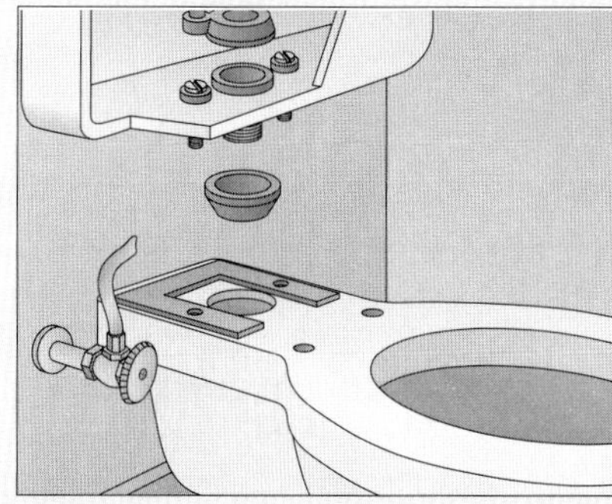

4 ATTACH THE TANK Attach the gasket and tank bolts if they were not preinstalled. Place the rubber cushion, if there is one, on the bowl. Set the tank in place so that the bolts drop into the holes in the bowl. Slide washers over the bolts and tighten the nuts with an adjustable wrench. The nuts should be snug enough to hold the tank securely to the bowl, but avoid overtightening.

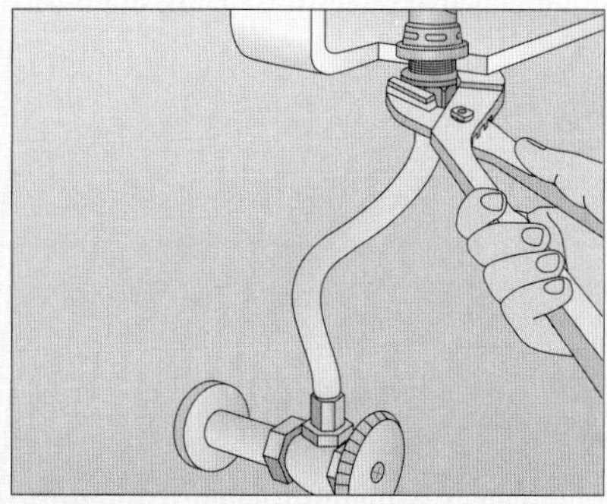

5 HOOK UP THE WATER SUPPLY If necessary, install a new shutoff valve. Buy an angled valve if the stubout comes out of the wall, and a straight one if it comes out of the floor. Attach the supply tube to the shutoff valve and the bottom of the toilet. Turn on the water supply and check for leaks. Flush the toilet a few times and make sure water is not leaking.

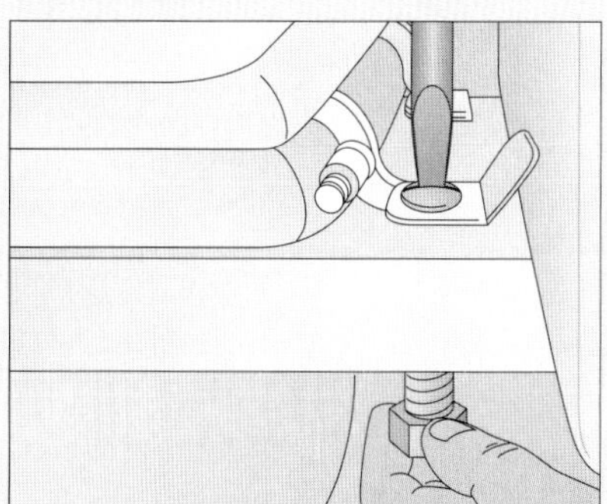

6 INSTALL THE SEAT Align the seat with the holes in the bowl. Install the bolts and tighten the nuts just enough to hold the seat firmly. If your seat has bolts attached to it, slip the bolts through the holes in the bowl and secure the nuts.

Garage Conversions

Converting a garage into living space can be a relatively easy task. Access to the space is usually cut and dried: if the garage is attached, an entry to the house already exists; if an exterior entry to the house is required, it can be done easily.

This chapter opens with a close look at a nicely executed garage conversion that is sure to inspire and encourage you. That look is followed by guidelines on how to assess the status of your garage and the possibilities for its conversion. The focus then turns to what is often the biggest dilemma in a garage conversion: removing and replacing the bulky garage door.

Following tips on preparing the floor for its new function, you will learn some special techniques for heating, cooling, and insulating a garage that were not covered in the general discussion of these subjects earlier in the book. Finally, by using landscaping as well as carpentry, you will see how you can recreate an exterior that looks more like an extension of the house itself than a storage depot for mowers and Mazdas.

A Case in Point When Kurt Lavenson decided that his architectural practice had outgrown the small workspace in his house, his eyes wandered across the patio to an old garage. For years the building had been used for tool storage and as a makeshift dressing room for friends and family wanting to swim in the pool. Lavenson quickly determined that he could make better use of the structure.

From Garage to Office

Lavenson's plan called for creating a new garage space and converting the existing garage to an office and guest room. A poolside wet room and bathroom complete the space.

Lavenson began by gutting the building down to the studs and plywood sheathing and by stripping the roof to the decking. Next, he removed the interior partitions and the huge 6-inch by 12-inch header that spanned the two-car garage door entrance. The result was a clean and empty 25-foot-square space.

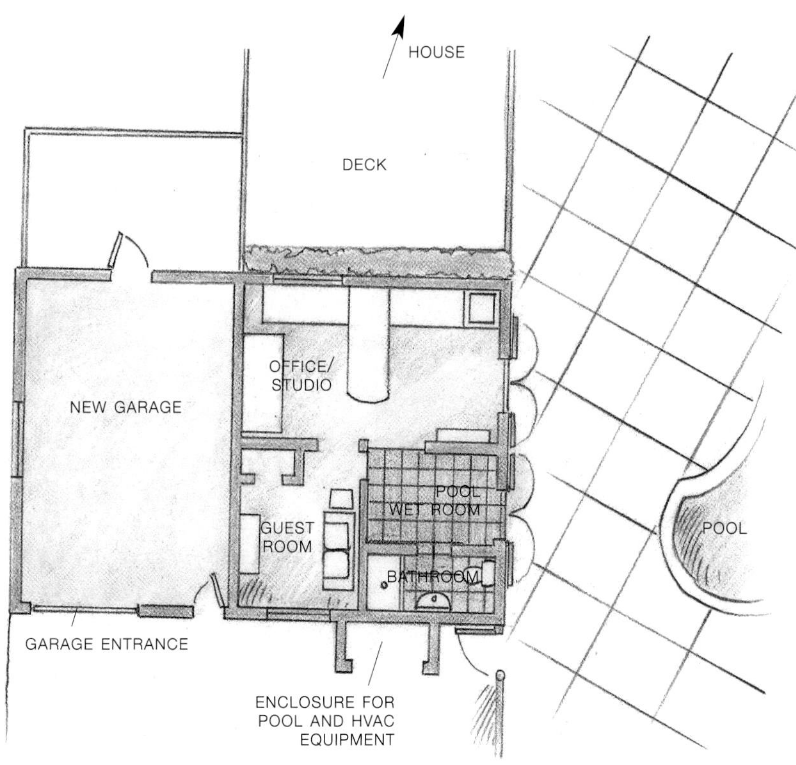

Although the garage had electrical service, Lavenson decided to remove the old wiring back to the conduit that supplied the building and install a new electrical subpanel. (As a one-time general contractor, he felt competent and comfortable doing the electrical work himself, but most do-it-yourselfers might prefer to hire a professional for such a job.) He insulated the roof with rigid foam panels installed between 2 x 4 sleepers attached to the old decking, and he insulated the walls while they were open.

Lavenson followed his plan to reframe the walls for French doors and windows. He divided the interior into four equal quadrants, two of which are now used as workspace. Another quadrant functions as a guest room, TV room, and quiet reading spot, and the final quadrant contains a full bathroom and a wet room for pool users. At the center of the building is a new 6 x 6 post that sits under the old ridge beam. The post serves as a symbolic central point, and all of the large pocket doors close against it. Lavenson's wife, Lesly, sanded and finished the post with clear polyurethane to set it apart visually from the white walls and white ridge beam.

Car access to the old garage had been cut off long ago by the addition of a swimming pool. As they planned the new garage space (the framed walls can be seen on the right), the homeowners decided to place the new garage entry out of sight from the house, with a new driveway that wraps around the back. Viewed from the house, as here, the converted garage was designed to look more domestic than vehicular. Large overhanging eaves provide shelter from the hot California sun.

Starting from the new subpanel, Lavenson added several electrical circuits for office equipment as well as the furnace and air conditioner. He ran three phone lines and a TV cable into the building through underground conduits. New plumbing was installed. Finally, after hiring someone to dig a trench from the house to the garage, Lavenson tied the drain and waste lines into the main line from the house, then ran hot and cold water pipes.

ABOVE: To level the sloping garage floor, Lavenson set a form board across the bottom of the large opening and leveled it with the highest point on the interior slab. He then poured a layer of a self-leveling mortar compound, which resulted in a smooth, level slab set slightly above the patio. The walls were then framed and secured to the floor with anchor bolts installed through the new slab and into the old foundation. A small addition (visible at the left of the building) was constructed to house HVAC and pool equipment. Ducts for the heating and air conditioning run horizontally along the ridge beam.

LEFT: With the framing completed, Lavenson sheathed the walls in plywood. Then he hired a subcontractor to plaster the walls with colored stucco.

Half of the converted garage now functions as the architect's home office and studio. When closed, the large pocket doors, which are mounted on heavy-duty rollers, shut the office off from the guest/TV room (visible in the back) and the pool wet room and bathroom beyond the door at the left of the photograph. When the doors are rolled into the walls, the space has an open, roomy feel. The floors in the bathroom and wet room are covered with 16-inch by 16-inch slate tiles; the other floors are carpeted. The ceilings are the exposed bottom sides of the original tongue-and-groove roof decking, painted white.

Assessing Your Garage

Garages come in a great variety of sizes, shapes, conditions, and locations around the property. Some are hidden out back, others are the most prominent feature on the street side of the house. Garages on newer houses tend to be attached, while those on older houses are more often detached.

Attached garages are more likely to be converted to living spaces because the process is relatively simple. Access to the rest of the house is already in place. Extending the heating and cooling system and bringing in plumbing and wiring are often easy.

However, be sure to consider the garage location in relationship to the rest of the house as well as traffic patterns through the space. A den or family room off a kitchen with easy access to the back yard may be ideal for a growing family; the same space, turned into a master bedroom suite or office, may prove to be too noisy or lacking in privacy.

You will also need to consider how the garage will look from the outside. Some attached garages are such an integral, understated part of the overall house design that masking their former role is really quite simple. Others, however, are so prominent and obviously intended for cars that providing them with a more domestic façade would require a major effort.

Conventional wisdom says that it usually doesn't make much sense to convert a detached garage; there are special difficulties involved in turning one into living space. For one, because the garage is, indeed, detached from the house, you are required to go outside to get there. And, since it does not share a wall with the house, extending an existing heating and cooling system to it is virtually out of the question. Bringing plumbing and wiring into the remote space is also more challenging.

Depending on your needs, however, a detached garage can be a perfect location for living space that requires some privacy

Running Underground Cable

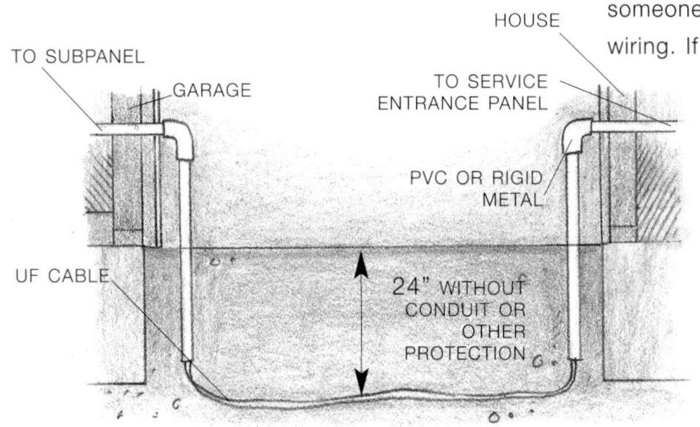

Running electrical cable to a detached garage is not a particularly difficult task for someone with a good knowledge of basic wiring. If your needs are modest, you can tap into an existing circuit in the house. For more involved electrical power needs, though, plan to run one or more circuits from the service entrance panel to a subpanel mounted in the garage. Be sure to use type UF (underground feed) cable for all exposed conduit or buried cable outside.

If covered with a layer of concrete, rigid nonmetallic (PVC) conduit can be buried just 12 inches deep. Otherwise, bury it at least 18 inches deep. Rigid metal conduit may be buried as little as 6 inches deep, with or without a concrete cap. Thinwall (EMT) conduit should not be used underground.

When burying UF cable, dig as deep as possible, but to at least 12 inches. Lay a rot-resistant or pressure-treated board on top of the cable before covering it with dirt to reduce the danger of inadvertently driving a shovel through the cable later. If you don't use a protective covering, bury the cable at least 24 inches down. Be sure to check your local code before you begin running cable.

and separation from the hubbub of the house. Plus, if the garage is located just a few steps away from the house, you can always build an enclosed walkway between the two. The converted garage featured on pages 102–103 is a good example of the possibilities of a detached garage, combining the needs of work, play, and guest housing in a single, thoughtfully designed remodel.

The following pages provide suggestions and instructions for tackling some of the biggest problems involved in garage conversions. The issues below will also need to be considered:

Wiring

Even if the garage has electricity, you will probably want to add at least one more dedicated 20-amp circuit to handle the additional needs. Electrical wires to a detached garage are often buried in the ground, requiring type UF cable; you may be required to run the cable through an underground conduit. It may be possible to run phone and cable lines through the same conduit, but check with an electrician or the phone or cable company first.

Plumbing

Adding new plumbing to a garage is often a difficult and expensive proposition. A plumber could quickly inform you of your options. If the garage is attached to the house, the transition between the two structures may be a utility room, which you might be able to convert into a bathroom.

Headroom

If raising the level of the garage floor would result in a ceiling that is too low, talk to a contractor about raising the ceiling. In many garages, this is not a particularly difficult job.

Security

Plan on installing secure doors and windows, with adequate locks. A detached garage may be particularly vulnerable to break-in, so consider installing an alarm system.

Loss of Storage and Parking

If you hate the idea of leaving your car fully exposed to the elements, consider building a carport. Alternatively, consider the approach used in the example on pages 102–103, in which the old garage was turned into living space and a new garage was built in back, with the driveway redirected.

Garage Styles

RANCH-STYLE HOUSE WITH ATTACHED GARAGE

SPLIT-LEVEL HOUSE WITH ATTACHED GARAGE UNDER LIVING SPACE

TRADITIONAL HOUSE WITH DETACHED GARAGE

Replacing the Garage Door

The first major chore in most garage conversions is removing the bulky garage door. And often the biggest challenge is filling in the resulting hole so that the finished product looks good. In this section you will find instructions on removing a typical garage door and suggestions on how best to replace it.

Older garages were often built with swing-up overhead doors, but most garage doors consist of four or five sections connected by hinges. The doors move on rollers sitting in overhead tracks. Springs handle most of the lifting and lowering, which can be done manually or by using an electric door opener.

If your garage door has an electric opener, it will have to be removed before the door can come off. Unplug the power unit and disconnect the wires to the switch. Pull the manual release cord, then disconnect the support arm from the garage door. While a helper holds it steady, remove the bolts securing the trolley to the power unit on one side and to the wall or ceiling on the other. Remove the bolts holding the power unit to the ceiling and all other brackets, bolts, and hardware supporting the unit. Remove all components of the opener.

Before proceeding, you will need to determine the type of spring mechanism the garage door uses (see the illustrations below) and decide if you can release the tension on the springs. Instructions for removing a garage door are shown on the facing page.

Extension Spring Mechanism

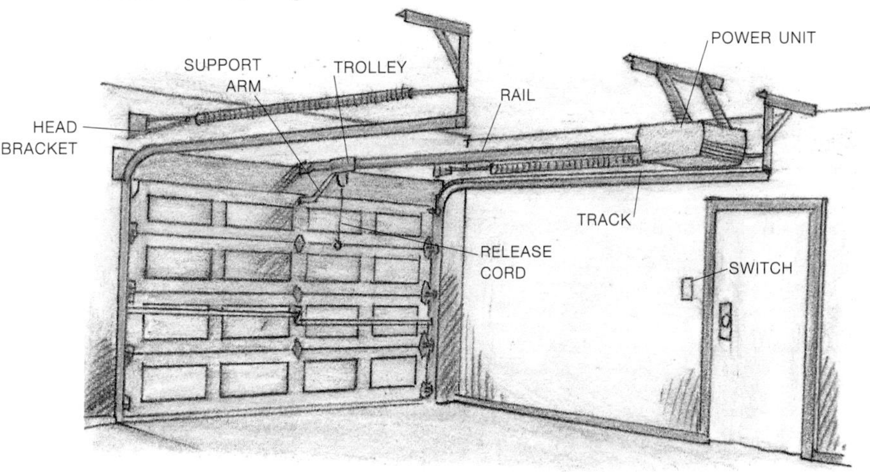

Torsion Spring Mechanism

Extension springs are found above the upper tracks on both sides, while torsion springs are mounted on the header over the closed door. If your garage door is equipped with a torsion spring, call a garage door professional to release the tension. This job requires special tools and experience; the lack of either could result in serious injury. If you have extension springs, you can proceed with the next step, as shown on page 107.

Removing a Garage Door

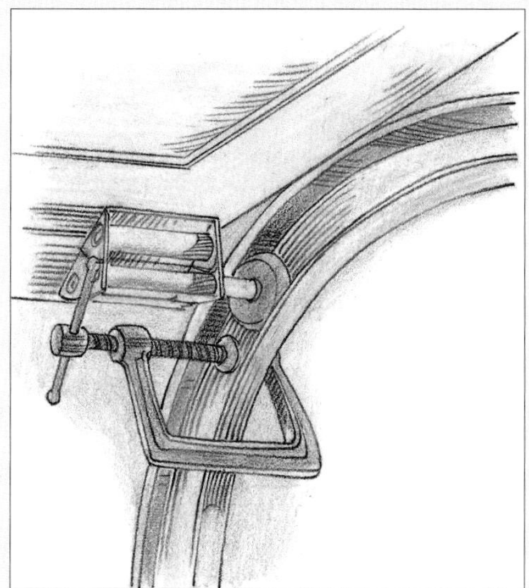

1 DISASSEMBLE THE SPRINGS
To release the tension on side-mounted extension springs, raise the door and prop it fully open with clamps on both sides, as shown. The clamps will prevent the door from rolling down when the springs are removed. Tie or tape each spring to the track, then use a pair of pliers to remove the lift cables from the lower brackets on each side. Disassemble the spring and pulley assemblies.

2 DISMANTLE THE DOOR
While a couple of helpers hold it up, remove the clamps supporting the door. Set a block of wood under the door landing spot to prevent pinching fingers when it is lowered. Lower the door. Remove the brackets holding the top two door sections together. Lift off the top section, then move on to the next one.

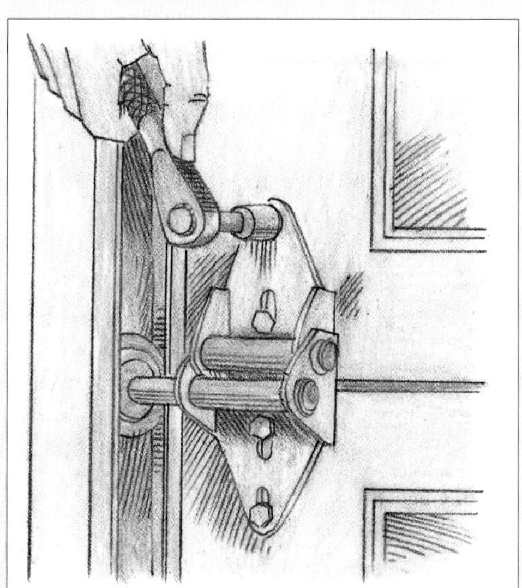

3 REMOVE THE ROLLER HINGES
Unbolt and remove the roller hinges on each side. Remove the tracks and any remaining hardware.

4 REMOVE THE DOOR JAMBS
Use a pry bar and hammer to remove the door jambs on both sides of the door. This should expose the existing curb and wall framing on top of it.

INSTALLING A PATIO DOOR

A patio door is a natural replacement for a garage door, since the major part of the framing (the header) has already been done. All you really need to contend with is choosing the right size of door unit and filling in any gaps between it and the existing rough opening. If your garage has a sloping floor that you want to level, you will need to tend to that job before tackling the patio door.

Choosing a Door

Patio doors are available in two principal styles: sliding and hinged. Each has some advantages and disadvantages, depending on your circumstances and design plans.

Sliding doors provide much light and visibility. When equipped with a screen, they can also vastly improve ventilation. Since the door slides on an integral track, these are good choices when you don't want to lose any space to allow for door swing.

Hinged doors, often referred to as French doors, are more formal and elegant than sliding doors. Because the doors swing open and shut, you will need to allow for the space required. With doors that swing to the interior ("in-swinging"), that can amount to a significant loss of floor space. Fortunately, major manufacturers of patio doors offer out-swinging French doors, such as those on the converted garage on pages 102–103.

Both types of patio doors are available in a wide variety of sizes and designs. You can even find sliding doors that, when closed, look more like hinged doors. With either style, you can simplify installation dramatically by buying a preassembled unit.

Installation Know-How

Always check carefully with the manufacturer of the door you choose for specific installation instructions. Here are a few tips that help you in most circumstances.

Prepare the floor The concrete slabs in garages are usually sloped toward the door so that water and snow that fall off a parked car will flow out. Sometimes the slope may be so gradual that you decide to ignore it. More often, though, you will want to level the floor (see page 113), which may raise the floor about 6 inches in the door opening. This work should be done before you order, much less install, a new door.

Patio Door Styles

Choose the right size door Once the garage door and door jambs have been removed and the floor is leveled, carefully measure the framed opening from top to bottom and side to side. Then choose a door with a rough opening requirement less than these dimensions. Try to avoid choosing a door that requires you to enlarge the existing rough opening.

Level the floor Set a 2-foot or 4-foot level along the edge of a very straight 2 x 4 that spans the full width of the rough opening where the door's threshold will rest. If the floor is out of level, place wood shims along the opening every 6 inches to create a level resting place for the door. Use silicone adhesive to secure the shims to the concrete.

Frame the opening Using 2 x 4s and, if necessary, pieces of plywood, fill in the gaps between the old garage door opening and the new patio door opening. The illustration above right gives a typical example of what this process entails. The floor height has been raised 6 inches to make it level, two 2 x 4 wall extensions have been constructed and fastened to the floor and old framing, and the top has been filled in with 2 x 6s resting on their edges. If the garage has a layer of sheathing beneath the siding, add the same thickness of sheathing to the new framing. The new framing should be flush with the old framing on both sides. The entire rough opening should be plumb and level. Test-fit the door in the rough opening.

Install the door Cut 8- to 10-inch-wide strips of building paper or roofing felt, then wrap them around the framing lumber. Secure with staples or silicone adhesive.

Framing for a Patio Door

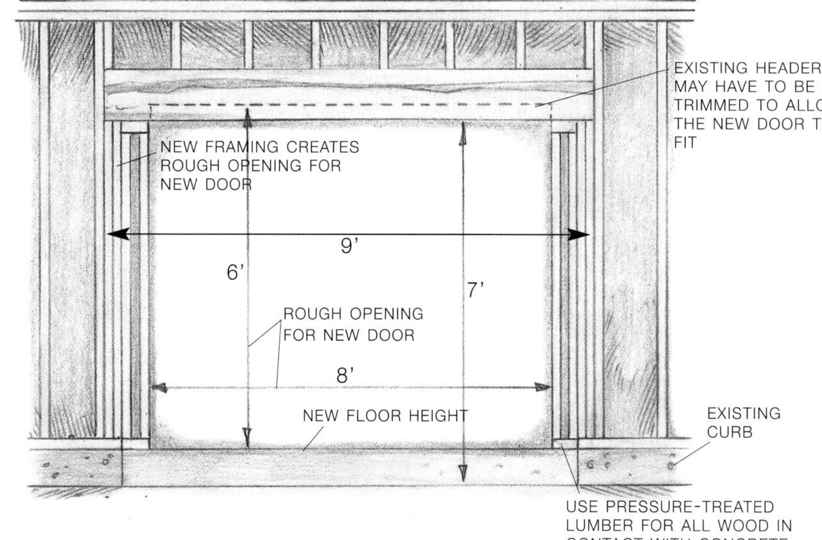

Installing a Patio Door

Apply a thick bead of silicone adhesive along the floor where the door's threshold will rest. Set the door carefully into place and center it in the rough opening. Check for plumb and level, using wood shims as necessary. If you are installing a hinged door, add additional shims along the strike plate section of the door frame.

When the door is properly positioned, begin driving 10d finish nails through the jambs and shims and into the framing. Space nails about 12 inches apart, with extras in the corners. When finished, countersink the nails with a nail set. Fasten the threshold to the slab with concrete anchors. Before installing siding and trim, place a piece of drip edge along the top of the door.

INSTALLING A WINDOW

You may be able to keep windows that are already in place in your converted garage, but in most cases you will want to replace the existing garage windows with new, nicer, larger, more secure and energy-efficient models. The first place to consider for installing a new window should be where the old garage door used to reside. The structural framing has already been done; all you need to do is choose a window (or windows), then build a nonstructural frame to fill the space around them. Here are some tips to help you choose the right window.

BAY WINDOW

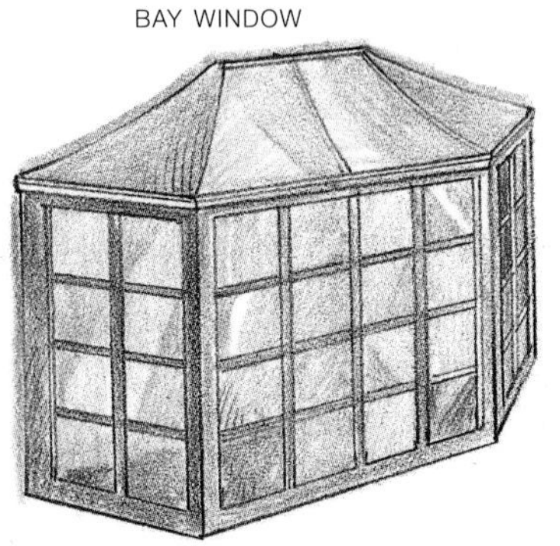

PICTURE WINDOW

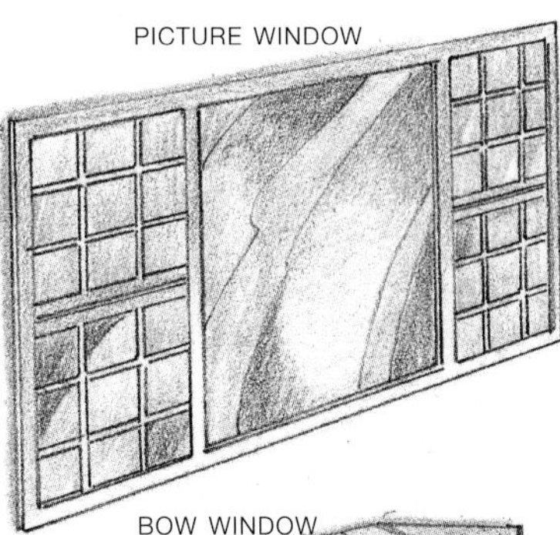

BOW WINDOW

Assess the light Consider the direction the window will face. A south-facing window will let in the most light, while a window facing the north will let in less, and more diffuse, light. Light from east- and west-facing windows requires careful management to control its intensity during the summer, because of the low sun angles in the morning and late afternoon.

Consider the view If a great view begs for a large window, consider breaking up the large piece of glass with muntins. The small panes create a multitude of framed views while adding a sense of security and shelter. If you plan to keep the driveway as is, you may want to de-emphasize the view with small windows. Ideally, the windowsill should be below eye level. In a living room, this can mean placing a window about 12 to 18 inches above floor level, while bedroom windows usually are about 4 feet above the floor.

Plan for ventilation Think about how much air movement you want to allow with the new window. Much of the ventilating capacity of a window depends on the placement of other windows in the house or room and whether it opens fully or only halfway. Air entering through one window and exiting through another window on the opposite wall creates cross ventilation, a great relief on warm summer nights.

Think energy Good-quality, energy-saving windows cost more than their more drafty cousins, but if you expect to be heating or cooling the converted garage on a regular basis, the extra expense up front will likely pay for itself many times over in the long run. Aluminum-frame windows might be a good, durable low-cost choice if energy efficiency was not a concern, but they are energy siphons. Low-emissivity (low-e), gas-filled windows offer the best choices for saving energy dollars.

Installation Know-How

With the garage door header serving as the header for a new window, much of the work has already been done. The following steps will help you prepare the space for a new window. For complete instructions on installing windows, see page 87.

Build a new curb It is not always necessary to build a new curb when you are replacing a garage door with a patio door, especially if you want to minimize the step up and down. When installing a window, however, you should first extend the concrete curb between the door jambs. The curb both keeps water out of the converted space and allows framing lumber to rest above ground level and away from potential moisture damage. See page 112 for instructions on how to build a new curb.

Frame the opening

With the curb extension in place, you can frame the opening to accept your new window. The illustration at right provides a typical example of the new framing that will be required. Use 2 x 4 framing lumber unless the existing framing differs. The height of the sill is determined by the length of the cripple studs that support it. It is usually best to keep the top line of the window on the same plane as that of other windows and doors on the house.

You can frame the wall in place, one stud at a time, but it will be easier to frame the entire wall on the ground and then lift it into place. Begin by cutting a sole plate to span the full width of the opening, then prepare the anchor bolt holes as shown below.

For more complete instructions on wall framing, see pages 22–27.

Framing for a Window

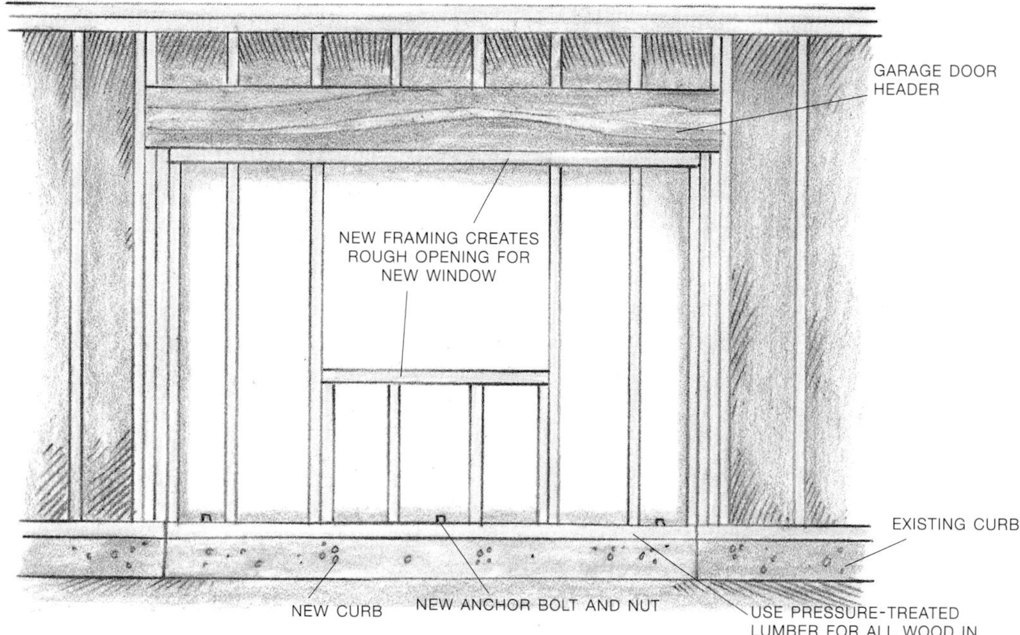

Raise the wall Cover the top of the curb with a sill sealer of caulk or fiberglass. With one or more helpers, carefully raise the wall and lift it onto the new curb, making sure that the anchor bolts slide through the drilled holes in the sole plate. Check the wall (especially the window rough opening) for level and plumb, and align it with the existing framing on both sides. Drive 16d nails through the studs into the old framing. Secure the sole plate with nuts screwed on over washers, as shown at right. Tighten with an adjustable wrench or socket wrench.

Preparing the Sole Plate

Since the sole plate sits directly on the new concrete curb, you should use pressure-treated lumber for this part of the new wall only. The sole plate will be held in position with anchor bolts that were set in the curb when it was being built. It is easiest to mark and drill holes for the bolts before the sole plate is attached to the rest of the wall.

Cut the plate to length and then set it on top of the bolts, aligned with the existing plates on either side. Over each bolt, hit the plate with a hammer hard enough to mark the lumber. Turn the plate over and drill ⅝-inch holes (for ½-inch bolts) at each mark. With the holes already drilled, you can easily drop the assembled wall into place.

Preparing the Floor

The typical garage rests on an uninsulated concrete slab. The floors of attached garages may sit 4 to 6 inches below the level of the house floors to comply with building codes. Slabs should be at least 4 inches thick, poured over 4 inches or more of gravel and a moisture barrier. Wire mesh adds strength to the concrete.

Slab on Grade

Slab with Deep Footing

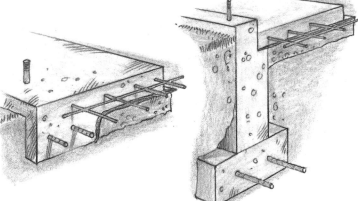

A footing runs around the perimeter of the garage. In mild climates a slab on grade is suitable (see illustration), while in cold climates the foundation is more likely to rest on a deep footing. These differences are not universal, however; it is possible to adapt a slab-on-grade foundation to a cold climate.

Garage slabs are usually sloped toward the garage door or a floor drain. The amount of slope usually ranges between 1/8 inch to 1/4 inch per foot. If the slope is mild, you may choose not to bother leveling it before converting the garage. But in many cases you will be happier with the results if you take the time to level the floor (see the instructions on page 113).

Garage walls can be framed and raised directly on the slab surface, but often they sit on a 6- to 10-inch curb that spans the

Extending the Curb

1 ADD REINFORCING BARS
Reinforcing bars (commonly called "rebar") are used to strengthen concrete slabs and foundations. Here the rebar ties the existing curb to the new one. You will need a hammer drill (available at most tool rental stores) and a 1/2-inch masonry bit. Drill two horizontal holes 6 inches into each curb. Center the holes and space them an equal distance from the top and bottom. With a small sledgehammer, tap 12-inch pieces of rebar into each hole, leaving 6 inches exposed.

2 BUILD THE FORMS
Rip two pieces of lumber, if necessary, to match the height of the curb. Normally you can use 2 x 6s or 2 x 8s; be sure to buy boards that are 3 to 4 feet longer than the width of the opening. Secure the form boards with concrete blocks or other heavy objects on the ends and in the middle. For added strength you can bolt the forms to the existing curb.

3 MIX AND POUR THE CONCRETE
Mix bags of ready-mix concrete with water in a wheelbarrow or large tub. Shovel the concrete into the forms, adding small amounts at a time. When the forms have been filled, use a float or mortar trowel to smooth the tops. Bags of ready-mix concrete have mixing instructions printed on them. Be sure to buy enough concrete to fill the forms completely. For a 6-inch by 6-inch curb in a 9-foot opening, you will need about 2 1/4 cubic feet of concrete.

perimeter. If your garage has a curb, you will want to extend it through the garage door opening before building a new wall (see below).

It makes little sense to construct a living space over a garage floor that is in poor condition. If your slab is severely cracked or crumbling, talk with a construction professional about your best options. It may be possible to repair the most seriously damaged sections of the slab; if headroom allows, you may also be able to pour a new 4-inch-thick slab on top of the old one. For minor repairs to concrete floors, see pages 48–49.

Extending the curb The foundation curb extension will help keep water out of the converted garage and moisture away from the framing. The new curb should be the same height and thickness as the existing curb. It is not difficult to pour a new concrete curb, even if you have never worked with concrete before. The garage door should be removed (see pages 106–107). Remove the jambs around the garage door to expose the wall studs and existing curb.

4 INSERT ANCHOR BOLTS While the concrete is still wet, insert ½-inch anchor bolts in the center about 12 inches from each end and every 4 to 6 feet along the curb. Plan ahead so that you don't place anchor bolts where wall studs will be located.

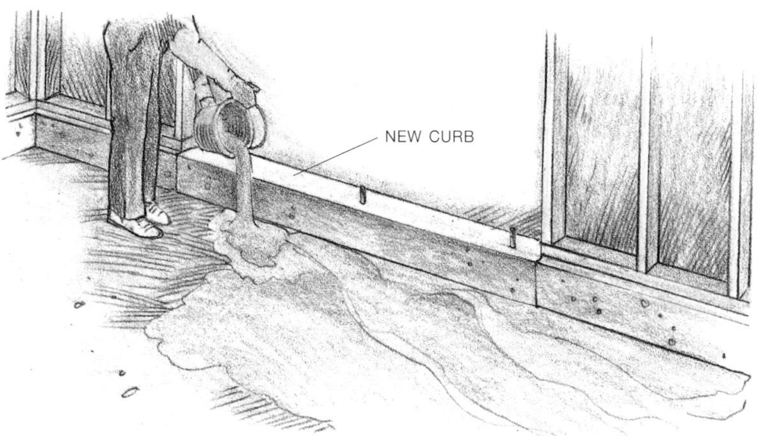

Self-leveling compounds offer a quick solution to sloping floors.

Leveling the floor To level a sloped garage floor, use a self-leveling concrete or gypsum-concrete mixture. These compounds are really quite easy to work with, but be sure to choose a product that is suitable for the maximum depth you require. If you are not installing a new foundation curb, place a single 2x form along the outside of the garage foundation to hold the compound in place. Clean and prepare the existing slab as directed by the manufacturer. Mix the compound into a pourable consistency, then pour over the slab. The compound will seek its own level and dry to a smooth finish without troweling. Wait a couple of days before walking on the surface, and at least a week before installing any floor covering.

If you are planning to insulate the floor, you can level the floor using 2 x 4 sleepers with shims. See page 116 for more details.

Heating and Cooling

If your garage is attached to the house, your first option should be to extend the heating and cooling system from the house into the converted space. Often this can be done quickly and inexpensively, but it is work that is best left to a professional. If extending the system is not viable, then you will need to explore the many options available for independent systems.

For general information on heating and cooling options, see pages 46–47.

CHOOSING THE RIGHT SIZE

The first step is deciding how much heat or cooled air you need. Heating and cooling capacity is generally measured in British thermal units (BTUs). Your goal should be to find a heating and/or cooling unit that can match the BTU needs of the space as closely as possible: an oversize unit can be every bit as inconvenient and inefficient as one that is not powerful enough.

The size of the space to be served is only one part of the equation for calculating BTU needs. You also need to consider the amount of insulation; the relative exposure to shade and direct sunlight; the quantity, quality, and location of windows; and other factors. Consult with the manufacturers of units you are considering for advice on buying the right size.

HEATING WITH WOOD

A new woodstove or energy-efficient fireplace can provide all the heat you need for a relatively modest investment. The tradeoff is that these heat sources require regular care and maintenance to function efficiently and safely.

Modern woodstoves are far less polluting and inefficient than their ancestors. A well-designed airtight woodstove requires very little combustion air and generates a minimal amount of pollution. Woodstoves should always be installed in accordance with the recommendations of the manufacturer and local building codes. Woodstoves require a metal or masonry chimney, which should be installed by a professional.

WOOD STOVES CAN BE VENTED THROUGH THE WALL OR THROUGH THE ROOF

Conventional fireplaces, for all their charm and tradition, tend to be very poor sources of heat. Modern, prefabricated fireplaces, however, can keep a converted garage comfortable. You can find models that burn wood, gas, or special pellets. A wood-burning fireplace that meets EPA emission standards will provide the most cost-effective heat, but gas-fired units require less hands-on care.

DIRECT-VENT SPACE HEATERS

A direct-vent space heater can be an excellent choice for a converted garage. These heaters use natural gas, propane, or kerosene, and do not require a chimney. Instead, combustion air is brought in and

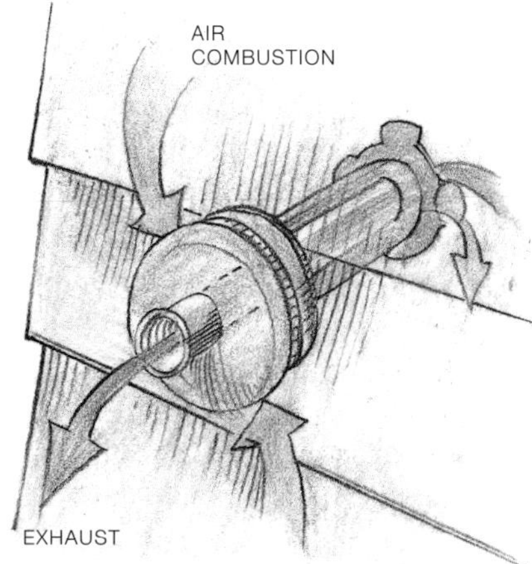

exhaust expelled through a pipe in the wall. Super-efficient models can cost twice as much as standard heaters, but will use much less energy over the long run.

Although many people balk at the idea of heating with kerosene, fearing the smelly and dangerous models of the past, the new fuel-injected, sealed-combustion heaters are clean and safe, and kerosene is a much more affordable fuel in most areas than natural gas or propane. The biggest drawback of kerosene is that it requires a large fuel tank outside the house.

Installing a direct-vent heater is pretty straightforward. You can choose from heaters that are wall-mounted or sit on the floor. Most direct-vent heaters are installed on an outside wall, preferably in a central location. Using a template supplied by the manufacturer, drill a hole (typically 2½ or 3 inches) through the wall for the vent pipe (check for wiring and plumbing before drilling the hole). The vent pipe assembly consists of two parts, one installed from inside and the other from outside. The fuel line connection should be installed by the fuel supplier.

VENT-FREE SPACE HEATERS

Vent-free gas or kerosene heaters are not permitted in many areas due to safety and health concerns. If your converted space is going to be used infrequently, though, a vent-free unit might be worth investigating. Newer models burn very clean, but are best used in rooms that will be heated for only a few hours at a time.

AIR CONDITIONERS

Room air conditioners can be installed in a window or in the wall. Air conditioners are frequently evaluated by leading consumer magazines. Another helpful source of information is the Association of Home Appliance Manufacturers. The AHAM Web site offers a handy worksheet to calculate the size air conditioner you need (www.aham.org/consumer/coolload. doc).

Ventilation

Fresh air can be brought in by adding screens to windows and the entry door. A bigger concern arises when you plan to convert only part of the garage, leaving the other part for your car. In that case, you need to be concerned with exhaust fumes from the car finding their way into the living space. At the very least, be sure to equip the living space with a carbon monoxide detector. Talk to a contractor about strategies for sealing the area from car exhaust.

Insulating a Garage

Most garage conversions will require insulation in the ceiling, walls, and floor. Open walls can be stuffed with batts and then covered with drywall or paneling. If the walls are already closed in, blown-in cellulose is a good choice (see right). If the garage is under the house, you don't have to worry about the ceilings, but if the garage has a ceiling, you will want to insulate there as well. For more information on installing insulation, see pages 52–55.

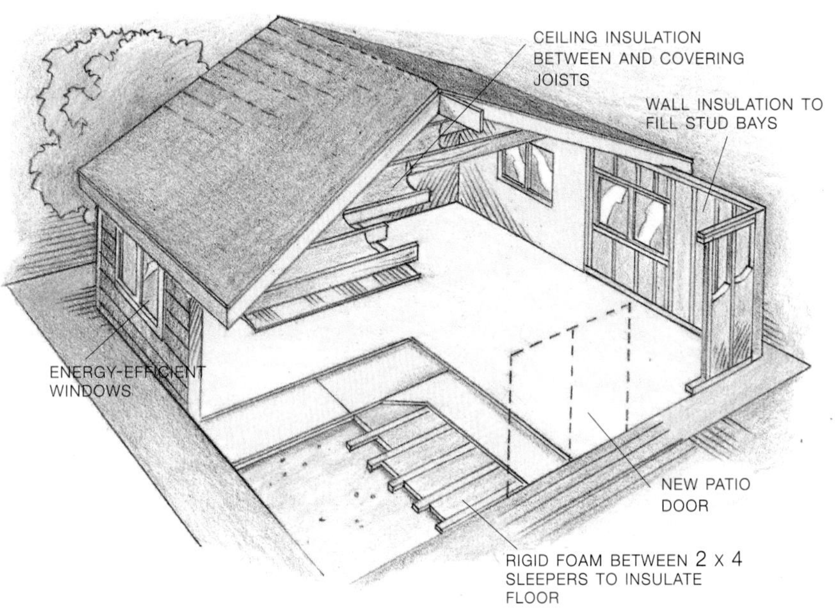

INSULATING GARAGE FLOORS

Concrete slabs in garages are usually uninsulated. In a mild climate, a carpet and pad may be sufficient for insulation. In colder climates, however, those slabs can get very cold.

The technique described on the facing page results in a solid plywood subfloor that can be covered with just about any finish flooring material you desire. Keep in mind that an insulated subfloor will reduce headroom in the garage. Consider the total thickness of floor and ceiling materials to determine the ultimate headroom in the finished space.

You can avoid using 2 x 4 sleepers on the floor entirely by using compression-grade rigid foam insulation instead. Lay full sheets over a 6-mil polyethylene vapor barrier. Tape the joints between panels and leave a ¼-inch gap around the perimeter, which can be filled with spray foam. Add a layer of ½-inch plywood perpendicular to the long dimension of the foam, spacing the panels ¼ inch apart, with a ½-inch gap around the perimeter. Then lay a second layer of ½-inch plywood perpendicular to the first, with the same spacing. Fasten the plywood together with ⅞-inch screws or staples. This technique

Heating with the Sun

Large slabs of concrete become very cold and uncomfortable. But with a little planning, they can just as easily become a source of low-cost solar heat. Passive solar heat utilizes "thermal mass" to store heat generated by the sun, which is then released gradually as the ambient temperature declines later in the day. Concrete slabs are an ideal form of thermal mass.

For solar energy to work properly in a converted garage, windows must be chosen and positioned correctly so that the ideal amount of sun strikes the concrete during the day. Good-quality windows will let in solar heat in the winter and prevent it from leaking out.

Passive solar design is a complex process that varies by geographical location, type of climate, orientation of the building, type and location of windows, and other factors. If the subject intrigues you, spend some time in the library reading current literature on solar energy, or talk with an experienced designer.

Adding Blown-in Cellulose

With the framing exposed, fiberglass batts are the best choice for do-it-yourself insulation. In some cases, however, garage walls and ceilings were covered long before you decided to undertake a conversion. If you would rather leave those surface materials in place, yet still want to add insulation, consider blown-in cellulose.

Cellulose is a loose-fill insulation product composed primarily of recycled newsprint that has been treated for fire and pest resistance. The most effective means of installing cellulose is through a process known as "dense packing," in which a blower machine sends the insulation through a hose fished into joist and stud bays. Dense packing fills the cavity completely, including around wires and pipes, and it simultaneously seals air leaks, which means that you don't have to worry about adding a separate vapor barrier.

You can buy the insulation and rent or borrow a blower at large home centers. It is a messy job, and a bit trickier to accomplish successfully than it might appear, so you might want to give this job over to a trained insulation contractor. If you want to do it yourself, cut 2½- to 3-inch holes with a hole saw in each stud bay (save the cutouts and glue them back in when you are finished). Feed the hose deep into the cavity and have a helper start the blower and control the mix of air and cellulose. As the bay starts to fill up, gradually pull the hose back out of the hole. Keep a rag around the hose to prevent insulation from escaping through the hole.

Cellulose must be blown into a sealed cavity. For attics, therefore, it is best to gain access from above, either through the roof or a hole cut into the ceiling. To avoid walking on the ceiling joists, you may need to tape a long rod to the hose to direct the insulation into joist bays that are otherwise out of reach.

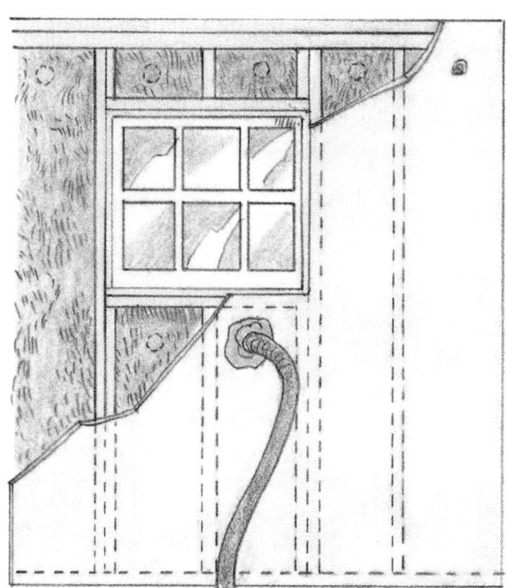

Adding Insulation to a Garage Floor

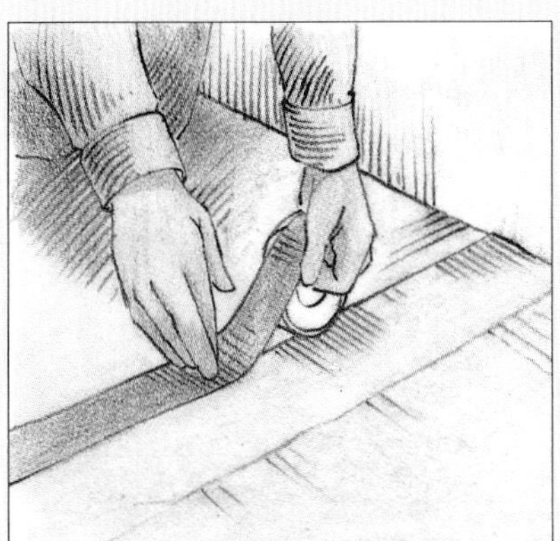

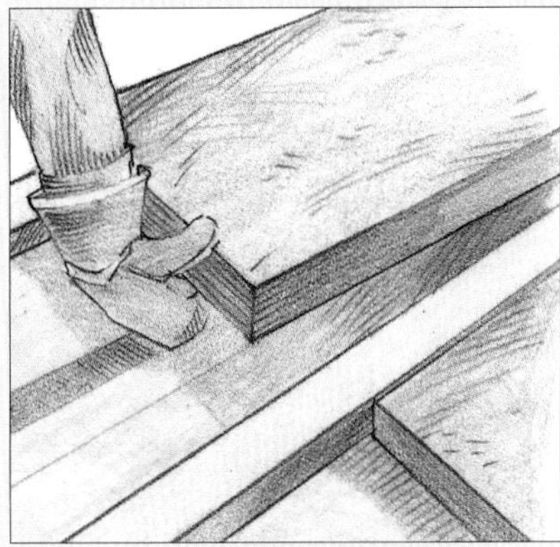

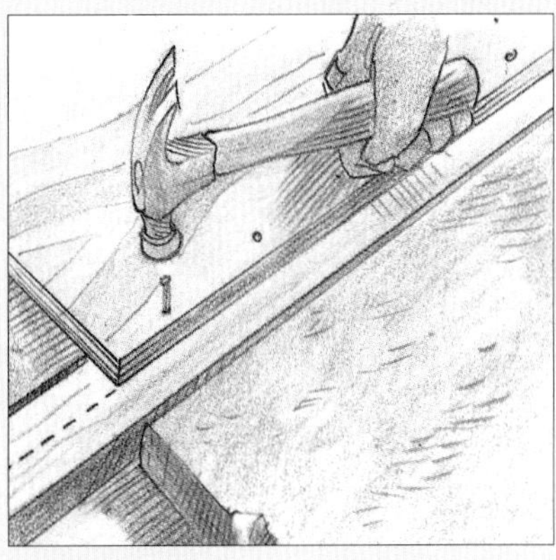

1 INSTALL A VAPOR BARRIER Vacuum the floor thoroughly, then cover it with a 6-mil polyethylene vapor barrier. Overlap the seams at least 6 inches and tape the seams. Run the vapor barrier up the sides of the walls several inches. If the poly keeps slipping on the floor, use dabs of caulk to hold it on the concrete slab.

2 ADD SLEEPERS AND FOAM Using pressure-treated 2 x 4s laid flat, set sleepers around the perimeter of the garage. Attach the sleepers with a powder-actuated nailer or 2¼-inch masonry nails. Then install sleepers on the rest of the floor, centered every 16 inches. Cut 4-foot-wide panels of rigid foam insulation (1½ inches thick) into three 12½-inch strips each and lay the strips between the sleepers.

3 ATTACH THE PLYWOOD Lay ¾-inch plywood perpendicular to the sleepers. Fasten the plywood to the sleepers with 6d ringshank nails or 2-inch galvanized screws. Stagger the edges of the panels.

Blending In

The decision to convert a garage is nearly always driven by needs inside the house—usually, the need for more space. By its nature, however, a garage conversion can have a profound effect on the exterior appearance of your house. The worst result would be an exterior that looks like a former garage, while the best result would be a façade that looks as though it was part of the original house design. The biggest factor separating these two extremes is planning. Don't start working on the inside until you have a clear idea of what the exterior will look like.

The plain garage and parking area of this South Carolina home have been transformed into a sun room opening onto a flower-filled terrace.

If you feel stymied by trying to design an attractive new exterior tying your original house in with your converted garage, consider talking with an architect or a landscape architect for some ideas. Some design decisions are relatively easy, however:

- Think about the whole house, not just the converted section. Design a new landscaping theme around the perimeter of the whole house to tie structures together. Paint the entire house, not just the converted section. Replace old windows and doors with new, more energy-efficient models to match those on the remodeled garage.
- When shopping for new doors and windows, match the size and style of those already on the house.
- The tops of windows and doors are often on the same horizontal plane around the house; if that is the case on your house, make sure to install the new ones on the same plane.
- Reproduce the trim, siding, and colors as best you can. If you have to install new siding (to fill in part of the space formerly occupied by the garage door, for example), it may make more sense to repaint the entire wall or even the entire house than to try and match a new color with an older one.
- Use shrubs and other plantings to give the front of the house new life.

The most attractive way to install siding where the garage door used to be is to remove much or all of the existing siding, then install new siding with staggered joints (left side of drawing). The simplest—and least attractive—option is to install new siding alongside existing siding, creating a vertical line of butt joints (right side).

With the garage door gone, you will probably want to move, remove, or otherwise readjust the driveway. There are many options: You could rip out the driveway and plant some new grass; redirect the driveway to the side or back of the house (perhaps to a new carport); or remove the section of driveway closest to the house and replace it with a flower bed.

Breaking Up Is Hard to Do

With the garage door removed, you will need to decide what to do about the driveway leading up to the threshold of the newly converted space. If the driveway leads to the side or back of your property, you may be satisfied with simply transforming it into a patio off a new patio door. If the garage door faced the front of the house, however, or a highly visible side of the house, you will probably want to get rid of some of it.

If you have an asphalt driveway, visit your local tool rental store. They should have a gas-powered saw made for cutting asphalt. You could also use a jackhammer equipped with a thin blade; the jackhammer approach is particularly recommended if you need to cut a square or angled corner.

The key to cutting concrete is choosing the right tools. For most jobs around the house, you can use a standard circular saw equipped with a special blade or wheel made for cutting concrete and other masonry. The least expensive option is a masonry cutoff wheel made with silicon carbide. Costing only a few dollars each, cutoff wheels are fine for small jobs, but can be time consuming for larger ones. They wear quickly, can make only shallow cuts, and create lots of dust.

Dry-cutting diamond blades, though costing $60 or more, cut much faster and cleaner and will last far longer than cutoff wheels. You can use them for cutting concrete, cement block, brick, and ceramic tile. A diamond blade will easily outlast several dozen cutoff wheels, making them potentially a much better long-term investment. For best results, make a straight cut through the top inch or so of a concrete slab, then use a sledgehammer to break off the rest. If you need to cut a lot of concrete, consider renting a gas-powered masonry saw.

Attic Conversions

In new house construction, the attic truly "ain't what it used to be." In much of North America, houses built before the 1930s often had spacious attics, ripe for storage or conversion to living space. Modern ranch houses, bungalows, and other styles have drastically reduced the size and convertibility of attics, however, or filled them with trusses that make conversion nearly impossible. But if you have a house with an attic large enough to provide comfortable living space, it is definitely worth considering.

This chapter begins with a look at a successful completed conversion, then focuses on identifying and solving the most common and most critical issues homeowners generally face when converting an attic. You will learn some tricks for creating a bathroom, as well as the fine points of insulating, heating, and cooling. You'll also find ideas that can solve a number of problems, including adding dormers and skylights and creating storage that takes maximum advantage of an attic's unusual space.

A Case in Point When you have designed as many attic conversions as architect Glen Jarvis, you collect a large bag of tricks that can help you solve complex problems. On some projects, such as the one shown here, you need to dig deeply into that bag in order to create a safe, functional, and comfortable living space.

Part of the attic in this 1920s French Provincial–style house had been previously turned into a bedroom, but the homeowners wanted to create a more substantial suite with a full bathroom, fireplace, lots of light, and a spectacular view of the Golden Gate Bridge and San Francisco Bay. The attic appeared to be large enough to accommodate the remodeling plans, but as Jarvis poked around the structural frame of the house he discovered some substantial hurdles.

The first big problem concerned the second-floor ceiling joists, which were 2 x 4s and would not support the new attic floor. New 2 x 10 joists would solve this dilemma, but would also raise the level of the finish floor enough to create headroom problems, especially in the bathroom. The solution: the builder installed new 2 x 10 joists between the existing 2 x 4s, cutting the ends of the 2 x 10s to match the angle of the roof. Once the floor was framed, a subfloor of plywood was attached with glue and screws.

The second structural problem was that the complex roof had been framed with 2 x 4 rafters and collar ties that created a complex tangle of lumber. To increase the living space, the collar ties had to be removed along with stud walls that were supporting rafters in the roof's valleys. New beams were installed to replace the stud walls, and new 2 x 4s were sistered to existing rafters to distribute the load and provide a flat surface for drywall installation.

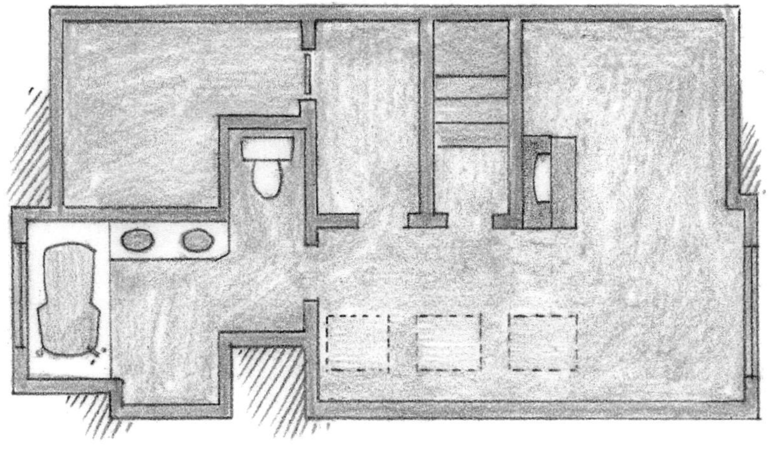

Because of the earlier partial conversion, access to the attic had already been resolved with a set of stairs. The bathroom was set in the narrow back portion of the attic, which offered easy access to the plumbing runs below. Drains were routed through a second-floor closet. The homeowners wanted a freestanding shower as well as a tub, but there wasn't enough space. The builder solved this problem by recessing the shower floor into the floor joists and its ceiling into the rafters.

This attic conversion required the combined talents of a creative architect, a skilled builder, and a structural engineer. The design and structural work were well beyond the abilities of a do-it-yourselfer, but the project demonstrates the advantages of turning to qualified professionals to help solve complex challenges. Even when much of the complicated work is left to the pros, cost-conscious homeowners can save a lot of money by taking care of the finish and decorating work themselves.

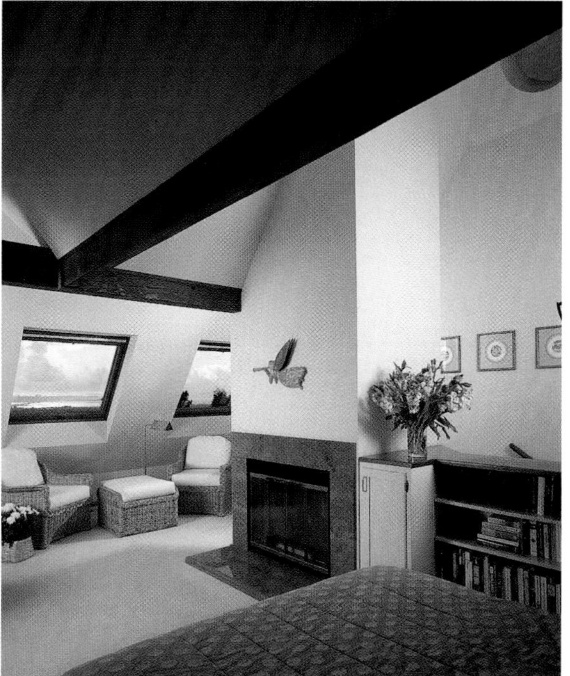

LEFT: The bed alcove, with its fireplace and spectacular view, is both cozy and dramatic. Large beams above replace attic stud walls.

BELOW: The view from the bathroom shows a new, custom-built half-round window resting above three awning windows. With additional skylights along the side, the new space is full of light and has plenty of ventilation. The bed alcove and entry are to the far left, under exposed beams.

LEFT: The new bathroom is compact but luxurious. It has twin sinks and a 5- by 7-foot whirlpool tub next to a skylight that offers a great view of the bay in complete privacy. A small round skylight over the tub provides light for reading. Near the entrance to the bathroom stands a shower stall that had to be recessed into both the floor and the ceiling to accommodate its height and width.

Assessing Your Attic

Many attics cannot be turned into living space without major, expensive alterations. The biggest obstacle often is the simple lack of space itself; the amount of space available is directly related to the pitch of the roof, as shown in the illustration. A roof with a steep 12-in-12 pitch is often the best candidate, while 4-in-12 roofs often can barely accommodate the squirrels.

Steep roofs are most common in areas that receive plenty of snow and rain, and are associated with house styles such as Victorian, Cape Cod, and Colonial. Shallow roofs are more prevalent in drier, more moderate climates, and are particularly associated with ranch and bi-level styles.

Houses that fall between the two roof extremes can be more difficult to assess. Though many potential problems have very adequate solutions, it is best to gauge the overall suitability of your attic by considering the factors discussed on this page.

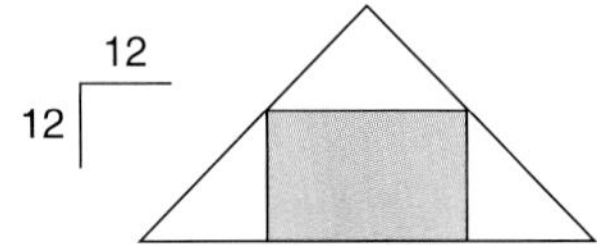

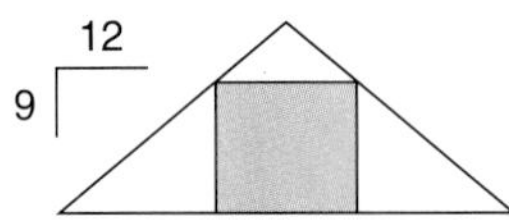

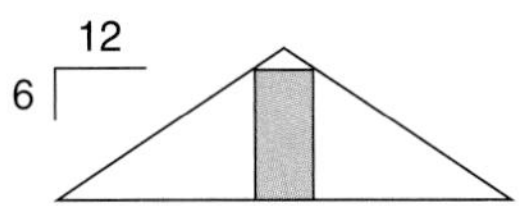

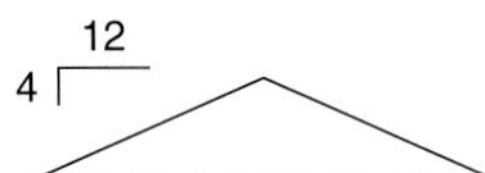

Potential living space in an attic declines as the roof pitch flattens. The shaded area in each drawing indicates the living space available.

Headroom Building codes often require that a finished space has a ceiling height of at least 7 feet 6 inches over at least half of the available floor space. If the distance between the ridge and the joists is not at least 9 feet, you will probably have to install dormers to meet the code requirement. However, if collar ties restrict available headroom, a contractor may be able to move or remove them.

If all else fails, you can explore the possibility of redesigning or even lifting the roof to create the headroom you need. Before taking such a drastic step, however, check with your building inspector; some local codes do allow less headroom in spaces that are defined as "recreational."

Floor space Building codes usually require that a habitable room has a minimum of 70 square feet of floor space (i.e., 7 feet by 10 feet). Any parts of the room with a ceiling height under 5 feet would not be counted as living space.

Access If you plan to use the converted attic on a regular basis, you will want to install a fixed stairway if one does not already exist. As a general rule, stairs must be at least 36 inches wide, with at least 6 feet 8 inches of headroom. Meeting these requirements can be a particularly difficult proposition, however, and may call for the

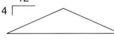

Does Your Attic Measure Up?

Before turning your attic into living space, make sure that the finished space will be large enough.

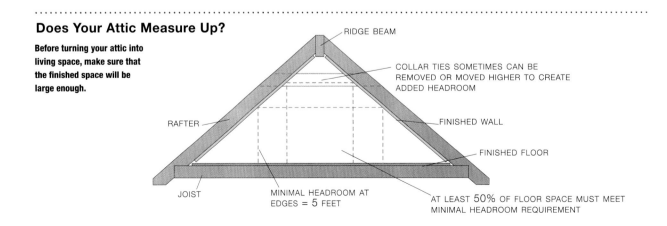

RIDGE BEAM
COLLAR TIES SOMETIMES CAN BE REMOVED OR MOVED HIGHER TO CREATE ADDED HEADROOM
RAFTER
FINISHED WALL
FINISHED FLOOR
JOIST
MINIMAL HEADROOM AT EDGES = 5 FEET
AT LEAST 50% OF FLOOR SPACE MUST MEET MINIMAL HEADROOM REQUIREMENT

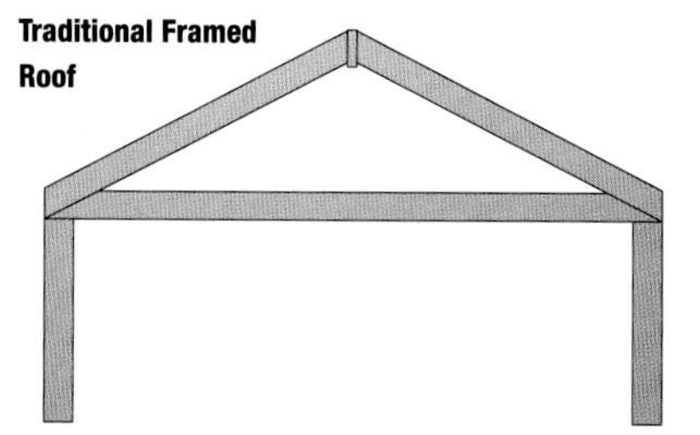

Traditional framing creates plenty of unused space.

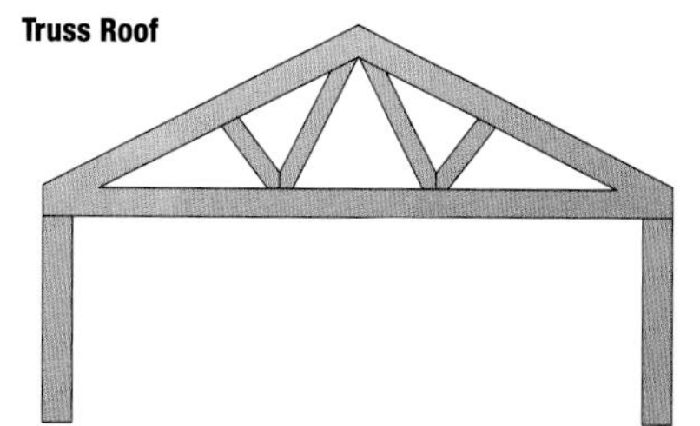

Webs in trusses make conversions impossible.

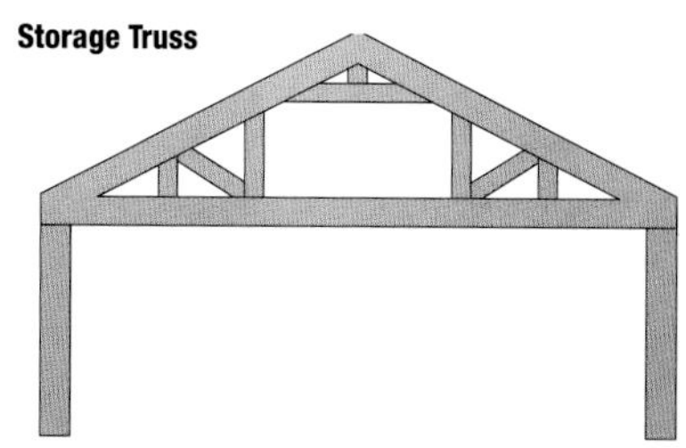

Special trusses can permit living or storage space.

creative efforts of a good contractor or architect. Hallways and even rooms may have to be reconfigured to make room for the stairs. Fold-down or drop stairs may not be allowable by code, although spiral stairs may be permissible.

If you plan to use the attic more modestly—as a playroom or a quiet spot to read, work, or meditate, for example—you may not have to meet such stringent access requirements. A ladder or fold-down stairway may be all you need.

Floor framing The ceiling joists that constitute the floor framing in an attic are often not designed to support the weight of people, furniture, and office equipment. Fortunately it is usually not difficult to reinforce the framing with additional joists. You can then cover the joists with a plywood or OSB subfloor before installing the finish flooring of your choice. **Caution:** Before you start moving around in your attic to assess its potential for conversion, take a moment to consider what you will be walking on. While the joists will support your weight, the space between them usually will not. As shown on page 126, use a catwalk or piece of plywood to help you navigate.

Roof framing Traditional stick-framed roofs are composed of rafters that span from the ridge to the top plates on walls. This design leaves the interior of the attic open for potential conversion.

Newer truss roofs are factory made of lumber joined in a carefully engineered web, and should never be cut and cannot be modified for living space. Storage trusses, on the other hand, are designed to leave an open, central space for living or storage purposes.

Temperature and circulation If your house is insulated, chances are that the attic is not within the "thermal boundary," or insulated area. You can leave existing insulation in what will be the floor, if you like, to act as a sound barrier. But you will want to add insulation along any new walls and ceilings that you construct.

Good ventilation will keep the attic from overheating. Many houses rely on a system of ridge, rafter, soffit, and gable end vents to provide ventilation, but attic conversion may require windows and skylights that can be opened to provide fresh air during warm weather.

Moisture Before proceeding with any major work on your attic, have your roof inspected thoroughly. Even a small leak can lead to serious trouble, and it is much easier to make major roof repairs before work on the attic begins. Dormers and skylights can be built and installed more easily while repairing or replacing a roof than after the fact.

Beefing Up the Joists

In the terminology of house framing, the structural lumber members supporting the floor beneath your feet are called floor joists, while the structural lumber members separating your upper ceiling from the attic are called ceiling joists. What's the difference? Plenty.

Ceiling Joists Versus Floor Joists

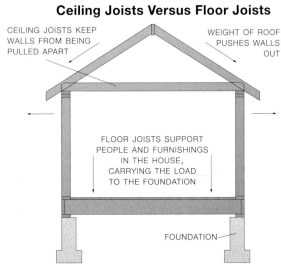

CEILING JOISTS KEEP WALLS FROM BEING PULLED APART

WEIGHT OF ROOF PUSHES WALLS OUT

FLOOR JOISTS SUPPORT PEOPLE AND FURNISHINGS IN THE HOUSE, CARRYING THE LOAD TO THE FOUNDATION

FOUNDATION

Floor joists are sized and spaced to support the weight of people and furnishings in the house, carrying the load to the foundation. They also provide the surface upon which the subfloor is installed.

Ceiling joists, on the other hand, primarily serve to counter the outward pressure on walls created by the weight of the roof assembly. They also provide the mounting surface for drywall or other finish material. While ceiling joists can support some weight from above (lightweight storage or one person), they are usually made with smaller lumber or spaced farther apart than floor joists. Converting a typical attic to living space, therefore, requires turning the ceiling joists into floor joists.

INSPECTING THE JOISTS

To determine if the existing ceiling joists can function as floor joists, you will need to get into your attic with a flashlight, tape measure, and, for handling fiberglass insulation, a pair of gloves and dust mask. Don't assume the ceiling joists beneath an existing floor can support a lot of weight. Before you start moving around, make sure you have an adequate surface to walk on. If the joists are not covered with plywood, install a catwalk as described below. If the joists are covered, remove the panels to gain access.

STRENGTHENING THE JOISTS

If you determine that your ceiling joists are not strong enough to support a floor, you will need to reinforce them. There are two common ways of adding strength to a floor frame (see "Sistering Techniques"). If you have any doubts about what size lumber to use for the reinforcement, consult a building inspector or contact a structural engineer.

Add a Catwalk

Attic joists are usually strong enough for one person to walk on as long as they are not split or damaged, but never step between joists. To make maneuvering easier and safer in an attic with exposed joists, make a temporary catwalk to reach all parts of the attic. Use several 1 x 6s or 1 x 8s next to each other or pieces of ¾-inch plywood cut into strips that you can fit into the attic. Attach the catwalk to the joists with screws (hammering nails can loosen plaster or drywall in the ceiling below).

Adding Joists

Installing additional joists can effectively reduce the on-center spacing by half, which is often more than sufficient reinforcement. Ideally, you will be able to add joists that are the same size as the existing ones, but if necessary you can install deeper joists. Attach the new joists by toe-nailing them on both sides to the top plates on the wall. In some attics, you may have better luck sistering the joists instead.

Sistering Joists

The technique of joining a new joist to an existing one effectively increases the size of the joist. Use lumber the same size as the existing joists, and make sure that the new joists are long enough to span between supports. Fasten the two joists together with plenty of 16d nails. If you are concerned about disturbing the ceiling below, use 2½-inch screws or a pneumatic nail gun.

Sistering Techniques

Short joists can be lapped (left) or spliced (right) over a bearing wall. Blocking between the joists provides added strength.

Determining Joist Strength

Your building department should be able to supply you with a floor joist span table. With the dimensions calculated as shown on the facing page, you should be able to determine if your joists can provide enough strength to support a floor. Take the following measurements from several locations around the attic. **Caution:** The minimum spans shown here are approximate distances. Check your local building code for recommendations in your area.

Span tables often provide separate requirements for different types of lumber; if you cannot determine the species and grade of lumber used for your joists, assume they are the weakest choice.

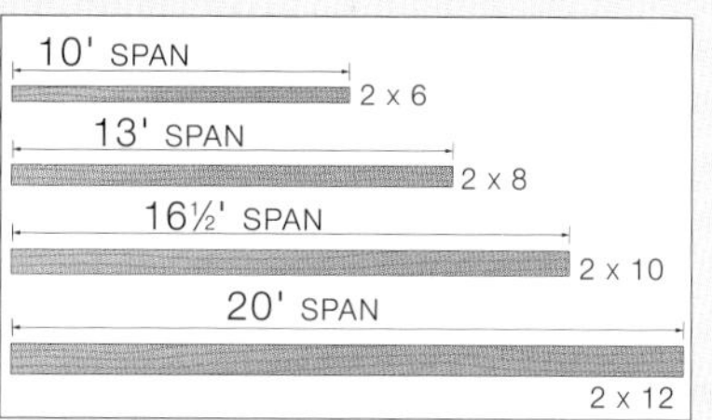

1 MEASURE THE SIZE OF THE JOISTS

If the joist bays are filled with insulation, slide it out of the way. Measure the depth of the joists and the width. Then redefine the actual measurements as nominal measurements (for example, a joist that actually measures 1½ inches by 5½ inches would be considered a 2 x 6). Note that in older houses, it is not uncommon to find joists and other framing lumber rough-cut and installed in full sizes (thus, a 2 x 6 actually measures a full 2 inches by 6 inches). Ceiling joists are frequently 2 x 6s or 2 x 4s.

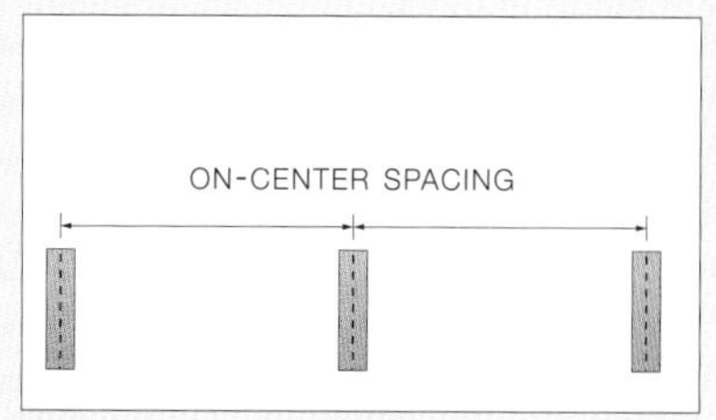

2 FIND THE SPACING

Measure across the tops of the joists, calculating the distance from centerline to centerline; this figure is called the "on-center spacing." Ceiling joists are commonly spaced either 16 or 24 inches on center.

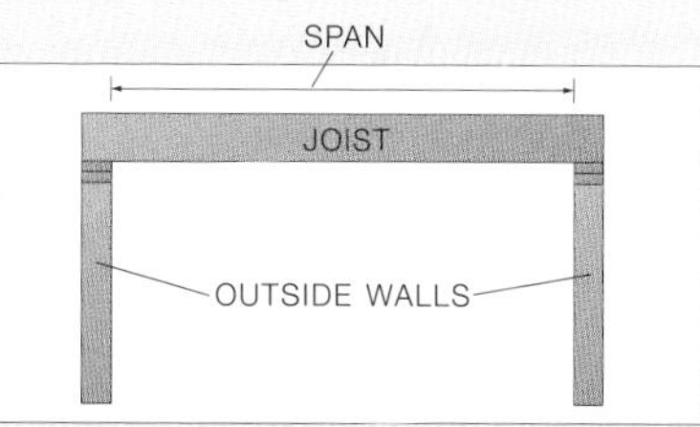

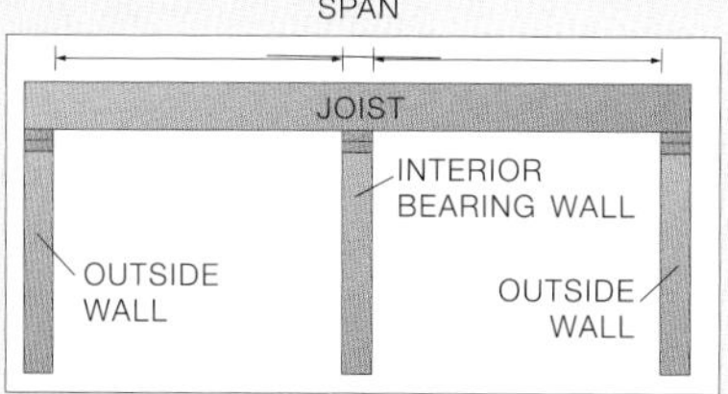

3 CHECK THE SPAN

The distance a joist travels between supports is called the "span." Joists can sometimes span the distance from one exterior wall to the opposing exterior wall, but frequently spans are broken up by intermediary supports in the form of bearing walls. Interior bearing walls allow the use of shorter, smaller joist stock, which is lapped or spliced (with blocking) over the wall, as shown at left. Check your measurements with a span table.

Repairing Roof Framing

Some attic conversions add little, if any, weight to the roof, while others can add quite a bit of weight (especially with new drywall or other material on the ceiling). Either way, it would be foolish to proceed with the remodel without carefully inspecting the rafters and ridge and tending to any necessary repairs while the roof framing is still exposed.

A SAGGING RIDGE MAY REQUIRE REPAIRS TO OR ADDITIONAL SUPPORT FOR THE RIDGE BEAM

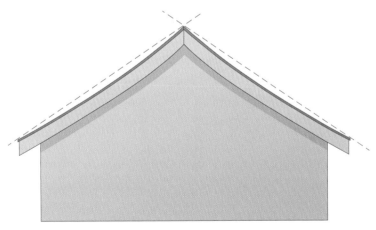

SAGGING RAFTERS MAY INDICATE AN OVERLOADED ROOF OR UNDERSIZED RAFTERS

INSPECTING THE FRAMING

The best place to begin your framing inspection is outside, far enough away from the house so that you can see as much of the roof as possible from each side. Examine the ridge from the side: It should be straight and level. If you notice a sag in the middle or a tilt in one direction, the ridge may need additional support or other repair. Does the roof line from ridge to eave appear flat and straight, or does it sag? If it's the latter, the rafters may need attention.

Continue the inspection from inside the attic, installing a catwalk first (see page 126) if the floor is not already covered with plywood or boards. Because sagging rafters are not always easy to spot, stretch a string line along the bottom edge of several rafters. If you find a consistent sag of ½ inch or more, talk with a building professional to determine the cause. It is possible that the rafters in your house were too small or spaced too far apart when the house was constructed.

Also consider if you will be installing new roofing directly on top of the old. Building codes generally allow two or three layers of asphalt shingles on a roof, depending on the slope. But these regulations apply to newer houses with carefully engineered roof frames; older houses often cannot support the same load.

Walk through the attic, carefully inspecting each rafter for cracks, open knot holes, or other defects. It is usually possible to repair rafters, but those with severe damage should be replaced.

Cracked Rafters

Any rafters you find with cracks, splits, or large holes should be repaired. In most cases, the best way to do this is by sistering on another rafter to act as a splint over the damaged area. This kind of repair is most effective when the rafter is very straight. If

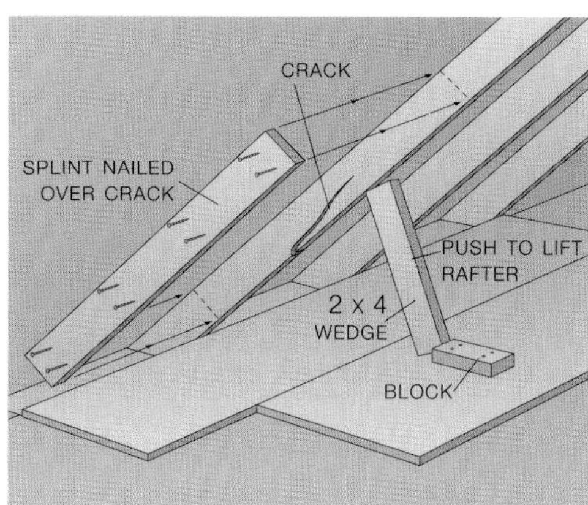

it is sagging near the damaged area, wedge a 2 x 4 between the rafter and a block nailed to the floor, as shown above. By applying pressure on the wedge, you should be able to force the rafter back into alignment.

When sistering a rafter, cut the new rafter long enough to reach about 2 or 3 feet beyond the damaged spot on both sides, then fasten it to the existing rafter with 16d nails or, even better, bolts.

Undersized Rafters

If you determine that the rafters are undersized, this would be a good time to give them the strength they need. This can be done by adding full-length sistered rafters to each existing rafter, as shown below. Add plywood gussets at the peak to further stiffen the frame. If the rafters are already sagging, it is probably easier to add support in the form of a kneewall (see page 144). This type

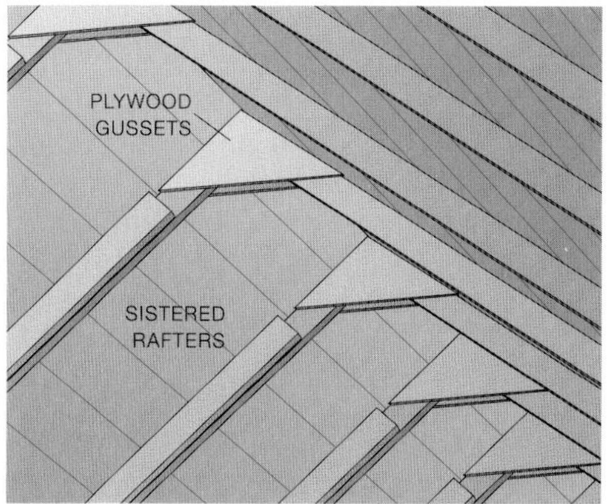

of structural kneewall, however, requires that the joists or bearing wall beneath it be strong enough to support the new load.

Sagging Rafters

A very effective way to add support to rafters that are undersized or overloaded is with a kneewall. Properly constructed, the kneewall (below) effectively reduces the span of the rafters, adding significantly to the strength of the roof assembly. Adding a kneewall is particularly appealing when you are converting an attic to living space because kneewalls serve as wall framing to enclose the space. For details on building a kneewall, see page 144.

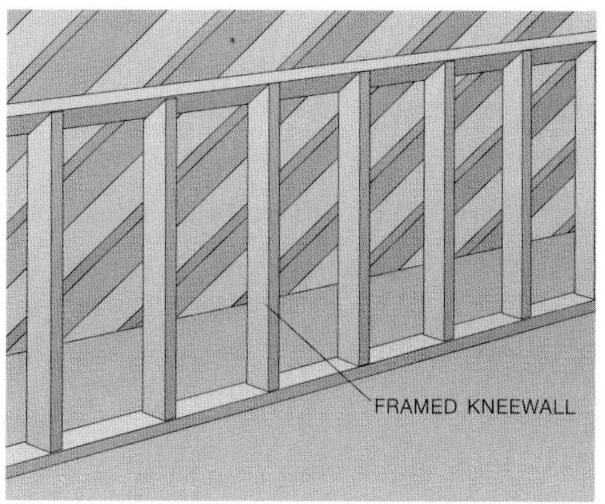

A Thorough Examination

While you are assessing the roof frame, take some time to look for other potential problems that could cause trouble in your converted space later on. Moisture is always a threat to the integrity of a roof assembly. Look for water stains around all penetrations through the roof, such as vents and chimneys. Dry rot or fungus on rafters is a clear sign of moisture trouble.

Moisture condensation in an attic may not be due to a roof leak. It can also originate in the basement or crawlspace, then find its way up through the house and walls to the attic. For instructions on dealing with a wet basement, see pages 153–161.

Even if you don't find evidence of moisture getting into the attic, you may still want to look for potential leaks. With the sun overhead, move around the attic looking for signs of light breaking through the roof. If you can see the underside of shingles or other roofing between boards nailed across the rafters, you ought to consider removing the roofing and boards and installing a new roof over solid sheathing.

If a chimney passes through the attic, check it for crumbling mortar or evidence of leaking water or creosote. If the chimney is out of service, you might want to tear it out completely.

Building Dormers

In attic conversions, dormers are often the most critical elements. Dormers can add a substantial amount of headroom to an attic that otherwise would not be a suitable candidate for conversion. Even if dormers are not required, they are worth considering for the added light and elbowroom they provide. Also, well-designed dormers can make the exterior of the house much more appealing.

Sometimes the best approach is to build gable dormers on the front side of the house and a shed dormer in the rear.

There are two primary types of dormers: gable and shed. Gable dormers are often preferred for their traditional styling and good looks, but shed dormers provide more usable space and are easier to build.

Size and scale are critical aspects of dormer design. Gable dormers are often built too small, and can look out of place on a large roof. Shed dormers, on the other hand, seem to work best when they are very large or very small.

PLANNING A SHED DORMER

A shed dormer requires a roof opening, a front wall, side walls, and new rafters. You will need to decide where to place the opening, what the slope of the new rafters should be, and how much floor space and headroom you want.

To maximize floor space, the front wall is sometimes positioned directly above the bearing wall below; however, the dormer

GABLE DORMERS

SHED DORMERS

Traditional gable dormers (top left) align with the lower-level windows and match window styles. European-style (top right) gable dormers share the front wall with the lower level. Gable windows align with windows and doors beneath them. A partial shed dormer (below left) adds more headroom than twin gables, but lacks their charm. A full shed dormer (below right) replaces nearly the entire roof on the front side of the house.

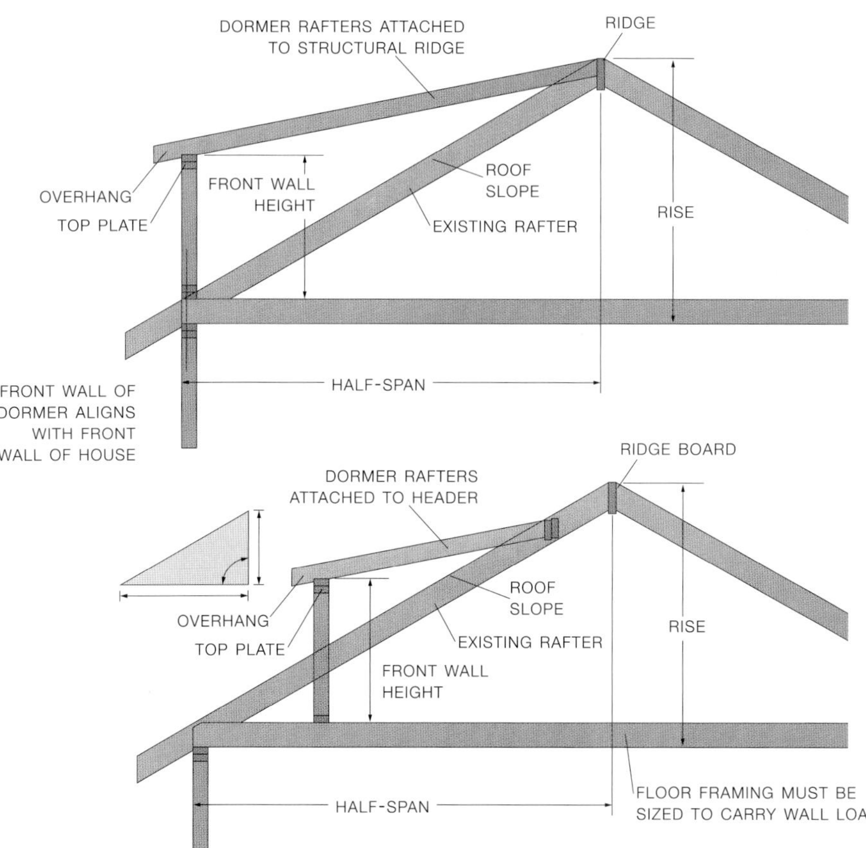

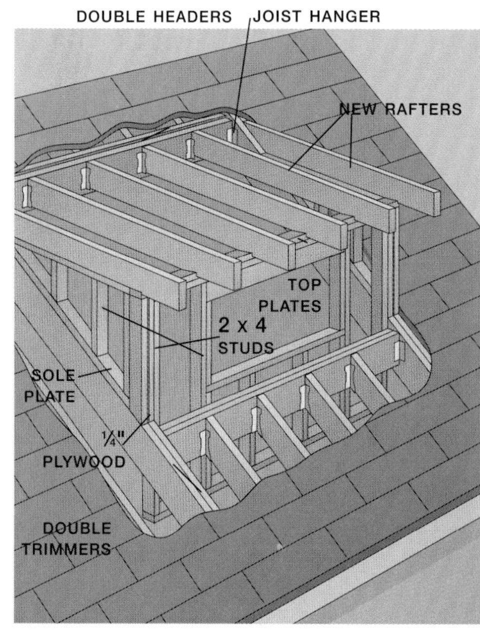

The basic parts of a dormer frame are shown above left. The front wall of the dormer is often seen directly over the wall beneath it (top left), but many prefer the appearance when the wall is moved back a little (bottom left).

looks better if it is moved back a bit, as shown in the illustrations. Rafter slope should be integrated visually with the existing roof line and must be at least the minimum required by code for the roofing material you're using.

The front wall's height affects both the rafter slope and available headroom: attic conversions typically must have 7½ feet of headroom over at least half of their area, and there may be a minimum requirement of 4 or 5 feet at any given point.

Begin by drawing a side view of your existing roof. Figure the roof's half-span (the horizontal distance from top plate to ridge) and the vertical rise at the ridge; then lay these features out to scale. Note that dormer rafters can be attached to a structural ridge, or to a nonstructural ridge if collar ties are added. (Check with a structural engineer or an architect about these matters.) The choice is primarily an aesthetic one, although tying dormer rafters to the ridge can create a little more headroom.

Next, lay tracing paper over your original plan and sketch dormer profiles like those shown in the illustrations on page 130 until you find one that you like. With this method

Dormer Design Tips

- Control the width. Keep the dormers wide enough for a window and corner trim, but not much more.
- Match the existing windows. Use windows in dormers that match the size and style of windows below.
- Watch the overhangs. Don't use a large overhang on a small dormer; keep overhangs proportional.
- Repeat the roof pitch. On gable dormers, try to match the pitch of the main roof.
- Minimize siding. Use about 8 inches of siding under the dormer window—enough for snow clearance if you live where it snows—but not much more.

Building a Shed Dormer

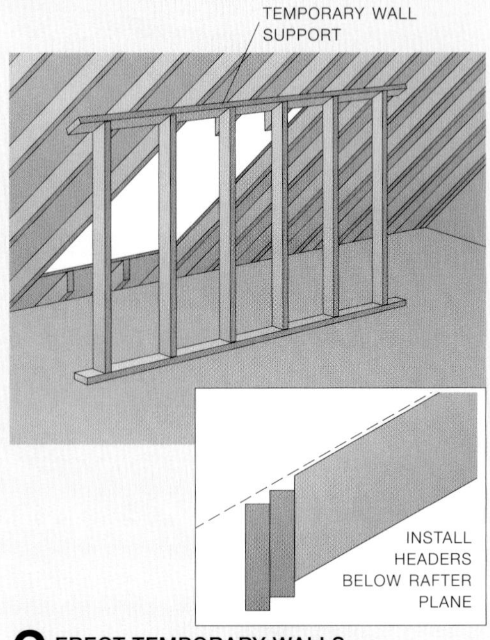

1 LAY OUT THE ROOF OPENING
Use the existing roof rafters for trimmers if possible. Double the trimmers, as shown on the previous page. From inside, drive nails through the roof of each corner. Mark the layout on the roof, then cut away the roofing materials and sheathing within the opening.

2 ERECT TEMPORARY WALLS
Temporary walls are needed to support the roof rafters above and below the opening. Once built, cut the rafters within the opening and install doubled headers, fastening them to the trimmers with double joist hangers. The lumber for the headers should be the same size as the existing rafters. Be sure to position the headers just below the rafter plane so that sheathing can be added.

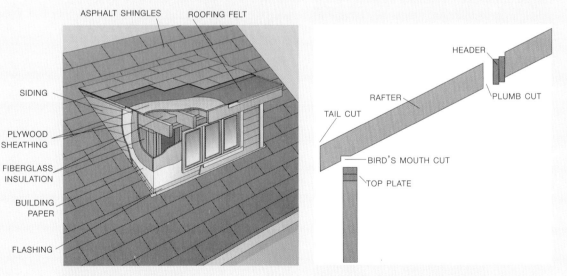

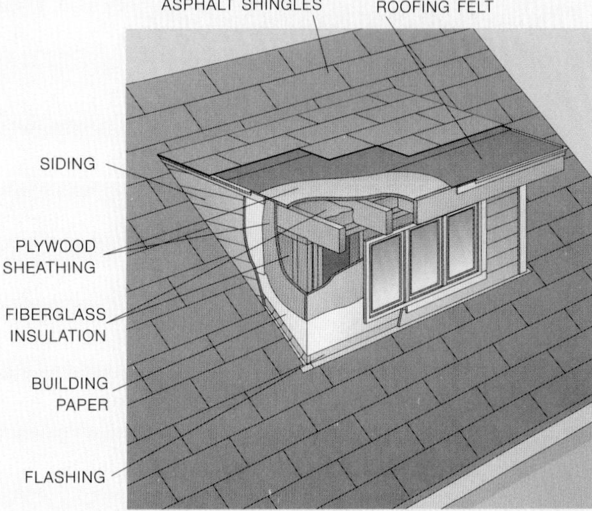

HEADER
PLUMB CUT
RAFTER
TAIL CUT
BIRD'S MOUTH CUT
TOP PLATE

3 FRAME THE DORMER
Frame the dormer's front wall, building it to the width of the opening (see pages 22–27). Swing the wall up into place, plumb and brace it, then nail it to the attic floor joists. Add corner posts at each end and nail a second top plate over the entire wall.

4 ADD THE DORMER RAFTERS
To lay out the dormer rafters, you will need to figure three cuts: (1) the plumb cut (where the rafter meets the header), (2) the bird's mouth (the notch for the front wall's top plate), and (3) the tail cut (forming the dormer roof's overhang). You can figure these cuts by trial and error or by laying them out with a rafter square.

you can also easily check the effects of any choices—such as front wall height or placement—on all the remaining factors, such as rafter slope.

THE BUILDING SEQUENCE

When you are ready to build, consider these general guidelines: choose a day with zero probability of rain and, where possible, do your work while standing on solid footing, such as the attic subfloor, rather than on the roof. When you must work on the roof, rent or buy roof jacks to support you. The jacks are nailed through the sheathing into rafters; planks are then set on the jacks to provide a level working surface. To climb up and down the roof safely, equip your ladder with a pair of ladder hooks.

The basic procedure for building a shed dormer is shown at left.

Once one rafter fits, use it as a pattern to cut the rest. For the end rafters, the ends of which sit atop the trimmers, first cut the bird's mouths; then hold each rafter against its respective trimmer, trace the correct angle, and cut the ends.

Next, add the sole and top plates for the side walls; then cut angled studs to fit between the plates.

Finally, apply the exterior finishing materials. Inside you will need new wall and ceiling coverings. For more on installing drywall to walls and ceilings, see pages 60–67.

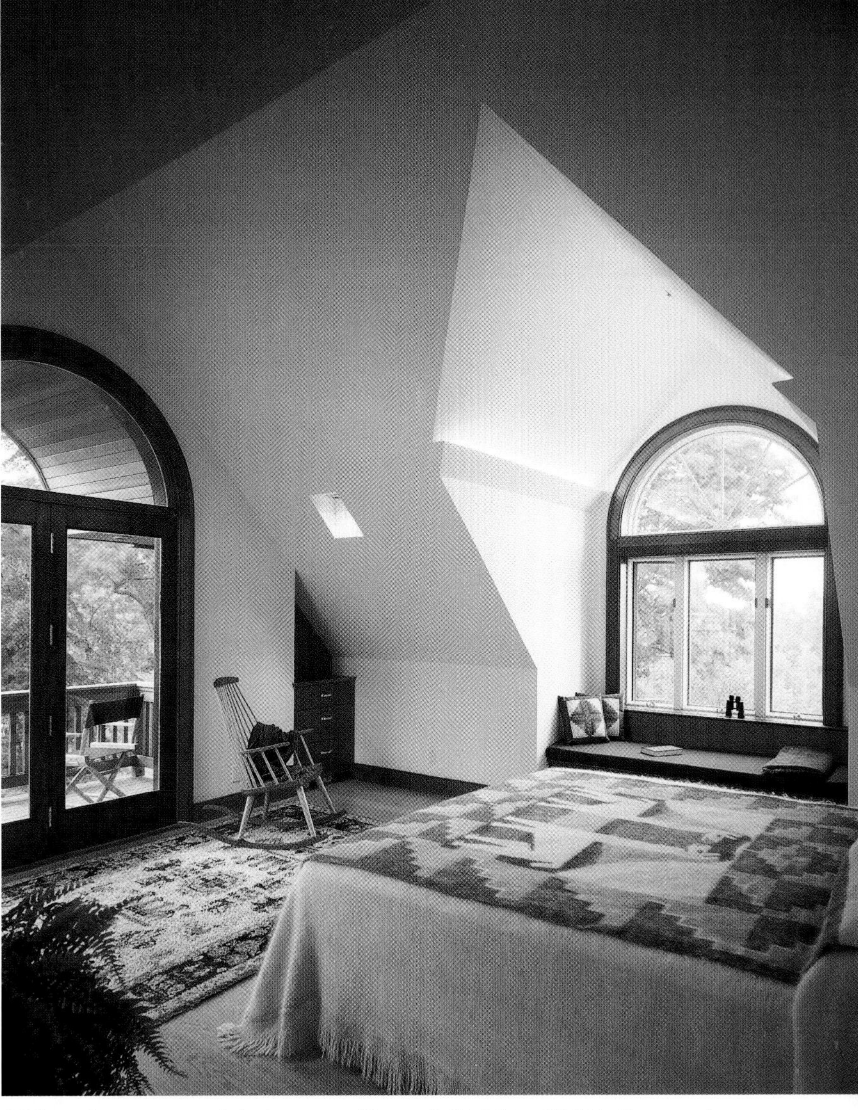

Adding a dormer to an attic bedroom provides needed height and light to the room. In this case, it also creates architectural interest and a terrific view.

Do It Yourself?

The process of building a dormer is not beyond the abilities of an experienced do-it-yourselfer, but it is not a task to be taken lightly. The principal steps involved are straightforward enough: cutting a hole; framing dormer walls and a small roof; adding siding and interior wall surfaces; and installing windows, flashing, and roofing.

Two factors make the project a bit more intense than the sum of its parts, however. First, you will be working on the roof, which is always an awkward and potentially hazardous undertaking. Second, the work has to be done quickly; any time you cut a hole in your roof, you must try and seal that hole again as soon as possible.

But if you possess the skills, confidence, and stamina—and the assistance of a good helper or two—you should be able to tackle a dormer project successfully. Before you dive in, though, show your plans to a structural engineer or architect to make sure your house structure can handle the new load.

Gaining Access

A nicely remodeled attic will not be used and enjoyed the way it should be if access to it is restricted. Building codes are usually quite stringent in their requirements for access to any part of a house deemed living space; check these first before building. The hardest part about creating good access, however, usually isn't the physical effort involved in building stairs; very often it is finding the space on the floor beneath the attic to locate the stairs.

You may be lucky to have a full stairway to the attic already. More likely, though, you gain access through a small panel in the ceiling, or perhaps use a fold-down stairway. When space is not a problem, you can choose the style of stair that suits you. But when you are hemmed in, you may be restricted to a stair style that requires little floor space.

Types of Stairs

There are dozens of stair configurations, and a good builder or architect can often design a safe, legal stairway to fit a seemingly impossible spot. Each type of stair consumes floor space differently, and you may have to choose based on that criterion alone. But stair preference is also an aesthetic matter; plus, any time you add a landing or turn in a stairway, you add an element of privacy between the levels.

Straight stairs Straight stairs are the most common type. And, because the stringers, treads, and risers are all identical, they are also the easiest to build (see pages 174–181). Because they are long, however, straight stairs won't always fit in a floor plan. They are usually best built against a wall.

L-shaped stairs An L-shaped stair consists of two straight sections set at right angles that are separated by a landing. L-shaped stairs don't require as long a piece of floor space as straight stairs, but they do require as much, if not more, total floor space. They are usually built in a corner. The flexibility of this design is enhanced by the fact that the landing can be located at, above, or below the midpoint.

Winders Winders are a variation on the L-shaped stair, offering a 90-degree turn but in a much more compact design. But winders are not as safe as straight stairs or those with a landing. Because of their irregularly shaped treads, winders force users to adjust their movement as they work their way around the corner. Also, users who try to climb the stairs along the narrow section of the treads may find insufficient support

Typical Stair Dimensions

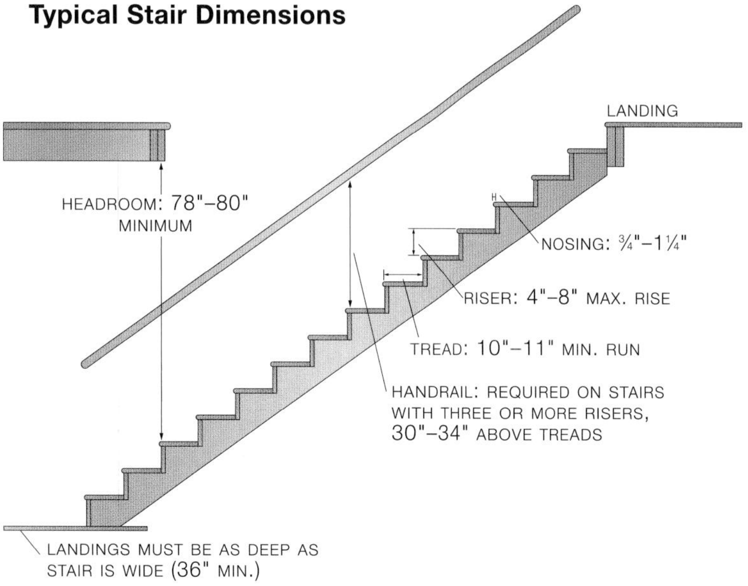

LANDING
HEADROOM: 78"–80" MINIMUM
NOSING: ¾"–1¼"
RISER: 4"–8" MAX. RISE
TREAD: 10"–11" MIN. RUN
HANDRAIL: REQUIRED ON STAIRS WITH THREE OR MORE RISERS, 30"–34" ABOVE TREADS
LANDINGS MUST BE AS DEEP AS STAIR IS WIDE (36" MIN.)

for their feet. For these reasons, winders are often closely restricted by building codes.

But winders can be designed to satisfy most codes. Talk with your building department and an experienced stair builder or designer for advice on how best to plan a winder for your attic access.

Switchback or U-shaped stairs Switchback or U-shaped stairs are similar to L-shaped stairs except that they make a full 180-degree turn. This is made possible by making the landing much larger. This style of stair is a good choice when you have more headroom than floor space.

Spiral stairs Because they can take up the least amount of floor space, spiral stairs are quite popular for gaining access to converted attics. A spiral stair can climb up to 15 feet using the same amount of floor space as a straight stair climbing only 9 feet. But just because they can be compact does not imply that spiral stairs must be squeezed into a tight space. In fact, many spiral stair designs offer a very graceful and roomy stairway.

Spiral stairs are not necessarily the best choice, however, if you have other options. Because of their winding design, they are less safe than other types of stairs. Also, they do not permit you to move furniture and other large objects up and down. Most spiral stairs are built from kits.

Manufactured Stairs

Today you can choose from a wide variety of high-quality prebuilt and ready-to-assemble stairs that are relatively affordable and easy to install. They come in spiral, circular, straight, and other configurations. A large home-improvement center or lumberyard may be your best source for information on manufactured stairs. You may also want to search the Internet or check ads in construction-related magazines.

When ordering manufactured stairs, first make sure that you are familiar with the requirements of your local building code. Pay special attention to where measurements must be taken. Many codes restrict head clearance and railing construction, and for spiral stairs demand a minimum 9- to 10-inch tread depth at a point 12 to 14 inches from the narrow side.

Spiral stairs are available in one-piece units that can be installed in less than an hour and as kits that require assembly. Manufacturers make them from steel, aluminum, hardwood, and combinations of these materials in a few basic designs that you can customize. When ordering a spiral stair, you will need to specify the diameter and, with some types, the direction of the twist.

Fold-down stairs are very affordable and relatively easy to install. They are only a good choice, however, for an attic that will be used infrequently and just for recreational purposes. Some manufacturers also build conventional straight and sweeping circular hardwood stairs in unassembled, unfinished sections, ready to connect end to end or at landings. These can be put into a preframed opening in a couple of hours by factory installers. For do-it-yourselfers, you might want to consider a disappearing one-piece stairway, which works much like a fold-down stairway but is much stronger and easier to operate.

Stair Types

Straight Stairs

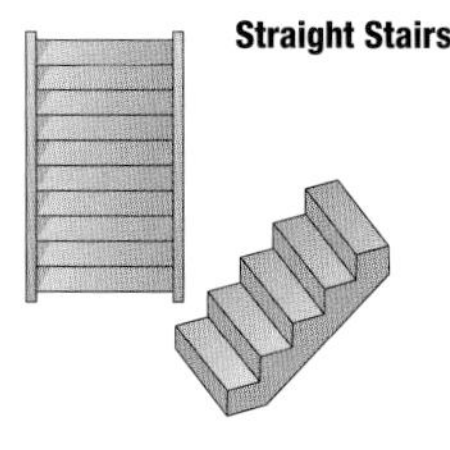

L-shaped Stairs

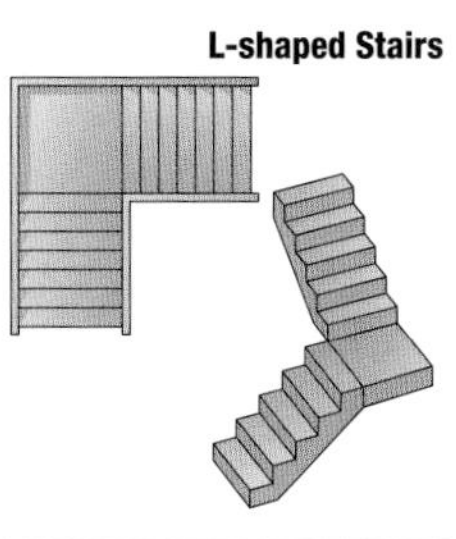

Winders

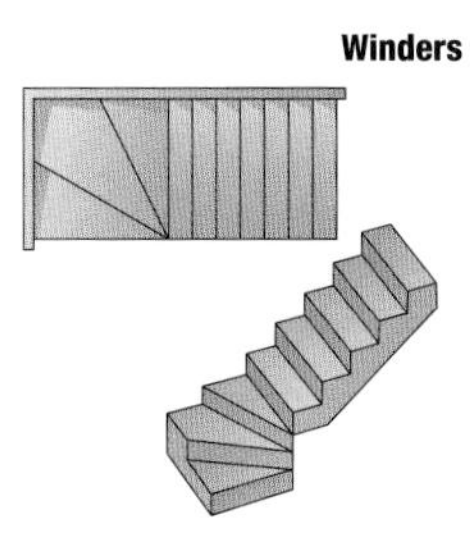

Switchback or U-shaped Stairs

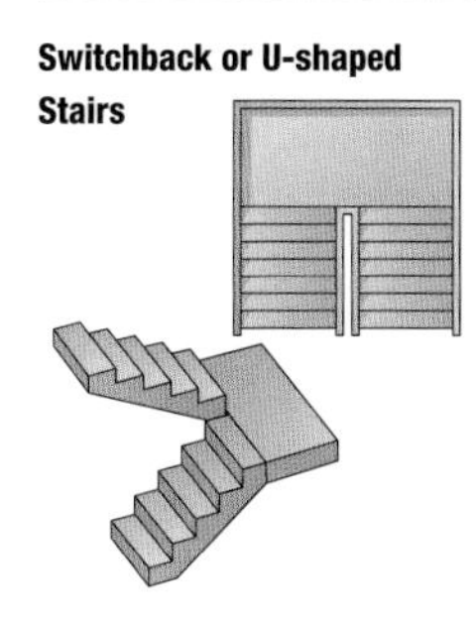

Spiral Stairs

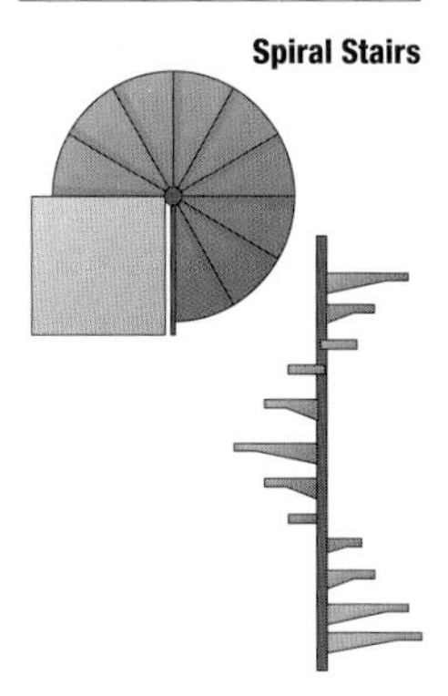

An Attic Bathroom

Adding a bathroom to your converted attic is strictly optional, but if you plan to use the space regularly it is not likely that you will regret the addition. Even if a full bathroom seems out of the question, a half bathroom (toilet and sink) might be greatly appreciated.

The most difficult part of the job may be tapping into existing hot and cold water supply lines as well as a drain and vent. In most cases this work will be easier if you locate the attic bathroom directly above an existing bathroom.

Plan the location of the fixtures carefully. Rough-in dimensions are pretty standard for most fixtures and most locales, but if you are off on the rough-in locations by even an inch or two, you may run into trouble when it comes time to install the fixtures. Whenever possible, tend to the rough plumbing before installing the finish wall and floor surfaces.

A bathroom sink is fairly easy to plumb and install. Toilets are the most troublesome fixture to install in a house because they require their own vent (2-inch minimum) and at least a 3-inch drain. If it is on a branch drain, a toilet cannot be located upstream from a sink or shower.

Ventilating the Bathroom

If your bathroom contains a shower or tub, you should install a ventilating fan. Even if you have only a toilet and sink, you may want to consider adding ventilation.

It is important that your fan have adequate capacity; it should be capable of exchanging the air at least eight times every hour. Ideally, the fan should be mounted as close to the shower or tub as possible. The exhaust duct should also be as short and direct as possible.

Tackling Tight Spaces

Perhaps you like the idea of a new bathroom in the attic but suspect that there isn't enough space. True, bathrooms do take up a fair bit of room, but with some creative planning you may be able to find just enough space. Often the biggest problem with attics isn't a lack of floor space, but

Roughing-in a Bathroom Sink

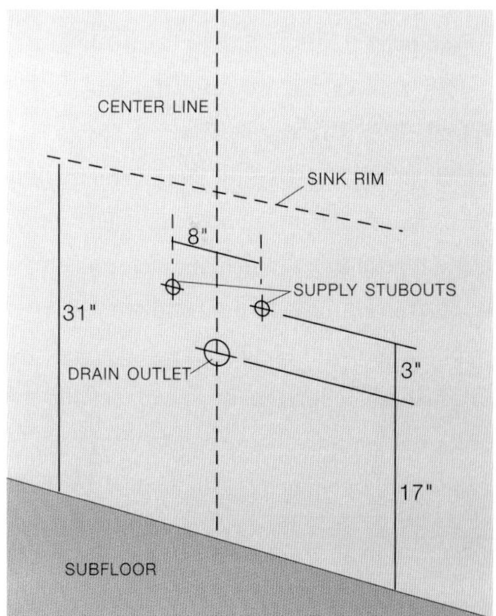

Plumbing a New Bathroom Sink

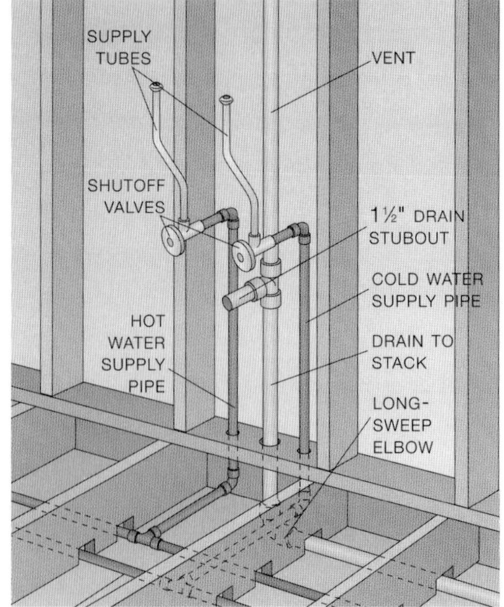

Roughing-in for a Toilet

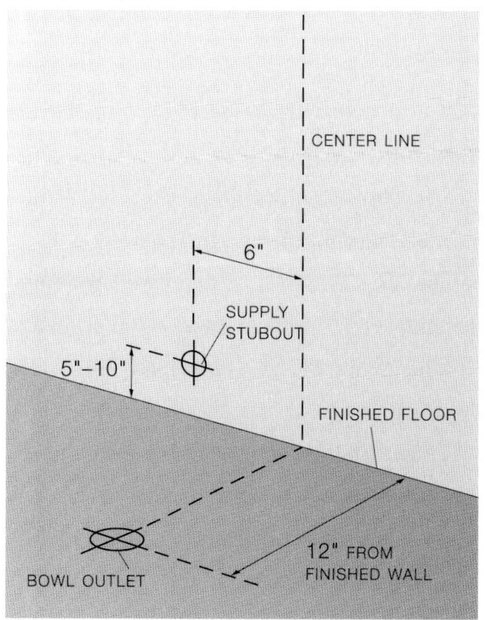

Plumbing a New Toilet

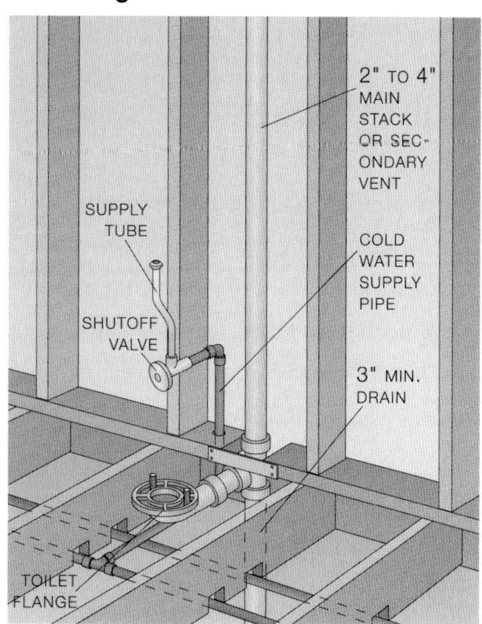

restricted height caused by sloping ceilings. For more information on bathroom floor plans, see pages 10–11.

The illustrations below demonstrate some of the critical height dimensions you must keep in mind with bathrooms. They also provide some layout approaches that take maximum advantage of the room that is available. Sometimes installing a skylight can add just enough headroom to make the project feasible.

The illustration at right provides an example of creative carpentry and plumbing. By cutting away part of the vanity and working with an experienced plumber able to surmount the odd arrangement, this sink was made to fit without jeopardizing headroom in the stairway.

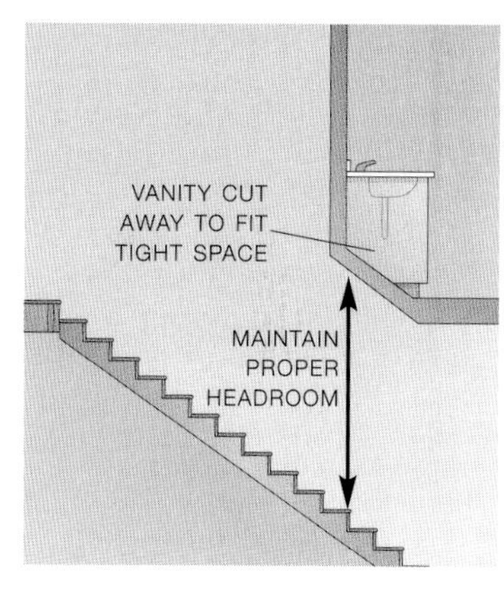

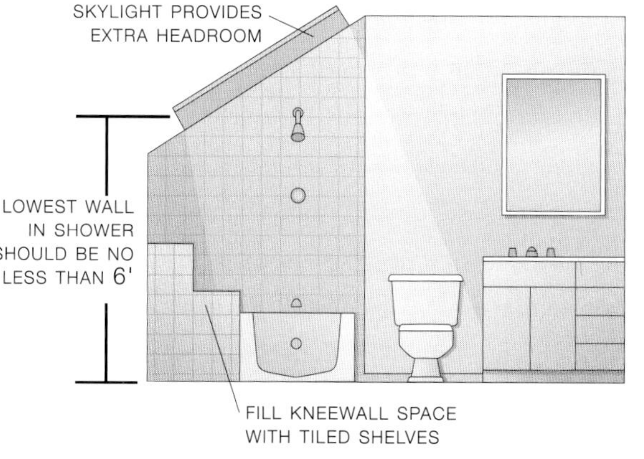

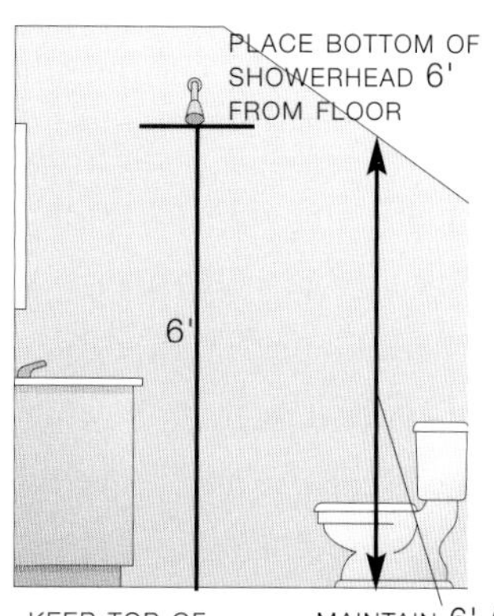

Installing Skylights

A skylight can be a very attractive and functional addition to a converted attic. Before you decide to install one, however, consider carefully what benefit you expect to receive from it. If all you really need is increased natural lighting, try to solve the problem with windows, which are less expensive, easier to install, and much less likely to leak. If windows simply won't give you the effect you want, then look for a top-quality skylight and insist on a first-rate installation—by either yourself or a professional.

Skylight types include (clockwise from top left) bubble-shaped curb-mounted; flat self-flashing; and trim venting model with integral curb.

Comparing Skylights

Skylights are available in a wide assortment of glass types and coatings, which are changing all the time. Generally, though, performance is measured by the following categories, which you can use for comparison.

U-factor is the measure of heat that is transferred through the glazing system. U-factor ratings generally range between 0.20 and 1.20, with the best insulators having the lowest ratings.

Solar heat-gain coefficient (SHGC) is the relative amount of solar-heat gain you should expect. SHGC is expressed as a number between 0 and 1; a lower number means less heat gain. SHGC is especially important in warm climates.

Visible transmission (VT) is a measure of how much light can pass through the glass, expressed as a number between 0 and 1. Tinted glass will have a low VT.

UV blocking refers to the amount of ultraviolet radiation from the sun that is blocked by the glass. The more ultraviolet radiation you block, the less fading you will experience in furniture and flooring, so the higher the blocking number, the better.

Another critical element that separates top-quality skylights from the pack is the flashing, which is vital for keeping water from leaking through. The best flashing systems offer separate top and bottom flashings along with side flashings, use an EPDM rubber gasket that covers the top of the flashing, or have a solid flange running around the entire skylight. Look for a skylight with a flashing kit tailored to your roof type and pitch. Each type has its own specific installation process, so check the manufacturer's instructions. Note that some skylights require the use of felt paper in addition to the supplied flashing; failure to use the felt paper as instructed can result in substantial air leakage in cold weather.

Skylights are generally offered with two types of glass. Tempered glass is very strong; when it does break, it shatters into small

Locating Skylights

Skylights are typically installed in or near the middle of a sloped ceiling, providing a balanced look. But don't feel restricted to this location. You may want to set the skylight higher, for example, to block an unwelcome view or the neighbors' eyes.

Sometimes the best location is low enough so that the skylight can function as a window as well, offering a clear view outside to someone sitting nearby. By moving the sill of the skylight down, you can also make the room feel larger and more dramatic. Use one large skylight or two smaller ones stacked together for the desired effect.

Wherever you choose to place the skylight along the roof slope, try to find a location that does not require reframing the roof or moving any plumbing or vent work. Building codes often require that skylights be located a minimal distance (often 10 feet) from any plumbing vents.

pebbles. Laminated glass has a thin sheet attached to the glass. It is not as strong as tempered glass, but the lamination holds the glass together when it breaks. Some building codes specify the types of glass required for specific applications. Laminated glass might be required on a skylight above a bathtub, for example, although the exterior of these skylights will usually have tempered glass. Check your local code for requirements in your area.

Choosing Options

Skylights are available as either fixed or venting. Fixed models cannot be opened. They are the least expensive choice and are fine if you are primarily concerned with adding light to the attic. If you also want to increase air circulation, choose a venting skylight, preferably with a screen. This kind is especially recommended in kitchens and bathrooms. A compromise between the two styles offers a fixed skylight with a small ventilation flap along the top.

Skylights equipped with shades and screens can better deflect heat in summer and retain it in winter. On some models, these options can be operated by remote control.

Some skylights are equipped with water sensors that automatically close the window when it starts to rain. Choose a model with a battery backup and the window will close even if a storm knocks out the power. Likewise, temperature sensors will shut the window at a sudden change of temperature, such as during a fire.

Stock sizes and models are usually considerably cheaper than custom-order skylights. So if you cannot find the model you want from one manufacturer, shop around before placing a custom order.

Choosing the Best Size

Skylights are available in a wide variety of sizes. Most manufacturers offer models that will fit between rafters that are spaced 16 inches or 24 inches on center. Installing one of these units is especially easy since you don't have to cut any rafters. To gain extra lighting from these slim skylights, still without having to cut any rafters, you can gang two or more units using the special kit offered by some manufacturers for side-by-side installations.

Continued on page 140

Adding Light

Skylights are often installed in a rectangular well, but you can substantially increase the amount of light they let into the room by flaring one or more of the sides. A flared side will bounce additional light into the room.

Wider skylights may require that you cut rafters to fit, but do-it-yourselfers may want to stick with skylights that require removing only one rafter. Codes often require that when just one rafter is cut, the only additional framing required is to double the top and bottom headers (below left). When two rafters are cut, you may have to double the side rafters as well (below right). Never cut more than two rafters without consulting a professional.

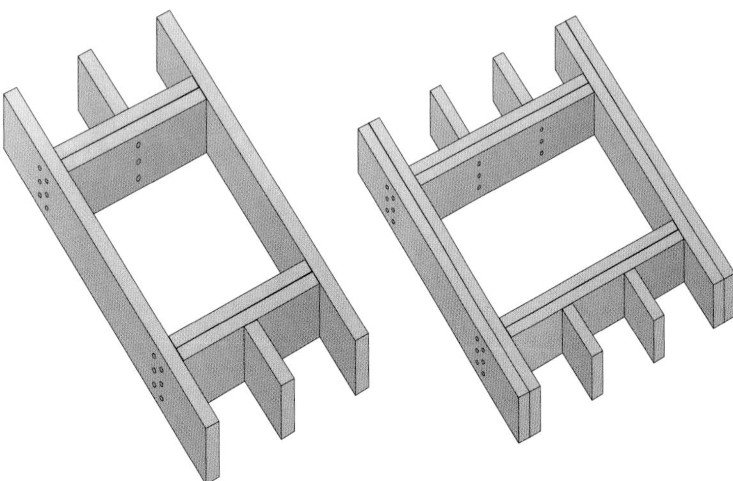

When thinking about size, keep in mind that larger skylights can produce a substantial amount of heat gain, which may be welcome in cold climates but very uncomfortable in mild climates.

Installing a Skylight

Before you start shopping for a skylight, inspect your roofing. If it is in poor condition, you should replace at least the section around the proposed skylight (preferably up to the ridge), if not the entire roof. Many professionals will not install a skylight if the existing roof is old and brittle, because this will make it difficult to effectively slip the skylight flashing into place.

Before you begin work, open the package and inspect all the parts that accompany your skylight. Make sure that nothing is missing, including the instructions. Read through the instructions; if you have any questions, call the manufacturer or your dealer for clarification. Each type of skylight has its own specific installation process, so follow only the instructions that come with the model you buy.

Begin by locating the corners for the rough opening on the underside of the roof. Drive nails through the roofing so that they are visible from above (see below). From outside, inspect the nails to be sure that you are satisfied with the location. If you plan to install multiple skylights, use the nails to gauge proper spacing and alignment.

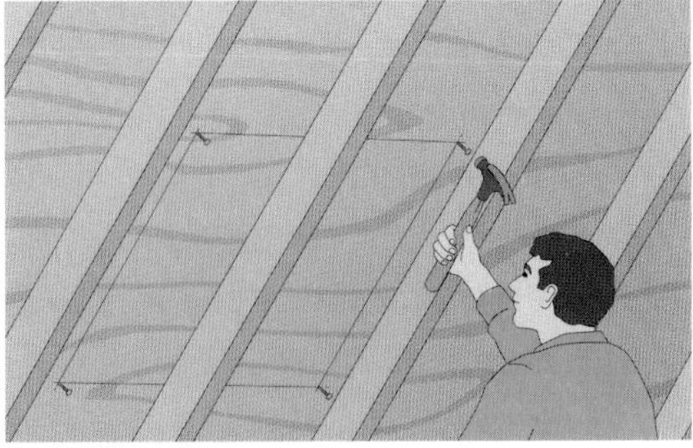

Working on the roof, cut a starter hole inside the nail holes just large enough to illuminate the attic. Go back into the attic and frame the opening, then cut the roof opening to size. Following this sequence will ensure that you do not cut an opening that is too big. To contain the mess in the attic, surround the work zone with plastic sheeting taped to the rafters.

Once the skylight has been installed, spray it forcefully with a hose to check for leaks. If you find any, use a good-quality sealant at the leak site. If it appears that the leak is due to a defective window, replace it.

Attic Comfort

Central heating and cooling systems can usually be extended into a converted attic. It is always easiest to rough-in forced air and hydronic systems before new floors and kneewalls are installed, however, so talk with a heating and cooling contractor before you get too far along with your building plans. You will probably have to provide details of your heating and cooling plans when you apply for a building permit.

For more on heating and cooling choices, see pages 46–47 and 114–115.

Staying Warm

When tapping into the existing heating system is too troublesome or expensive, an independent heating source, as discussed on page 47, can be a reasonable alternative.

One useful heating system for converted attics is a radiant wall. If your house is heated with a boiler, talk with a contractor about extending the system into the attic by running tubing in the kneewall. Heating the wall rather than the floor is often a better choice as long as the wall is not lined with large bookcases or other furniture. Kneewalls, because of their low profile, are a good choice for such an approach.

Keeping Cool

Even in cool climates, attics can become uncomfortably warm. If your house is not equipped with central air conditioning, or if you cannot reasonably extend the existing system, here are some options to consider.

A window or wall air-conditioning unit is simple to install and, if you choose a model properly sized for your space, very effective. But there is no way around the fact that a window or wall unit can be an unsightly addition to your house's exterior.

Ductless, or split, air-conditioners are an increasingly popular choice in residential applications. They are composed of a compressor and a condenser that sit outside the house and send cold refrigerant through small lines that can be run up the walls into the attic. Cold air is delivered through an air handler, which can be mounted on the ceiling, wall, or floor; the air handler also provides an air return to the compressor.

While a ductless system may not cool a large area as effectively as central air conditioning, it can be much less expensive to install. Ductless systems are also very quiet, in contrast to many window or wall units.

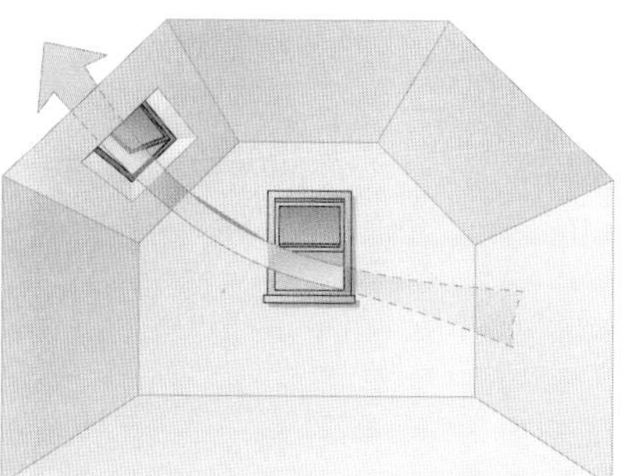

Natural Cooling

Before installing an expensive mechanical cooling process, consider how you might add to the comfort of your attic through natural, non-mechanical means. Ventilation can be provided by windows and skylights, but their effectiveness can vary depending on size and location. Cross ventilation can move air through the space. Here are a few rules of thumb for making the best use of cross ventilation:

- Let air enter on the side of the house that receives prevailing winds most often and have it exit on the opposite side.
- Place the inlet low and the outlet high, creating a natural draft that can move air effectively even when there is no wind.
- Make the outlet larger than the inlet for maximum air flow.

Insulating the Attic

With attic conversions, headroom is almost always a major dilemma. When you add the need for insulation, the dilemma can grow into a major bottleneck. Depending on where you live, you may be required to insulate the attic to R-38 or even more. But even if you don't face this requirement, you would be wise not to skip insulation: attics can get very hot in the summer and cold in the winter.

Existing attic insulation is most likely concentrated in the floor. With the creation of new living space, however, that insulation boundary must be moved out to the new walls and ceiling, which is often the roof itself. You may want to leave the existing insulation in place to reduce sound transmission through the floor, although you will have to remove any that sits on top of the joists to make room for the new subfloor. For more information on insulation products and techniques, see pages 60–67.

Dense Packing

If the spaces behind the kneewalls and above the ceiling are small, you might be better off hiring a contractor to insulate them with dense-pack cellulose, which will seal and insulate at the same time. The cellulose can be blown under the kneewalls and around all penetrations for a very effective thermal envelope. See page 53 for details about cellulose.

Mix and Match

Insulation requirements are generally given in terms of R-values, which is a simple comparative measure of the effectiveness of the product. The higher the R-value, the more effective the insulation. But R-values are not necessarily related to thickness. By using different products—or combinations of products—you can achieve identical R-values with varying thicknesses of insulating materials.

When space is tight, as it often is in a converted attic, look for insulation products that offer a high R-value per inch. Rigid foam boards can be a very good choice, offering R-5 to R-7 per inch. Standard fiberglass batts, by contrast, provide R-3 to R-3.5 per inch, although high-density batts can reach in excess of R-4.

To achieve a value of R-38 using standard fiberglass, you would need to install batts to a thickness of 12 inches (below left). By

Can't Be Done?

Sometimes it is just plain impossible to meet code requirements for both headroom and insulation in an attic conversion. If you face that situation, talk with your local building department. Inspectors often will permit you to lower the insulation requirement enough to allow you to finish the attic with adequate headroom. In situations where restricted headroom prohibits effective insulation in the rafters, it may be necessary to add rigid foam to the outside of the sheathing or decking, along with new roofing. This is an expensive and tricky procedure, though, and should only be done by a contractor.

You can achieve the same level of insulation in less space by using rigid foam boards and high-density batts.

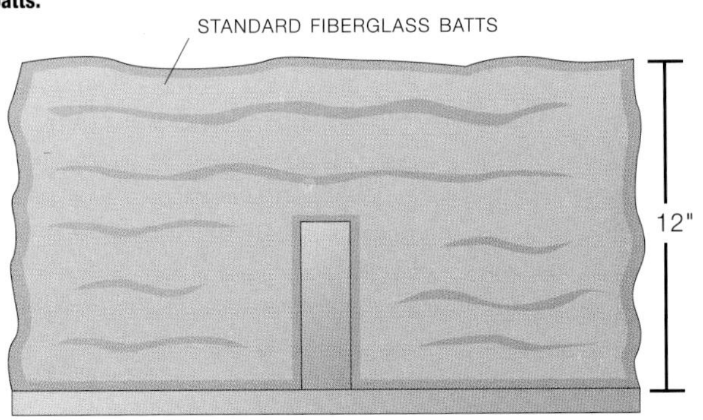

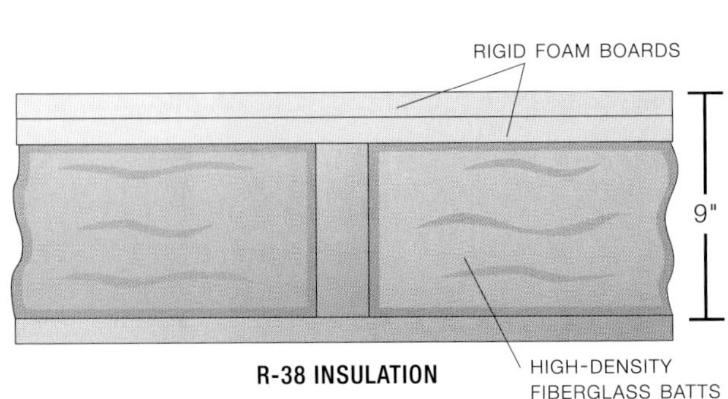

using high-density batts between rafters, then covering the rafters with rigid foam, you could reduce this thickness by several inches, depending on the depth of the rafters and the choice of materials available to you.

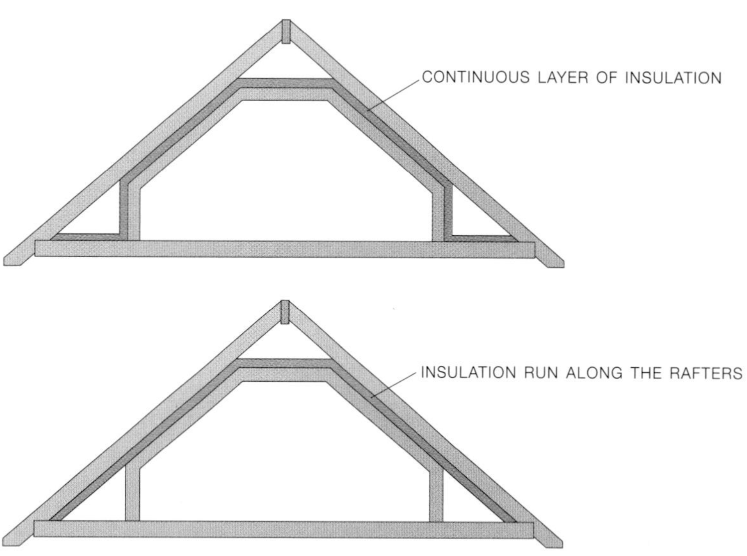

Two Approaches

The most effective strategy for insulating is to create a tight thermal envelope around the living space. If you plan to completely enclose the kneewalls, run insulation directly behind the walls and up to the ceiling, as shown at right, above. If, however, you want to use the space behind kneewalls for storage, as explained on pages 144–145, run the insulation up the rafters, then over the ceiling, as shown above right, below.

Attic Insulation Tips

If your roof is equipped with soffit and ridge vents, you should plan to install rafter vents or air chutes in each rafter bay. Once they are stapled to the roof sheathing or decking, the vents allow a continuous air flow from the soffit to the ridge even after batts of insulation have been placed over them.

Technically, rafter vents are beneficial only when the roof has rafter bays running from the soffit to the ridge. If your roof does not have this, you might want to talk to a building professional about the feasibility of adding this effective technique for venting attics, especially if you foresee a new roofing project in the near future. But even in the absence of soffit and ridge vents, rafter vents can keep moisture from the roof sheathing or decking from soaking any insulation in direct contact with it.

With rafter vents in place, fill the bays with fiberglass insulation. Choose batts with the same depth as the rafters and that fit snugly between the rafters. As with all insulation, be sure to add a vapor retardant, as discussed on page 53.

Finally, add rigid insulation with nails or screws driven into rafters. When it comes time to add drywall or other finish material to the walls and ceiling, be sure to use fasteners long enough to pass through the rigid insulation and firmly into the rafters.

The exterior walls of your converted attic should also be insulated. See pages 52–55 for more information on how to install insulation on walls.

Beware of Recessed Lights

If the ceiling beneath the attic contains recessed lights or any other heat-producing fixtures, keep insulation and flooring materials away from them. IC (insulation contact) light fixtures can, however, be covered with insulation. Check with a building professional if you have any questions.

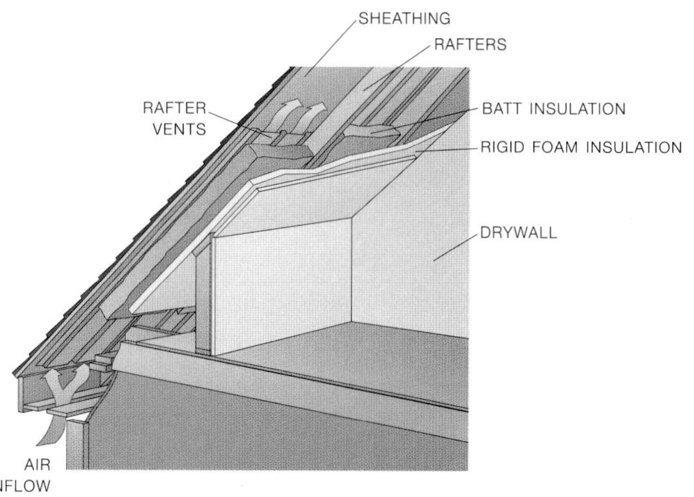

Attic Storage

To make the most efficient use of the attic space you have, try to locate some storage units along the kneewalls. Kneewalls are short partitions that extend from the floor to the rafters. They help to give a finished look to a converted attic, but are generally too short to allow much use of the nearby area. Nonstructural kneewalls can easily be framed to house an assortment of shelving and cabinetry options. Keep in mind that not all kneewalls are nonstructural. If your attic already has kneewalls in place, check with a construction professional before cutting any part of them.

Baskets and built-ins give a crisp look to a bright white attic office. Cubby hole cases that follow the roof pitch provide much-needed additional storage.

Framing a Kneewall

The first step in creating a kneewall storage unit is framing the kneewall. The process is similar to framing full-size partition walls (see pages 22–27) except for the top, which must allow for the slope of the rafters. The top plate, usually a 2 x 6, is nailed to the rafters after its inside edge has been cut at an angle to provide a flush face. The easiest way to make the angled (or bevel) cut is on a table saw, although you can also use a circular saw adjusted for the proper angle. The 2 x 4 studs also need to be cut at an angle to rest against the top plate.

To find the angle of the bevel cut, nail a 2 x 4 to the side of a rafter. Use a level to plumb the 2 x 4, then use a bevel gauge, as shown below, to establish the angle formed. Adjust your saw to that angle and cut the top plate. Then nail the top plate to the rafters so that both sides are evenly spaced from the floor.

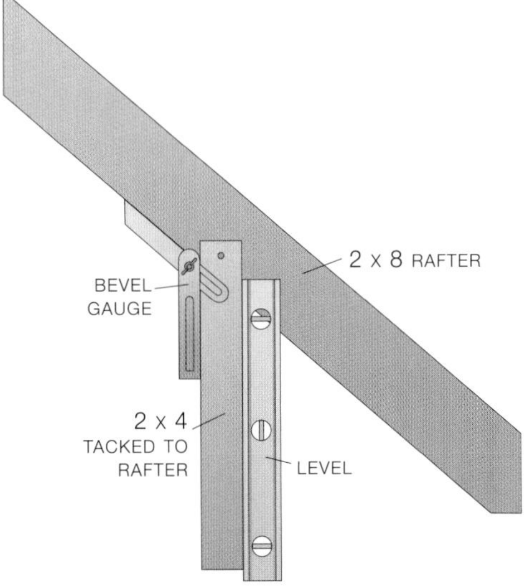

Use a level or plumb bob to transfer the alignment of the inside face of the top plate to the floor. Then nail a 2 x 4 sole plate to the floor. Use the previously set bevel gauge to mark each stud for its top cut.

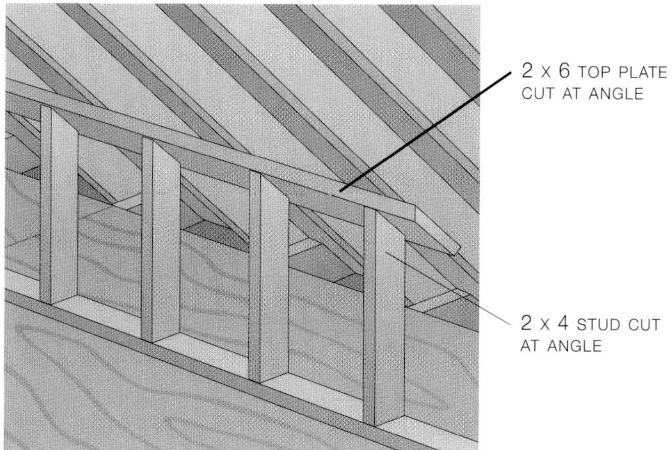

Make the bevel cut first, then cut the stud to finished length with a straight bottom cut. The distance between top and bottom plates may vary somewhat, so measure before cutting each stud. Attach the studs to the plates by toenailing each end with four 8d nails.

To provide a continuous nailing surface for ceiling drywall or other finish material, cut backing blocks to fit between the rafters.

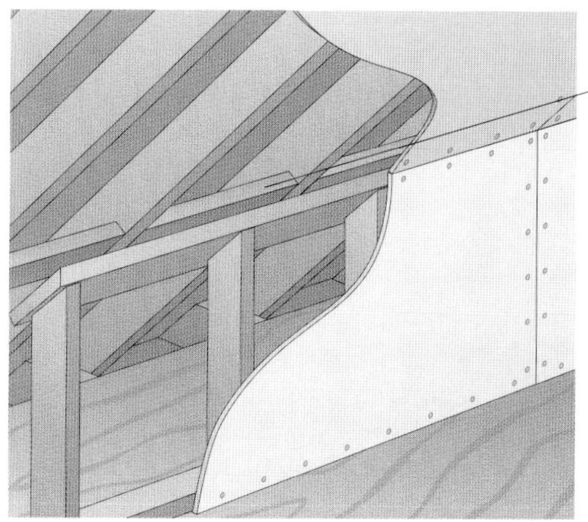

Nail the blocks to the rafters before securing the kneewall, or drive nails or screws through the top plate and into the blocks after the wall is up.

Adding Storage

You can place any number of storage units in a kneewall; shelves, roll-out drawers or bins, and file cabinets are all likely choices. Frame the openings much like you would for a window (see pages 87). Remove one or more studs, then install a header and sill. For a nonstructural kneewall, you can use a single 2 x 4 installed on flat to form the header. Use ¼-inch plywood to enclose the back of a shelving unit and the back and sides of drawer or bin openings. Shelving hardware, wheels, and casters are available at home centers and woodworking suppliers.

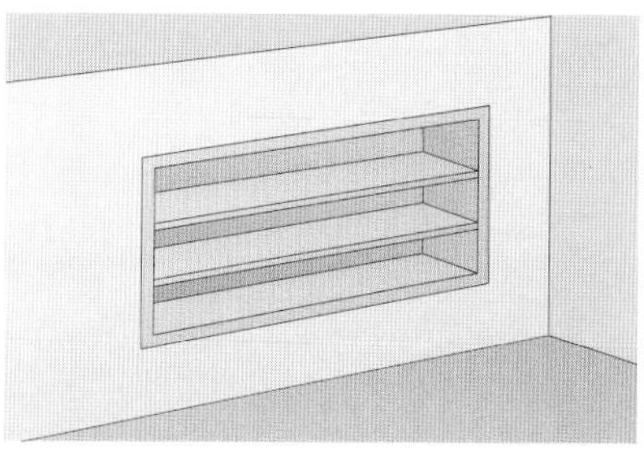

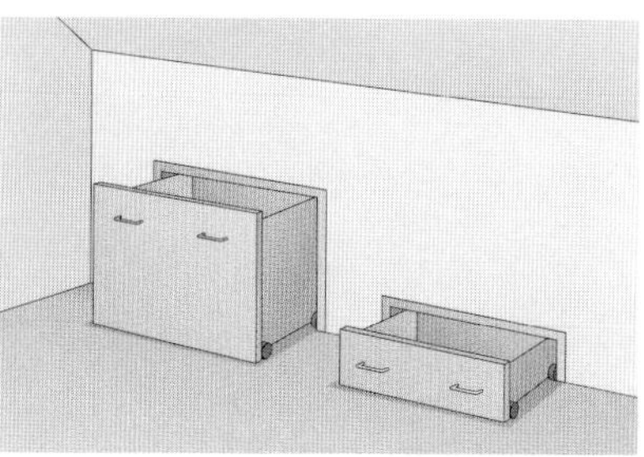

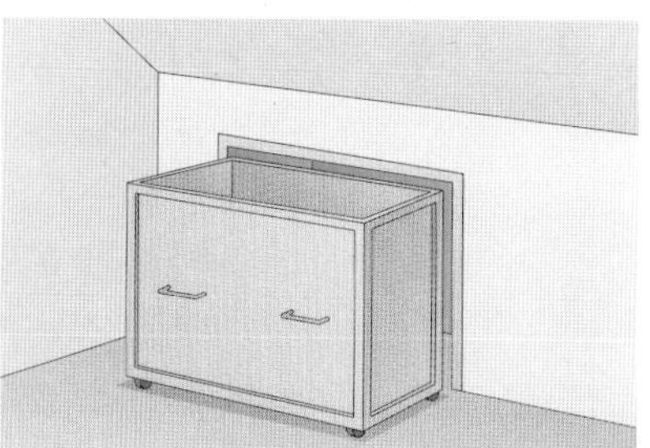

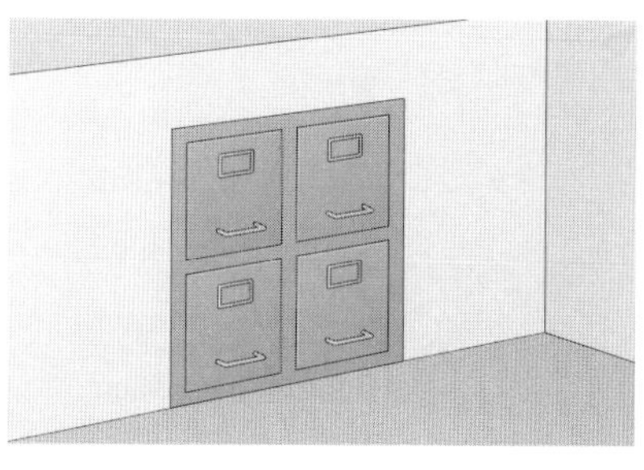

Basement Conversions

Because basements usually are roomy, converting them to living space often takes a prolonged period, and sometimes happens in piecemeal fashion. The result can be somewhat less than satisfying, with separate spaces cobbled together as they satisfy one immediate need or another. If that process describes the evolution of your basement, chances are good that you have developed a new appreciation for careful, thoughtful design and have formulated some strong ideas about how you would like to make use of the space.

Making a basement useful is often quite easy—making it attractive and comfortable is generally the bigger dilemma. The detailed information offered here will make you better prepared to diagnose and cure any current or potential moisture issues. You will also learn how to hide the unsightly pipes, wires, and ducts that are such prominent components of a basement ceiling. Finally, this chapter will show you how to turn your basement into a fully functional living space, with kitchen and bathroom facilities.

A Case in Point Doug Walter's architectural firm has designed dozens of basement conversions over the years. Walter often reminds potential clients that a converted basement can be a very cost-effective way to add space to the home. One of his goals in a conversion project is to make the basement as nice, or even nicer, than the upstairs. The key elements to a successful conversion, he has learned, are access, light, and detail. All of these elements are apparent in the two conversions shown here.

OFFICE DOWN UNDER

On paper, this basement conversion looked quite simple. But the transformed space is really quite remarkable. Structurally, the only changes involved enlarging the windows to provide more light and suitable egress. Furring strips were attached to the walls, providing room for insulation and a nailing surface for the drywall. The ceiling was insulated and then covered with a suspended acoustic ceiling installed diagonally.

Plenty of light was added, with both recessed and decorative hanging fixtures. Two computer workstations were custom-built and installed to wrap around the office area. A television and a stereo were also included for evening enjoyment.

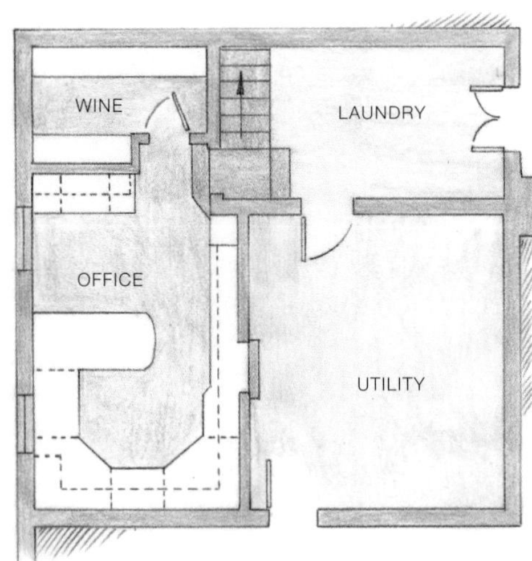

The new floor plan differed little from the original basement. An open storage area became separate office and wine rooms divided by a new wall and door. The door between the office and the utility room was removed, and a new door was installed between the laundry and utility rooms.

When the homeowners first needed to find more room, they converted their attic into a generous master suite. When they needed to expand again ten years later, they invited the architect and contractor back to turn their unfinished basement into a deluxe home office. Bikes and boxes now have their own storage space, adjacent to the office, and the wine collection is now neatly arranged and illuminated.

The stairs coming down from the kitchen were rebuilt to provide a safer rise and run. Halfway down a formal railing was provided, adding to the openness of the new space. A dropped ceiling hides the steel beam and ductwork, while octagonal coffers over the home theater and pool table create a sense of height. As with most of his basement conversions, Walter designed the space to have an abundance of artificial lighting.

PLAY IN STYLE

Walk-out basements are ideal candidates for transformation, since part of the space is not underground at all. The part that is below ground can be used for spaces that do not require much light, such as the home theater, pool table area, and bathroom in this example. The play area, guest room, and exercise areas, however, are located next to the window-filled outside wall.

Before

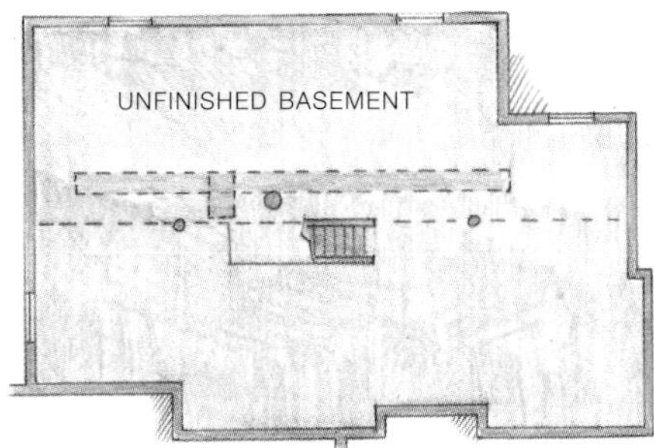

After

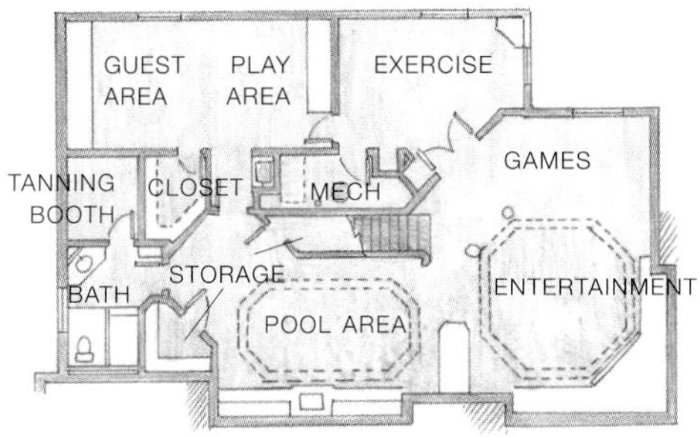

The other side of the room houses the large television screen, placed in the corner at a 45-degree angle to provide a wide viewing area.

Assessing Your Basement

The extent to which your basement is suitable for conversion often depends a great deal on how old it is. Basements in newer houses, with concrete floors and walls and substantial headroom, can make great living spaces.

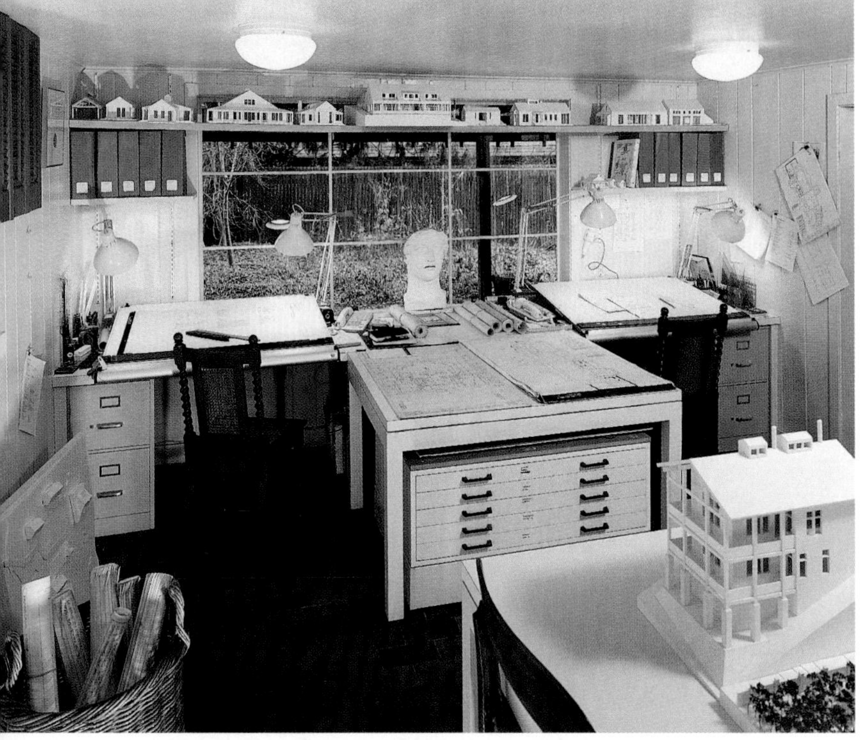

This compact basement office opens to a backyard view and fits four drawing tables around a central conference table.

But basements in old houses tend to be poor candidates; frequently they are dark and very moist, and the ceilings are too low. It is possible to tackle each of these issues in a remodeling job, but the cost may well exceed what you would spend on a new addition.

Some of the major problems you might face in converting a basement to usable living space are outlined here.

Moisture Some moisture problems are obvious, some are not. If water or dampness is apparent in your basement, do not proceed with any major remodeling project without addressing the moisture's source.

If you think your basement is dry, it is still wise to check for moisture infiltration or condensation that may be too subtle to see. Even a moderate level of dampness can create an unhealthy environment that can damage furniture and equipment. Fortunately, the most common sources of basement moisture are relatively easy to address; see pages 153–161 for a full discussion of moisture problems and cures.

Egress Egress windows are defined by building codes as windows large enough to allow a person to escape through in the event of an emergency. You probably will not be required to provide an egress window unless you plan to add a bedroom as part of your conversion. But if you do want to add direct access to the basement from the outside, talk with a contractor about the feasibility of installing a bulkhead door.

Another, albeit expensive, option is to excavate along a section of the foundation and install a sunken patio with a door to the basement. Basement door and window choices are covered on pages 170–173.

Headroom As in attic conversions, most building codes require that the distance between the finish basement floor and the finish ceiling be at least 7 feet 6 inches over at least half the room. Even if your unfinished basement exceeds this requirement, be sure to remember the reduction in headroom that will result when you add a new floor covering or cover the ceiling. Any rooms you intend to use as living space must have at least 70 square feet of floor space.

Stairs Old basement stairs are often very steep, have inadequate headroom, and lack a handrail and balusters. To turn your basement into a living space that will satisfy the building code, the stairs to it may have to be reconstructed.

Repositioning the stairs may also be the best way to create a functional floor plan in the basement. One solution to the basement stair dilemma is to replace a straight run of stairs with an L-shaped design, which consumes little additional floor space but can make for a less steep stair with an appealing entry to the basement. The space beneath the stairs can be turned into an enclosed storage closet.

This day-lit basement office is comprised of several linked-use areas and features a stylish conference area brightened with sponge-painted walls and halogen lighting.

Noise Sound can easily pass through the ceiling of an unfinished basement. Acoustic tile panels (see pages 56–59) can block some of the noise. Adding insulation between the joists before covering the ceiling is another effective strategy. For more on soundproofing, see page 55.

If you are bothered by noise from a furnace or other mechanical device in the basement, talk to a contractor about the merits of building a partition wall or enclosing the offending units in their own closet. This step may require the use of fire-retardant materials and special measures to ensure adequate combustion air.

Lighting Most basements receive little, if any, natural light, and artificial lighting alone may not be sufficient. You may be able to add windows to your basement provided the foundation is strong enough. But you may not want to add windows where privacy or security may be jeopardized, such as near a sidewalk.

Building codes will require that the bottom of any window rest about 6 inches above the ground. Often this allows for only a very narrow window, but you can increase the size of the allowable window by adding a window well. South-facing windows will collect the most sunlight during the winter.

Plan to supplement whatever natural light you can gather with a well-designed artificial lighting scheme that provides plentiful ambient, task, and, perhaps, accent lighting. Because of restricted ceiling heights, overhead light fixtures can be a problem in a basement. If they are, you can create ambient lighting with wall sconces or even lamps that direct light toward the ceiling.

You may also want to explore using recessed lights in the ceiling. Task lighting can be provided with lamps or spotlights

Dealing with Dirt

For old basements with dirt floors, often the first step toward conversion is pouring a concrete floor. For best results, the ground should first be compacted, then covered with a 4-inch layer of gravel or sand. Once this base has been compacted and leveled, cover it with a vapor barrier before pouring a reinforced 4-inch slab. Provisions must be made for supporting any posts, heating equipment, and other utilities. Note that this process can only work in a basement with a high ceiling.

Extreme Measures

Old houses often have basements that are barely deep enough to stand in, or have small basements combined with a much larger crawl space. If this describes your house, you may think that a suitable conversion is simply out of the question. Before jumping to this conclusion, though, you may want to consult with a contractor or two about the possibility of digging your basement deeper or wider. Such work may involve supporting the entire house on temporary steel beams while a new basement and foundation are prepared (a professional house mover may be the best person for this job). It is an expensive proposition, but if you are unable to build an addition and are pressed for space, it can be a good solution in the long run. Also, if your cramped basement has persistent moisture problems, a new one would offer a good chance to eliminate them once and for all.

mounted on walls or the ceiling. And the atmosphere of a converted basement can be improved dramatically with a few pieces of art or other decorative elements highlighted by accent lights.

Comfort and Appeal The most important consideration in converting a basement to a living space is whether it will be a usable space year-round. Some of the biggest challenges homeowners face are ensuring that the overall room temperature remains comfortable and that the room itself is inviting.

Basements tend to remain cool in the summer, which can be a big advantage. Come winter, however, the story often changes as the basement becomes too cool to enjoy comfortably. The first step in adding heat to a basement is to insulate the walls and floors. If your home's heating system is located in the basement, it may give off enough heat to warm the well-insulated room. A small space heater could be used occasionally as a supplement.

Finishing a basement ceiling so that it is attractive can be a challenge. Unfinished, such ceilings are ugly, and filled with ducts, wires, and pipes running in all directions—creating a room that is more industrial than inviting in feel. An effective yet low-cost solution is to install a suspended ceiling, with acoustic tile panels installed in a frame of metal channels hung from the joists. The panels provide a light, attractive surface, yet can be easily removed for temporary access. A suspended ceiling is only possible, however, if your basement has a high ceiling to begin with.

Another option is to cover the ceiling with drywall or paneling, building boxes around ducts and pipes. See pages 164–167 for more specific recommendations.

Finally, if your basement conversion is focused on fun (games, toys, exercise, relaxation), take some of the darkness away by using bold, bright colors on the surfaces and for your furnishings. Since the basement is separate from the rest of the house, you can use any style and tone you like.

A converted basement is an ideal choice for a home theater. Wall sconces provide indirect lighting.

Dealing with Moisture

With most basement conversions, the first question to ask is: Can I keep it dry? It is not unusual for basements to have a higher level of humidity than the rest of the house, but it is not a good sign if the basement experiences standing water, even if only occasionally.

Some typical symptoms of moisture problems are shown in the illustration below, and may include dry rot on sills or joists, rust on metal objects, or even just a musty or sour smell. If your basement has any of these symptoms, you will want to track down the cause and take steps to alleviate the problem. Some basement moisture problems are complex, but the overwhelming majority of them are pretty simple.

Primary Causes of a Wet Basement

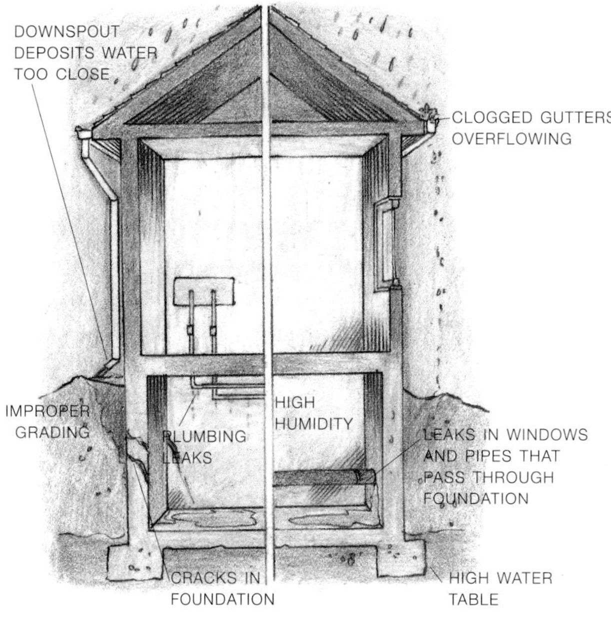

FINDING THE SOURCE

There are many possible causes of a wet basement; the primary ones are shown in the illustration above. Condensation occurs when warm, moist air meets a cool surface. In a basement, moist air can be given off by damp walls or floors, or it can enter through windows and doors during periods of rain or high humidity. The most common source of moisture is saturated soil caused by poorly

Signs of Moisture Problems

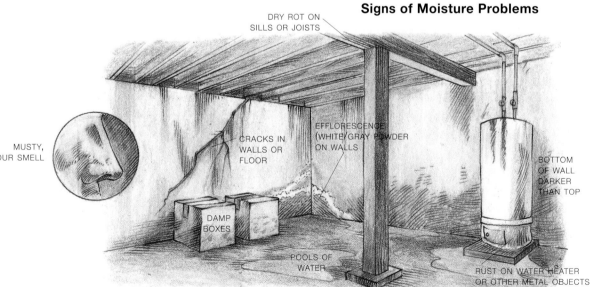

DRY ROT ON SILLS OR JOISTS
MUSTY, SOUR SMELL
CRACKS IN WALLS OR FLOOR
EFFLORESCENCE (WHITE/GRAY POWDER ON WALLS
BOTTOM OF WALL DARKER THAN TOP
DAMP BOXES
POOLS OF WATER
RUST ON WATER HEATER OR OTHER METAL OBJECTS
MOISTURE DAMAGE ON SUPPORT POSTS

LOW TEMPERATURE OUTDOORS
CONDENSATION
HIGH HUMIDITY INDOORS

functioning downspouts and gutters or inadequate grading around the house. Sweating water pipes can also be a source of high humidity in a basement. Leaking pipes or windows or a high water table can produce excess moisture in the basement.

If you find evidence of moisture damage in the basement but cannot determine the source, the easy procedure shown below should help make the diagnosis. If you find moisture on top of the squares, that is a sign of condensation from high humidity. Moisture underneath the squares is due to seepage through the masonry. If both sides are damp, you will have to contend with both sources of moisture.

REDUCING CONDENSATION

Condensation is a fact of life, but under certain circumstances it can become a problem. When warm air, which can hold more moisture than cold air, hits a cold surface, such as a window or a basement wall, it condenses into visible moisture. This same effect occurs when cold water passes through copper pipes that are located in a warm space, such as a basement; condensation develops on the outside surface of the pipes and starts to drip.

In an unfinished basement, you may not be aware of an ongoing cycle of condensation. But once you start altering the climate of the basement (through mechanical heating and cooling) and adding moisture-absorbing materials (such as furniture and carpeting), routine condensation can become a routine headache.

The following tips on reducing condensation are really worth considering in any basement conversion, even if you don't think you have an existing moisture problem. Taking a few precautionary—and inexpensive—steps early on might save aggravation later.

Checking for Moisture Sources

1 FASTEN PLASTIC
With duct tape, fasten heavy plastic or aluminum foil to any suspected damp areas of the basement walls or floor.

2 CHECK FOR MOISTURE
Check the square every few days. Moisture on top of the square indicates high humidity. Moisture under the square indicates seepage through the masonry.

Control sources of humidity The humidity level in a house can rise dramatically from cooking, bathing, washing, and other household activities. You can keep this moisture from causing problems by installing—and using—exhaust fans in the bathrooms and kitchen, and by making sure that your clothes dryer is vented to the outdoors (not to the attic or basement).

Provide ventilation If condensation is only a mild and infrequent problem for you, ventilation may be a sufficient solution. Open windows in the basement, when the weather permits, to encourage air circulation.

Add insulation You can reduce condensation by making cold surfaces warmer; that is the job of insulation. Air sealing and vapor retardants assist in this process by preventing warm, moist air from passing through building materials. See pages 52–55 for more information on insulation materials and techniques.

Wrap pipes Many homeowners have long insulated hot water pipes to conserve energy, but you can use the same approach on cold water pipes to control condensation. The easiest way to wrap pipes is with foam sleeve insulators. Measure the total length of

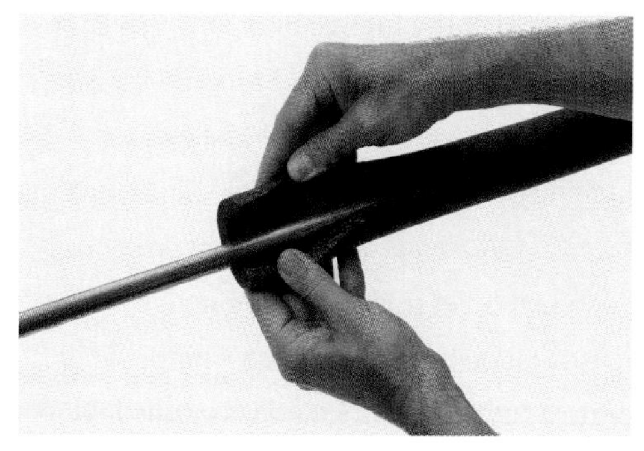

uninsulated water supply pipes in your basement, then buy sleeves to fit the pipes' diameter (typically ½ inch).

Foam sleeves are easy to install. They come already slit, so you can usually just slip them into place over the pipes. Use a utility knife or large scissors to cut the foam to length; make neat miter cuts around elbows to maximize coverage. For added protection, add tape around all joints and gaps.

Seal ducts Duct systems on forced-air heating and cooling systems are supposed to operate as a closed loop. Heated or cooled air should pass from the furnace or air conditioner to and from supply and return grills throughout the house by way of airtight connections. But these ducts are often poorly sealed, which can cause excessive moisture to be deposited where it shouldn't be. Humidifiers on central air conditioners are a particularly troublesome piece of equipment. If

Mold and Mildew

High relative humidity can produce more than condensation—mold and mildew are more likely to thrive in such an environment. While both are almost always present in buildings in at least moderate amounts, they are especially prevalent when the air is moist.

Mold and mildew can create unpleasant odors, stain surfaces, produce slippery stairs, and, in certain circumstances, even pose a health threat to inhabitants. To address the issue, first get rid of the moisture that is causing the problem. There's no sense in cleaning and replacing moldy materials if they are only going to wind up in the same environment that produced the original problem.

Second, remove all moldy materials. If the problem is severe, wear a respirator. Wrap or double-bag all materials before discarding them. Wash all surfaces with a 50-50 solution of bleach and water.

Finally, chose new materials for the basement that are less likely to provide fuel for mold and mildew: hardwood or vinyl rather than carpet on floors; metal blinds rather than curtains on windows; vinyl chairs rather than cushioned recliners.

you have a humidifier, consider trying to live without using it. If you need to add moisture to maintain a comfortable home, set the humidity level as low as possible and make sure that the ducts are thoroughly sealed.

To seal holes and joints in ductwork, use mastic (shown below), which will fill small crevices and dry to a long-lasting, airtight seal (especially if it is reinforced with fiberglass mesh). Duct tape, despite its name, really is not particularly good at sealing ducts.

Use a dehumidifier The science is pretty basic: When you remove moisture from your house, you are less likely to experience condensation on cold surfaces. Modern houses are often equipped with mechanical systems that remove moisture from the home. When you don't have that option available, the next best solution is to use a dehumidifier.

Before shopping for a dehumidifier, you need to know two things: the square footage of the room (length times width) and the level of humidity in the room (from moderately damp to very wet).

A dehumidifier works best at normal room temperatures of 65°F to 70°F. If you operate the unit at cooler temperatures, frost may form on the coils, which can both reduce air circulation and cause damage to the appliance.

Plug the dehumidifier into a grounded outlet, allowing at least a 12-inch airspace on all sides. It's best to avoid placing the unit in a corner or near large pieces of furniture. For the first few days of operating your dehumidifier, set it at "extra dry," if possible, then adjust it to a more suitable comfort level.

Also during the first few days of using your dehumidifier, check the collector tank several times a day; you may be surprised at how quickly it fills with water. To avoid having to empty the tank regularly, attach a hose to the drain hose connector, then run the hose to a floor drain, if you have one.

At least once a month, wash the collector tank with a mild detergent. (Always unplug the unit before cleaning.) Clean or replace the filter at the same time. Once or twice a year, vacuum the coils behind the filter and add oil to the fan motor as instructed by the manufacturer.

CONTROLLING RUNOFF

Often, basement moisture problems are caused by rain and melting snow falling from the roof, saturating the soil surrounding the foundation. The water penetrates the soil, seeking a crack or hole through which to trickle into the basement. Keep that water away from the house, and you can eliminate most of this effect. The following tried-and-true methods are your first line of defense against outside water getting into your basement.

Grading One of the best ways to keep moisture out of the basement is with proper grading of the soil surrounding the house. Normally, the soil is graded when the house is built. Over time, however, the backfill that was deposited around the foundation can settle. When that happens, water soaks into

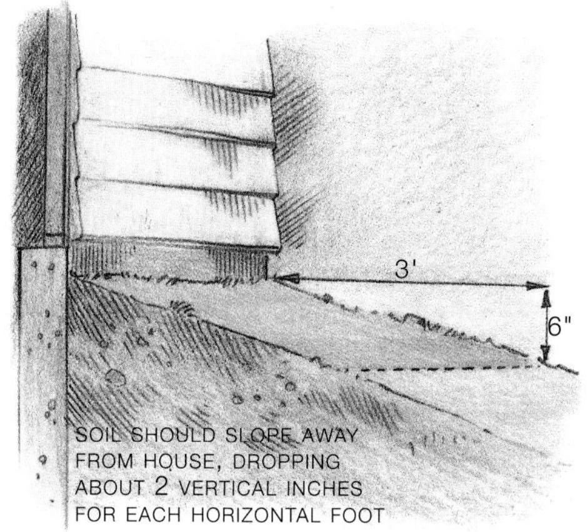

the ground next to the foundation rather than several feet away.

The soil on all sides of the house should slope away from the foundation for at least 3 to 4 feet, dropping a total of 6 to 8 inches over that distance. Use a 4-foot carpenter's level and tape measure to check the slope on each side of your house. If the grading seems inadequate, you will want to order some soil to build the necessary slope. Also use soil (not gravel) to fill low spots near the house.

Adding gutters and downspouts Gutters and downspouts are critical elements in keeping your basement dry. Gutters collect water from the roof and direct it to downspouts, which direct the water to ground level and away from the house. Without gutters, rainwater and melting snow fall around the entire perimeter of the house, very close to the foundation.

Gutters and downspouts rely on gravity to do their job. Each section of gutter should

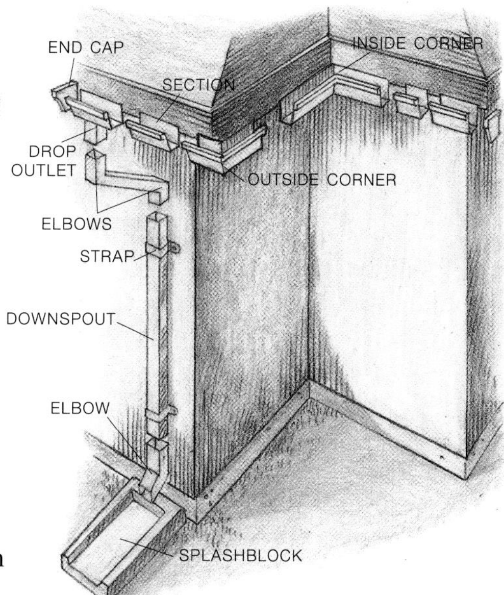

slope slightly toward a downspout—about ¼ inch for every 4 feet of horizontal run is usually best. Run water in all gutters to see that it flows to an outlet. If it doesn't, readjust the slope by adding or moving the hangers, brackets, or spikes that hold the gutters in place.

Gutters and downspouts require regular maintenance. Clean and flush the system in the spring and fall. Remove leaves, twigs,

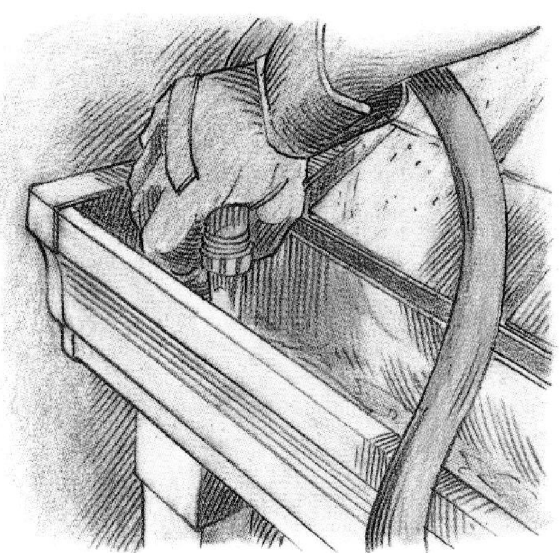

Maintaining Gutters

Left: Remove leaves, twigs, and other debris from gutters (wear gloves). Loosen dried dirt with a stiff brush. After you have removed as much as you can by hand, hose the gutters clean.

Right: Use a garden hose turned on full force to clean out the downspouts. If you encounter a clog, try removing it with a plumber's snake. If that fails, disassemble the downspout to clean it out.

and other debris. Loosen dried dirt with a stiff brush. Then use a garden hose turned to full force to clean out the downspouts. If you encounter a clog, try removing it with a plumber's snake. If that fails, you will have to disassemble the downspout to clean it out.

Once the gutters and downspouts are clean, probe for weaknesses with a small screwdriver. Holes or cracks should be patched with plastic roofing cement (or a sealant recommended for your type of gutter). Badly damaged sections may have to be replaced.

Splashblocks While downspouts funnel water to ground level, it is up to splashblocks to carry the water away from the house. Place a ready-made concrete or plastic splashblock below each downspout elbow. Ideally the splashblock should extend at least 4 feet and be sloped away from the house.

Water can also be diverted from the house with outlet extensions. Gutter manufacturers offer pivoting metal extensions, which can be raised out of the way when you need to mow around them. Flexible plastic extensions (shown above left) are especially versatile, and aren't so easily damaged by foot traffic.

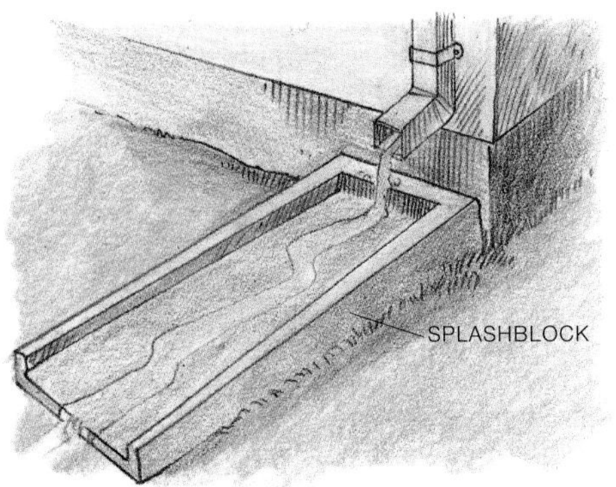

Dry wells Dry wells are another way to collect water from downspouts. If you live in a very wet climate, you may need a dry well to handle all the runoff. Typically located 10 or more feet from the house, dry wells allow water runoff to slowly soak into the ground. Their success depends, however, on how well the surrounding soil drains.

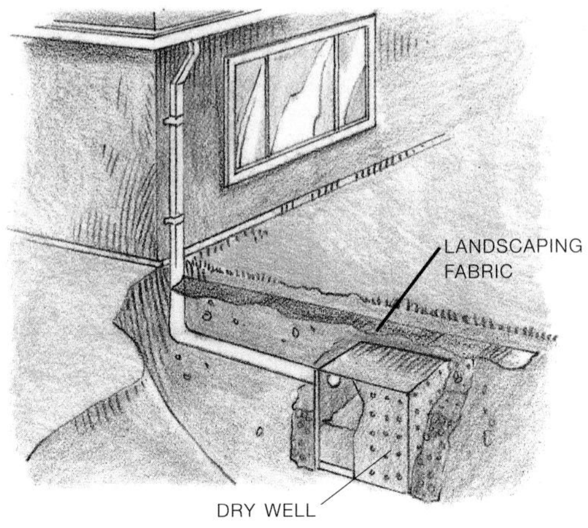

A dry well can be a simple hole in the ground (2 to 4 feet wide and 3 feet deep) filled with rocks or gravel. The top of the dry well should be at least 18 inches below ground level and covered with landscaping fabric or roofing felt; the bottom should be above the water table. More elaborate installations use a 1,000-gallon precast concrete or perforated plastic dry well surrounded by gravel.

One or more underground drainage pipes, sloped ¼ to ½ inch per foot, carry water away from the downspouts to the dry well. Before installing a dry well, check local building codes and your property lines for any restrictions.

SEALING LEAKS

Creating and maintaining a dry basement often requires a series of steps. Reducing condensation and diverting water from the foundation are two of the most important measures you can take, and no basement should be remodeled until that work is done. But even with the best moisture-control strategies, holes will need to be patched and cracks filled to keep moisture at bay.

The first step in sealing off leaks is to determine where moisture can enter the basement from outside the house. Leaking basement doors and windows can allow a lot of water to get inside. Repair cracked or broken glass, and use caulk and weather-stripping to maintain a tight seal.

If a driveway runs near your house's foundation, water can find its way through the concrete or asphalt surface into your basement. Patch all driveway cracks with concrete or asphalt patching compound, depending on the type of driveway.

If your basement walls are constructed with concrete block, inspect the top of the wall to see if the cores are open. Open cores can introduce a large amount of moisture into the basement—and the rest of the house—by providing a passage for evaporating groundwater. You can easily seal the cores, however, by spraying expanding foam into them, as shown below.

There are a wide variety of products on the market that can seal basement walls and floors against water penetration. Shop carefully and read the instructions on the label before committing yourself to any one product. Some can be applied with a brush or roller, others are trowelled on. Some of the general techniques and products are described below. In addition to filling holes and cracks, seal all penetrations in the wall.

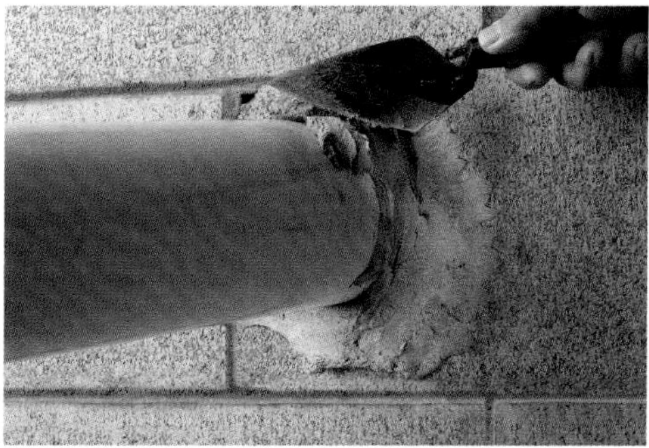

Filling holes and cracks To fill holes or cracks over ¼-inch wide, use a masonry repair compound or a hydraulic cement product. Hydraulic cement is ideal for sealing walls even when water is trickling through. It comes in powdered form and must be mixed with water.

To apply, undercut the hole or crack a bit with a masonry chisel, brush clean, then force cement into the hole. Have a wet brush handy to smooth and feather the edges. The cement will begin expanding and setting within minutes. To fill a long, narrow crack, use a polyurethane masonry caulk.

Waterproofing walls Basic waterproofing paint can do a satisfactory job of keeping moisture from migrating into a basement. Coatings that contain portland cement and a synthetic rubber are better at bonding to and sealing masonry surfaces.

Although some products can be applied to damp walls, most waterproofing paints will adhere best if they are brushed or rolled onto a dry surface. If possible, wait for a dry season and run a dehumidifier in the basement for several days before applying the coating. Use a stiff brush and cleaning compound made especially for concrete to remove dirt, grease, and salty efflorescence from the walls. Repair all holes or cracks (see page 159). Let the wall dry, then apply at least two coats of the waterproofing paint.

Dealing with a High Water Table

One of the most difficult situations to control is the moisture problems that result from a high water table. The water table is defined as the line between saturated and unsaturated soil. It can vary by season and by location, and even a heavy rainfall can cause the water table to rise. It is not likely that there is much you can do to change the water table, but if you determine that the source of your basement moisture problem comes from below, here are some steps that you can take to keep the basement dry.

Adding interior perimeter drains A perimeter drain system collects moisture at the bottom of basement walls and directs it to a floor drain or, more often, to a sump pump.

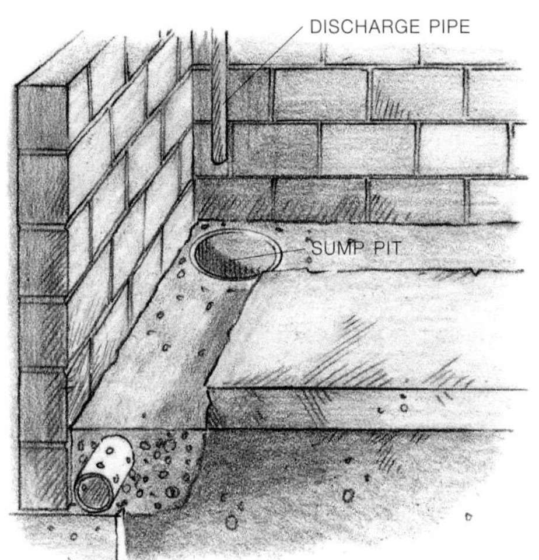

The most effective approach is to dig a trough around the perimeter of the basement floor. Then run a 4-inch perforated plastic drainpipe in gravel around the trough, sloping the pipe to a sump pit, as shown below left.

A less involved approach is to install a manufactured interior gutter system around the perimeter of the basement as shown below. Lengths of plastic gutter are glued to the concrete floor, pitched toward an outlet (floor drain or sump pump).

If a high water table or poor exterior drainage causes serious problems, talk with a contractor about breaking up the concrete floor and installing a more elaborate drainage system in gravel, then pouring a new slab.

Adding a sump pump Sump pumps can be very effective at keeping water from getting into the basement. The pump is set in a tank, or sump pit, which should be installed at the lowest spot in the basement floor or along a perimeter drain system. Sump pits, which can be purchased at lumberyards and home centers, can be made of fiberglass, concrete, plastic, or metal. As the water level beneath the basement floor rises, water begins to fill

Submersible Sump Pump

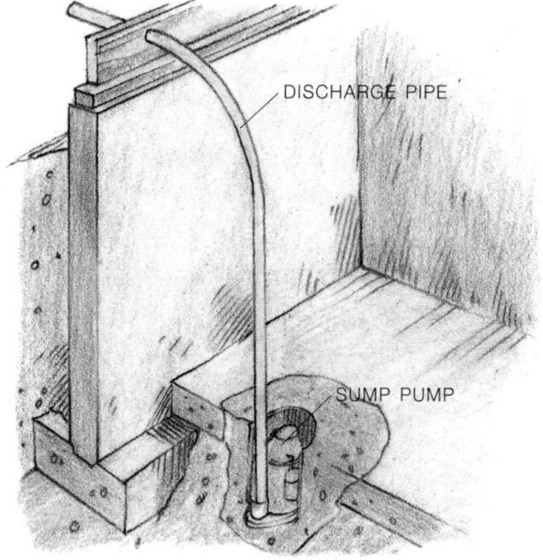

Pedestal Sump Pump

the sump pit, the pump is activated, and water is discharged to a drain or directly out of the house. Once the water level falls, the pump shuts off.

There are two types of sump pumps used in houses: submersible pumps are fully concealed in the sump pit, while pedestal pumps are only partially concealed, with the motor resting above water. Pedestal sump pumps tend to cost a bit less than submersible models, and they are easier to repair and maintain. But submersible pumps are quieter, and therefore a better choice for living areas.

Sump pumps usually come with long cords, allowing you to plug them into a receptacle protected by a ground fault circuit interrupter. Do not use an extension cord with a sump pump.

Adding an exterior drainage system An exterior drainage system is the most effective strategy for keeping water out of the basement. Unfortunately, it is also the most expensive and time consuming to install, and should only be considered as a last resort. This is a job for a trained contractor.

The typical process involves excavating around the house to the bottom of the foundation. Any cracks or holes in the exterior foundation wall are patched, then the wall is waterproofed (a wide variety of products can be used for this step), with special attention paid to the joint between the footing and the wall. The wall is covered with rigid insulation or drainage board. A 4-foot perforated plastic drainpipe is set in gravel along the footing, connected to a drain line that slopes away from the house. Often, landscaping fabric is wrapped around the drainpipe or laid across the gravel. The perimeter is then backfilled, tamped, and graded to ensure that surface water drains away from the house.

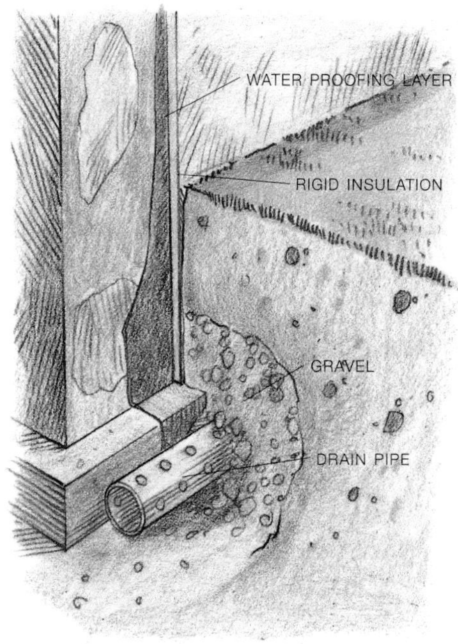

Dealing with Radon and Asbestos

Indoor air quality is an important issue throughout the house, but it deserves special attention when you are converting a basement into living space. That's because the basement often contains a furnace or boiler, water heater, and other combustion devices that can pollute the air. In addition, the heating ducts and pipes in the basements of older homes are frequently insulated with materials containing asbestos. The basement is also the port of entry for radon gas (see below). The following section contains tips for dealing with these possible environmental problems and for ensuring that the air in your converted basement is healthy and comfortable.

RADON

Radon (Rn) is an odorless, colorless, tasteless, radioactive gas that is released when trace amounts of uranium in rocks and soil decay. Radon is released into the outdoor environment all the time, but causes little health concern because it quickly dissipates. Indoors, however, radon can become much more concentrated. Breathing high amounts of the gas over a long period of time can result in lung cancer. Thousands of lung cancer deaths each year in the United States are attributed to radon.

Radon can seep into basements through cracks in the floor or walls, and through floor drains and sump pump pits. It can be found in old as well as new houses.

Fortunately, testing for radon is simple and inexpensive. Charcoal canister testers are commonly used for short-term testing. They are placed in the house for several days, then returned to a lab for analysis. Alpha-track detectors are used for long-term testing. They are usually left in the house for three months to a year, and offer a more balanced assessment of radon levels.

Short- and long-term radon testers are available at reasonable cost from the National Safety Council (800-767-7236; www.nsc.org).

Basement Smoke Detectors

Be sure to install at least one smoke detector in your converted basement that is wired to detectors in the floors above; if people in the basement are listening to music or the TV at a high volume, they might not hear a smoke alarm going off in another part of the house. Some codes require this wiring, but it is a worthwhile addition even if your local department's code does not.

Old Test, New Test

If your house was tested in the past for radon and did not contain high levels, don't take that finding as the last word. Radon testing is typically done in parts of the house designated as "primary living areas," such as a first floor living room. The assumption is that even if the radon level in the basement is a bit high, much of the gas will pass outside and not reach upper floors. Before turning your basement into a living space, you should conduct a test there to determine the existing level of radon.

Whether or not you've tested before, don't be surprised if a test turns up some level of radon. The Environmental Protection Agency estimates that the average indoor concentration is 1.3 picoCuries per liter (pCi/l), but does not suggest taking any action unless the level reaches 4 pCi/l. It should be noted, though, that even that higher level poses very little risk to nonsmokers. If you are a smoker and the radon level in your house measures 4 pCi/l or more, the best remedial action you can take is to quit smoking. Also be aware that radon levels are generally higher in winter than in summer. If possible, take a measurement in both seasons, then average the two results.

You can reduce the amount of radon entering your basement by sealing all cracks and holes in the floor and walls and covering the sump pit, if you have one. For more substantial reduction, however, you should talk with a contractor experienced in radon remediation. One common and successful strategy involves installing a piping system that captures the radon beneath the slab and vents it to the outdoors.

For more information on radon, contact your local health department, cooperative extension service, the American Lung Association (800-LUNG-USA), or the Environmental Protection Agency (800-490-9198; www.epa.gov).

ASBESTOS

Asbestos is a mineral fiber that was widely used in household products before the 1970s. It was also used in construction materials, including insulation used around pipes and heating ducts, paint, adhesives, and flooring. Inhaling it can cause cancer and other health problems.

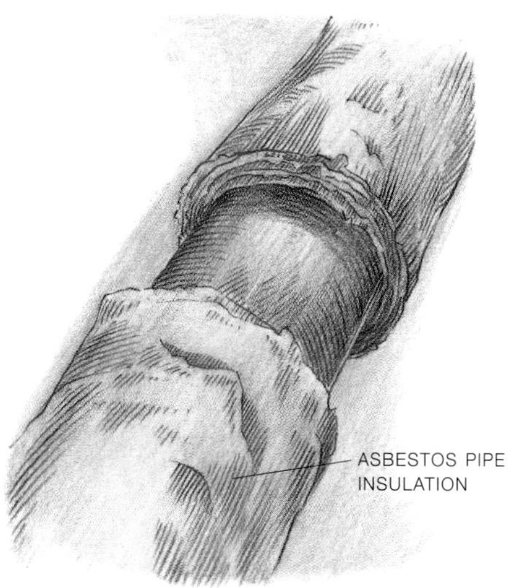

Asbestos is dangerous stuff, but it poses a health risk only if particles are airborne. Loose or cracked material containing asbestos can often be wrapped tightly or coated to enclose the fibers. However, some materials may have to be removed by a specialist. An asbestos inspector, certified by the EPA, can inspect your house and suggest remedies.

Caution: Carbon Monoxide

Carbon monoxide (CO) is an odorless, tasteless gas that is emitted by fireplaces, furnaces, gas appliances, water heaters, and other combustion appliances. Under normal circumstances, carbon monoxide is carried safely out of the house by vents and chimneys. But members of your household can be exposed to dangerous levels of carbon monoxide when a chimney becomes clogged or a vent pipe becomes disconnected.

Protect your family from this deadly gas by regularly inspecting all fuel-burning equipment and venting systems in your home. For added protection, install at least one carbon monoxide detector. For recommendations, check with the American Lung Association, your local health department, and consumer magazines.

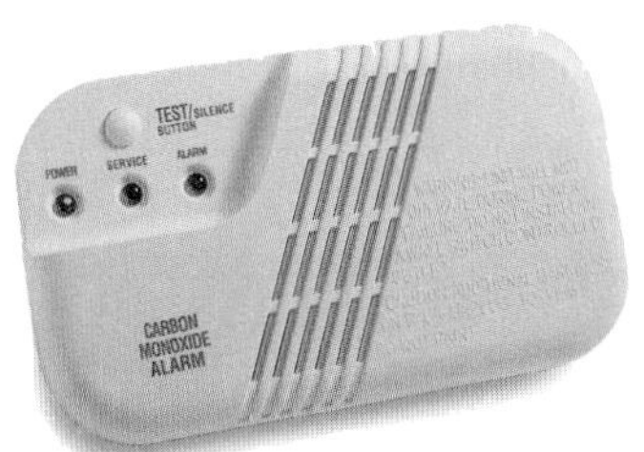

Hiding Ducts and Pipes

You probably will not be able to transform your basement into the brightest part of your house, but with some relatively simple cosmetic touches you certainly can make it cozy, attractive, and less basement-like. Some of the most important steps that you can take in that regard are hiding or disguising the posts, beams, pipes, and ducts that are such prominent features of the basement landscape.

While it is possible to move, reconfigure, or even eliminate some posts and beams in a basement, it is not a job for a do-it-yourselfer. If these structural components are a serious obstacle to your conversion plans, or if you would just like to learn about your options, talk to a contractor or structural engineer. Likewise, ductwork can often be moved, but you should talk with an HVAC contractor to make sure that service and

Sometimes the best way to hide ducts and pipes is not to hide them at all. In this converted basement, the pipes and ceiling have been painted to match the walls, giving the office a contemporary high-tech look. To soften the edges, the windows look out on a garden path that flanks the basement wall. Interior Design: Gail Woolaway & Associates.

efficiency won't be affected. Plumbing drain lines can also be rerouted as long as you are able to maintain the required slope (see pages 185–187). Wiring and small-diameter water and gas lines are usually quite easy to reroute through joist bays or newly framed walls. The most simple strategy is to paint the offending features to make them blend in with the walls and ceiling.

MAKING OBSTRUCTIONS DISAPPEAR

With careful planning, it is often possible to make unsightly basement obstructions simply disappear into the walls and ceilings. Posts and beams can be enclosed in new partition walls, for example, while beams and ductwork can be incorporated into a soffit above built-in cabinets or shelving as shown at right. If basement posts are too big to be buried in a 2 x 4 partition wall, you can frame the wall with 2 x 6s instead.

continued on page 166

A soffit with recessed lights serves two purposes: it conceals any ductwork or beams while providing additional lighting for a dark wall.

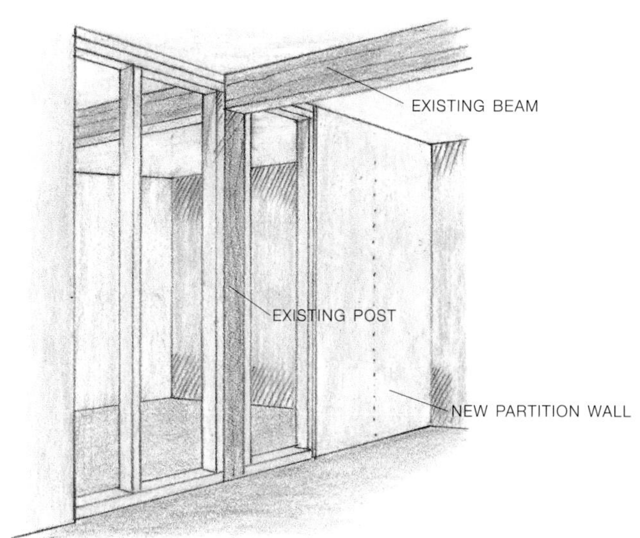

Existing posts and beams can be hidden by building partition walls to cover them. This will decrease the amount of floor space in the room.

Something Simple

A basement conversion does not need to be too involved. You can make your basement much more livable and inviting with just a few surface treatments. If no moisture or headroom problems need to be addressed, a coat of paint on the walls may be all you need to liven things up.

Prepare the walls by removing dirt and loose mortar with a brush, filling and patching any cracks or holes (see pages 48–49), then washing with soap and water. When dry, apply a good quality latex paint or, if necessary, use a waterproofing paint as described on pages 159–160.

Paint the floor too, if you like, or install some commercial-grade carpet squares that can be set on the concrete surface without any adhesive. To blend unsightly pipes, ducts, wires, and joists with the rest of the room, consider spraying all surfaces in the basement the same color.

Concealing Ducts

Heating and cooling ducts can be concealed quite successfully in a simple box, or soffit, constructed with 2 x 2s and 1 x 2s. The sides should be built like ladders and joined by bottom braces.

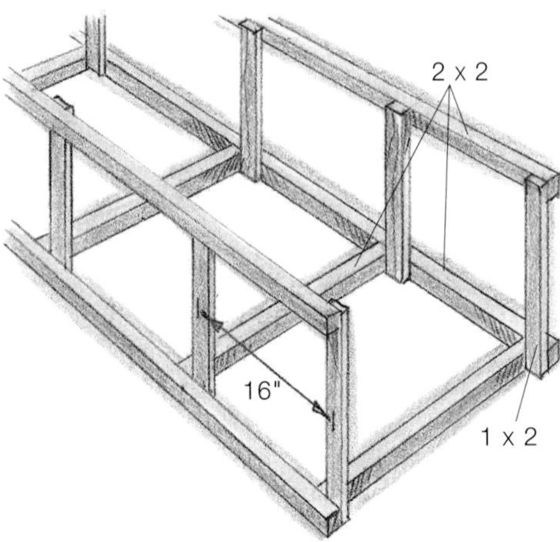

Build the frame on the floor, then attach it to floor joists. Leave an airspace of about 1 inch on all three sides of the duct to be concealed, then seal it before enclosing (see page 155–156). Once installed, the box can be covered with drywall, wood, or paneling.

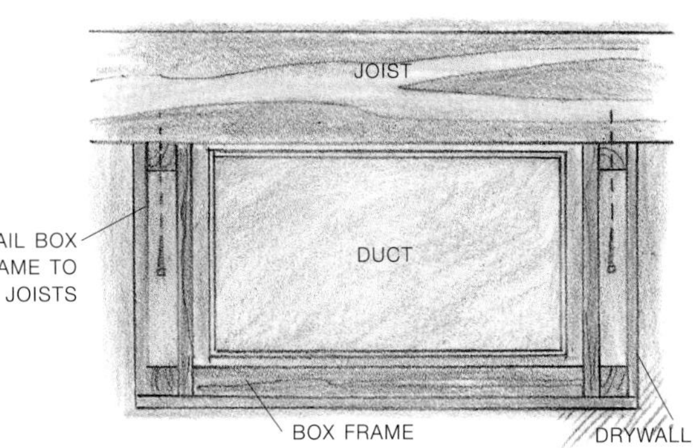

If you need to build wider boxes (to enclose ducts and pipes running side by side, for example), use 2 x 4s rather than 2 x 2s for the bottom framing members. Cover the frame with plywood or OSB (oriented strand board) before adding drywall or another finish surface.

Steel beams can be enclosed using the same technique.

Hiding Posts

Round steel posts, or lally columns, can be dressed up quickly by gluing carpet to them. To hide them more completely, frame a box around them using 2 x 4s, as shown below. Attach the top of the frame to the beam with nails or screws and the bottom to the floor with construction adhesive.

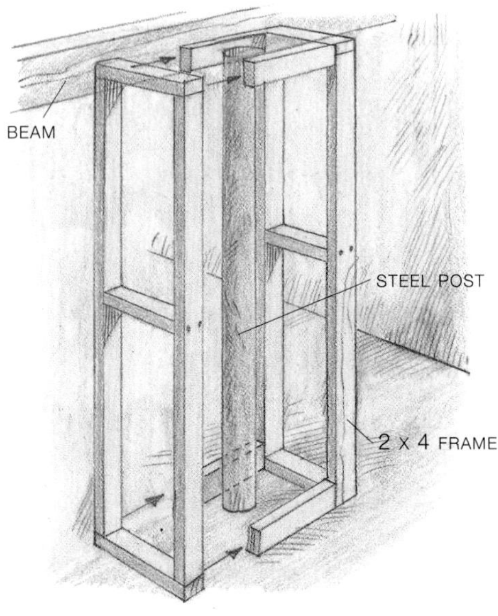

Once the frame is in place, cover it with drywall and finish it to match the other walls in the room. Or, to create a focal point, consider covering one or more sides with any number of other decorative surfaces, such as cork, for use as a bulletin board, or even with a mirror.

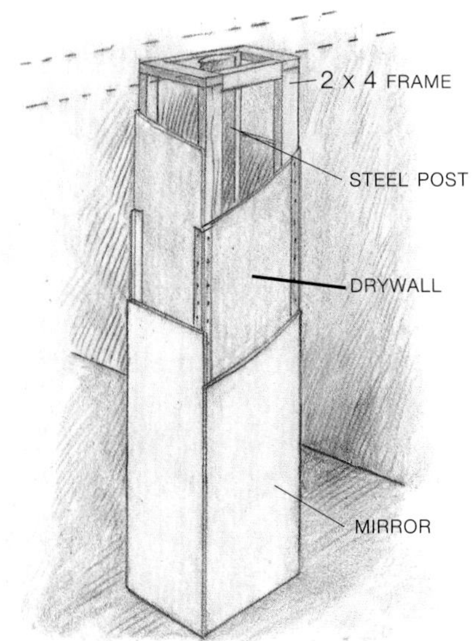

The Silent Treatment

If you have not spent much quiet time in your basement, you may be surprised at just how noisy some of the plumbing pipes can be. Waste lines, in particular, can make quite a racket when water is running through them. Your converted basement will certainly be a better place to relax if you take some time to soundproof the pipes.

Plastic drainpipes are considerably noisier than cast iron, so one way to reduce noise is to replace sections of plastic with cast iron. Or you can wrap a layer or two of dense carpet pad around the pipes and seal the pad with duct tape. If you then plan to cover the pipe with some form of enclosure, stuff the box with insulation before completing the enclosure.

Supply pipes can also make noise, vibrating when water runs through them. You can add pipe hangers or isolators to reduce this source of noise.

Enclosing Pipes

Pipes can be hidden in much the same manner as ducts and posts. Build a sturdy frame, attach the frame to the joists, then cover the assembly with drywall or other material.

When dealing with drainpipes (and often supply pipes as well), you will have to contend with the slope of the pipe (typically ¼ inch per foot). To build an enclosure that is perfectly level, cut the horizontal framing 2 x 4s long enough to reach the lowest part of the pipe run. For best results, use a carpenter's level when nailing the 2 x 4s to the joists. Attach the horizontal 2 x 4s, then the drywall. You will need to add soundproofing or insulation to the pipes before building the frame (see "The Silent Treatment," above).

If there is a cleanout in the pipe that will be concealed, you might want to build an access panel so that the cleanout can be reached without having to damage the enclosure.

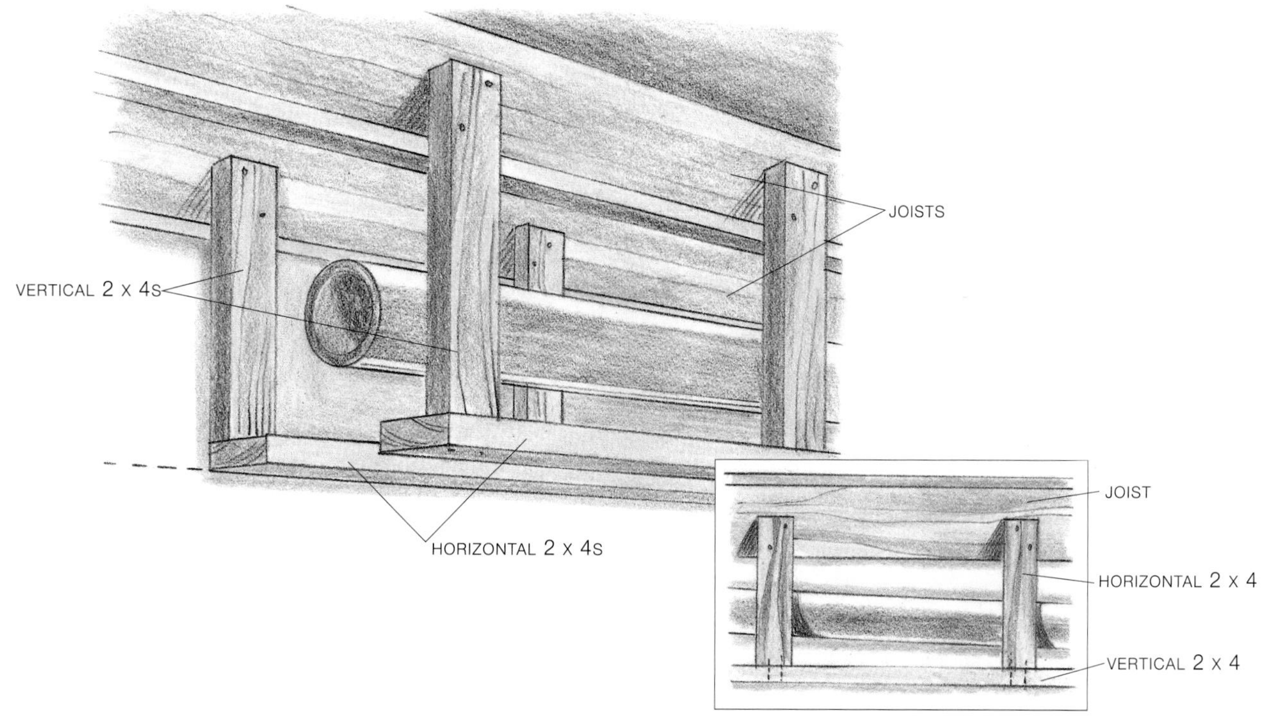

Adding Surface-Mounted Wiring

Running electrical wiring is usually easy work in a basement, because the service panel is generally nearby and wiring runs are relatively short and uncomplicated. If you are framing new walls, wiring can be routed before the finish surface is installed.

If you need to run cable and mount switches and receptacles on a masonry wall, however, you should use a surface-mounting system. Modular surface-wiring systems usually consist of protective channels, or strips, that allow you to mount wiring and boxes on practically any floor, wall, or ceiling material. Cable is fished through the channels.

The materials in surface-wiring systems differ by manufacturer. Consult with your electrical supplies dealer for more information about the various systems available.

You may also want to consider using metal or plastic conduit, which can be mounted to a basement wall.

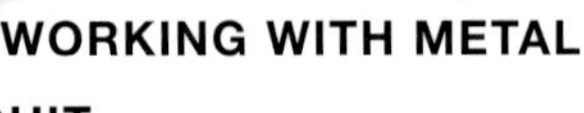

WORKING WITH METAL CONDUIT

Thinwall metal conduit (type EMT) is a good choice for exposed wiring in a basement. When creating a conduit system, you have to cut, bend, and join the conduit, then run wires through it. Professionals often bend conduit with a conduit bender, but most homeowners find it more practical to use prebent sections.

Metal housing boxes must be used with metal conduit. Screw the boxes to walls or ceilings through their backs; use masonry screws or expanding anchors for masonry surfaces, or panhead wood screws for wood framing.

How to Cut EMT

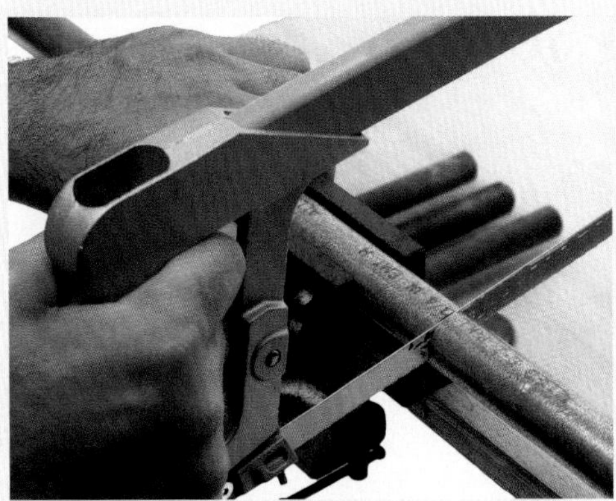

1 CUT CONDUIT TO LENGTH Clamp it firmly in a vise. Cut it with a hacksaw. You will get a cleaner cut if you support the cut end with your free hand during the last few saw strokes.

2 CLEAN THE EDGES Smooth the inside of the cut end of the conduit with a round metal file. This step will remove all burrs and sharp edges that could damage insulation on the wires.

Routing conduit If your conduit run contains more than 360 degrees in total bends (such as four 90-degree bends or three 90-degree bends plus two 45-degree bends), plan to use a pull box to help ease wires around turns. Pull boxes are used only for pulling and connecting wires. The photo below shows a square junction box with a single-device adapter plate used as a pull box. After the wires are pulled, a blank faceplate should be added. An alternative is to use corner elbows that break apart for pulling and then are sealed with cover plates. Always plan to install a pull box at a T intersection where a conduit run splits in two. EMT should be anchored with conduit straps within 3 feet of every box and with additional straps at least every 10 feet.

Making connections Use threadless setscrew couplings to join sections of conduit. Simply slip the conduit inside the coupling's shoulder, then tighten the screws. Elbow fittings come with their own setscrew connectors.

Joining conduit to boxes Conduit joins a square or an octagonal metal box through a knockout; you can't join conduit to a round box. Be sure the boxes have knockouts large enough to accommodate the size conduit you're using. If the housing box and conduit are mounted directly to the wall, you will need to connect them with offset fittings.

Grounding EMT To maintain grounding continuity, all couplings, connectors, fittings, and boxes must be metal, and all connections must be tight. To play it safe, some electricians run a separate grounding wire with the other wires inside the conduit.

Rigid Nonmetallic Conduit

Schedule 40 PVC conduit can be used in place of EMT in most areas (check your local code). It is a bit cheaper than EMT and easier to cut and join (use gray conduit cement). Place straps within 4 feet of each box and fitting, with additional supports at least every 4 feet.

Pulling Wires

You can pull wires with a fish tape. Unreel the tape through the conduit until it's exposed at the other end. Strip several inches of insulation off the end of each wire and bend the ends tightly over the fish tape loop. Wrap the splice with electrical tape, then pull the wires by rewinding the fish tape. For best results, smear cable lubricant (available at electrical supply stores) over the wires as they are fed into the conduit.

Basement Doors

If your basement does not have an access door to the outside, it is possible to add one. If it already has one, there's probably a good chance that it needs replacing. At the very least, you'll want to make an existing door more secure and attractive.

REPLACING BULKHEAD DOORS

If your basement has an old, rotting-wood bulkhead door, you will probably want to replace it with a new, secure, steel door. Home-improvement centers and lumberyards usually carry, or can special order, replacement bulkhead doors. They are not too expensive and can be quite easy to install.

Follow the manufacturer's instructions for measuring your existing foundation to determine the right size replacement door to buy. If the bulkhead foundation is angled, buy a flat door; if the foundation is flat, buy an angled door. Bulkhead doors lock from the inside, although some manufacturers offer keyed locks that allow entry from the outside. Installation will vary somewhat, depending on the type of door you need.

Begin by removing the old door or doors. Flat replacement doors often rest on foundation plates, which can conceal small holes or rough patches of masonry. If the sidewalls are already flat and smooth, however, you can place the door frame directly on them. Secure the frame to the foundation with connectors supplied by the manufacturer, then install the doors.

Flat Bulkhead Door

Angled Bulkhead Door

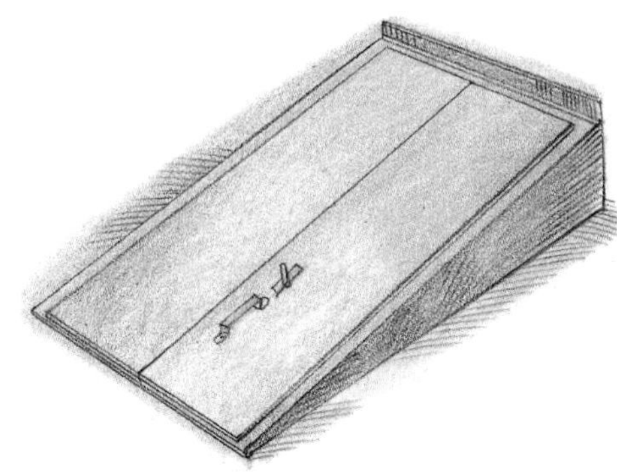

Angled doors may require that you remove some siding. The frame must rest on a smooth, flat surface. Use concrete anchors to secure the frame to the foundation, then install the doors. Paint the doors with a glossy paint recommended for use on metal.

REPLACING THE PASSAGE DOOR

If you need to replace an old passage door into your basement, consider installing a new

door with a large window in it. The glass can let a substantial amount of natural lighting into a dark basement. Be sure to choose a door suitable for exterior use. If the frame around the old door is rotting, replace that too with pressure-treated lumber.

INSTALLING A NEW ENTRY

Installing a new basement entry is probably a job for a professional contractor, and it can be expensive. The convenience it provides, however, may well be worth the cost. A basement entry can provide an emergency exit (although it may not satisfy your local building code's requirements for a bedroom egress), and it can greatly facilitate moving large objects in and out of the house. During mild weather, the doors can be left open to aid cross-ventilation in the basement.

ADDING A PREFABRICATED UNIT

Another option for basement access is to install a prefabricated basement entry unit. These units have walls and stairs made of concrete, steel, or lightweight plastic, usually with a steel bulkhead door. Once the hole is dug, a prefabricated entry unit can usually be installed in a single day, often for less than a custom-built entry. Talk with a building contractor about the types of prefabricated units available, or check the Yellow Pages under "Excavating Contractors."

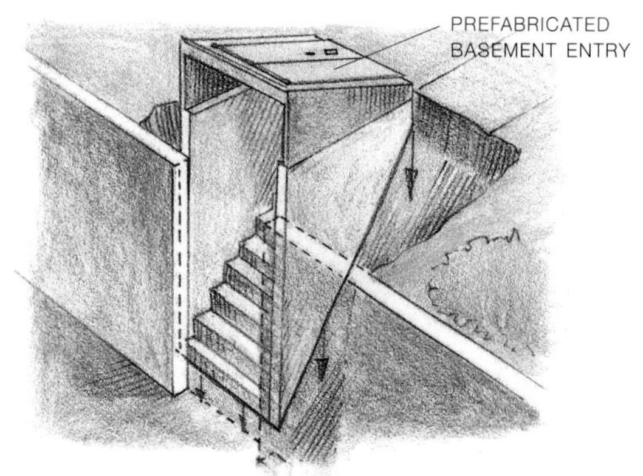

Installing a New Basement Entry

1 DIG THE HOLE
A standard basement entry installation requires that you dig a hole 8 to 10 feet square next to the foundation.

2 ADD THE WALLS
Sidewalls and stairs are then formed with concrete, and a doorway is cut in the foundation. Steel bulkhead doors are installed at the top of the opening, and an exterior-grade passage door is installed in the foundation opening. The hole must then be backfilled and graded.

Basement Windows

Many people don't spend a lot of time thinking about windows when designing a comfortable living space in the basement, but they should. Windows are a critical element in providing natural light and cross-ventilation, and they can also be required by code for emergency access and exit. Not every remodeled basement requires new windows, but many do.

Privacy can become an important issue once your basement becomes a more popular part of the house. If you are thinking of adding windows, try to avoid locating them next to sidewalks or in direct sight of neighboring houses. Add plantings, fences, or curtains to promote privacy. If you want to maximize the amount of sunlight—and solar heat—entering the basement during the cold season, place new windows on the south side of the house.

Installing and enlarging basement windows can be a challenging job for most do-it-yourselfers. Part of the foundation must be removed, which involves cutting concrete or concrete block, and a properly sized header must be added. Before cutting through the foundation, ask a contractor or an engineer to confirm your plans. Cutting the foundation can be messy, difficult work. If you have doubts about your ability to handle the job, let a contractor do it.

A LEGAL EXIT

Building codes usually have stricter requirements for sleeping spaces than for general living spaces. In most cases, if you are planning to create a bedroom in the basement, you will be required to provide an emergency egress window. The egress window serves two purposes: it offers a quick escape from the basement in the event of a fire, and it offers easy access to the space for firefighters and other emergency personnel. Basement fires are not uncommon, and ignoring these requirements can be both dangerous and illegal.

National building codes generally stipulate that a bedroom egress window meet

Minimum Egress Window Requirements

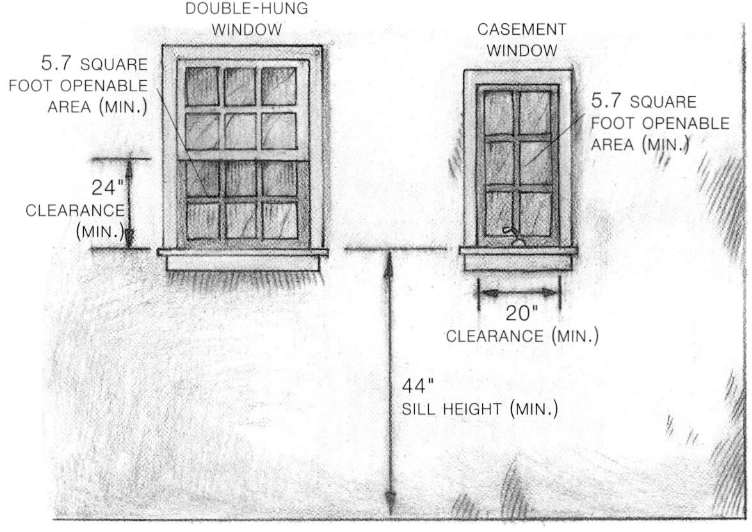

Window Well Requirements

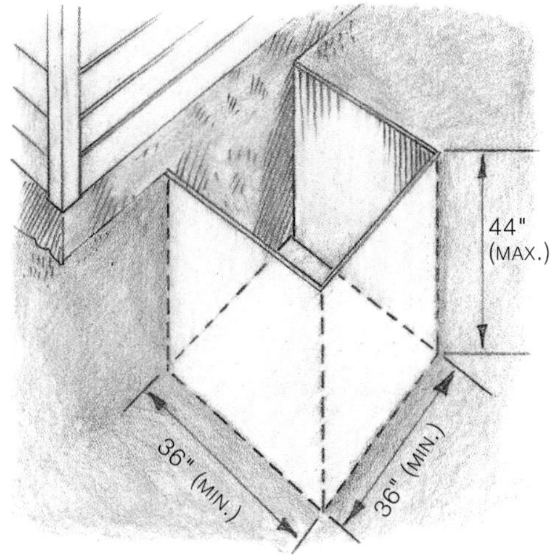

certain requirements. Codes do vary, so check with your local building department for requirements in your area.

In a deep basement, it can be a challenge to satisfy the rule regarding maximum sill height. A very large window well may be needed to accommodate a window that can pass the test. A relatively easy and inexpensive solution is to install a prefabricated window well system. This type of system is made of lightweight plastic with a foam core, and snaps together. The inside panels provide a terraced step, which can hold planters.

INSTALLING WINDOWS

Installing a new window and enlarging an existing one require the same steps. Remove the old window and dig a hole about 4 feet square and at least 6 inches below the bottom of the planned window opening. Mark a cut line on the foundation (inside and out) with chalk or a grease pencil.

Use a circular saw with a masonry blade or rent a gas-powered concrete saw (especially if you will be cutting through solid concrete). Wear eye and ear protection and a dust mask. Make a shallow cut first, then a deeper cut halfway through the wall. Repeat this process on the inside. Use a heavy hammer and masonry chisel to knock out the foundation and smooth the edges.

Build a box for the window using pressure-treated wood. Secure the box to the foundation with construction adhesive and concrete nails, or use a powder-actuated fastener (see page 26). Attach the window to the box. If necessary, fill gaps or cracks around the frame with mortar. Cut and install window trim, then caulk the seams around the trim. Prime and paint the trim.

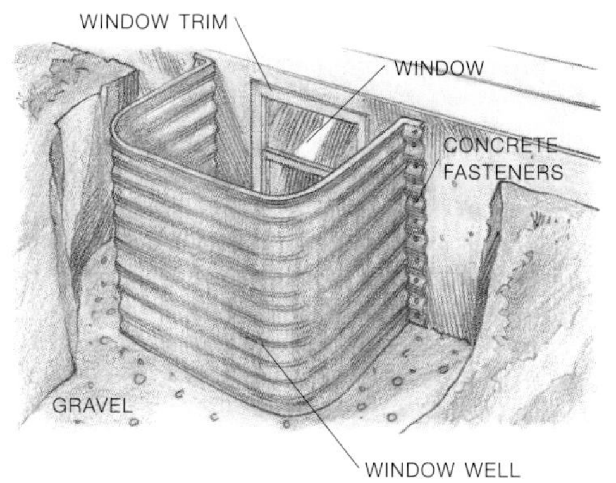

Attach a window well to the foundation with concrete fasteners. Place at least 3 inches of gravel in the bottom of the well, then backfill around the outside of the well with about 6 inches of gravel topped by soil, tamped, and graded.

GLASS BLOCK WINDOWS

Glass block is a wonderful material to use for basement windows (though not for egress windows). It is durable, secure, easy to maintain, and surprisingly simple to install. You can install individual glass blocks yourself provided you are able to assemble blocks to fit the size of your opening.

For many do-it-yourselfers, however, prefabricated glass block panels are a smarter choice. Large home centers usually carry glass block panels in a range of sizes. You can also have panels custom-made to your specifications by a fabricator (check under "Glass" or "Glass Block" in the Yellow Pages). Choose clear glass for maximum light and visibility or frosted glass for more privacy.

Buy or order a panel that is ½ inch less than the length and width of the rough opening. Use small wedges to align the panel in the opening, then mix a small batch of mortar. Slide some mortar under the panel, then let this base harden before you pack the sides with mortar. Slope the mortar edges so that water will drain away. Apply silicone caulk in the joint along the top of the panel.

If your house has a drain system along the footing, you can dig a hole in the bottom of the window well all the way down to the gravel around the footing. Fill the hole with gravel.

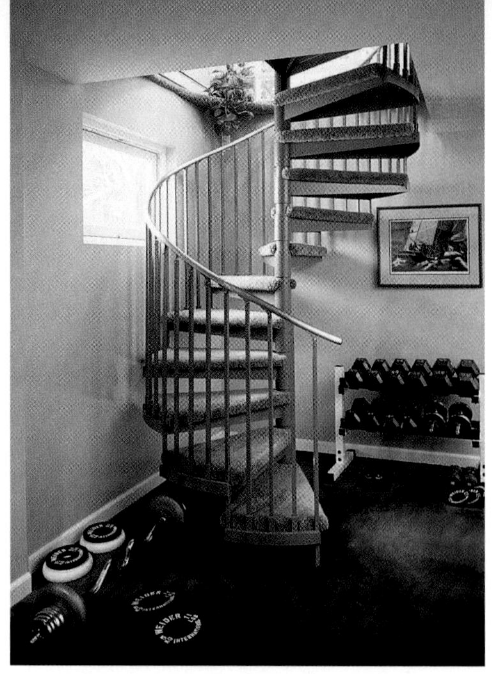

Building Stairs

Basement stairs often fall into the category of "made to be used, not seen." Unlike stairs to upper levels of a house, those to the basement are usually fairly bare bones. In older homes, basement stairs may also be in poor condition. Since the stairs to your converted basement are likely to see an increased traffic load, you should plan to make them as safe and as pleasant to use as possible. You may want to move the existing stairs to another part of the basement to create a more open floor plan.

Building codes often distinguish between primary stairs and secondary stairs in residences. Primary stairs connect two living spaces (first floor to second floor), while secondary stairs connect a living space to an unconverted basement or attic. By turning your basement into living space, you may be required to upgrade the stairs. The following pages will guide you in that effort.

Stair building is a challenging yet extremely rewarding job for the do-it-yourselfer. It used to be one of those tasks that was left to the most experienced member of a carpentry crew, or even given over to a specialist. Modern materials and techniques, however, make it possible for the motivated homeowner to build stairs.

THE PARTS OF A STAIRWAY

The basic frame is composed of a stairwell, which is the framed opening in the upper floor through which the stairs pass, and the stringers (also called carriages), which support the treads and risers. A stairwell usually has doubled headers and doubled trimmers around its perimeter. If you need to frame a new stairwell or enlarge an existing one, make it wide enough to accommodate the width of the stairs plus any wall surfaces you need to add. The stairwell must also be long

Parts of a Stairway

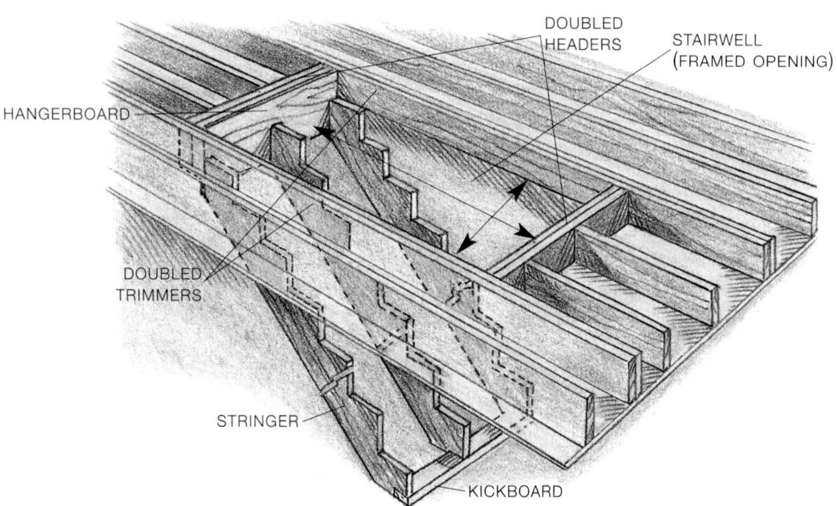

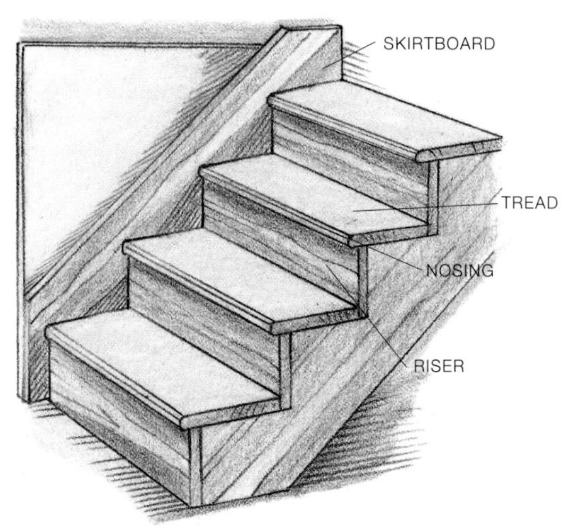

enough to provide adequate headroom. Stringers are attached to a ¾-inch plywood hangerboard at the top and to a 2 x 4 kickboard at the bottom.

Finished stairs consist of treads, which you step on when going up and down, and risers, which are the vertical sections between treads. Risers are not often used on basic basement stairs, but they do add strength and formality to a stairway. "Open-riser" stairs do not include risers; "closed-riser" stairs do. For safety's sake, a closed-riser stair generally must include a nosing, which is the part of a tread that overhangs the riser.

A skirtboard is a piece of trim between the stairs and the wall. It protects the wall from damage and also creates a nicer-looking stairway. If you plan to use a skirtboard, attach it to the wall before installing the treads and risers; otherwise the skirtboard will have to be notched to fit.

CODE REQUIREMENTS

Stairs are subject to a host of regulations, all of which vary from place to place and time to time. Check your local code before you start building or upgrading your stairs. The dimensions given in the illustration at right are typical.

Headroom is measured from the nosing to the ceiling (or any other overhead object). Most codes require a minimum of 80 inches, although 82 to 84 inches is more suitable for tall folks. Stair width is the clear tread width, measured from finish wall to finish wall in an enclosed stairway. The normal minimal width allowed is 36 inches, but 40 to 42 inches is more comfortable.

A handrail is required on stairs with three or more risers. If there are no walls on either side of the stairway, you will need two handrails—one on each side. In an enclosed stairway, you may need a handrail only on one side unless the stairs are especially wide. But, again, these are minimal requirements; placing handrails on both sides adds a level of safety and comfort regardless of whether or not they are required. The size of a handrail is usually spelled out in the building code, as is the distance a handrail must be located from a wall (to ensure that it can be grasped easily).

Tread depth is often stipulated in terms of unit run, and riser height as unit rise. Unit run is the horizontal distance from the face of one riser to the face of the next, and you are usually required to make that distance a minimum of 10 inches (11 inches is preferred). Unit rise is a vertical measurement from the top of one tread to the top of the next. While codes may allow a maximum rise of 7¾ inches (or even more), most people are more comfortable with a 7-inch step up or down. Though the nosing is a part of the tread, it is often addressed separately in the code. Typically, nosings must be between ¾ inch and 1¼ inches.

Common Stairway Dimensions

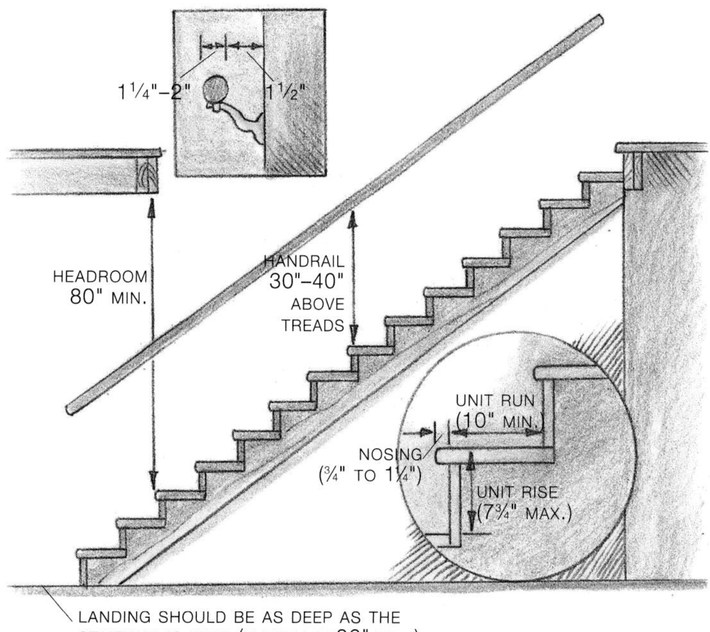

CALCULATING STAIR DIMENSIONS

Stair safety demands careful planning and calculation. Building codes require that rise and run be nearly identical from step to step (you may be allowed up to a ⅜-inch difference in height between risers, but uniformity should be your goal). By following the steps below in order and checking your math at each stage, you will be able to find the right formula for your stairs. Working in decimals rather than fractions (see chart) will give you the best results. Note that the following directions use dimensions from an example stairway to help you understand the process; for your own stairs, you will need to use your own dimensions.

Calculating Stair Dimensions

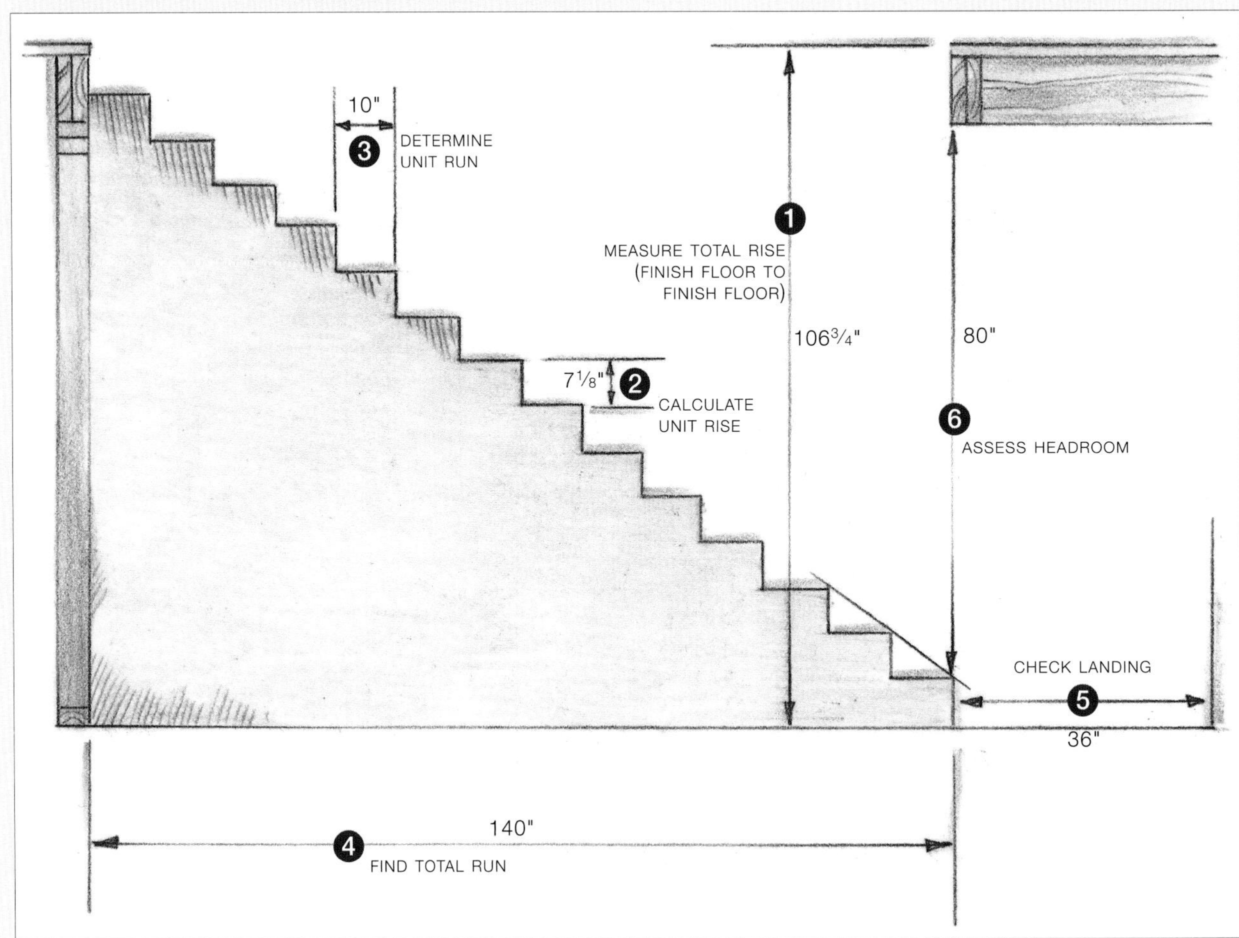

Converting Fractions to Decimals

1/32	0.0313	3/8	0.3750	23/32	0.7188
1/16	0.0625	7/16	0.4375	3/4	0.7500
3/32	0.0938	15/32	0.4688	13/16	0.8125
1/8	0.1250	1/2	0.5000	27/32	0.8438
3/16	0.1875	17/32	0.5313	7/8	0.8750
7/32	0.2188	9/16	0.5625	15/16	0.9375
1/4	0.2500	19/32	0.5938	31/32	0.9688
5/16	0.3125	5/8	0.6250	1	1.0
11/32	0.3438	11/16	0.6875		

1 MEASURE TOTAL RISE

The total rise is the distance the stairs must travel vertically, and should be measured from finish floor to finish floor. For the most accurate results, set your measuring tape alongside a plumb-bob line. Measure from each corner of the stairwell; if the measurements differ, use the shortest dimension as your total rise and plan to shim under the stringers when they are installed. In our example, the total rise is 106¾ inches.

2 CALCULATE UNIT RISE

The unit rise is the height of one step. Codes typically mandate that the maximum step height be 7¾ inches, so divide the total rise by this amount:

106.75 divided by 7.75 = 13.77

Round this figure up to 14, which is the minimum number of risers the stairs will require. Now go back and divide the total rise by the number of risers:

106.75 divided by 14 = 7.625

This staircase could be constructed with 14 risers, each rising 7.625 (7⅝) inches. But that is only one option. Many people find a riser height closer to 7 inches to be more comfortable. By adding another riser to the formula,

106.75 divided by 15 = 7.117

you come up with a better solution. Before making a final decision, however, find the unit run and total run, then see if you have adequate headroom and landing space.

3 DETERMINE UNIT RUN

Unit run, or tread depth, is measured from the face of one riser to the face of the next. You may be required to maintain a minimal unit run of 9 inches, but 10 to 11 inches is safer. Stair builders often refer to the following formulas to match tread depth and riser height:

rise plus run = 17 to 18
rise times run = 70 to 75

Apply these formulas to your target riser height (7.117, or 7⅛, inches):

7⅛ plus 10 = 17⅛
7.117 times 10 = 71.17

Both results fall within the formula ranges, making a 10-inch unit run a good choice.

4 FIND TOTAL RUN

Now multiply the unit run by the total number of treads to find the total run. Stairs have one less tread than riser (the bottom landing effectively serves as one tread), so with 15 risers the stairway will have 14 treads: 14 treads times a 10-inch unit run results in a total run of 140.

5 CHECK THE LANDING

The landing, the space between the bottom riser and the wall, should be at least 36 inches. If you find that your calculated total run leaves too little room for a landing, you will have to adjust your rise/run formula. Try reducing the unit run, reducing the number of treads, or reducing both to make the stairs fit. If the numbers still don't work, you may have to build a different type of stairs; for this, you may want to talk with a contractor.

6 ASSESS HEADROOM

Once you've determined where the stairs will end, you can measure the clear space between the stairs and the ceiling, called headroom. Headroom is often measured from an imaginary line running across the nosing of each tread vertically to the closest part of the ceiling or other overhead object. Codes usually insist on a minimum of 80 inches of headroom. If you find that your stair design has too little headroom, try reducing the unit run or the number of treads. If that doesn't work, talk with a contractor about enlarging the stairwell.

Know Your Cuts

A novice stairbuilder can get lost in the maze of cuts required to produce an accurate stringer. Take a few moments to study this illustration before you pick up your saw.

PLUMB AND LEVEL The top and bottom of the stringer require finish cuts that carry the layout lines to the edge of the board: The level cut is along an extended tread line, while the plumb cut extends the riser.

DROP THE STRINGER The bottom of the stringer must be reduced by the thickness of one finish tread; otherwise, the first step would be higher than the others, and the top step would be lower. If you are using 1-inch-thick treads, for example, cut an additional 1 inch from the bottom of the tread.

KICKBOARD NOTCH Finally, the bottom of the treads are secured by means of a 2 x 4 kickboard on the floor. Cut a notch to fit over the kickboard.

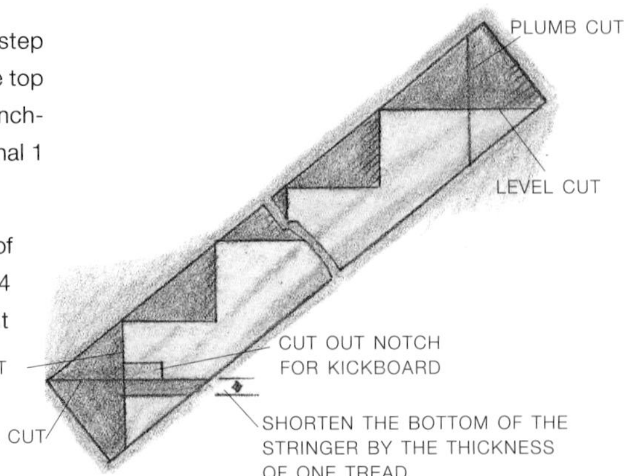

PREPARE THE STRINGERS

Stringers, or carriages, are the backbone of the stairs, and are usually made with 2 x 12s. You will want to choose stringer boards carefully; look for clear, straight lumber that is relatively free of knots and splits. If the ends are split, and they often are on lumber this size, you will need to trim them.

Stairs that are wider than 30 inches are usually required to have three stringers. Even if you do not face that obligation, you will find that a three-stringer stair is much stronger than a two-stringer stair, especially in an open riser design (risers add support to the stairs).

Calculate Stringer Length

Before buying lumber for stringers, you will need to calculate how long the boards should be. The most accurate way to find this dimension is to use a calculator and the Pythagorean theorem ($A^2 + B^2 = C^2$), where A is the total rise, B is the total run, and C is the board length.

A simpler way to approximate the length of board needed is to use a framing square and tape measure, as shown below, and assume that 1 inch on the framing square equals 1 foot. Convert the total rise and total run into feet (106¾ inches equals 8⅞ feet total rise; 140 inches equals 11⅔ feet total run). Measure the distance between these marks on the framing square (about 14¾ inches), and convert that to feet. Since dimension lumber is normally sold in 2-foot increments, you would need 16-foot boards to make these stringers.

In truth, most standard basement stairs can be built with 16-foot stringers (if the ends are split, though, you should buy 18-footers and trim them).

Lay Out the Stringer

You will need a framing square and stair buttons (or stair gauges) to lay out the first stringer. Set one button on the outside edge of the long arm of the square to the run depth (10 inches in our example) and the other one on the outside edge of the short arm to the riser height (7⅛ inches here). With the stringer flat across sawhorses, place the square as shown below and mark along the outside edges. Slide the square down the stringer so it aligns perfectly with the previous mark, and mark again.

Note that the bottom of the stringer needs to be shortened by the thickness of one tread. If it isn't, the first step will be too high and the top step too low. Set a piece of the tread stock along the bottom cut-off line on the stringer and draw another line. The stringer should be cut off at this line.

Cut the Stringer

Clamp the stringer to the sawhorses and use a circular saw to cut up to the spot where the tread and riser lines meet. Cutting beyond this line with a circular saw will weaken the stringer. Instead, finish the cut with a handsaw, as shown above.

Cut the Kickboard Notch

Trace the outline of a 2 x 4 along the bottom front corner of the stringer. Cut along the lines to create a notch for the kickboard.

Set the cut stringer in the stairwell and check the fit. If you are satisfied, use the cut stringer as a template to mark the layout on the other two boards before cutting them.

continued on page 180

Play It Safe

Cutting stringers takes time, and buying lumber for stringers takes money. Before you commit to either effort, it might be wise to take a few minutes to double-check your calculations.

A simple way to do this is to make a story pole out of a straight, long 2 x 4. Use dividers set to the unit rise on your stairs, or cut a piece of scrap wood to that size. Starting from the edge, carefully mark the 2 x 4 in riser increments. Set the story pole in the stairwell (make sure it is plumb), and check that the top mark aligns with the finished floor of the upper level. If it doesn't, you may need to calculate the unit rise again.

Installing Stringers

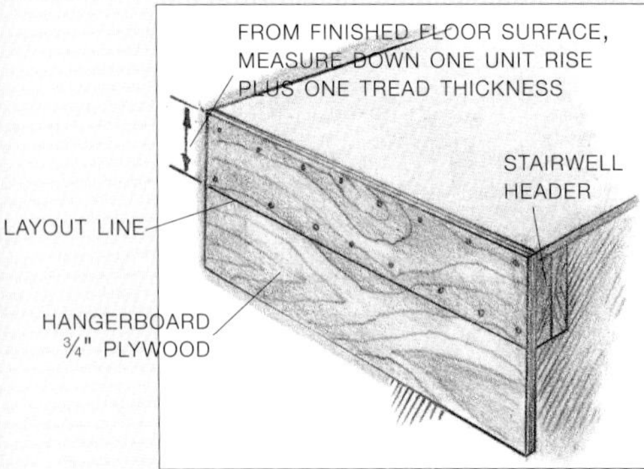

1 ATTACH THE HANGERBOARD Nail the hangerboard to the header in the stairwell with 8d nails. Measure down from the finished floor height one unit rise (7⅛ inches in our example) plus the thickness of the tread and make a level mark across the hangerboard. The stringers will be installed along this line.

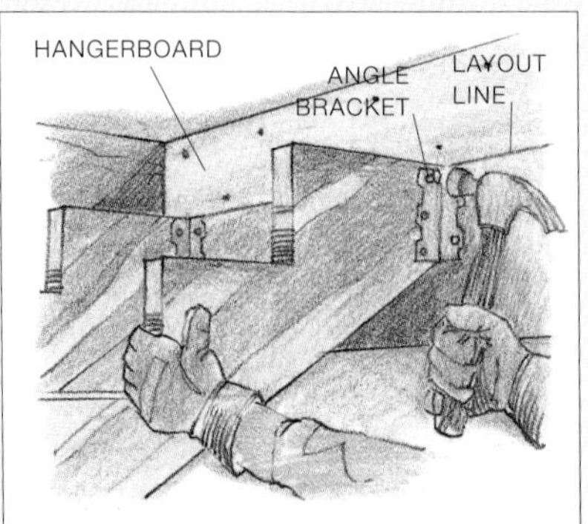

2 HANG THE STRINGERS Attach each stringer along the layout line with a single nail (if possible, drive the nail through the back of the hangerboard into the stringer). Center the middle stringer in the stairwell. Check the fit. The stringers should lie flat against the hangerboard and flat on the floor. Adjust the stringers for plumb and level, then attach metal angle brackets to the stringers and hangerboard. If there is a wall on one or both sides, you can nail the stringers directly to the wall framing instead.

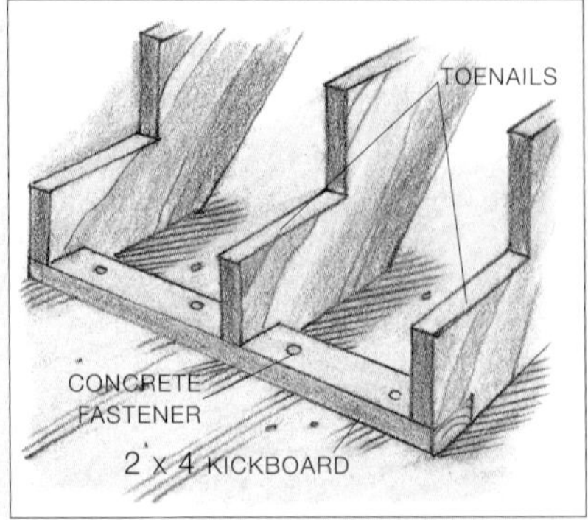

3 ANCHOR THE BOTTOM Cut a 2 x 4 kickboard to length. Align and space the stringers at the bottom, then slip the kickboard into the notches. Use concrete fasteners, or a powder-actuated fastener, to attach the kickboard to the concrete floor. Toenail the stringers to the kickboard.

INSTALL THE STRINGERS

The easiest way to install stringers is to use a hangerboard at the top and a kickboard at the bottom, as shown above. The hangerboard is a piece of ¾-inch plywood, cut long enough to fit in the rough opening and about two risers wide (14 to 15 inches).

ATTACH TREADS AND RISERS

Treads for basement stairs can be made out of 2 x 6s or solid hardwood. With 2 x 6 treads, you may want to use 1 x 8 pine for the risers. If you use hardwood for treads (e.g., oak or maple), you should use the same wood in the risers. Cut and install the risers first, then the treads. Use glue and 2 ¼-inch screws to attach 2 x 4 treads; use glue and 1½-inch screws to attach 1 x 8 risers; use glue and finish nails for hardwood treads and risers.

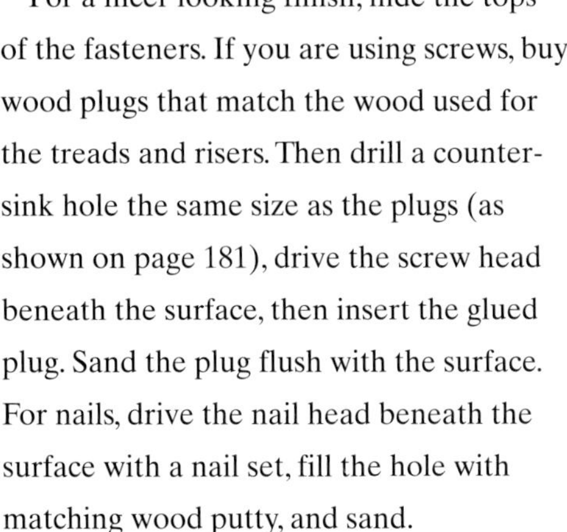

For a nicer looking finish, hide the tops of the fasteners. If you are using screws, buy wood plugs that match the wood used for the treads and risers. Then drill a countersink hole the same size as the plugs (as shown on page 181), drive the screw head beneath the surface, then insert the glued plug. Sand the plug flush with the surface. For nails, drive the nail head beneath the surface with a nail set, fill the hole with matching wood putty, and sand.

If the stairs are open on one or both sides, you might want to let the treads overhang the stringer by an inch or so. It looks nicer and decreases the chance of splitting the treads when attaching them. You can also dress up the edges a bit with a router and round-over bit. The treads on closed-riser stairs are usually required to have a nosing, as shown on page 175.

If the stairs are closed on one or both sides, you may want to install a skirtboard, which protects the drywall and gives stairs a more finished look (see pages 174–175). A skirtboard is usually made of 1 x 12 hardwood, pine, or medium-density fiberboard (MDF). It is set between the drywall and the treads, and nailed to the wall framing. Treads and risers are then cut to fit snugly against the skirtboard.

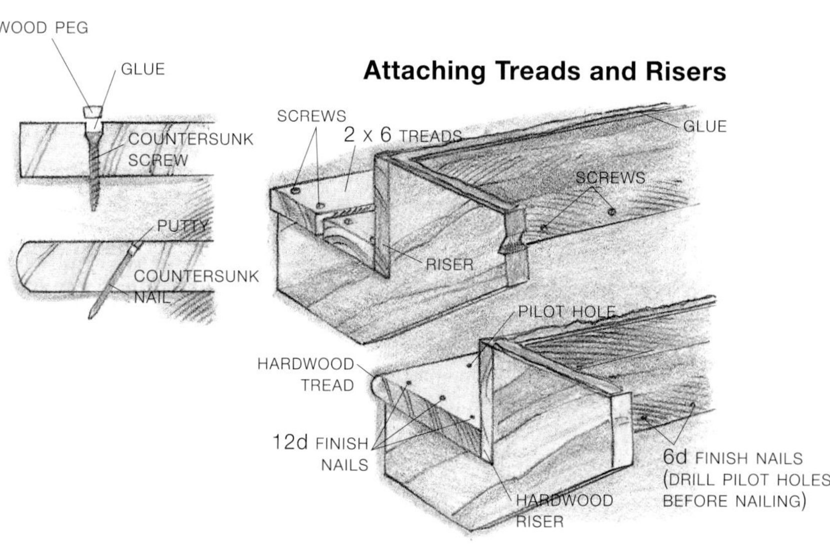

INSTALL HANDRAILS

Your stairs are not complete until you have installed at least one handrail. For stairs sitting next to walls, you can use simple handrails available at lumberyards and home centers. Some handrails come with brackets already attached; otherwise, brackets are screwed to the underside of the handrail. The brackets must then be secured with screws long enough to penetrate at least one inch into the wall studs or blocking. Your handrail may have to be cut to length.

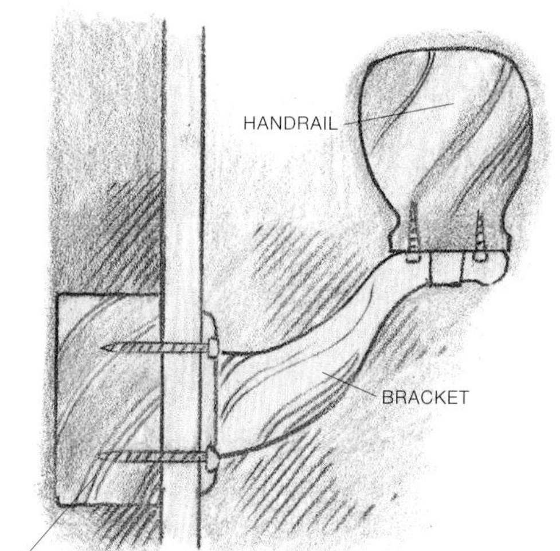

The open side or sides of a stairway should be enclosed with a railing system, or balustrade. Many styles are possible, but for simplicity as well as good looks it is hard to beat the design shown at right. Just be sure to maintain the handrail height dictated by your building code.

With this style, three 4 x 4 posts are bolted to the stringers to provide support for the railing. The posts must be perfectly plumb. Cut 1½-inch-deep notches in the posts by making a series of passes with a circular saw. Then clean out the waste with a chisel. Next, attach a 2 x 4 bottom rail and a 2 x 6 top rail to the posts with nails or screws. Nail 2 x 2 balusters to the rails with 8d finishing nails, maintaining a maximum spacing between balusters of 4 inches. If you are required to do so, nail a 2-inch-wide cap on the top rail.

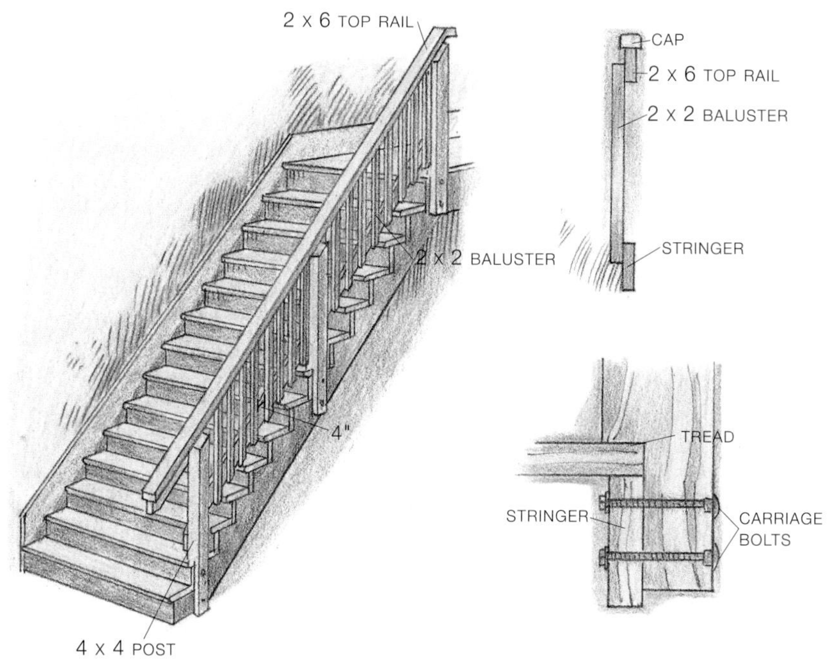

Finishing Basement Walls

Basement walls can be finished in any number of ways. The choice is often based partly on function and partly on aesthetics. Just keep in mind that a finished basement wall should not be viewed as a solution to moisture problems. If you have a damp basement, take all necessary steps to eliminate the source of the problem before you decide on the finished look of the walls (see pages 153–161).

In addition to function and aesthetics, your choice of wall finish may also depend on where you live. In a warm, dry climate you may be happiest with walls that have been painted with a good quality masonry paint. This approach can maintain the basement as a cool escape from the warmer parts of the house. In cooler, moister climates, however, you are more likely to want an added measure of waterproofing on your walls along with insulation to keep the basement comfortable.

Basement partition walls need no special treatment, but the foundation walls around the perimeter often do. That's because the material they're usually made of is concrete or concrete block and because they are in contact with the outside and its ever-changing climate. To add both insulation and a more finished look, you will probably want to build a stud wall.

Basement floors can be insulated and finished much like garage floors (see pages 112–113 for techniques).

ABOVE: Color adds new life to this basement closet turned office alcove.

BELOW: Built-ins warm this potentially "cold" basement space with glowing wood tones.

Building a Stud Wall

Building a 2 x 4 stud wall around the perimeter of the basement offers many benefits. It provides cavities for batt insulation, room to hide electrical wiring and plumbing pipes, and a solid backing for drywall or other surface material. And since masonry walls often aren't straight, building a separate wall structure allows you to create a smooth, flat surface. To save a few dollars and a few square feet, you could frame the walls with 2 x 3s, although doing so would reduce the amount of insulation you could put in the wall. See pages 22–27 for a full discussion of wall framing.

When framing walls over concrete floors, use pressure-treated lumber for the sole plate and for any other wood piece that will be in direct contact with masonry.

Adding a Vapor Retardant

Most construction specialists agree that a basement stud wall should include a vapor retardant, usually a layer of 6-mil polyethylene. But there is little consensus on where to locate it. One school argues that it should be placed against the masonry wall to keep moisture from the soil outside from getting in the basement. To be most effective, this approach also requires that the walls be coated with a waterproofer before the vapor retardant is installed.

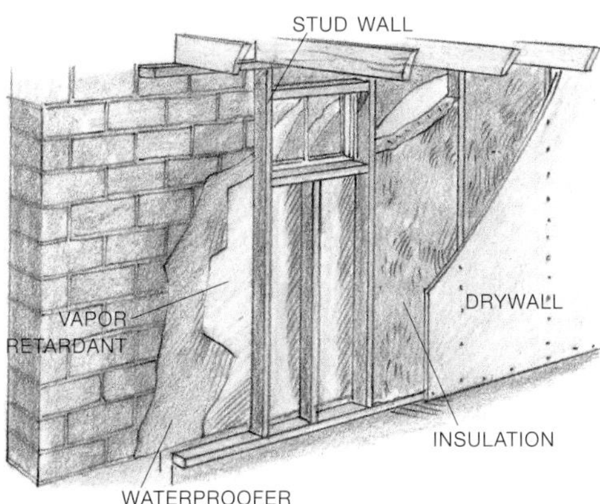

Another school maintains that the basement should be treated just like the upper floors, where the vapor retardant is usually placed on the warm side (normally the inside) of the framed wall. With either

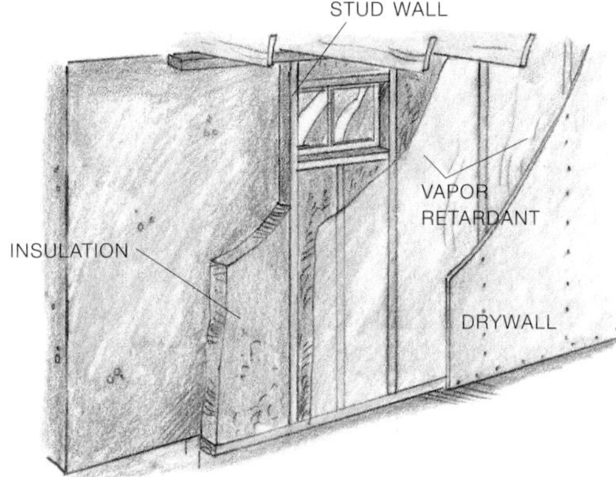

approach, some contractors favor leaving a 1- to 2-inch air gap between the stud wall and the basement wall to allow any moisture that finds its way between the walls to evaporate.

Wherever you locate the vapor retardant, the success of the approach may depend on your specific circumstances. Climate, soil conditions, and the construction of your house (especially the foundation) can make a big difference. If the exterior of your foundation was waterproofed and drains well, especially if it is solid concrete, then moisture is less likely to pass through the wall. In this case, placing the vapor retardant on the warm side of the stud wall makes the most sense.

If, on the other hand, you are not as confident that moisture can be kept out of the basement walls, even though you've done as much as you reasonably can to control the situation, then it might be better to waterproof the inside of the basement wall and cover it with a vapor retardant before building the wall.

Unfortunately, there is no standardized answer. Your local building code may decide the matter for you, but if it doesn't and you are too uncertain to take any action, take some time to talk with builders, designers, and knowledgeable folks at your building supply store to see what local customs are.

Insulation Tip

When insulating a basement wall, be sure to add insulation in the rim (or band) joist, which is the open section at the top of the foundation. Cut pieces of fiberglass batts or rigid boards to fit snugly in the spaces.

Installing Rigid Foam Insulation

1 ATTACH THE BOARDS Use an adhesive to attach the boards to the walls. Cut the boards to fit as snugly as possible around pipes and other obstructions, and fill any gaps with caulk or spray foam. Be sure to use products recommended by the foam board manufacturer for sealing and gluing.

2 ADD FURRING STRIPS With the foam board in place, you can attach furring strips with fasteners driven through the board and into the masonry wall, or proceed to build an insulated stud wall.

Using Rigid Foam

Another insulation option is to place rigid polystyrene foam board directly on the basement walls, as shown above. A big advantage of this approach is that it keeps moist interior air from coming into contact with the cold foundation surface, thus eliminating a major source of basement condensation.

Basement Wall Systems

Manufacturers of rigid insulation have introduced products designed specifically for use on the walls of basements being converted to living space. One product is billed as a "Basement Finishing System." It utilizes prefabricated wall panels that offer built-in insulation, vapor protection, and noise suppression. PVC channels provide room for wiring runs, plus the surface is prefinished and you can choose from several types of molding. The wall panels can be easily removed as needed for inspection. However, the system is not a do-it-yourself option; you will need to hire a factory-trained installer.

If a wall system is not to your liking, there are other products that are available too and can easily be handled by the homeowner. These include rigid insulation boards with integrated channels that allow 1 x 3 furring strips to be installed flush with the face of the board.

One product, made with extruded polystyrene (XPS), is available in 2-foot by 8-foot boards with recessed edges. Another, made with expanded polystyrene (EPS), comes in 4-foot by 8-foot boards with channels located 16 inches on center. With either product, you install the boards by driving masonry screws through the furring strips, then use regular drywall screws driven into the furring strips to install your finish wall surface.

A Basement Bathroom

For many homeowners, a new bathroom is right at the top of their wish list for a basement conversion. Given the basement's ready access to drain, waste, and supply lines, many assume that plumbing a new basement will be easy. Life is not always so convenient, however, and adding a bathroom or other features that require new plumbing in a basement can often be quite a challenge. Once any drainage issues are dealt with, you will be able to add additional plumbing and bathroom fixtures as you would in any other space. For more information on plumbing, see pages 28–32 and 95–99. For more detailed information, see Sunset's *Complete Home Plumbing.*

DEALING WITH DRAINAGE

Drain lines are the primary obstacle when adding new plumbing to a basement; because they depend on gravity, they must be installed with adequate slope, and this can be difficult. The first step in adding a bathroom should be tackling the drain and vent systems.

If your main drain line exits your house beneath the basement slab, you may be able to tie into it with new drain lines from a toilet, sink, and shower. Tying in will require removing part of the slab—a messy but not particularly difficult job. You may also want to move some existing drain lines to fit the layout of your bathroom.

Basement Drainage

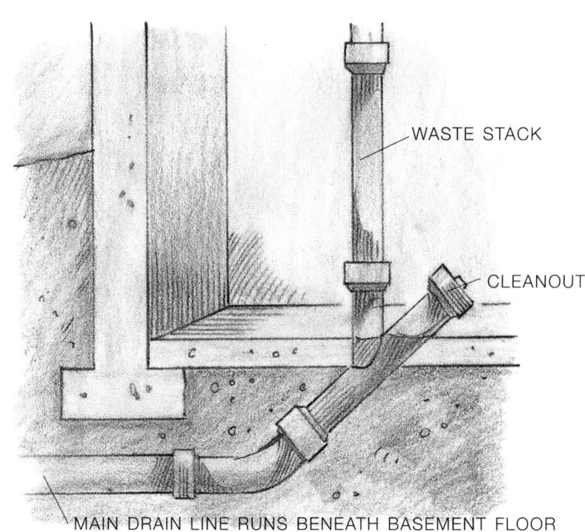

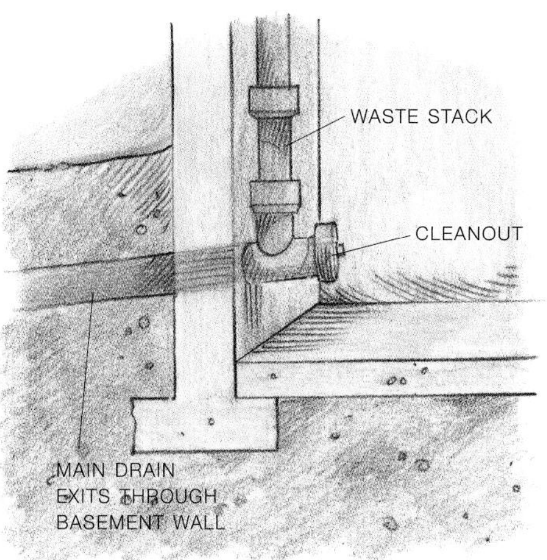

If, however, the main drain line exits your house through the basement wall, you will not be able to rely on gravity to handle the drain lines. Instead, you will need to rely on mechanical means to establish functioning drains (see page 187).

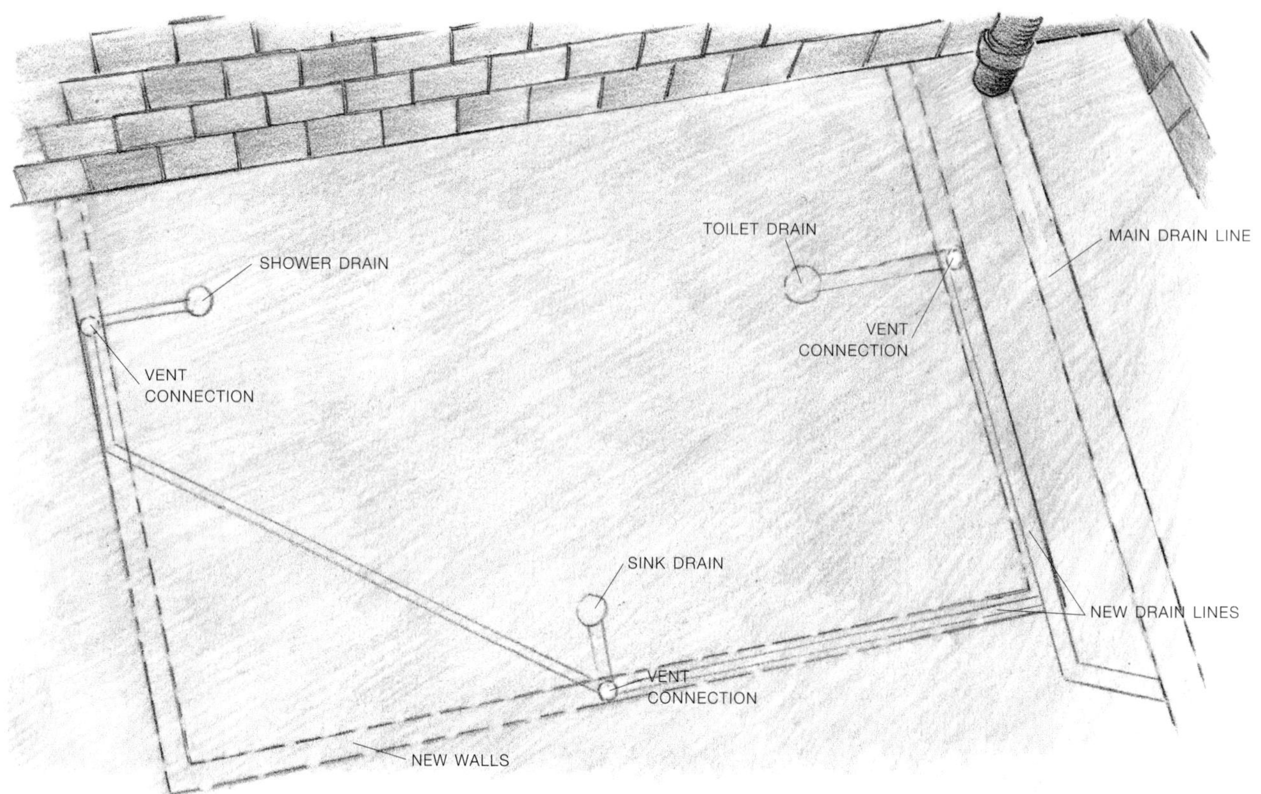

Moving a Drain Line

Try to locate the new bathroom as close as possible to the main drain line, so that it will be easier to maintain a slope of ¼ inch per foot. If possible, find suitable spots for the fixtures before situating walls and doors. Use chalk or tape to mark the location of the main drain line and to lay out new lines.

To cut through the concrete slab, start by using a circular saw with a masonry or diamond blade to score lines along the planned opening. Make two or more cuts, increasing the depth on each pass. You will make a lot of noise and kick up a lot of dust cutting through concrete, so be sure to wear leather gloves, eye and ear protection, and a dust mask. Break up the concrete with a sledgehammer or a rented electric jackhammer. (If you use a jackhammer, take care not to cut into the drain line!) Remove the concrete and dig out the dirt around the drain line.

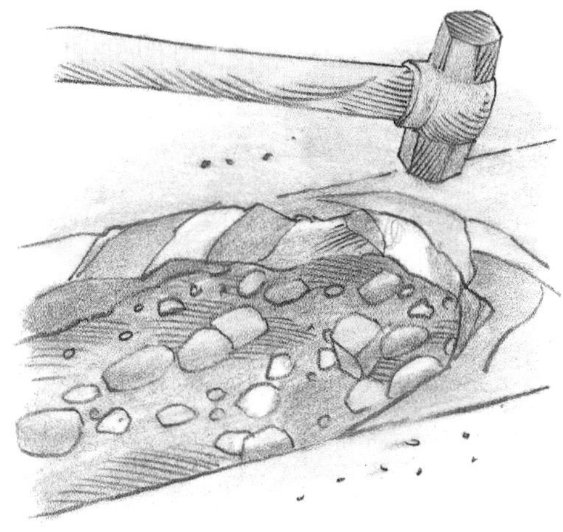

The next step is to remove a section of the main drain line and install a Y fitting, which will tie in with the drain lines from the new fixtures. For information on cutting and joining pipe, see pages 31–32. Use PVC or ABS plastic pipe for the new lines. Cut drain and vent stubs long enough to rest above the slab, and place temporary caps on them to keep sewer gas from escaping into the basement.

Venting New Fixtures

Every new plumbing fixture must be vented, but there are several ways to run the vent lines. First, you can create a new vent stack that serves only the fixtures in the basement, and run it outside and up along the side of the house to the roof. Second, you can route a new vent stack through the interior of the house, perhaps through closets or other out-of-sight locations, then through the attic and out the roof. Or, third, you can tie into the existing vent if it is near the location of your new bathroom.

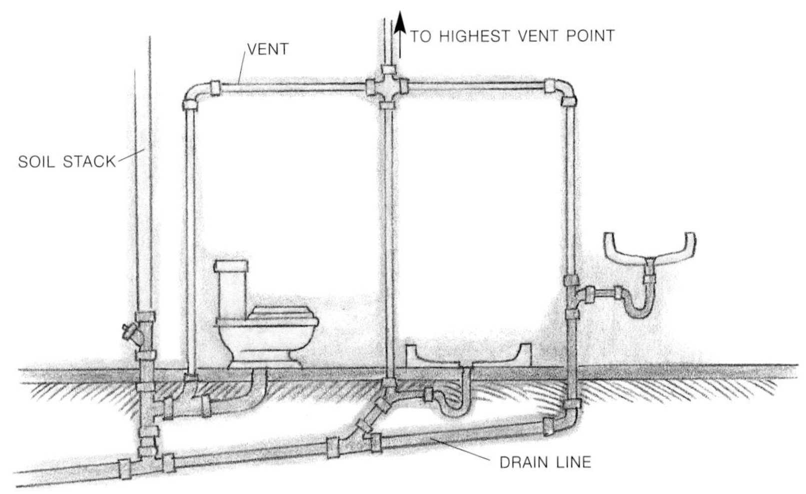

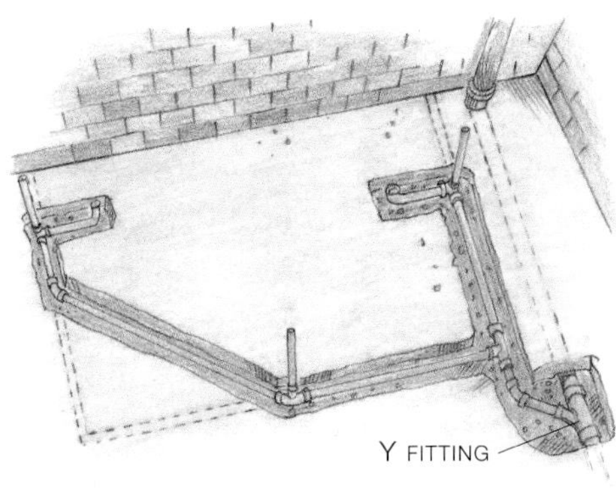

The area around the shower drain must remain accessible after the concrete is patched so that the trap can be connected. Your local plumbing supplier may sell plastic tub boxes for this purpose; or you could build a 1-foot-square wood frame around the drain. You should also wrap the stub for the toilet drain with a cardboard sleeve, available at plumbing suppliers. This will keep concrete far enough away to allow the toilet flange to fit.

After the new plumbing has been inspected, return dirt and gravel to surround the pipes, then add a 3-inch layer of concrete to patch the hole. Smooth the concrete with a 2 x 4 board, working it back and forth to level the surface, then smooth with a steel trowel. You are now ready to frame the bathroom walls, run new water supply lines, and install the new fixtures.

Flushing Uphill?

If your drain pipe leaves the house above the floor of the basement, you obviously cannot rely on gravity to drain the lines. But you can connect toilets to overhead drain lines by using a sewage ejector. Sewage ejectors pump waste up through a discharge pipe to the main drain line.

There are two types of sewage ejectors. An in-floor system requires that part of the slab be cut out to make room for a basin, which contains the pump, and piping. An above-ground system is usually easier to install, although it can look a bit odd. The pump tank rests at floor level, requiring that the toilet be installed on a platform about 6 inches high to make room for the waste line. The tank can be hidden behind a wall near the toilet. Check with a plumbing supplier for more information.

A Basement Kitchen

A basement kitchen can be a convenient step-saver—or a real necessity. Kitchen design is a well-honed craft, and you will almost certainly find your new kitchen easier to use if you apply some of the basic design principles outlined below.

Kitchen Layouts

Designers evaluate kitchen efficiency by means of the work triangle. The three legs of the triangle connect the refrigerator, sink, and range (or cooktop). An efficient work triangle greatly reduces the steps a cook must take during meal preparation; the ideal sum of the three legs is 26 feet or less, with no leg shorter than 4 feet nor longer than 9 feet. The distance between the sink and cooktop should be the shortest leg. The work triangle should not be interrupted by traffic flow through the kitchen.

The concept of the work triangle is rooted in kitchen studies done in the 1950s. Today, that concept is being challenged by two-cook layouts, elaborate island work centers, peninsulas, and the presence of specialized appliances. But the work triangle still offers a valuable starting point for planning kitchen efficiency.

Kitchen Basics

An ideal floor plan eases the cook's work and enables others to enjoy the kitchen's warmth and fragrance without getting in the way. Though the dimensions of your room and your particular needs will determine the final plan, you will probably want to consider some of the following kitchen basics.

Where to eat To plan an efficient eating area, think first about how you'll use the space. If the kitchen will be used for quick snacks and an occasional meal, all you probably need is a seating counter on the outside of a peninsula or an island with stools or chairs that tuck underneath. For every-day meal use, however, you will probably want a separate table, located out of the main traffic flow. To conserve space, consider a banquette of fixed, upholstered seats or a bench.

Cooking Small

If space is tight, or if you just need a small kitchenette in the basement for occasional use, you may want to look into manufactured mini-kitchens. You can find models that include a miniature sink, refrigerator, microwave oven, and cabinets, yet fit inside a typical closet. You can also shop for small-sized fixtures and appliances aimed at apartment dwellers and college students.

Sample Kitchen Layouts

An ideal floor plan makes a kitchen more convenient and efficient. The floor plans shown here utilize the space well and incorporate an efficient work area. The dimensions of your room and your particular needs will determine the final plan.

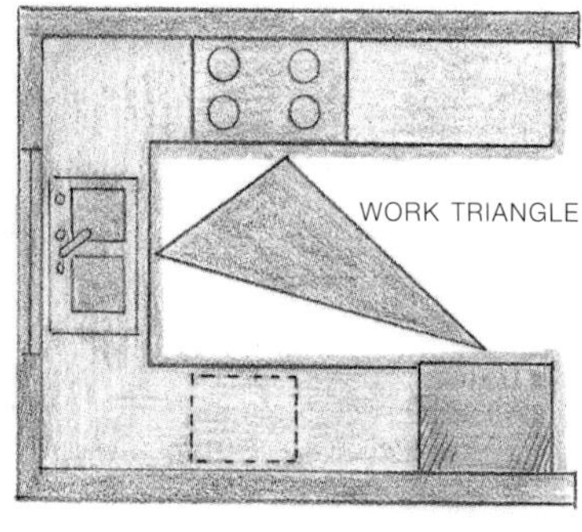

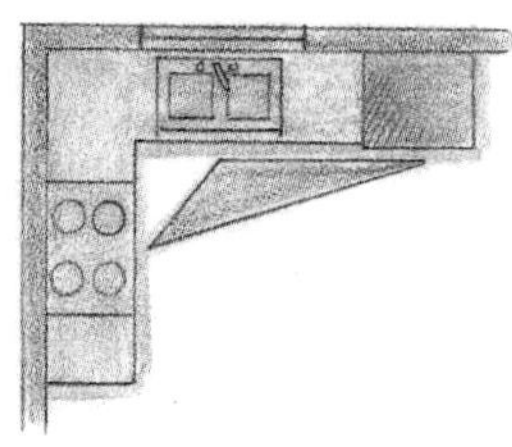

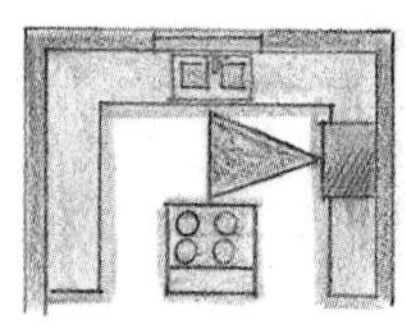

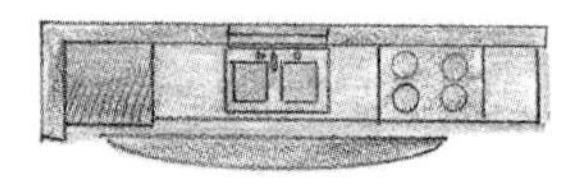

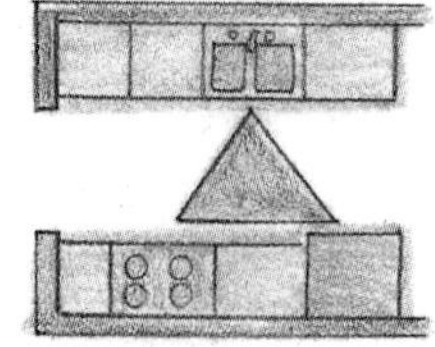

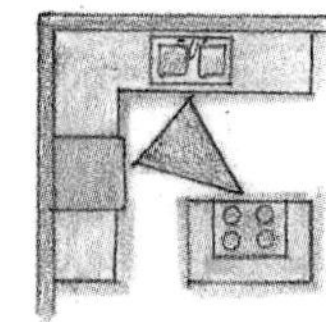

Heights and clearances The standard minimum clearances for kitchens ensure enough space for a busy cook as well as occasional foot traffic. They also provide enough door clearance for unhindered access to cabinets and appliances, and room for diners to sit comfortably.

Lighting Good kitchen lighting works together with an efficient layout and modern fixtures and appliances to create a safe and pleasant place to cook and dine. A good lighting plan provides shadowless, glare-free illumination for the entire room as well as bright, uniform light for specific tasks. Decide early on in your kitchen design where you want to place light fixtures and what kind of light you want them to provide.

Plumbing Even a modest kitchenette will require a water supply and drains. The more complex you wish to make the kitchen, the more new plumbing you are likely to have to install. The fundamentals of basement plumbing are covered on pages 185–187. If you are unable to tie into existing drain lines, you will have to explore the various sewage ejector pump systems available. To simplify construction and keep costs down, you may want to think hard about the need for a dishwasher, garbage disposal, and elaborate fixtures and appliances in your basement kitchen.

Wiring Electrical codes have very specific requirements for kitchens. Plug-in outlets and switches for small appliances and a refrigerator must be served by a minimum of two 20-amp circuits. Light fixtures do not connect to these circuits, but share one or more 15-amp circuits. Any outlets on the countertop should be protected with a ground-fault circuit interrupter (GFCI).

If you are planning to install both a dishwasher and a disposal, you will need a separate 20-amp circuit for each. Most electric ranges use an individual 50-amp, 120/240-volt major appliance circuit. A wall oven and a separate cooktop may share a 50-amp circuit. For more information on wiring, see pages 33–45.

Cabinets It's possible to spend a small fortune on kitchen cabinets, but you don't need to. If you are particularly handy or motivated, you could build some simple cabinets and open shelves of your own. Many good books on kitchen cabinet construction are available, as is good quality hardware. Ready-to-assemble (RTA) or knock-down (KD) cabinets are an excellent choice for those who want to save money and don't mind putting the cabinets together themselves.

If you prefer to use manufactured cabinets, compare prices and products at several home centers, lumberyards, and kitchen-products dealers. Standard-sized stock cabinets are usually the least expensive option.

Standard Heights

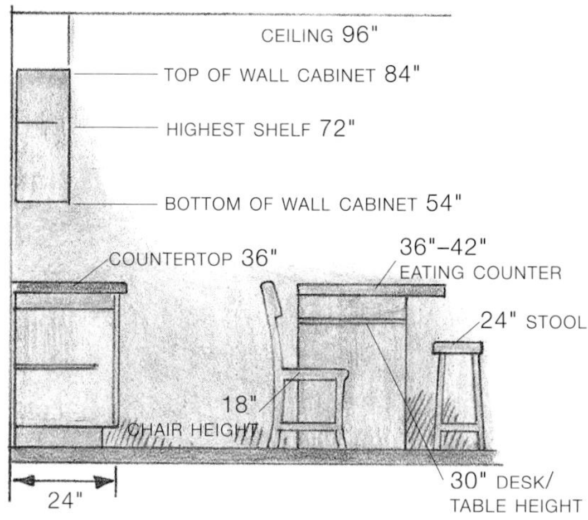

Standard Clearances

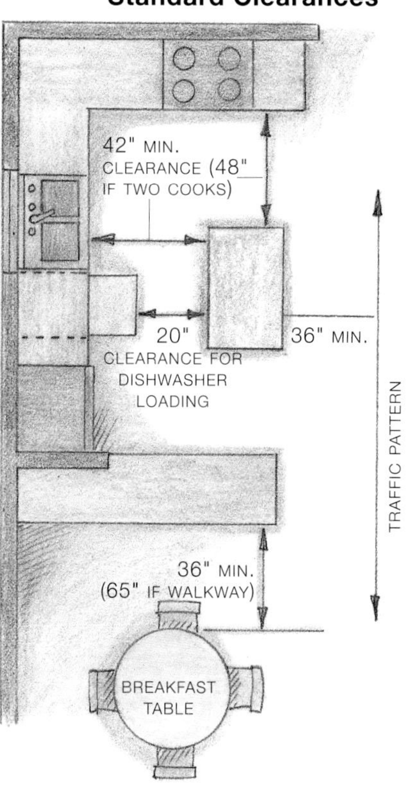

INDEX

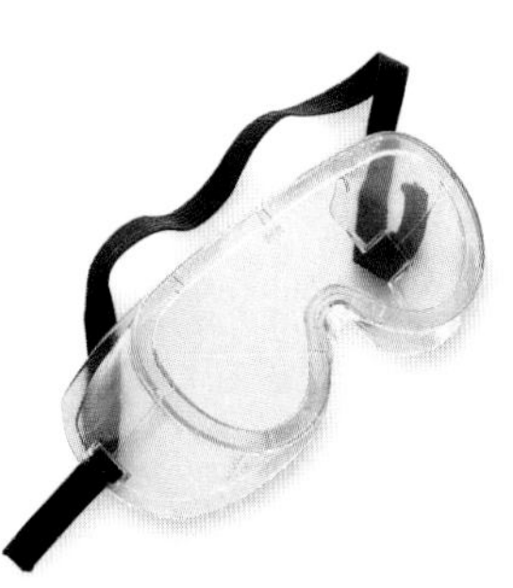

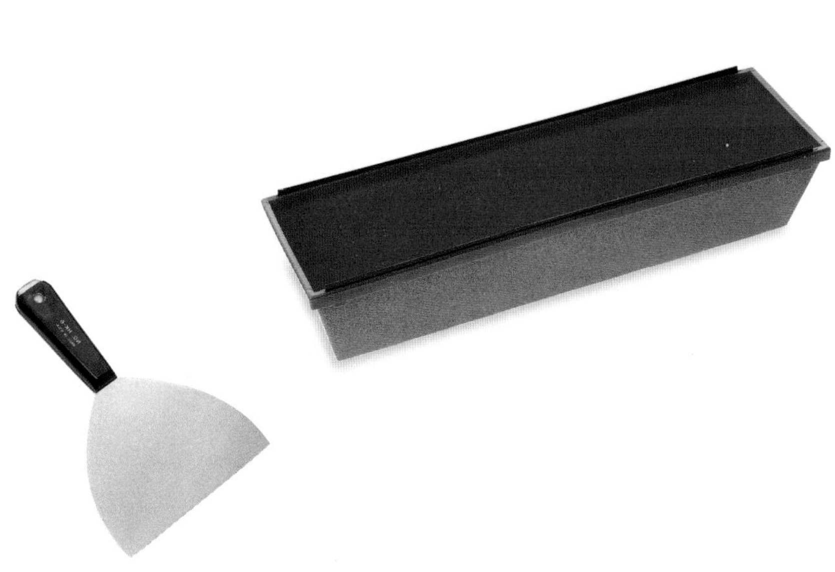